ROGUE HEROES

ROGUE HEROES

The History of the SAS, Britain's Secret
Special Forces Unit That Sabotaged the Nazis and
Changed the Nature of War

BEN MACINTYRE

CROWN
NEW YORK

Copyright © 2016 by Ben Macintyre Books Ltd.

Published in the United States by Crown, an imprint of the Crown Publishing Group, a division of Penguin Random House LLC, New York.
crownpublishing.com

CROWN is a registered trademark and the Crown colophon is a trademark of Penguin Random House LLC.

Simultaneously published in the UK by Viking, an imprint of Penguin Random House UK, and in Canada by Signal, an imprint of Random House Canada.

Photography credits can be found on page 365.

Library of Congress Cataloging-in-Publication Data is available upon request.

ISBN 978-1-101-90416-9
eBook ISBN 978-1-101-90417-6

Printed in the United States of America

Book design by Lauren Dong
Maps: copyright © Jeff Edwards, 2016
Jacket design by Elena Giavaldi
Jacket photograph: SAS Regimental Association Archive

10 9 8 7 6 5 4 3

First Edition

You are "the best of cut-throats": do not start;
The phrase is Shakespeare's, and not misapplied:
War's a brain-spattering, windpipe-slitting art,
Unless her cause by Right be sanctified.

LORD BYRON, *Don Juan*

Contents

List of Maps

Foreword

By the Rt. Hon. Viscount Slim

MANY BOOKS HAVE BEEN WRITTEN ABOUT THE ORIGINS AND formative years of the SAS during the Second World War, and most are excellent in their own way.

Here, however, for the first time, is the full early story of the SAS based on our own Second World War Diary, personal accounts of those involved, and never-before-released archive material. Ben Macintyre has drawn together a gripping tale which follows the Regiment's exploits through North Africa, to Sicily and Italy, before D-Day saw it in France and then the final thrust deep into Germany taking SAS jeep patrols to the shores of the Baltic.

Joining 22SAS on its formation in 1952, I was privileged to command the Regiment from 1967 to the end of 1969. I had the good luck to know David Stirling well, together with many of the Originals such as George Jellicoe, David Sutherland, Pat Riley, and Jim Almonds.

I believe the author has done an outstanding job in capturing the audacity of the operations and teasing out the eccentricities of the very different characters involved; how they related to one another and fought together in these early operations was key to the success of the Regiment.

The darker side of war cannot be ignored and Macintyre does not shirk from exploring the effects on all involved as the fighting becomes bloodier and more desperate in the final months of the conflict. Events have also been placed in the wider strategic context of the war in Europe. This is important, as he recognizes both the core ethos of the SAS and the fact that its role and impact were strategic. This remains true to the present day.

The SAS in the Second World War became the blueprint upon which other special forces around the world are based. This is the first SAS authorized history. It is a cracking good read and made even more fascinating because it is true.

John Slim
Patron
The Special Air Service Regimental Association

Author's Note

LIKE WAR ITSELF, BATTLEFIELD COURAGE TAKES MANY FORMS. This is a book about a style of warfare that was quite different from anything that preceded it, an unexpected species of hero, and perhaps a different sort of bravery.

The Special Air Service pioneered a form of combat that has since become a central component of modern warfare. It began life as a raiding force in the North African desert, but grew into the most formidable commando unit of the Second World War and the prototype for special forces across the world, notably the US Delta Force and Navy SEALs.

Yet throughout the war, and for many years afterward, the activities of this specialized regiment were a closely guarded secret. This book, describing the origins and wartime evolution of the SAS, has been written with full and unprecedented access to the SAS regimental archives—an astonishingly rich trove of unpublished material including top secret reports, memos, private diaries, letters, memoirs, maps, and hundreds of hitherto unseen photographs.

The most important single source has been the SAS War Diary. This is an extraordinary compilation of original documents, gathered by an SAS officer in 1945, bound in a single, leather-clad volume of more than five hundred pages. Held in secrecy for the next seventy years, it is now preserved in the SAS regimental archives.

This is an authorized history, not an official one; I have been generously aided by the SAS Regimental Association at every stage of its production, but the views expressed herein are entirely my own, and not those of the regiment. It is not a comprehensive history. If such a thing were possible, it would be unreadable. For reasons of space and continuity, I have tended to focus on key individuals and events; many men who played gallant roles in the early days of the regiment do not appear in these pages; a few major operations have been omitted, to avoid repetition, as have many minor ones. I have also given more prominence to the British elements of the SAS than their French, Greek, and Belgian counterparts. This is not a specialist military history but a book for the general reader, and I have tried to keep to a minimum the particulars of rank, unit numbers, medal awards, and other military details when these are not essential to the narrative. A full list of wartime SAS operations and the regiment's roll of honor is included at the end.

Many books have been written about the SAS. Some are excellent, but often these have focused on a single individual, consequently downplaying the impact of others; some veer toward the hagiographic; many are somewhat overmuscled, tending to emphasize machismo at the expense of objectivity, physical strength over the psychological stamina that was the hallmark of the organization in its earliest incarnation. While many members of the wartime SAS exhibited extraordinary qualities, they were also human: flawed, occasionally cruel, and capable of making specular mistakes. The SAS has become a legend, but the true story contains darkness as well as light, tragedy and evil alongside heroism: it is tale of unparalleled bravery and ingenuity, interspersed with moments of rank incompetence, raw brutality, and touching human frailty.

At the time of its founding, the SAS was an experiment, and an unpopular one among many of the more traditional-minded officers in the British Army. The idea of inserting small groups of highly trained men behind enemy lines, to carry out special operations against high-value targets, ran contrary to all the accepted notions of symmetrical warfare, in which armies faced one another across a defined battlefield. Originally a British unit, formed in the North African desert in 1941, the SAS drew fighting men from all over the world: American, Canadian, Irish, Jewish, French, Belgian, Danish, and Greek. The regiment started small, and expanded hugely in the space of three years.

Some exceptional warriors appear only briefly in what follows, but a handful of individuals fought in the SAS from its inception to the war's end, from the sands of Libya to the coasts of Italy to the hills of France and into Germany. Recruits tended to be unusual to the point of eccentricity, people who did not fit easily into the ranks of the regular army, rogues and reprobates with an instinct for covert war and little time for convention, part soldiers and part spies, rogue warriors. They were, as one former SAS officer put it, "the sweepings of the public schools and the prisons." Success in the ranks of the SAS required a particular cast of mind, and this book is, in part, an attempt to identify those elusive qualities of character and personality.

At the end of the war the SAS was disbanded, on the erroneous assumption that such specialized troops would no longer be necessary. The importance of special forces in the prosecution of modern war has grown steadily ever since.

In 1947, the SAS was re-formed by the British government as a long-term, deep-penetration commando force. The regiment went on to fight in Korea, Malaya, Oman, Borneo, and Northern Ireland. In 1980, the shadowy unit gained sudden notoriety after an SAS squad successfully stormed the Iranian embassy and liberated 25 hostages, killing 5 of the 6 hostage-takers in 11 minutes. The assault was broadcast live on television, bringing instant worldwide fame to a regiment whose continued existence had been known to few outside the military special operations community.

The techniques employed by the SAS have changed radically over the last seven decades, but its essential nature has altered little since 1941: an elite force deployed on clandestine, highly dangerous missions beyond the scope of conventional forces. Today, special forces are deployed more widely, and more effectively, than ever before. In 2006, the SAS and the US Army Delta Force launched multiple surprise raids against Al Qaeda targets in and around Baghdad that tore apart the terrorists' leadership structures. At the time of writing, special forces are combating the march of ISIS, the brutal self-styled Islamist caliphate, in Iraq, Syria, and once again in Libya, where the SAS story began seventy-five years ago. The US defense secretary recently described the role of special forces in carrying out missions against ISIS targets: "We have the long reach . . . You don't know at night who's going to be coming in the window. And that's the sensation that we want all of [ISIS] leadership and followers to have." That is definition of the role of special forces that David Stirling, the founder of the SAS, would have recognized and applauded.

The SAS was at the sharp end of the war's toughest assignments, and inflicted immense damage on enemy forces, both material and psychological. In the desert, SAS raiding parties wrecked fleets of aircraft, terrified Rommel's troops, carried out vital espionage operations, and forged a myth; in Italy they spearheaded the Allied invasion; on or before D-Day, they parachuted into occupied France to conduct guerrilla operations that helped to turn the tide of war. They paid a heavy price, in blood and sanity. The hallucinatory hell of war echoes through these pages, as well as the delight of comradeship, the pleasure in destruction, and the horror of senseless death.

Bravery sometimes comes in unexpected forms, and in places far from the battlefield. The wartime history of the SAS is a rattling adventure story, but in the following pages I have also tried to explore the psychology of secret, unconventional warfare, a particular attitude of mind at a crucial moment in history, and the reactions of ordinary people to extraordinary wartime circumstances.

This is a book about the meaning of courage.

A Note on Sources

THE MAJORITY OF SOURCE MATERIAL FOR THIS BOOK COMES from the SAS regimental archives, most notably the War Diary. I am also indebted to those who have preceded me in exploring the history of the regiment, notably Gavin Mortimer, Gordon Stevens, Martin Morgan, Alan Hoe, Damien Lewis, Lorna Almonds Windmill, Stewart McLean, Virginia Cowles, Hamish Ross, Paul McCue, John Lewes, Anthony Kemp, Martin Dillon, Michael Asher, and many others. A great debt is owed to those historians who had the foresight to record, on paper, film, or audiotape, the memories of the participants before it was too late, and I have been fortunate to be able to draw on these. Only a small handful of SAS wartime veterans now remain, and I have spent many happy hours talking about the past with Mike Sadler, Keith Kilby, and Edward Toms. The family of former SAS intelligence officer Robert McCready kindly shared his wartime diaries and other artifacts. Archie Stirling generously enabled me to explore the David Stirling papers. In addition to the unpublished firsthand accounts held in the archives, much valuable information is contained in the postwar memoirs published by several former soldiers, including Malcolm Pleydell, Johnny Cooper, Vladimir Peniakoff, Alan Caillou, David Lloyd Owen, Roy Close, Fitzroy Maclean, and Roy Farran.

Prologue

INTO THE DARK

On a November evening in 1941, five elderly Bristol Bombay transport aircraft lumbered along the runway of Bagush airfield on the Egyptian coast, and then wheeled into the darkening Mediterranean haze. Each aircraft carried a "stick" of eleven British parachutists, some fifty-five soldiers in all, almost the entire strength of a new, experimental, and intensely secret combat unit: "L Detachment" of the Special Air Service. The SAS.

As the planes rumbled northwest the wind began to pick up, bringing the electric inklings of a brewing storm. The temperature inside dropped quickly as the sun slipped below the desert horizon. It was suddenly intensely cold.

The fledgling SAS was on its first mission. Code-named Operation Squatter, it ran as follows: to parachute at night into the Libyan desert behind enemy lines, infiltrate five airfields on foot, plant explosives on as many German and Italian aircraft as they could find, and then, as the bombs exploded, head south to a rendezvous point deep in the desert where they would be picked up and brought back to safety.

Some of the men strapped in and shivering in the rushing darkness at eighteen thousand feet were regular soldiers, but others were not: their number included a hotel porter, an ice-cream maker, a Scottish aristocrat, and an Irish international rugby player. Some were natural warriors, nerveless and calm, and a few were touched by a sort of martial madness; most were silently petrified, and determined not to show it. None could claim to have been fully prepared for what they were about to do, for the simple reason that no one had ever before attempted a nighttime parachute assault in the North African desert. But a peculiar camaraderie had already taken root, a strange esprit compounded in equal parts of ruthlessness, guile, competitiveness, and collective determination. Before takeoff, the men had been informed that anyone seriously injured on landing would have to be left behind. There is no evidence that any of them found this odd.

The wind had reached gale force by the time the bucking Bombays neared the Libyan coast, two and a half hours after takeoff. Storm-driven sand and pelting rain completely obscured the flares on the ground, laid down by the Royal Air Force to guide the planes to the drop zone, twelve miles inland. The pilots could not even make out the shape of the shoreline. German searchlights on the coast picked up the incoming planes, and flak began exploding around them in blinding flashes. A shell ripped through the floor of one plane and missed the auxiliary fuel tank by inches. One of the sergeants made a joke, which no one could hear, though everyone grinned.

The pilots indicated that the parachutists should prepare to jump—although, in truth, they were now flying blind, navigating by guesswork. The parachute canisters—containing explosives, tommy guns, ammunition, food, water, maps, blankets, and medical supplies—were tossed out first.

Then, one by one, the men hurled themselves into the seething darkness.

Part I

WAR IN THE DESERT

Chapter 1

COWBOY SOLDIER

FIVE MONTHS BEFORE OPERATION SQUATTER, A TALL, THIN soldier lay, grumpy and immobile, in a Cairo hospital bed. The twenty-five-year-old officer had been brought into the Scottish Military Hospital on June 15, 1941, paralyzed from the waist down. A letter to his mother from the War Office stated that he had suffered "a contusion of the back as a result of enemy action."

This was not, strictly speaking, true. The injured soldier had not set eyes on the enemy: he had jumped out of a plane, without a helmet or proper training, ripped his parachute on the tail, and plummeted to earth at roughly twice the recommended speed. The impact had knocked him out and badly injured his spine, leaving him temporarily blinded and without feeling in his legs. The doctors feared he would never walk again.

Even before his parachuting accident, the officer's contribution to the war effort had been minimal: he lacked the most basic military discipline, could not march straight, and was so lazy his comrades had nicknamed him "the Giant Sloth." Since being posted to Egypt with the British commando force, he had spent much of his time in Cairo's bars and clubs, or gambling at the racecourse. The nurses at the hospital knew him well, for he frequently popped in during the morning, whey-faced and liverish, to request a blast from the oxygen bottle to cure his hangover. Before his parachute jump landed him in the hospital, he had been under investigation to establish whether he was malingering and ought to be court-martialed. His fellow officers found him charming and entertaining; his senior commanders, for the most part, regarded him as impertinent, incompetent, and profoundly irritating. On completing officer training, he had received a blunt appraisal: "irresponsible and unremarkable."

Lieutenant David Stirling of the Scots Guards was not a conventional soldier.

The writer Evelyn Waugh, a fellow officer in the commando force, came to visit Stirling about three weeks after his admission to the hospital. Waugh had been misinformed by the matron that one of Stirling's legs had already been amputated, and he would likely lose the other. "I can't feel a thing," Stirling told his friend. Embarrassed, as Englishmen tend to be when faced with disability, Waugh kept up a steady stream of meaningless small talk, perched on the edge of the bed, and studiously avoided the subject of his friend's paralysis. Every so often, however, he would sneak a surreptitious glance to where Stirling's remaining leg ought to be, and whenever he did so Stirling, with extreme effort, would wiggle the big toe of his right foot. Finally, Waugh realized he was being teased, and hit Stirling with a pillow.

"You bastard, Stirling, when did it happen?"

"Minutes before you came. It takes a bit of effort, but it's a start."

Stirling was regaining the use of his legs. Others might have cried for joy; for Stirling, however, the first sign of his recovery was an excellent opportunity to play a practical joke on one of Britain's greatest novelists.

It would take two more weeks before Stirling could stand upright, and several more before he was able to hobble about. But during those two months of enforced inaction he did a great deal of thinking—something that, in spite of his reputation as a feckless gadabout, he was rather good at.

The commandos were intended to be Britain's storm troops, volunteers selected and trained to carry out destructive raids against Axis targets. Prime Minister Winston Churchill had decided that the ideal theater in which to deploy the commandos would be North Africa, where they could conduct seaborne raids against enemy bases along the Mediterranean coast.

In Stirling's unsolicited opinion, the concept was not working. Most of the time the commandos were inactive, awaiting the order for a great assault that never came; on the rare occasions when they were deployed, the results had been disappointing. The German and Italian troops fully expected to be attacked from the sea, and were primed and waiting. The commando forces were simply too large and cumbersome to launch an assault without being spotted; the element of surprise was immediately lost.

But what if, wondered Stirling, the combat troops attacked from the opposite direction? To the south, stretching between Egypt and Libya, lay the Great Sand Sea, a vast, waterless expanse of unbroken dunes covering forty-five thousand square miles. One of the most inhospitable environments on earth, the desert was considered by the Germans to be virtually impassable, a natural barrier, and they therefore left it largely unprotected, and entirely unpatrolled. "This was one sea the Hun was not watching," Stirling reflected. If mobile teams of highly trained men, under cover of darkness, could be infiltrated onto the enemy's desert flank, they might be able to sabotage airfields, supply depots, communications links, railways, and roads, and then slip back into the embracing emptiness of the sand sea. A commando force several hundred strong could attack only one target at a time; but a number of smaller units, moving quickly, raiding suddenly and then retreating swiftly, could destroy multiple targets simultaneously. The opportunity to attack the enemy in the rear, when he least expects it, is the pipe dream of every general. The peculiar geography of North Africa offered just such a possibility, reflected Stirling, as he lay half paralyzed in his hospital bed, trying to wiggle his toes.

Stirling's idea was the result of wishful thinking more than expertise; it had emerged not from long hours of reflection and

study, but from the acute boredom of convalescence. It was based
on intuition, imagination, and self-confidence, of which Stirling
had plenty, rather than experience of desert warfare, of which he
had none.

But it was an inspired idea, and the sort of idea that could only
have occurred to someone as strange and remarkable as Archibald
David Stirling.

STIRLING WAS ONE of those people who thrive in war, having
failed at peace. In a short life, he had tried his hand at a variety
of occupations—artist, architect, cowboy, and mountaineer—and
found success in none of them. Privileged by birth and education,
intelligent and resourceful, he could have done anything, but had
spent the early part of his life doing little of any consequence. The
war was his salvation.

The Stirling family was one of the oldest and grandest in Scotland, an aristocratic clan of great distinction, long military traditions, and considerable eccentricity. David Stirling's mother was
the daughter of Lord Lovat, the chief of Clan Fraser, with blood-
lines stretching back to Charles II. His father, General Archibald
Stirling, had been gassed in the First World War, served as an MP,
and then retired to Keir, the fifteen-thousand-acre Perthshire
estate that had been the family's seat for the previous five centuries. The general presided over his sprawling lands and unruly
family like some benign but distant chieftain observing a battlefield from a remote hill. David's formidable mother, Margaret, was
the more forceful presence: her children were in awe of her. Keir
House, where David Stirling was born in 1915, was a vast edifice,
freezing cold even at the height of summer, filled with old hunting trophies, noise, and devilment. The Stirling parents drummed
good manners into their six children, but otherwise largely left
them to get on with their lives. The four Stirling boys, of whom
David was the second in age, grew up stalking deer, hunting rab-

bits, fighting, and competing. One favorite game was a form of sibling duel using air rifles: two brothers would take potshots at each other's backsides in turn, moving closer by a pace after each shot.

Despite this aristocratically spartan start in life, David Stirling was not a hardy child. Dispatched to Ampleforth, a Catholic boarding school, at the age of eight, he caught typhoid fever and was sent home for an extended period of recovery. A speech impediment was eventually cured by surgery. He disliked sports, and did his best to avoid them. He grew at an astonishing rate: by the age of seventeen, he was nearly six feet, six inches tall, a gangly beanpole, willful, reckless, and exceptionally polite. Largely by virtue of his class, he was awarded a place at Cambridge University, where he misbehaved on a lavish scale, spending more time at Newmarket racecourse than he devoted to studying. "If there was a serious side to life it totally escaped me," he later admitted. If he ever opened a book, the event was not recorded. After a year, the master of his college informed him that he was being sent down, read out a list of twenty-three offenses that merited expulsion, and invited him to select the three that he considered "would be least offensive" to his mother.

David Stirling decided he would become an artist, in Paris. He had little talent for painting. But he did have a beret, and a yen for the bohemian life. Some have detected "a strange mixture of beauty and the macabre" in his paintings. His French art tutor, however, did not, and after a year and a half of louche Left Bank life, he was told that while he might one day make a half-decent commercial draftsman, his "painting would never achieve any real merit." Stirling was profoundly upset; his failure as an artist marked him forever, and perhaps explained the consistent ripple of insecurity that lay beneath the carapace of confidence.

He returned to Cambridge to study architecture, but soon dropped out again. A job with an Edinburgh architect was short-lived. His mother now intervened, and told her second son that he must stop drifting and do something with his life. Stirling announced that he intended to become the first person to climb Mount Everest.

Stirling was quite the wrong shape to scramble up rocks. He had little experience of serious climbing. He also suffered from vertigo. Intrepid British mountaineers had been trying to scale the world's highest mountain since 1921; dozens had perished in the attempt. Climbing Everest was an expensive, dangerous, demanding business, and Stirling was broke—none of which dented his determination to succeed where other, qualified, experienced, well-funded mountaineers had failed. He spent a year climbing in the Swiss Alps, bankrolled by his mother, before joining the supplementary reserve of the Scots Guards, his father's regiment, in the hope that part-time army training might bolster his mountaineering quest. He soon drifted out of uniform, repelled by the mind-swamping boredom of the parade ground. In 1938, at the age of twenty-three, he went to the United States with the intention of climbing the Rockies and riding across the Continental Divide. He was south of the Rio Grande, having spent several months herding cattle in the company of a cowboy named Roy "Panhandle" Terrill, when he learned that Britain was at war—the run-up to which had, it seems, almost entirely passed him by. His mother sent a telegram: "Return home by the cheapest possible means." Stirling flew to Britain on a first-class ticket, and rushed back into uniform.

The David Stirling who turned up at the Guards Depot in Pirbright in the autumn of 1939 was a strange mixture of parts. Ambitious but unfocused; steeped in soldierly traditions but allergic to military discipline. A boisterous exterior belied a man prone to periodic depressions, whose extreme good manners and social ease masked moments of inner turmoil. Stirling was a romantic, with an innate talent for friendship but little desire or need for physical intimacy. He appears to have lost his virginity in Paris as an art student. With Panhandle Terrill he had enjoyed the company of "some of those dark girls down in Mexico." But his natural shyness coupled with a stern all-male Catholic education seems to have left him in fear of women. "The totally confused, guilt-ridden years of puberty exerted an awful pressure," he once remarked. He spoke of "predatory females"; his few romantic encounters were described as "close escapes," as if he feared entrapment. "Bonds of any sort are a pressure I find very difficult to bear," he admitted. He had many women friends, and according to his biographer was "not unattracted to the opposite sex." Yet he seemed to relax only among men, and "in wide open spaces." Like many convivial people, he was slightly lonely. A warrior monk, he craved action and the company of soldiers, but when the fighting was over, he embraced solitude.

Stirling was also possessed of a profound self-belief, the sort of confidence that comes from high birth and boundless opportunity. He was blithely unconstrained by convention, and regarded rules as nuisances to be ignored, broken, or otherwise overcome. He was elaborately respectful toward his social inferiors, and showed no deference whatever to rank. Strikingly modest, he was repelled by braggarts and loudmouths: "swanks" (swanking) or "pomposo" (pomposity) were his gravest insults. His manner seemed vague and forgetful, but his powers of concentration were phenomenal. Despite an ungainly body and a patchy academic record, he had a stubborn faith in his own abilities, intellectual and physical. Stirling did exactly what he wanted to do, whether or not others thought his aims were sensible or even possible. The SAS came into being, in part, because its founder would not take no for an answer, either from those in authority or from those under his command.

Just as he had been bored by the logistics of mountaineering, so Stirling found the practical preparations for war indescribably tedious. Like many young men, he was hungry for the fight, but instead found himself shackled to a regime of endless marching, kit inspections, weapons drill, and all the other rote elements of military life. So he rebelled. Slipping away from the Guards Depot at Pirbright, he would frequently head to London for a night of drinking, gambling, and billiards at White's club; just as frequently he was caught, and confined to barracks. Stirling was a nightmare recruit: impertinent, indolent, and often half asleep as a result of his carousing the night before. "He was quite, quite irresponsible," recalled Willie (later Viscount) Whitelaw, a fellow trainee officer at Pirbright. "He just couldn't tolerate that we were being trained along the lines of the last major conflict. His reaction was just to ignore everything."

It was at the bar of White's, one of the most exclusive gentleman's clubs in London, that Stirling first learned about a form of soldiering that seemed much closer to the adventure and excitement he had in mind: a crack new commando unit intended to hit important enemy targets with maximum impact. Stirling's cousin Lord Lovat had been among the first to volunteer for the commandos.

Formed under the command of Lieutenant Colonel Robert Laycock, the force—christened Layforce—would consist of more than 1,500 volunteers formed into three commando regiments, recruited from the Foot Guards (the regular infantry of the Household Division) and other infantry regiments: an elite troop of specialized, highly trained raiders and marauders. Lord Haw-Haw, the British traitor who broadcast radio announcements into England for the Nazis, would describe the commandos as "Churchill's cut-throats."

Stirling immediately volunteered. Soon he found himself stomping through the wilds of western Scotland, familiar boyhood terrain and far from the parade ground he loathed. For weeks the commandos trained in the bogs and bracken of the Isle of Arran: route marches, unarmed combat, endurance, fieldcraft, navigation, and survival techniques. Even at this early stage, some of the other volunteers noticed something different about the tall young officer: Stirling was a natural leader, with an understated but adamant faith in his own decisions and a gentlemanly insistence on doing everything he asked of his men, and more. On February 1, 1941, Layforce sailed for the Middle East. Finally Stirling was heading into battle, leaving behind a long string of unpaid bills—from his bookmaker, his tailor, his bank manager, and even from a cowboy outfitter in Arizona, seeking payment for a saddle.

Layforce had been deployed to disrupt Axis communication lines in the Mediterranean, and to spearhead the capture of Rhodes. But by the time the commandos arrived in Egypt, the military situation had changed: the arrival in Cyrenaica (eastern coastal Libya) of the Afrika Korps, the German expeditionary force under Erwin Rommel, had transformed the strategic picture. The British were now scrambling to oppose the German advances, and the first stage of the seesaw war in North Africa was under way. Initially deployed to shore up the Italian defense of their North African colonies, the Afrika Korps moved with alarming speed, driving the British back to the Egyptian border with Libya and laying siege to the coastal town of Tobruk. Instead of storming Rhodes, the commandos were split up and variously deployed to garrison Cyprus, cover the evacuation of Crete, reinforce the defense of Tobruk, and carry out raids along the coasts of Cyrenaica and Syria. An assault on the Libyan coastal town of Bardia achieved little, with 67 of the British raiders taken prisoner. Of the 800 commandos sent to cover the evacuation of Crete in May, fewer than 200 managed to escape—among them Evelyn Waugh, who boarded the last ship to leave. In June, the commandos successfully established a bridgehead on the Litani River in Lebanon against Vichy French forces, but lost a quarter of their attacking force.

Stirling, based in Egypt with the Layforce Reserve, was bored and frustrated. He had yet to fire a gun in action. "We were involved in a series of postponements and cancellations, and that was extremely frustrating," he later recalled. Before the departure of the commandos, the director of combined operations had told them they were about to "embark on an enterprise that would stir the world." So far, Stirling had barely stirred. As always when he was underemployed, he turned to revelry. Peter Stirling, David's younger brother, was serving at the British embassy in Cairo, and his comfortable diplomatic flat in the Garden City district became the venue for riotous parties and nocturnal forays into the city's fleshpots.

Stirling began to miss parades, and make excuses. His claims of ill health were not wholly untrue. He was stricken by a nasty bout of dysentery. Then, returning from a night exercise, he tripped over a tent rope and gashed an eye socket, requiring stitches. Stirling found the American hospital particularly comfortable, and began to contrive to spend his days there, claiming to be suffering from fever. "In a sense, I was pretty ill," he later argued. "Because I would go out in the evening, having recovered from the appalling hangover caused by the previous night's activities in Cairo, and re-establish my illness by my activities the following night." Alerted by the hospital matron, Stirling's superiors began to question just how unwell he really was. He was drinking and partying himself into serious trouble when his life was changed by a conversation, in the mess, with Lieutenant Jock Lewes, a fellow officer in the commandos who was as self-disciplined and uptight as Stirling was dissolute and nonchalant.

Lewes told Stirling that he had recently obtained a stock of several dozen parachutes, destined for a paratroop unit operating in India but accidentally shipped to Port Said, where he had appropriated them. Colonel Laycock had given Lewes permission to attempt an experimental parachute jump in the desert. Stirling asked if he could come along, "partly for fun, partly because it would be useful to know how to do it," and mostly because he was very bored. So began an important and unlikely partnership between two men who could hardly have been more different.

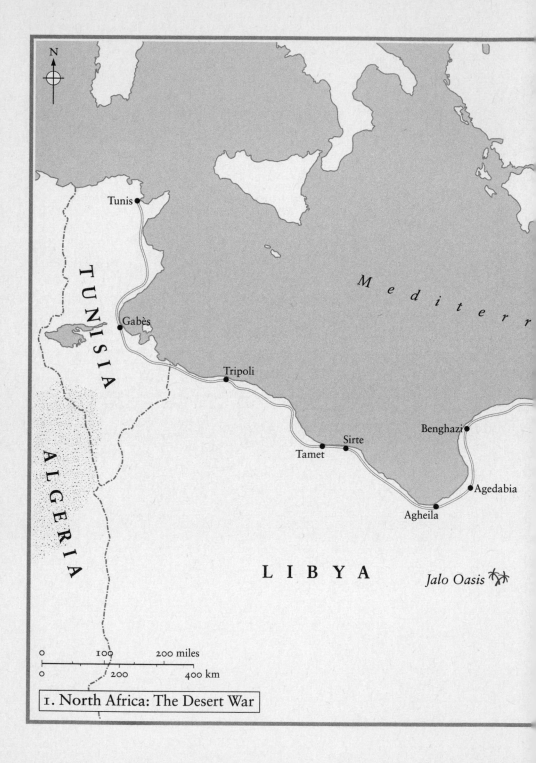

N

TUNISIA

Tunis

ALGERIA

Gabès

Tripoli

M e d i t e r r

Benghazi

Sirte

Tamet

Agedabia

Agheila

L I B Y A

Jalo Oasis

0   100   200 miles
0   200   400 km

1. North Africa: The Desert War

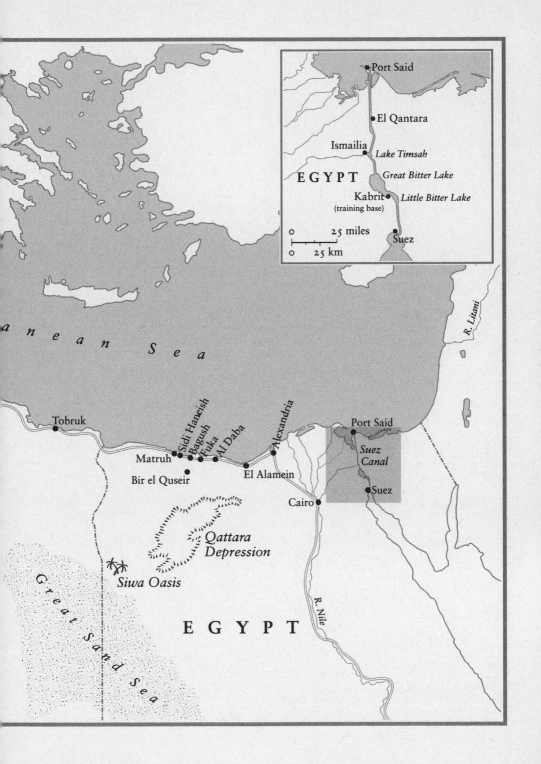

Port Said

El Qantara

Ismailia · *Lake Timsah*

EGYPT · *Great Bitter Lake*

Kabrit · *Little Bitter Lake*
(training base)

25 miles
25 km

Suez

Tobruk

Sidi Haneish
Bagush
Fuka
Al Daba

Matruh

Bir el Quseir

Alexandria

El Alamein

Port Said

Suez Canal

Suez

Cairo

Qattara Depression

Siwa Oasis

Great Sand Sea

EGYPT

R. Nile

R. Litani

an e a n   S e a

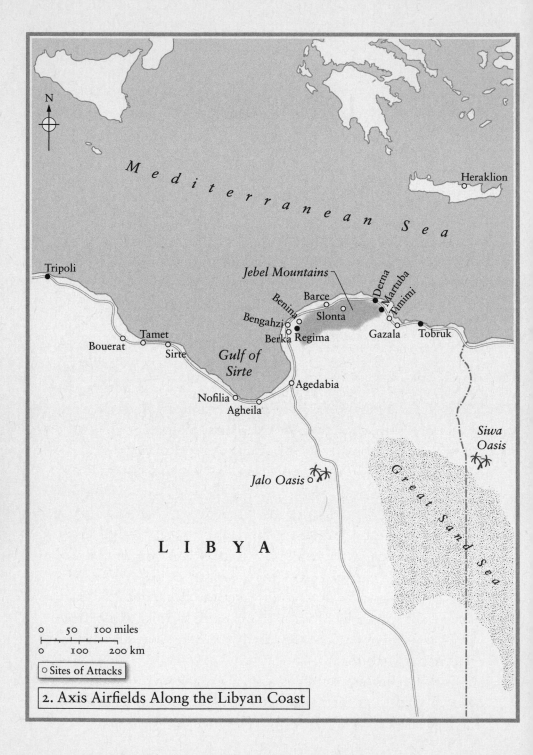

N

Heraklion

Mediterranean Sea

Tripoli

Jebel Mountains

Barce
Benina
Bengahzi   Slonta
Berka Regima

Derna
Martuba
Timimi

Gazala   Tobruk

Tamet
Bouerat
Sirte

Gulf of Sirte

Agedabia

Nofilia
Agheila

Siwa Oasis

Jalo Oasis

Great Sand Sea

L I B Y A

0   50   100 miles

0   100   200 km

○ Sites of Attacks

2. Axis Airfields Along the Libyan Coast

Chapter 2

L DETACHMENT

Lieutenant John Steele Lewes was a paragon of military virtue, a man of rigid personal austerity, and a martinet. Born in India to a British father and Australian mother, he had captained the Oxford University Boat Club, graduated from Christ Church, and seemed destined for a career in politics or the upper reaches of the army. Having joined the Welsh Guards on the outbreak of war, he was appointed regimental training officer and billeted at Sandown Racecourse. There he was painted by the artist Rex Whistler, a fellow officer and friend, sitting on the steps of the grandstand with a Bren gun across his knees, looking as if he was about to mow down the runners and riders in the 3:15.

"Jock" Lewes was almost too good to be true. "Be something great," his father had told him, and Lewes intended to fulfill that injunction. He was athletic, rich, patriotic, and handsome, with glinting blue eyes and an immaculately tended Douglas Fairbanks Jr. mustache. He appeared in the society magazines, and was courting a wellborn and sensible woman named Miriam Barford, whom he lectured on the importance of sacrifice and hard work. "We acquire more merit on this earth in doing gladly those tasks set us which are least attractive than by any amount of enjoyable labour," he wrote.

Jock Lewes was stern, workaholic, and slightly priggish, with a deep "contempt for decadence," according to his biographer. He had no sense of humor, and "his austerity could be simply too much for other mortals." "You wouldn't find Jock catching a quick drink in Cairo or taking a flutter at the racecourse," observed Stirling, who was usually to be found doing one or the other.

The two officers did, however, share an urgent desire for action, and a belief that the commandos were not being properly used. A rising star in Layforce, Lewes had already demonstrated his pluck and ingenuity in several operations, including a successful attack using motorized gunboats on an enemy air base near Gazala on the Libyan coast. Lewes had been impressed by the Germans' use of paratroops in the conquest of Crete, and thought that a parachute force might prove a useful addition to future Allied commando operations. He began lobbying senior officers to be allowed to form his own, hand-picked unit, and wrote home that he had been given "that which I have longed for—a team of men, and complete freedom to train and use them as I think best." Stirling was struck by Lewes's calm demeanor, great professionalism, and experience. According to one version of the story, he had got wind of what Lewes was up to and deliberately sought him out in the officers' mess. Others say the conversation was purely accidental. Either way, the ideas of Lewes and Stirling were converging.

There was, however, another, secret side to Jock Lewes that might have given Stirling pause, had he known about it: Lewes had flirted with Nazism.

On a cycling tour to Germany in 1935, Lewes had been deeply impressed by the organization and strength of the nascent Third Reich. "England is no democracy and Germany far from being a totalitarian state," he wrote to his parents. "Dazzled" by National Socialism, he visited Germany several times in the following years, returning home more smitten from each visit: he mixed with German high society, attended a 1938 ball where Hitler and Goebbels were guests of honor, and fell in love with a young German woman, Senta Adriano, an enthusiastic member of the Nazi Party. He mooned over Senta's "frankness and sincerity," her "golden hair, eyes greeny blue and well spaced, fine delicate eyebrows—not plucked." Plucked eyebrows would have been a mark of frivolity.

Then came *Kristallnacht*, the night of broken glass, as Nazis rampaged through Germany and Austria, smashing and looting Jewish shops, businesses, and synagogues. Jock Lewes may have been politically naive, but he was not a fool: the events of November 1938 provoked in him a violent and painful change of heart. Suddenly, with horrible clarity, he understood the true nature of the regime he had appeased, politically and emotionally.

"I have been struggling to retain my belief in German sincerity but only a fanatic faith could withstand the evidence they choose to put before us," he wrote. "I swear I will not live to see the day when Britain hauls down the colours of her beliefs before totalitarian aggression." He broke off his engagement to Senta, and became, almost overnight, a ferocious opponent of Nazism. "I shall willingly take up arms against Germany," he wrote. He felt he had been duped, both by the Nazis and by the fascist woman he loved. "He took the lie personally"; he was out for revenge.

Lewes's determination and ruthlessness, his utter dedication to the task of fighting Germany, was the reaction of a man who has been wronged by a faithless lover, one who has made a terrible mistake and needed to make amends.

The light was already fading when Lewes, Stirling, and four other men climbed into an elderly biplane to perform the world's first desert parachute jump: for Stirling, a jaunt; for Lewes, the next stage in his campaign of revenge against Nazi Germany. The Vickers Valentia, on loan to the Royal Air Force, was used to deliver mail; it was almost comically unsuitable for parachuting. The parachutes purloined by Lewes were designed with static lines to be clipped to a steel cable, attached fore and aft. As the parachutist left the plane, the line would pull out the folded parachute until fully extended, at which point a connecting thread would snap and the parachute canopy would fill with air. There were no parachute instructors in the Middle East, but a friendly RAF officer advised them to "dive out as though going through into water." The team practiced by jumping off the plane wings, a fall of about ten feet. By way of a test, Lewes tossed out a dummy parachutist, made from tent poles and sandbags, at a height of eight hundred feet. "The parachute opened okay, but the tent poles smashed on landing."

Lewes and Stirling agreed they were ready to go: they would simply tie the parachute lines to the legs of the passenger seats, open the door, and dive out. The pilot took off from the small airfield fifty miles south of Bagush, circled once, and then gave the signal to jump. Lewes and his batman went first, followed by a volunteer named D'Arcy and then Stirling. D'Arcy later wrote: "I was surprised to see Lieutenant Stirling pass me in the air." But not half as surprised as Lieutenant Stirling. His parachute had snagged on the tail of the plane and badly ripped. Realizing that he was not so much parachuting as falling, he closed his eyes and braced himself for the impact.

Stirling did not regain consciousness until he awoke, half paralyzed, in a bed at the Scottish Military Hospital. "I was a bit unlucky," he said, with resounding understatement.

Lewes, predictably enough, had "made a perfect landing," and felt moved to write a poem about the romance of parachuting.

> *Green for Go! Now! God, how slow it is!*
> *The air doesn't rush and earth doesn't rise*
> *Till you swoop into harness and know it is*
> *Over, look up and love the white canopy*
> *Steadfast above you, an angel in panoply*
> *Guarding the skies.*

Stirling did not feel that way. His first experience of parachuting had been extremely unpleasant. He would suffer back pain and migraines for the rest of his life as a result of his spinal injury. The fall had almost killed him, but it had given him a very good idea.

It was eight weeks before Stirling could walk again. In that time, he gathered every map of the coast and inland area he could lay his hands on, jotting down notes on airfields, roads, rail lines, and enemy positions along the coast. When Lewes visited him in hospital, Stirling laid out his plans: "I believe it would be possible, not too difficult in fact, to infiltrate small numbers of men into selected German positions from the desert flank. I think we could then have a pretty dramatic effect on their efficiency and morale by sabotaging aircraft, runways and fuel dumps."

With typical generosity, Stirling would later credit Lewes with much of the thinking behind this plan. Yet at this stage Lewes was skeptical. How would parachutists be able to carry sufficient explosives to do real damage? Who would authorize such an operation? And how would the raiders get away after an attack across hundreds of miles of sand? "Have you thought about training for walking in the desert?" he asked. Lewes's doubts may have had less to do with the feasibility of the plan than with misgivings about the character of Stirling himself, a man with a rakish reputation and many of the traits Lewes despised. He may also have felt that Stirling was interfering with his own plans. Lewes was heading back to besieged Tobruk. They agreed to discuss the concept of parachute raiding once more when he returned. "If you manage to get anywhere with the idea, talk to me again," said Lewes, as he got up to leave. "I don't hold out much hope."

By mid-July, Stirling had written the outline of a proposal, giving credit to Lewes and noting that the plan was "largely based on Jock's ideas."

Stirling's original memo was handwritten in pencil, and does not survive in the SAS archives. Its outlines were straightforward: Rommel's eastward advance along the North African coast had swung the battle in favor of the celebrated German commander, but it had also created an opportunity, leaving the enemy supply lines extended and coastal airfields vulnerable to attack. Most were only thinly defended. Some even lacked perimeter fencing. On a moonless night a small group of highly trained commandos could be dropped by parachute, as close as feasible to enemy airfields; they would then split into small teams, each no more than five strong, which would penetrate the aerodromes under cover of darkness, plant time bombs on as many aircraft as possible, and then retreat back into the desert, where they could be picked up by the Long Range Desert Group—the British reconnaissance unit that, Stirling had learned, was capable of driving deep into the desert. Up to thirty separate attacks might be launched in a single night. To maintain security and secrecy, such an operation would have to be approved by the commander in chief in the Middle East. The new unit would need special status, access to military intelligence, and its own secluded training ground. Stirling was suggesting "a new type of force, to extract the maximum out of surprise and guile."

With hindsight the plan seems obvious. At the time it was revolutionary.

Many middle-ranking officers in the British Army had fought in the First World War, and clung to an old-fashioned, classical conception of warfare: men in uniform clashing on a battlefield, and then fighting until one side emerged victorious. So far, although the battlefront had moved back and forth, the war in North Africa was following this pattern. What Stirling proposed would leapfrog the front line and take the battle directly into the enemy camp. In the eyes of some, this was not only unprecedented, but unsporting, like punching a chap when he is looking the other way. Blowing up planes in the middle of the night and then running away, some felt, was a job for saboteurs, mercenaries, and assassins, not for soldiers of His Majesty's armed forces. It was not war, as they knew it, and it was not cricket. Worse than that, Stirling's idea represented a threat to the very concept of rank. The chain of command is sacrosanct in every army, but Stirling was proposing to bypass that too, and report only to the most senior commander—in this case General Sir Claude Auchinleck, the newly appointed commander in chief of Middle East Command. Stirling was a mere lieutenant, and an undistinguished one at that, who was proposing to subvert centuries of military tradition by speaking directly to the top boss, in order to create and command what looked suspiciously like a private army. To the traditionalists among his superiors, this was more than just impertinent; it was positively insurrectionary.

Stirling had no illusions about how his plan would be received by the staff officers at Middle East Headquarters. He was openly contemptuous of the mid-level military bureaucracy, which he referred to, variously, as "a freemasonry of mediocrity" and "layer upon layer of fossilized shit." If his idea was to have a chance, he would need to get the proposal directly into the hands of the most senior officers, before anyone lower in the hierarchy had a chance to kill it. If it passed through the normal channels, the plan would perish on the desk of the first staff officer who read it. Stirling's radical approach to the "fossilized shit" was similar to his attitude toward the front line: he did not intend to try to go through it, but to go around it. How he did so has become the stuff of myth.

British Middle East Headquarters was housed in a large block of commandeered flats surrounded by barbed wire in Cairo's Garden City. Still on crutches, Stirling hobbled up to the entrance, only to find his way barred by two guards demanding he show a pass, which he did not have. So, waiting until a moment when the guards were preoccupied, he climbed through a gap in the fence. As he was entering the building, the guards spotted his abandoned crutches and gave chase. Going as fast as his stiff legs would carry him, he flew upstairs and burst into a room marked "Adjutant General." There he found himself confronted by a red-faced major, who just happened to be one of his former instructors at Pirbright. The senior officer remembered Stirling as one of his least attentive students and swiftly sent him packing: "Whatever lunatic idea you have, Stirling, forget it . . . Now, get out."

In the corridor, hearing the guards thundering upstairs, he entered the next room, which turned out to contain General Sir Neil Ritchie, the deputy chief of staff. Stirling handed over his proposal, which he had condensed into a short paper. Ritchie leafed through it with, according to Stirling, growing interest. Then he looked up: "This may be the sort of plan we're looking for." The adjutant general was summoned from next door and instructed, to his astonishment and barely suppressed fury, to give the young officer all the assistance he needed. "I don't like you, and I don't like this business," hissed the adjutant general, after Ritchie had left. "You will get no favours from me." Three days later, Stirling was summoned back to see General Auchinleck.

This is an almost perfect Stirling story, containing the characteristic admixture of self-deprecation, bluff, and impudence, describing an act of daring crowned with unlikely success, while taking a swipe at the military bureaucracy he disdained. It has the patina of a tale polished, told, and retold after dinner. It might even be true, or partly true.

But there is another, more prosaic explanation for Stirling's successful attempt to gain access to the top brass. Auchinleck was an old family friend of the Stirlings. Ritchie had been grouse shooting at Keir. Both were Scots, and both had fought in the First World War alongside General Archibald Stirling, David's father. This was an age when family and class connections counted for much: if there was one junior officer who could get to see a general simply by asking, that was David Stirling. "I knew I could argue with a general," he later said.

Generals Auchinleck and Ritchie were both present at Stirling's next interview, along with Major General Eric Dorman-Smith—a man considered by one colleague to be close to lunacy, but one of the few senior officers who appreciated the way war was swiftly evolving with new technology and motorization.

The three officers quizzed Stirling closely on his outline proposal, and listened attentively as he laid out his ideas.

Auchinleck, universally known as "the Auk," had only recently taken over as commander in chief, and was already under intense pressure from Winston Churchill to strike back at Rommel and reverse the tide of the North African war. A major counteroffensive would be taking place sooner (if Churchill had his way) or later (if Auchinleck had his), and Stirling's band of raiders might possibly play an important role in hampering enemy airpower at a critical moment. The decision had been made to disband Layforce, providing a ready pool of possible recruits, and unlike earlier commando operations, the plan would not require the use of expensive ships and the complexities of naval cooperation. Stirling's plan was cheap, in terms of manpower and equipment, and could pay hand-some dividends, if it worked. And if it didn't, all that would be lost would be a handful of adventurers. There may have been another reason for the generals' willingness to listen. All three had been in the thick of battle during the last war: Dorman-Smith had won the Military Cross at Ypres; Ritchie had won the same medal for his "coolness, courage and utter disregard of danger" under fire; Auchinleck had been mentioned in dispatches during the fierce fighting in Mesopotamia. The trio of generals may have heard this twenty-five-year-old soldier explaining how he intended to help win the war by fighting the Germans at close quarters, and seen in him a little of themselves.

At the end of the meeting, Stirling was told he would be pro-moted to captain, and authorized to raise an initial force of six officers and sixty men from the remnants of Layforce.

The new unit needed a name. It was provided by a little-known military genius with a unique talent for deception and subterfuge, and a taste for theatricality. Colonel Dudley Wrangel Clarke was responsible for strategic deception in the Middle East, the strange but vital offshoot of military operations dedicated to concealing the truth from the enemy and planting lies in its place. Clarke had emerged as one of the great deceivers of the Second World War: operating from a converted bathroom and then from the base-ment of a Cairo brothel, he perfected the use of fictional orders of battle, visual deception, double agents, and misinformation to confuse and mislead the enemy. He was flamboyant, charming, and very funny. He was also a bit odd. In October 1941, he would be arrested in Madrid dressed, rather elegantly, as a woman. This incident, never fully explained, caused much sniggering (the Span-ish police photographs were sent to Churchill), but it did his career no harm whatever.

One of Clarke's ruses in the Middle East had been the creation, in January 1941, of a fake paratroop brigade, to try to fool the Italians into fearing that the British might land airborne troops to assist the next attack. The aim was to soak up Italian forces by making them mount defenses against a nonexistent threat, inflate the apparent size of British forces, and generally corrupt enemy planning. The operation was code-named Abeam, and the bogus unit was given the invented name "1st Special Air Service Brigade." Clarke had planted fake photographs in Egyptian newspapers showing parachutists training in the desert, dropped dummy parachutists near prisoner-of-war camps, and had two men in bogus uniforms wander around Egypt pretending to be SAS paratroopers, convalescing from injuries sustained while parachuting. False documents identifying the 1st SAS Brigade were also planted on known enemy spies, including a Japanese consular official. Captured enemy documents appeared to indicate that Operation Abeam was working, but when Clarke got wind that a real parachute unit was being prepared, he sensed an opportunity to bolster the deception. If Stirling's small assault team took the same name, Clarke argued, this would surely reinforce the idea, in the mind of the opposition, that a full brigade of paratroopers was preparing for action.

Stirling readily agreed to name his force "L Detachment, Special Air Service Brigade." The letter "L" was selected to imply that detachments A to K were already in existence; Stirling later joked that it stood for "Learner." Clarke was "delighted to have some flesh and blood parachutists instead of totally bogus ones." In return he promised to use his extensive network of contacts to spread the word that Stirling was looking for recruits.

The SAS was formed as part of a larger contingent that did not, in reality, exist—an oddly appropriate start for a unit that had come into being through a most unlikely combination of good luck and bad, error, accident, and design.

Chapter 3

RECRUITS

O F THE NEW RECRUITS TO THE SAS, NONE WOULD BE MORE important, or harder to reel in, than Jock Lewes, the hard-minded and demanding Welsh Guards officer whose ideas about raiding behind the lines mirrored, and partly inspired, Stirling's own.

While Stirling was coaxing and charming the generals at Middle East Headquarters, Lewes had been fighting a series of bloody skirmishes in besieged Tobruk, one of the most active and unpleasant battlefronts of the North African war. The vital port was still in British hands, accessible by sea but encircled to the south by German and Italian forces, which kept up a steady bombardment.

On July 18, 1941, Lewes led a night raid on the Italian lines, attacking two rocky outcrops known as the "Twin Pimples." More than fifty enemy soldiers were killed, and Lewes wrote ecstatically of "winkling out the wretched wop from his entrenchments with the bayonet, or rolling in the hand grenades when he lay low." Lewes returned to his own lines, only to be told to go back and take a prisoner—which he did, capturing a luckless Italian soldier who had left his dugout to defecate. Lewes dragged him into camp with his trousers still around his ankles.

Lewes seemed to revel in the discomfort, the heat and flies, the acute boredom punctuated by episodes of extreme violence and raging adrenaline. Every other night a small force of commandos would venture into no-man's-land, navigating through minefields and across barbed wire. "I did most of the patrolling," wrote Lewes, "as desert sores, dysentery and the unspeakable squalor rendered most of the other officers temporarily unserviceable." A solitary, steely figure, he was deeply admired by his comrades (he was "by far the most daring of us all," wrote one), yet he was remote from them. A single-minded predator, he had little need of comradeship.

Stirling made no fewer than three trips to Tobruk, over a six-week period, to try to persuade Lewes to join his fledgling detachment as its first recruit. Lewes had expertise and discipline, to an almost brutal degree, and Stirling had concluded that this meticulous attention to detail would make him "the ideal officer for the unit's training programme." But Lewes held back, resisting all entreaties, and Stirling had enough self-knowledge to realize why: "He just didn't want to get involved if it was going to be a short-term flight of fancy . . . I suppose I'd come across to him in the past as a bit of a Good Time Charlie."

At the end of August, Lewes returned to Egypt for some desperately needed rest. Stirling found him lying in bed, "an absolute wreck," and therefore unable to escape Stirling's appeals. It was a neat reversal of their earlier meeting when Stirling had been immobilized. "I could really get at him," observed Stirling, who proceeded to deploy every argument he could muster to convince Lewes that his future lay with the SAS. Finally Lewes cracked and agreed to come on board as chief instructor of L Detachment, and Stirling's deputy.

The two men would never become close friends. "We got on well enough," said Stirling, a tepid commendation from a man who got on famously with almost everyone. They had very little in common, but their very dissimilarity would be a crucial source of unity and strength.

Lewes's first contribution to L Detachment was to bring with him some of the toughest soldiers in the British Army, men whose abilities he had witnessed at first hand during the commando raids around Tobruk. The first was an American.

Sergeant Pat Riley was a hard-grained native of Redgranite, Wisconsin, who had moved to England with his family in the 1920s. As a teenager, he had worked in the Cumbrian mines, alongside his father and grandfather, before falsifying his birth certificate and faking British citizenship in order to join the Coldstream Guards, the Foot Guards regiment second only in precedence to the Grenadier Guards. A huge man, with a wide Irish face and cheery grin, Riley was one of the most experienced soldiers among the early recruits. On arrival in the Middle East with Layforce he learned that, as an American citizen, he had been summoned to join the US Army. He ignored his call-up papers. Well over six feet tall and broad as a buffalo, Riley exuded an air of great latent power and complete calm: at moments of danger, he tended to hum cowboy songs. The younger men under his command jumped twice as high as he ordered, but also looked on him as a protective figure, instilling instant confidence. Soldiers tended to follow him instinctively. With the breakup of Layforce, several of Riley's fellow guardsmen had asked him what he was planning to do: "They decided they'd go wherever I went." In Tobruk, Riley heard the rumor that a special assault team was being formed, and approached Jock Lewes: "I gather it's a do-or-die unit that you people are forming?"

Riley brought with him another sergeant, Jim Almonds, a fellow veteran of Tobruk who had caught Lewes's eye by dragging a wounded soldier to safety during the Twin Pimples raid. Almonds had joined the Coldstream Guards at the age of eighteen, in 1932. His deceptively soft voice and courtesy had earned him the soubriquet "Gentleman Jim," and there was an old-fashioned air about him, grave, careful, and serious. "I don't think I was ever a vagabond, really," he said. Married, with an infant son at home, in many ways he was the least wild of the bunch. Intensely practical, Almonds was also a person of intelligence and sensitivity: his diary and letters depicting life in the early SAS are a trove of close observation and good sense.

The SAS would attract many rough and fierce individuals in the coming years, but in Riley and Almonds, the bedrock of the unit, it had two men who were anything but intemperate: older, married noncommissioned officers, combat veterans who were keen to fight but who also knew how to calculate the odds, retreat if required, and live to fight again. "I can't think of any better blokes," said Lewes, who advised Riley and his mates to take some leave in Cairo, and then report for duty at the new L Detachment headquarters.

Stirling, meanwhile, was mounting his own recruitment drive. Word swiftly spread among the remnants of Layforce that something unusual was in the offing. Most commandos had signed up in order to see action, and there was no shortage of volunteers. Stirling was careful not to reveal too much and would say only, "I'm forming a unit that is going to drop in behind enemy lines." That was sufficient enticement for most.

A few recruits were approached by Stirling in person. During training in Scotland, he had taken note of a private in the Scots Guards named Johnny Cooper. The most immediately striking thing about Cooper was that he looked barely old enough to be a Boy Scout, let alone a soldier. He came from a middle-class Leicester family, and had been educated at Wyggeston Grammar School, where his most notable achievement had been to play the part of Robin Hood opposite Dickie Attenborough as Maid Marian in the school play. Soon after the outbreak of war, at the age of seventeen, he quit an apprenticeship in the wool trade and bribed a recruiting sergeant to swallow the obvious lie that he was twenty. Cooper was slightly built, with a thin face and piercing eyes; his boyish looks belied a remarkable strength of will and almost unnerving resilience. He neither smoked nor drank, and he endured the demands of training, the pain of amoebic dysentery on the passage to the Middle East, and the monotonous inactivity in the desert without a murmur of complaint. Cooper was made of some light but tough material that seemed able to endure any kind of stress without breaking.

"Do you want to do something special?" Stirling asked him.

"Yes," said Cooper, without pausing to ask what "special" might involve. He was not yet nineteen, the youngest recruit to this new-born unit.

Stirling made a point of interviewing every man who volunteered. Many were rejected, for he had formed a clear idea of the sort of men he would need. Commandos were already some of the most highly trained soldiers in the army, but he was looking for something more profound, and rarer: an ability to think and react independently. Individuality and self-reliance are not always highly prized in an army. Indeed, many officers prefer soldiers to do exactly what they are told, without question or, indeed, thought. But Stirling was insistent that this unit would not be composed of biddable yes-men: "I always hoisted onboard guys who argued."

The men would also have to be willing to kill, at close quarters, and not merely for the sake of killing. "I didn't want psychopaths," he insisted. Stirling, then, was seeking a set of qualities that are not often found together: fighters who were exceptionally brave but just short of irresponsible; disciplined but also independent-minded; uncomplaining, unconventional, and, when necessary, merciless. People who simply wanted a change of routine were dismissed out of hand: "It is no good men volunteering for this type of work just for the novelty," Stirling believed. He even listed the traits he sought: "Courage, fitness and determination in the highest degree, but also, just as important, discipline, skill, intelligence and training."

Inevitably, Stirling's band attracted distinctive characters, as well as some very strange ones, and a few who were positively dangerous. Independent-minded soldiers, as Stirling was about to learn, are not always easy to control.

Reg Seekings was a very difficult man. An amateur boxing champion, he was chippy, irascible, almost blind in one eye, and not very bright. One historian has compared him to "a bad-tempered dog, snarling and scowling." He believed that every argument could be solved with his fists. If someone disagreed with him, he would threaten to fight them; if they declined (as most did, given that he was almost two hundred pounds, muscular and possessed of a famous right hook), he called them a coward. Like most aggressive people, Seekings was insecure, in part because he was dyslexic. Motivated by a sort of desperate competitiveness, he had a morbid fear of being found wanting. Ferociously loyal to those comrades he considered worthy, he was disdainful of everyone else. He once described himself as a "rough tough so-and-so." Many considered him a complete bastard.

But Reg Seekings had one asset that set him apart. He was hard, in the way that very few people are truly hard. He was prepared to do brutal things that others would never have had the stomach for. He never took a backward step, in the boxing ring or on the battlefield, and he had no compunction about the shedding of blood. This was not an attractive human trait, but in the experiment now under way it would prove a supremely valuable one.

Stirling had been allocated a base camp for his new unit, but almost nothing else. Kabrit was a desert headland, flyblown, sandflayed, and roasting, about one hundred miles east of Cairo, on the western shore of the Great Bitter Lake near the junction with the Suez Canal, on the edge of an existing military encampment. The new detachment arrived at the designated spot to find a signpost with the unit's name scrawled on it, three ragged tents, a single ancient lorry, and a couple of chairs. Stirling's battles with headquarters over equipment and supplies would become a recurrent, and rather boring, theme of the early days of the SAS. The unit required a camp, and urgently, so they did what soldiers at war have always done when faced with a lack of necessities: they stole what was needed. It is unclear whether Stirling gave a direct order for the act of larceny that now ensued, but he certainly did nothing to stop it.

A few miles from their designated area was a camp occupied by a New Zealand regiment, which happened to be away on an exercise. That evening the SAS recruits drove the lorry into the camp, and helped themselves to tents, bedding, tables, chairs, a gramophone, cooking equipment, hurricane lamps, rope, washbasins, and tarpaulins. They made no fewer than four round-trips that night, to load up with stolen goods and return to Kabrit. They even stole a piano and a table-tennis set. By morning, they had one of the best-appointed small camps in the Middle East. This story has become an SAS founding myth, combining many of the elements that would define the regiment: bold, successful, and joyfully breaking all the rules.

Stirling was an officer different from any other. A stooped, lanky figure, an unlikely pioneer of a regiment that would become famed for physical strength, he limped around the camp, making a point of getting to know each of the men. Most of the recruits were used to being disdained by their officers, bullied by their NCOs, and generally treated as a lower life-form. Stirling was exquisitely polite to all. "He did not bark orders," marveled Johnny Cooper. "He asked people to do things." While many officers existed in a state of permanent choleric meltdown, Stirling never raised his voice. Riley found him a "very quiet chap, very shy." Most of his recruits had never come across an officer who not only tolerated alternative views but encouraged them.

Other elements of Stirling's peculiar character seeped into the unit, including his natural modesty and talent for extreme understatement. From the earliest days, he insisted that there should be "no bragging or swanking." The members of L Detachment would be carrying out secret, perilous tasks that might well impress other soldiers and civilians, but they should never speak about them outside their own ranks. This was sound military policy, but it also reflected Stirling's personal allergy to boasting. The men of the SAS were expected to maintain a discreet silence about their activities.

As the mini-camp took shape, Jock Lewes set about devising a training program of spartan rigor, a regime so severe that many came close to quitting—which was, of course, exactly what Lewes wanted the quitters to do.

Lewes's intention was to create a force capable of landing in the desert, and then operating there for far longer than anyone else had attempted before. Training began almost immediately in explosives, first aid (including amputation in the field), radio operation, and identification of enemy aircraft. Navigation was of vital importance, given the vast and all but featureless terrain: there was training in map reading, compass use, and celestial navigation. Lewes instituted intensive weapons drills, using Thompson submachine guns and Webley pistols. Much of the training was conducted at night. During the day, the same operations would be carried out by blindfolded men, so the others could observe the way men move and react in nighttime conditions. Lewes also framed a program of memory training, to enable the filing of accurate intelligence reports, and initiative tests to see which men responded well to unexpected situations. They were even assigned homework to do in their tents, which had to be handed in the next morning. Reg Seekings found this particularly demanding: "The physical side was easy, but the writing, the mental side . . . Everybody else would be asleep and I'd still be struggling with my notes." Each unit of between four and six men would include a specialist navigator, a driver-mechanic, and an explosives expert, but with such small teams, and such a high probability of casualties, everyone had to be able to do everything.

"Lewes Marches" were a particularly telling example of the man's constructive brutality. Within days of arriving in Kabrit, Lewes began a series of route marches across the desert, "starting from 11 miles working up to 100 miles with full load," while gradually reducing the water ration. In order to work out how far a man could walk in the desert, Lewes first tested himself: he would set off alone, transferring a stone from one pocket to the other every hundred paces, and calculating the resulting overall distance on the basis that one stone was equal to eighty-three yards. Since he was covering huge distances, this created the added burden of slogging through the sand with his pockets full of stones. The men were permitted to carry water, but told not to drink it until the day's march was completed. Self-control in relation to water was a matter not just of life and death but of military discipline.

The men were instructed never to share their own water bottle with a friend, for in extremis such an act could create tensions that might explode in terrible ways: "You'd got to train your mind to carry the water, and leave the damned stuff alone." Such marches were not only demanding but very dangerous, since Lewes insisted that the desert treks be carried out without vehicle, medical, or radio backup. If something went wrong, if the navigator miscalculated, if someone fell ill, the results might well be fatal. Above all, he sought to instill supreme physical stamina and self-confidence, to make the men so inured to hardship that the reality, when it came, would feel almost easy. "The confident man will win," Lewes insisted.

As for Lewes himself, the disciplined deprivation seemed to give him strength. He wrote: "I can keep going almost indefinitely on one cup of tea at breakfast, and tea and one glass of water at lunch and supplemented by two or three oranges."

Training the men in parachuting was obviously of the first priority. Lacking any sort of formal parachuting expertise, Lewes took an experimental approach: he decided that jumping from the back of a moving vehicle would replicate the lateral and vertical movement of a parachute landing. It doesn't, but it is a very effective way to break bones. Lewes, as ever, used himself as a dummy. First he rolled forward off the tailgate of a truck moving at fifteen miles per hour. Then he rolled backward. Then he gradually increased the speed. Then he forced the men to do the same. One after another, they leaped into the desert at up to thirty-five miles per hour, landing (or more often sprawling) in an explosion of dust and sand. Rudimentary protection was provided by strapping on some borrowed American baseball gear, including kneepads and helmets. Several men were injured, some quite badly, in what was less a useful training exercise than a primitive test of nerve. Next Lewes devised a trolley that would hurtle downhill with a parachutist aboard before slamming into a buffer and hurling him out. "By the end of the first week's training," one NCO recalled, "every man in the unit was sporting a bandage or plaster, some were in splints." Finally, Sergeant Jim Almonds designed and built a wooden jumping platform, which was safer, though not much. "Very primitive equipment locally constructed and no qualified instructors available," a later report noted.

With Lewes on board, Stirling had five more officers to recruit. He chose with extreme care.

Lieutenant Bill Fraser seemed slightly baffled by life, too delicate for soldiering—but he had seen some hard fighting. Tall and thin, with protruding ears and a restrained manner, he had followed in his father's and grandfather's footsteps by joining the Gordon Highlanders. During the Litani River action, an assault on Vichy French positions, Fraser had been shot in the face, the bullet bouncing off his chin strap but leaving him with no more than a "slight concussion." Some of the soldiers considered him "a bit strange"—code for "homosexual"—and nicknamed him "Skin Fraser." He may well have been gay, but it is noticeable that, at a time of intense homophobia in army ranks, most of his comrades in arms (with some notable exceptions) could not have cared less. Fraser was a superb leader.

Another recruited officer was Eoin McGonigal, a Catholic Irishman who had signed up with the Royal Ulster Rifles and then joined the commandos. Two Englishmen, Lieutenants Peter Thomas and Charles Bonington (father of the future mountaineer Chris Bonington), were added to the roster.

Stirling's final choice of junior officer was both inspired and quite odd: inspired because the officer in question would set an unparalleled standard for courage and leadership in the SAS; and odd because he was also given to volcanic explosions of temper and sometimes violent insubordination. He was truculent, troubled, and dangerously unpredictable, particularly when drunk, which was often. A celebrated international rugby player, a frustrated poet and barroom brawler, this man was 240 pounds of highly volatile human explosive. At the time when Stirling set out to recruit him, he was also allegedly in prison for thumping his commanding officer.

Robert Blair Mayne, known by all as Paddy, was one of seven children of a prosperous Protestant family from Northern Ireland. Born in Newtownards in County Down in 1915, he had excelled at rugby as a schoolboy, and went on to read law at Queen's University Belfast, where he won the Ireland universities heavyweight boxing championship. Over six feet tall, broad-shouldered and swift, he first played for Ireland's national rugby team, in the position of lock forward, against Wales in 1937, and went on to represent Ireland on five subsequent occasions. In 1938, he was one of eight Irishmen chosen to take part in the Lions' tour of South Africa. One reporter noted his "quiet, almost ruthless efficiency." The war interrupted what had seemed destined to be a great rugby career. He signed up with the Royal Ulster Rifles, and then the commandos. After the Battle of Litani River in June 1941, he was mentioned in dispatches for the impressive way he had commanded his troop, achieving his objectives and bringing back a large clutch of prisoners.

All of which makes Paddy Mayne sound like some plastic model of academic, athletic, and military virtue. Which he most emphatically was not.

Mayne struck many, on first meeting, as a subdued, almost shy man. After a few drinks, he became boisterous; after a few more, he became argumentative and challenging; quite soon after that, it was time to get out of the bar.

His conduct during the Lions' tour of South Africa broke all records for drunken misbehavior, in a sport not noted for sobriety and tranquillity off the field. He repeatedly broke into his teammates' rooms after midnight and smashed all the furniture to splinters; in the company of Welsh player "Bunner" Travers, he headed down to the Durban docks to get plastered and pick fights with the longshoremen; he argued with the team manager, and then disappeared on a three-day bender. One night he found a team of convicts chained up beneath Ellis Park stadium, where they were being put to work erecting stands. This he considered barbaric, so he returned the following night with bolt cutters and set free at least one, and possibly all of them. In an attempt to impose some restraint on Mayne, he was made to share a hotel room with teammate George Cromey, a Presbyterian minister. One night, after an official dinner, Mayne vanished. Cromey was still waiting for him at 3:00 a.m. when Mayne, in bedraggled evening dress, burst in and announced, "I've just shot a springbok," before dumping a very bloody, very dead South African antelope on the floor. He had run into some hunters in a bar and gone off for a little midnight game hunting.

This was Mayne the amusing drunk. Mayne the vicious, fighting drunk was a different proposition altogether. In the latter state, he was liable to pick up people who had annoyed him and hurl them quite considerable distances, or simply beat them senseless. He never remembered what he had done the next morning. As one of his closest friends put it, Mayne was "a very nice and kind fellow, most of the time, although he could be roused to be something else . . . once he had gone beyond a certain point, drinking, he became somebody quite different." Inside Paddy Mayne there was a deep reservoir of anger that welled up in violence; it had found one channel on the rugby field, and another in alcoholic postmatch mayhem. On the battlefield, it would produce heroics; off it, Paddy Mayne's destructive demon could erupt without warning, and with terrifying force.

What was the source of Mayne's inner fury? He may have been subconsciously rebelling against a rigidly strait-laced Protestant upbringing. He had a strong aversion to the use of foul language. The only person he feared, it is said, was his mother—who was, admittedly, petrifying. Mayne was a deeply literate man, with a particular liking for the darker poetry of A. E. Housman, and he may have harbored dreams of becoming a writer; some have seen frustrated creativity as the root of his anger. There have also been suggestions that he had homosexual inclinations. Certainly, his relations with women were strained, and he never established a long-term heterosexual relationship. "How could any woman love a big, ugly man like me?" he once said to his brother. Male sexual banter on the subject of women could send him into a rage. He was intensely secretive about his emotional life, as he was about much else. Mayne's sexuality has no bearing whatever on his qualities as a soldier, except to the extent that the repression of his feelings may have contributed to an inner turmoil that made him a most complicated and angry man, but a very remarkable soldier.

Mayne was said to have been in prison, for striking a superior officer, in the late summer of 1941. The story is told that he was playing chess with Eoin McGonigal, his closest friend, when they were interrupted by his commanding officer, Lieutenant Colonel Geoffrey Keyes, an upper-class Old Etonian and the son of Sir Roger Keyes, the director of combined operations. Keyes was a brave man (he would die just a few months later in an abortive attempt to kidnap Rommel, winning a posthumous Victoria Cross), but he had the voice of Bertie Wooster and exactly the sort of patrician manner that lit Mayne's very short fuse. A row ensued, Mayne pushed Keyes, who fell over and cut himself on the edge of a table. According to some accounts, the confrontation ended with Mayne running Keyes out of the mess tent on the point of a bayonet. Soon afterward, Mayne applied to be transferred to the Far East. If he was arrested, there is no supporting evidence in the archives. Stirling, however, told and retold the story of how he had discovered Paddy in prison, and arranged for the charges to be dropped in order to get him into L Detachment. Mayne never denied it.

Mayne did not like posh people. As a militant Ulster unionist, he was instinctively anti-Catholic. He despised the way certain officers seemed to gain preferment through social connections. So the first meeting between Mayne and David Stirling—an upper-class, Catholic officer with unrivaled access to the old-boy network—was never going to be easy. According to Stirling, Mayne eyed him with dark suspicion as he laid out his plans and asked the Irishman if he would like to come aboard. Mayne listened, and then began asking questions in a "gentle, slightly mocking voice," with his light Ulster twang.

Finally, Mayne leaned back: "I can't see any real prospect of fighting in this scheme of yours."

Stirling was quick in response. "There isn't any . . . except against the enemy."

Mayne laughed. He was hooked. But, before they shook on it, Stirling had one condition: "This is one commanding officer you never hit, and I want your promise on that."

"You have it," said Mayne.

Stirling was only half joking. He would always remain wary of Mayne's "vicious temper, at times unnatural in its ferocity." Recruiting Mayne was like adopting a wolf: exciting, certain to instill fear, but not necessarily sensible.

THE OFFICERS UNDERWENT exactly the same training as the NCOs and other ranks: they marched together, leaped off the back of the lorry at the same speeds, and studied maps, compasses, and explosives together deep into the night. And when Lewes deemed that they were ready, they jumped together.

The first real parachute jump was scheduled for October 16, 1941. The RAF's 216 Squadron had agreed to provide a Bristol Bombay aircraft, which, though not ideal for parachuting, was a lot safer than the Vickers Valentia from which Stirling had so disastrously jumped four months earlier.

The first team, or stick, of ten parachutists jumped without incident, the static lines smoothly yanking out the parachutes and then safely disconnecting. Young Johnny Cooper drifted gently to earth, marveling at the view of the Gulf of Suez and beyond to the Great Bitter Lake. He landed lightly in soft sand, and "felt a sense of stupendous elation."

Then the second stick climbed aboard and the Bombay trundled into the air. The first to jump was Ken Warburton, a twenty-one-year-old from Manchester, a keen amateur pianist, who had done some fine pounding on the stolen piano in the mess. The second was his friend, a young Scotsman named Joe Duffy. Warburton jumped; Duffy followed him a few seconds later. The third man was about to leap, when the RAF dispatcher hauled him back with a look of horror.

The first two clips on the static line had twisted and sheared off. Warburton and Duffy were plummeting to earth with parachutes unopened, their screams clearly audible to those on the ground. There can be few more horrendous ways to die than the slow seconds as a fully sentient person tumbles through unresisting air. The two men landed close together, and were killed instantly. Duffy, it appeared, had still been desperately trying to pull his parachute out by hand as he hit the ground.

The deaths of Duffy and Warburton stunned the rest of the unit. Jock Lewes immediately called a parade and announced that the men had died due to a fault in their parachute lines, which had now been rectified; everyone would be jumping in the morning. This was the moment for faint hearts to back out. None did. "We made our way to the canteen, each man with his own thoughts but no one speaking . . . never in the history of the SAS has a canteen been as deathly quiet as it was that night."

David Stirling was first out of the plane the next morning, as he had to be. He had more reason than most to dislike parachuting, having barely recovered from his first attempt. He knew his classical mythology, and must have wondered if he was flying too close to the sun in his attempt to forge a unit of parachute raiders. It was, he later said, the hardest jump he ever made. He landed well, and rolled. One by one, the men followed. A cheery cockney named Bob Bennett played the mouth organ as he descended. One NCO recalled: "That night in the canteen we were again one big happy family of fifty noisy men, but we didn't forget to drink a toast to our two absent brothers."

Stirling had made it clear, from the outset, that failure would not be tolerated: anyone who did not fit in, or proved unable to reach Lewes's demanding standards, would be ejected. Several had already dropped out, unable to take the pace of training. "There will be no second chances," Stirling had told them. He tried "not to hurt feelings when rejecting someone," but reject them he did, in quite large numbers, politely but inflexibly. Fear of being "returned to unit" (RTUed, in army parlance) stalked the detachment, but also motivated and drove them on. "That fear of an RTU was with everybody," said Reg Seekings. "It was always there, at the back of the mind." The men with the right stuff were prepared to go to extremes to fulfill a training program others fled from. A note in the files records that one private soldier "walked 40 miles across the desert in stockinged feet rather than fall out after [his] boots gave way."

A dread of humiliation in front of one's peers may not be the most noble of motivations, but among many groups, particularly young males locked in physical competition, it often provides the most forceful impetus of all. In the SAS, one of the motors of success was the collective fear of failure. The only acceptable direction was forward. "Never run away," Jock Lewes instructed them. "Because once you start running, you've stopped thinking."

As numbers were whittled down, by death, dropouts, illness, and rejection, another kind of bonding mechanism began to emerge: the sense of belonging to an elite unit, barely one hundred strong, tested by trial, selected for survival. Even before it went into action, this strange and mixed bag of independent-minded individuals was beginning to forge a collective identity. "They weren't easily controllable," Stirling later admitted. "They were harnessable. The object was to give them the same purpose. . . . That band of vagabonds had to grasp what they had to do in order to get there."

All soldiers complain. Grumbling is a cherished part of military tradition, a form of pressure release that does not necessarily reflect genuine dissatisfaction. L Detachment grumbled as it bonded. An official investigation later noted that Lewes's training regimen was the "hardest ever undertaken in the Middle East," with the men being put through their paces an average of nine or ten hours a day, "plus night schemes." The food at the Kabrit camp was supremely nasty, consisting largely of bully beef, biscuits, herring, dried bread, and yams. While the men were becoming exceptionally fit, they were also permanently, ravenously hungry. One night, as a treat, the cook served jam-roll pudding. Reg Seekings decided his portion was too small, and reacted in the way he usually did: he pushed the plate into the face of the poor kitchen orderly. On another occasion after about a month of grueling training, a minor rebellion erupted: a group of men had been digging holes in the sand for hours; it was boring, boiling, and "appeared to be mindless." They downed tools and stomped off to the mess tent. According to Seekings, it was Jock Lewes who averted mutiny by turning the episode into a test of machismo. He jumped on a table and shouted: "You've all got a bloody yellow streak a mile wide down your backs! You just can't take it! Unless you can prove otherwise."

The uprising subsided, but tensions still simmered.

In such a small unit, close attachments and intense enmities rapidly arose. Friendships evolved slowly, and fights erupted quickly. Stirling had given orders that "scrapping" between the men would not be tolerated: "Toughness should be reserved entirely for the benefit of the enemy." But friction was inevitable.

Cooper and Seekings, the young grammar school boy and the pugnacious boxer, loathed each other on sight. Cooper, with his more refined accent and education, was a red rag for Seekings, who had left school at fourteen to work as a farm laborer, before joining the Cambridgeshire Regiment. Cooper had probably never met anyone quite as raw and belligerent as Seekings, and he did little to hide his opinion of the older man as a thug and a bully. "We hated each other's guts," recalled Seekings. "I was the country yokel, he was the public schoolboy." The two men avoided each other as much as possible.

Lieutenant Bill Fraser tended to keep to himself, spending much of his time alone in his tent with a stray dog, part dachshund, he had adopted and named "Withers." Paddy Mayne picked up on the rumors of Fraser's homosexuality and teased him brutally, a cruelty that in no way undermines, and may even reinforce, suggestions that Mayne was gay himself. "Paddy used to give him a hell of a time, because he thought he was that way inclined," one contemporary noted. "Paddy could be cruel, especially after a few."

The one man in the unit who was neither awed nor intimidated by Mayne was Eoin McGonigal. "Dark-haired, dark-faced, slim and neat," McGonigal had also fought at the Litani River, where he had won a reputation for coolness under fire. The two men had known each other since before the war. McGonigal's father had been a judge in County Tyrone, but the family had moved north after the partition of Ireland. The two young men probably met on the rugby field, and had visited each other's homes and families. Their friendship had deepened after they joined the Royal Ulster Rifles in early 1940, and then together applied to join the commandos. "They were absolutely inseparable," said one contemporary. McGonigal was slightly built and gentle, with a knack for conciliation and a liking for fair-haired women. "Apart from that, they seemed to have almost every other taste in common." When Mayne became drunk and aggressive, only McGonigal appeared able to calm him. As a Catholic Irishman from the South, McGonigal might easily have been the butt of Mayne's sectarian prejudice, but there is no evidence they ever exchanged a harsh word. It seems likely that Mayne urged Stirling to recruit McGonigal, and felt a strong sense of responsibility for his welfare. "McGonigal is here with me," Mayne wrote to his sister in September, like a schoolboy delighted to find himself in the same class as his best friend.

By October, the men had been training at peak intensity for two months, without having a clear idea what they were training for. The waiting exacerbated the tension. Stirling was forced to spend much of his time in Cairo, chivvying the "unfailingly obstructive and uncooperative" military bureaucracy for supplies and backup.

The work he was doing to meet the detachment's logistical needs was as important as any amount of training. Lewes acknowledged as much: "Together we have fashioned this unit. David has established it without, and I think I may say I have established it within." Yet Stirling was acutely aware that while the others were slogging through the desert and living under canvas, he was usually moving around pieces of paper and sleeping in a comfortable bed. During his long absences, the group was developing its own internal dynamics, frictions, and rivalries.

Stirling worried that "Paddy was emerging as the natural leader."

THE FIRST OPPORTUNITY to demonstrate the team's practical prowess came in the form of a bet. Heliopolis airfield, the home of the RAF's 216 Squadron, was ninety-four miles from Kabrit, and surrounded by a barbed-wire fence. An RAF group captain had told Stirling his chances of creeping onto a British airfield undetected were "practically non-existent." Stirling disputed this, and offered a wager to settle the matter. It was agreed that the fake attack would take place on a moonless night toward the end of the month.

The men selected were divided into five groups of ten, led by Lewes, Mayne, Fraser, McGonigal, and Charles Bonington. Each man carried a pack containing rocks equivalent to the weight of a full complement of explosives, along with four pints of water, half a pound of boiled sweets, biscuits nicknamed "sand channels" (because they were hard enough to drive a jeep over), and some raisins. They marched at night, and hid out during the day, each man covered with a strip of burlap that blended with the desert sand, as camouflage against being spotted from the air. The October sun was still roasting: lying out in the midday heat covered by a strip of cloth was a particularly brutal form of self-torture. After three days of dehydration, some of the men were hallucinating and close to collapse. "I was dreaming of a running tap every time I closed my eyes," Bennett, the cockney mouth organist, later recalled. On the fourth night they reached Heliopolis, cut their way through the outer perimeter, and began planting self-adhesive labels on the RAF planes parked in neat rows. Had the guards spotted them, they might have been shot. Each team deposited around forty stickers (some planes were later found to have several attached) and slipped out of the aerodrome by the same route they had entered. Then they turned themselves in at the army barracks in Abassea, where the guards, seeing a group of smelly, dirty, sunburned men emerge from the desert, initially assumed they must be surrendering Italians. Stirling won £10.

Destroying a plane, however, is far trickier than simply planting a sticky label on it. The most effective weapon against a stationary aircraft is a time bomb that simultaneously explodes and ignites, setting fire to the plane's fuel tanks. This meant combining two bombs into one, with two fuses and a clock timer, a cumbersome device weighing five pounds that took ten minutes to prime. Stirling needed a new sort of bomb: so Jock Lewes set to work, applying a very little knowledge gained from playing with his brother's chemistry set as a child and a great deal of determination. For several weeks he experimented, in a makeshift open-air laboratory away from the camp, with various combinations of gelignite, ammonal, and gun cotton. The sound of the explosions echoed across the desert. Finally, in triumph, he produced a solution: a pound of plastic explosive, rolled with a quarter pound of incendiary thermite and some motor oil. This could be triggered by a pencil detonator, a glass tube similar to a ballpoint pen, with a spring-loaded striker held down by copper wire; gently squeezing the glass vial at the top of the detonator released acid, which then ate through the wire and released the striker, quickly or slowly depending on the thickness of the wire. The detonator could be primed to go off with a delay of anything between twelve seconds and two hours. This homemade explosive-incendiary bomb would prove to be one of the more remarkable innovations of the war: lightweight, versatile, sticky enough to attach to the wing of a plane, hard to spot in the dark, and hugely destructive—an all-purpose time bomb that could be carried in a backpack and primed in seconds. Jim Almonds described it as "a nice little black pudding." The "Lewes bomb" would be a permanent addition to the military arsenal, the ideal desert-raiding explosive, and the first customized weapon created by and for the SAS.

Auchinleck's offensive would be the largest armored operation undertaken by the British to date. The aim of the commander in chief was to push Rommel out of Cyrenaica, relieve Tobruk, and retake the coastal airfields in order to provide vital air cover for the convoys to Malta. Code-named Operation Crusader, it would be launched on November 18.

On November 10, Brigadier Galloway of Middle East Headquarters issued an outline of Operation Squatter, enlarging on the plan laid out by David Stirling in his original memo: on the night of November 17, the night before Auchinleck's tanks began to roll west, fifty-five men of L Detachment would take off from Bagush airfield in Egypt, fly over enemy territory, and then parachute to the desert twelve miles from the coast. A heavy air raid on the airstrips beforehand would create fires that would enable the pilots to navigate toward the drop zone, which would also be identified by the RAF's marker flares. On landing, five teams of eleven men would then attack five forward airfields in the vicinity of Timimi and Gazala, with the aim of "destroying as many aircraft as possible." They would deploy Lewes bombs with staggered timers to ensure that they all detonated at roughly the same time. "The destruction of fighter aircraft is of greater importance than bombers, and German aircraft are of more importance than Italian," the order advised. There were estimated to be some three hundred planes on the five airfields; each team would carry sixty Lewes bombs. In theory, therefore, they should be able to destroy the lot.

Having completed the mission, the men would march some fifty miles inland to a point three miles south of the crossroads on the Trig al Abd, an ancient desert trading track running parallel to the coast. There, they would be picked up by a unit of the Long Range Desert Group (LRDG), a reconnaissance unit, transported to Siwa Oasis, and then flown back to Kabrit by transport plane. The LRDG would keep a watch by day for the returning SAS units, and hang a red hurricane lantern at the rendezvous point visible at night; they would wait for three days; and if at the end of that period the SAS had still not appeared, the LRDG would bury two twelve-gallon water containers and some tinned dates at a prearranged spot, and leave. The men would then be on their own in the desert.

The contribution planned for L Detachment would be small but important: a low-stakes gamble for potentially high returns. If it worked, it might seriously degrade enemy airpower at a pivotal moment; if it failed, at worst a few dozen men would be lost, a small drop in the great military wave surging westward.

Lewes was elated at the prospect of action at last. His letters home ring with the chivalric tones of a Crusader: "We wait to prove ourselves. . . . This unit cannot now die, as Layforce died, it is alive and will live gloriously. Soon our name will be honoured and our ranks filled with those who come seeking honour and nobility."

Chapter 4

INTO THE DESERT

Two hours before takeoff, the RAF laid on what was, by wartime standards, a banquet. There was as much food as the men of L Detachment could eat, and a bottle of beer each. It was even served by RAF officers. This "dinner fit for a king" was intended as a tribute to the departing parachutists, but some detected a melancholy aspect to the elaborate send-off: "We were treated like men going to the gallows." A small flicker of premonitory anxiety, like the rising wind off the desert, wafted through the RAF mess tent at Bagush airfield as the men ate their meal, and with good reason: Operation Squatter ought never to have taken place.

The weather forecast was atrocious. Winds of at least thirty knots were predicted, twice the maximum speed for safe parachuting, with heavy rain. Whirling sand could create serious navigation problems for the pilots, while the gusting wind would probably blow the parachutists, and the canisters containing their equipment, far off course. Visibility on this moonless night would be limited anyway, but in the midst of a desert storm regrouping on the ground would be a severe challenge. Brigadier Galloway of the general staff advised calling off the operation, but the final decision was left to Stirling. He consulted his officers. There was no question of postponement, since Auchinleck's main Eighth Army offensive would be taking place the following day, whatever the weather: the parachute drop would either have to go ahead or be canceled. The men had signed up because they were frustrated by the endless delays that had plagued Layforce; the effect on morale of another cancellation could be terminal. Stirling feared that his enemies at Middle East HQ might take the opportunity to disband his detachment altogether. He would later frame the decision as one in which the very future of the unit was at stake, although he cannot have been certain of this at the time. At the back of his mind must have been the knowledge that his own leadership status would suffer badly if he pulled the plug. "I swore when I started SAS that if we undertook to take on a target on a particular night, we'd do it utterly regardless," he told his biographer. "It seemed to me we had to take the risk." Jock Lewes and Paddy Mayne agreed; the decision was popular with the men. Stirling's choice was prompted by conviction, audacity, and hope. It was a brave decision, but the wrong one.

The day before the operation, Stirling wrote to his mother, with a jauntiness he may not have felt, revealing that he would soon be taking part in "the best possible type of operation [which] will be far more exciting than dangerous."

The five sticks of parachutists would be led by Stirling, Lewes, Mayne, McGonigal, and Bonington. Once safely on the ground, each group would split into smaller units of between four and six men, before moving on to attack the five separate airfields. Each plane also carried parachute canisters containing explosives, weapons, spare ammunition, fuses, and extra rations. The men were each equipped with an entrenching tool and a small haversack containing grenades, a revolver, maps, a compass, and rations (these consisted of dates, raisins, cheese, biscuits, sweets, and chocolate). They were dressed in standard desert uniform of khaki shorts and shirt, with rubber boots, helmets, and mechanics' overalls. The American Pat Riley and young Johnny Cooper would both jump with Jock Lewes; Seekings was under Mayne's command.

"The wind is getting up," one of the pilots remarked gloomily as the men climbed aboard.

Of the officers, Fraser was absent, left behind on account of a wrist broken in parachute training; he planned to travel with the LRDG and join the others at the rendezvous. Jim Almonds was also forced to remain in camp, since his young son was gravely ill with suspected meningitis and he expected to be recalled to Britain at any moment. "Watched them embark and the planes take off," Almonds wrote in his diary. "They are a fine crowd of lads. How many will I see again?"

DAVID STIRLING HIT the desert floor with such force that he blacked out. Just a few minutes earlier, the pilot of the plane, unable to navigate accurately in the storm, had asked if he should abort the jump. "No, certainly not," said Stirling. Then he jumped. When he came to, he found he was being dragged along by his parachute "like a kite" in a forty-mile-per-hour wind, whipped and grated across sharp gravel and rocks. After a struggle he managed to twist the clip of his parachute release, and the canopy flapped away into the storm. Stirling staggered to his feet in the darkness, covered in lacerations and pouring blood but otherwise unharmed. He switched on his torch and began shouting into the wind. The pilot had told him which compass bearing the men had been dropped on: by following that bearing, the first man dropped should come across the second, and so on. It took two hours to gather what remained of his team. One man had vanished; apparently unable to release himself from his parachute, he had probably been dragged to death. Another had broken an ankle and could not stand. The worst injury was to Sergeant Jock Cheyne, a tall twenty-five-year-old Scotsman from Aberdeen, "full of quaint Scots humour." Cheyne had broken his back on landing. The men had all been told that in case of serious injury their best chance of survival would be to "crawl to a roadside and hope." There was no road for miles, and poor Cheyne was unable to crawl anywhere. The supply canisters had vanished. Armed only with revolvers and a handful of grenades, and barely a day's supply of water, Stirling's unit was now useless as an attacking force.

Once his dismay had subsided, Stirling became practical. He would continue toward the coast and try to carry out a reconnaissance of the target airfield, and perhaps an attack, along with Sergeant Bob Tait, who, like himself, seemed to have suffered only superficial injuries. Sergeant Yates, the company sergeant major, would make for the LRDG rendezvous with the four men still able to walk. The two most badly injured men would be left behind. "It's an awful feeling," one of the departing men recalled, "to leave two friends, but you had to, couldn't carry them, just had to hope they would be picked up by the Germans." The two men were left with a supply of water and two revolvers. Few words were said. There was little to say. Cheyne lay unconscious, "huddled in the blankets that were brought him." The injured men were never seen again.

Paddy Mayne's team fared little better. Reg Seekings, to his intense and vociferous fury, was dragged across the desert for fifty yards and straight through a thorn bush, flaying hands, arms, and face. "I could feel the blood running down, and Jesus that got my temper up." Finally he wrenched himself free of the parachute. Mayne had landed unscathed, and gathered his bedraggled troop. They had come down, he estimated, at least a dozen miles from the drop zone. Dave Kershaw, a veteran who had fought on the Republican side in the Spanish Civil War, had broken an arm. Two other men were too badly injured to walk. Only two of the canisters were located, containing two tommy guns, eight bottles of water, six blankets, and some food and explosives. Mayne insisted the mission would go ahead as planned. The most injured men would be left with water and rations. "We shook hands with them, wished them luck, and set out to find our objective." (The two men were captured by an Italian patrol the next day.)

Of the five parachuting parties, only that of Jock Lewes had landed more or less intact. Their plane had come under attack from the coastal antiaircraft batteries, and the pilot, dodging searchlights and fighting the wind, shouted that he had only a vague idea of where they were. "We're jumping blind," thought Johnny Cooper as he leaped into the dark. The only sound he could hear as he descended was the wind howling though the rigging lines of his parachute. Below was pitch-darkness. The sudden impact with the ground knocked the wind out of him but, staggering to his feet, Cooper was astonished to find he had broken no bones. The dozen men in his team all survived the jump uninjured, despite discovering that extrication from a parachute harness in a raging wind was "a job for Houdini." Only two of the canisters were located, but at least these contained Lewes bombs and machine guns. They were still combat capable. "Well, fellows," said Lewes with unfeigned cheeriness, "I don't know where we are, so we can only carry out the operation assuming that we may be within five to ten miles of our original dropping zone." Led by the burly and reassuring figure of Pat Riley, they headed north, in what they hoped was the direction of the airfields.

The plane carrying Charles Bonington and his party was flown by Charlie West, a regular RAF pilot from Devon and a favorite with the men of L Detachment. With black storm clouds rolling in off the Gulf of Bomba, West flew in low, crossing the coast at three hundred feet, and immediately came under heavy attack from the ground; antiaircraft fire tore through the port engine, the cockpit instruments, and the fuel tanks. With the plane crippled, the mission was aborted and West wheeled eastward toward home—or what he thought was east, unaware that a piece of shrapnel had lodged beneath the compass. The plane was flying in a circle. Running low on fuel, West landed on a patch of scrubby desert, in the dark, in the teeth of the worst storm in the area for thirty years, an achievement later cited as an "impeccable feat of flying."

As dawn rose, the party discovered that they had come down just a few miles from the coast. They now faced imminent attack from the very planes on the Gazala airstrip they were supposed to be destroying. West immediately took off again, with what little fuel remained, in the hope of being able to "flop" the Bombay into Tobruk harbor, still in British hands, some thirty miles to the west.

West had wrestled the plane to a height of about two hundred feet when an Italian Breda gun opened fire from below, sending bullets thudding into the fuselage. Moments later a Messerschmitt 109, dispatched from Gazala, joined the attack. West's navigator was killed beside him. Several of the men were hit. West attempted evasive action and then somehow managed to land the stricken plane, which hit a series of low sandhills and slewed to a stop after a "violent tobogganing over the rough sandy ground." Some of the men were thrown clear; several more were trapped beneath the burning fuselage; West himself, with a fractured skull, broken ribs, and internal injuries, was still in the cockpit, miraculously alive. The soldier who had walked forty miles in his socks during training was mortally injured and would die the next day. The men prepared to make a fighting stand, but when the plane came under attack again from ground forces it became clear that the situation was hopeless. The unit surrendered to a Luftwaffe pilot at 7:00 a.m. Lieutenant Charles Bonington and the other survivors were all made prisoners. (West spent a year in various POW camps, before escaping from a train taking him from Italy to Germany by cutting through the floorboards.)

Eoin McGonigal's party was doomed from the moment of landing. McGonigal himself appears to have broken his neck on hitting the ground, and may never have regained consciousness. The team laid up overnight. By morning, McGonigal was dead. He was twenty years old. The others quietly buried him in the sand and then struck out for the rendezvous point. Lost, they wandered onto the Timimi airfield and were captured by Italian guards.

Back at Kabrit, Gentleman Jim Almonds fretted over the fate of his comrades.

> The lads are now 280 miles inside enemy territory, hiding in the sand and awaiting dark to start their reign of terror and destruction. After the massacre is over and the enemy planes blown up, there remains that terrible march back through the desert. No one who is sick or

wounded can possibly make it, and none can afford to help . . . I am not there. I sit back here in the safety of the camp and wish I were . . . Reality beats fiction for sheer, cold, calculating courage. Some of the lads cannot be beaten. Films and books of adventure fall far short of the real thing. More will be heard of the SAS should this raid go through as planned. My mates are somewhere in enemy territory . . . poor devils, they need all the luck possible.

For a few hours after the landings, the wind had seemed to abate, as the two teams under Mayne and Lewes set off in the dark, marching north. Then the skies opened. Not the spitting rain of the previous evening, but a blinding, soaking deluge. A desert storm and flash flood is a terrifying experience: dry riverbeds, or wadis, transform in minutes into raging torrents. "The water was up to your chest," recalled Johnny Cooper. Lewes ordered his men to a section of higher ground, now an island in the flood, and announced that he and Sergeant Riley would push ahead to try to locate the target airfield. They returned after a few hours, having seen nothing but an endless damp horizon of desert and convinced they must have been dropped far to the south of their target. "To get to the airfield before light is now out of the question," said Lewes. Using blankets as makeshift tents, the men huddled together for a sodden, freezing, hungry, sleepless night. "With constant wringing out of blankets and the occasional sip at the old rum stakes we managed to survive," one man recalled. As dawn broke the rain eased, but it was clear the operation would have to be aborted: the explosives were soaked and useless. Lewes ordered the men to turn around and head toward the rendezvous point. "At least we won't die of thirst," said Lewes brightly, as the men set off, alternately marching and wading across the still-sodden sands. Riley led the way, bullying, urging, and cajoling: forty minutes' marching, then twenty minutes' rest, then another forty minutes' marching, hour after hour.

Mayne's team was in a similar plight, although, unlike Lewes, Mayne had a good idea of where he was. In the five hours of darkness after landing, his team marched six miles. At dawn, they laid up in a wadi about five miles south of the target, Timimi airfield. Mayne conducted a swift reconnaissance and declared that they would attack that evening. Then the downpour started. "In the middle of the desert we had this raging torrent," recalled Seekings. "I've never been so cold in my life." Several haversacks were washed away. "It rained as I have never seen it before—clouds broke by the score, and our nice dry little wadi was transformed in a matter of minutes into a lake." The men were soaked to the bone; even their cigarettes were waterlogged, a source of deep annoyance for soldiers who craved tobacco more than food.

Mayne ordered the men to salvage what they could and scramble to higher ground, but the rain had already done irreparable damage to the sabotage equipment. "I tried two of the time pencils and they did not work. . . . I tried the instantaneous fuses and they did not work either." Mayne was prepared to continue, and attack the planes using only grenades. "We had a hell of a time talking him out of it," said Seekings. "But there was no point getting knocked off in a hopeless cause. You couldn't knock an aircraft out with a grenade." With ferocious reluctance, Mayne aborted the mission, and as night fell once more, the men set off on the thirty-five-mile slog to the pickup point.

Lewes and his men trudged south. It was beginning to grow dark, on the evening of November 19, the third day of the operation, when Johnny Cooper spotted a pole incongruously sticking out of the desert: a marker for the Trig al Abd, an old Italian signpost complete with fascist symbol on top, pointing toward Egypt in one direction and Benghazi in the other, and indicating that they were just a few miles from the rendezvous point. The men cheered. Some kissed the post. Then they headed west. As they walked, Cooper could see two stationary stars on the horizon, which gradually resolved themselves into hurricane lamps posted on twin hillocks, one hundred yards apart. The password was "Roll Out the Barrel"; the men broke into a loud rendition of that old drinking song. A voice emerged from the gloom: "Over here, Pommies." They had found R1 Patrol, a New Zealand unit of the Long Range Desert Group, their trucks encircling a small fire, and hidden in a shallow desert hollow. The welcoming feast of bully-beef stew washed down with rum-laced tea was "the best meal I have ever had in my life," said one of the survivors. The disheveled remnants of Mayne's team stumbled into the camp a few hours later.

The following morning, before the rest of the camp was awake, David Lloyd Owen of the LRDG was brewing up his tea when a tall figure emerged out of the dawn gloom. "My name is Stirling," the man said. "Have you seen any of my chaps?" Lloyd Owen had not, of course, for all of the other chaps on Stirling's team had been captured. Under Sergeant Yates, they had taken a wrong turn and stumbled into an Italian patrol. Stirling and Sergeant Tait had managed to reach the coastal escarpment, locating the coast road but not the airfield, before turning back and trudging fifty miles through the rain to the rendezvous. They were the only members of their stick to make it back.

Stirling remained at the desert rendezvous for two more days, scanning the horizon in the hope that other stragglers might eventually emerge. None did.

The L Detachment survivors tried to look on the bright side. They had encountered some cruel ill luck, weather even worse than forecast and conditions "almost unbelievably unsuitable for a parachute operation." The pilots, unable to see the coast or the drop-zone flares, had simply guessed at the right moment and altitude to drop the men, who had consequently landed "all over the bloody shop." Not one of the sticks landed within ten miles of its intended drop zone. No one could have anticipated the biblical flood of the next day.

Stirling pointed out that he had personally reached the coast road and seen the sea, having approached from the desert, which proved that "given the right conditions what I had thought of was possible." The men had performed admirably, under appalling conditions. "The whole section behaved extremely well," wrote Paddy Mayne, "and although lacerated and bruised in varying degrees by their landing, and wet and numb with cold, remained cheerful." Cooper was philosophical: "OK, we've had a beating. It's been a fiasco, but the weather did it all. The general plan was alright." Seekings, as usual, struck an uncompromising pose: "You can't sit around thinking about casualties. We joined to fight a war. We knew what it was about." But behind the bravado, even Seekings was rattled.

There was no disguising the grim truth: Operation Squatter had been an unmitigated disaster. Of the fifty-five men who parachuted into the gale on November 16, just twenty-one had returned. The rest were dead or injured, missing or captured. L Detachment had lost most of its strength without firing a shot, attacking the enemy, or detonating a single bomb. They had been defeated, not by force of arms, but by wind and rain. The mission had done nothing to support Operation Crusader. Worse than that, the failed operation had alerted the enemy that the British were conducting active sabotage behind the lines. Bonington's party, shot down and captured, was under orders to reveal only name, rank, and serial number to their German captors. But someone had blabbed.

Late on November 19, as the remnants of L Detachment were slogging back to the rendezvous, British code breakers intercepted and deciphered a message sent by the commander of Gazala airfield to the Luftwaffe and the panzer commanders of the Afrika Korps. "Reference the sabotage detachment of the Lay Force [*sic*] from the shot down Bombay. Attention is drawn to five [*sic*] further Bombays which operated over Cyrenaica in the night of 16–17/11. Accordingly you must count on the probability that further sabotage detachments were dropped."

One of the captives had apparently revealed that they were part of a larger sabotage team. On the return journey, the LRDG convoy carrying the SAS survivors had come under attack from an Italian Savoia-Marchetti fighter. The decoded message might explain why: the enemy was already looking for the other British sabotage units in the desert.

The men were deeply demoralized. Everyone had lost a close friend. Jock Cheyne, left in the desert with a broken back, had been a particular chum of Pat Riley's. Jim Almonds learned of the loss of Bonington's unit with a stab of guilt. "I should have been with that plane," he reflected. "The terms of fate are past all understanding." Though he never spoke of it, the loss of Eoin McGonigal devastated Paddy Mayne. "Eoin McGonigal was the one person who liked Paddy before he became a hero," said one who knew them both. One of Mayne's biographers goes further: "If there was a real love in [Mayne's] life, it was his friend Eoin McGonigal." Something snapped in Mayne when McGonigal died.

What should have been a triumphant first mission, Stirling conceded, had been "a complete failure." He had feared that canceling the operation might jeopardize the future of the SAS; by pushing ahead, he had very nearly destroyed it. "It was tragic . . . so much talent in those we lost," he reflected. The reduced detachment seemed quite likely to be disbanded.

But in disaster, as so often, lay the germ of salvation.

Chapter 5

THE LONG RANGE DESERT GROUP

I T MAY HAVE BEEN DURING THE TWO-HUNDRED-MILE JOUR-
ney back to Jaghbub Oasis, the Eighth Army's forward base,
that inspiration struck David Stirling. Riley claimed that the
idea came to Stirling while they were lying under a tarpaulin
with Jock Lewes on the night they reached the desert rendezvous.
Seekings insisted that Stirling's eureka moment came while they
were scouring the horizon for stragglers. The most likely source
of inspiration was David Lloyd Owen, a highly intelligent officer
who would go on to command the LRDG. But the most extraordinary aspect of this idea is that it seems, in retrospect, so blin-
dingly obvious: if the LRDG could get the SAS out of the desert
without difficulty, then the reconnaissance unit could surely drive
them in as well, thus cutting out all the danger and uncertainty
involved in jumping out of airplanes in the dark. Quite why this
glaringly good idea had not occurred to anyone before is one of
the enduring mysteries of the SAS story.

The Long Range Desert Group was the brainchild of Ralph
Alger Bagnold, soldier, explorer, scientist, archaeologist, sedimen-
tologist, geomorphologist, and the world's greatest living expert
on sand. Bagnold was the brother of Enid Bagnold, author of the
novel *National Velvet*; his own, less popular but no less durable
contribution to world literature was *The Physics of Blown Sand and
Desert Dunes*, first published in 1941 and today still influencing
NASA's ongoing research into sand dunes on Mars. A veteran of

the Somme and Ypres, a pioneer in desert exploration, inquisitive and indestructible, Bagnold spent much of 1930 driving a Model A Ford around the vast desert between Cairo and Ain Dalla in search of the mythical city of Zerzura. He made the first east-west crossing of the Libyan desert in 1932, driving more than three thousand miles and winning a medal from the Royal Geographical Society. Then he drove through the Mourdi Depression of northeastern Chad and back to Libya. He worked out that reduced tire pressure and wider tires increased speed across desert terrain; he invented a condenser that could be attached to a car radiator to prevent it from boiling over, and steel channels for unsticking vehicles bogged down in soft sand. He developed "Bagnold's sun compass," which, unlike the traditional magnetic compass, was unaffected by desert iron-ore deposits and was also impervious, in Bagnold's words, to "changes in the positions of magnetically uncertain spare parts carried in the vehicles." He spent so long being battered by the desert wind that his nose achieved a permanent roseate hue. "Never in our peacetime travels had we imagined that war could ever reach the enormous empty solitudes of the inner desert, walled off by sheer distance, lack of water, and impassable seas of sand dunes," Bagnold wrote. "Little did we dream that any of the special equipment and techniques we had evolved for very long-distance travel, and for navigation, would ever be put to serious use." But that, of course, is what happened. Nine months after the outbreak of war, Major Bagnold was given permission to form and command a mobile desert scouting force to operate behind the Italian lines: the Long Range Patrol (later the Long Range Desert Group) was born in Egypt in June 1940, to commit "piracy on the high desert."

The Libyan desert covers well over a million square miles of the earth's surface, an area roughly the size of India. Stretching a thousand miles south from the Mediterranean and twelve hundred miles from the Nile Valley to the mountains of Tunisia and Algeria, it is one of the most inhospitable places on earth and, in terms of humanity, one of the emptiest. Most of the North African war so far had been fought on a narrow coastal strip, along which a single paved road hugged the edge of the Mediterranean. Only a few ancient trading tracks traversed the interior. In daytime, the temperature could soar to 135° F, and then plummet below freezing at night. The only water is to be found in a handful of small oases. It was not an easy place to live, and a very easy place to die, but it offered an opportunity for warfare of a most unconventional and uncomfortable sort. In theory, this mighty desert was enemy-held territory; in reality, Bagnold calculated, the Italians and Germans had "only enough motor transport for a radius of action of a paltry 100 miles." The rest was his. So far from being an impassable, hostile wilderness, the desert was a place that men, with the right training and equipment, could cross and recross, navigate, watch, hide in, and survive indefinitely. To the uninitiated, the landscape appears bleak and monotonous, but the apparently flat expanse hid myriad dips and depressions, rocky patches, shelves, and escarpments, as well as treacherous seas of soft sand. There were points to navigate by, if one knew how to see them.

The broad purpose of the LRDG was to carry out reconnaissance and raiding, to find out what the enemy was doing where and, from time to time, to attack him. Initially, Bagnold recruited New Zealand farmers, leathery outdoorsmen used to surviving for long periods in harsh terrain; gradually, as the unit expanded, volunteers came forward from Rhodesian and British regiments. After long weeks in the desert, the sand buccaneers had developed a distinctly piratical look, sporting Arab headdresses, sandals in place of boots, and bushy beards. Equipped with adapted, lightweight, heavily armed vehicles, the LRDG carried out deep penetration and covert missions behind the lines, moving undetected across huge swathes of territory and perfecting the art of desert camouflage and evasion. LRDG units became adept at slipping unseen up to the coastal road itself and observing the movements of enemy troops; these "road-watching" operations provided some of the most important military intelligence of the war. Axis forces never adapted to the challenges of the desert in the same way. At the time when Stirling first encountered them, the LRDG were the masters of their terrain: "There seemed to be nothing they did not know about the desert."

Siwa Oasis in Egypt, about thirty miles from the Libyan border, was the operational headquarters and forward base of the LRDG, under the command of Colonel Guy Prendergast, another desert explorer who had traveled with Bagnold before the war. Waiting in Siwa for a plane to take him back to Cairo, Stirling asked Prendergast if the LRDG might be prepared to act as a transport service for the SAS to and from coastal targets. Prendergast said that this would be perfectly possible, so long as the task did not interfere with the unit's primary reconnaissance role. Thus began one of the most fruitful partnerships in wartime history, bringing together the fighters of the SAS with the expert desert navigators of the LRDG. The SAS would come to refer to the LRDG, with deep admiration, as the "Libyan Taxi Service." The hairy, hardened, experienced men of the LRDG were cabdrivers unlike any others.

STIRLING HAD FEARED that the abject failure of Operation Squatter might prove the death of the SAS. But, in truth, the brass at Middle East Headquarters had greater concerns than the loss of a few dozen men in a sideshow to the main battle. Operation Crusader was not going smoothly: Rommel's panzers had inflicted a major defeat on the British 7th Armoured Division, and the Afrika Korps had pushed into Egypt in a dramatic counterthrust. General Neil Ritchie, Stirling's initial backer and family friend, had taken over command of the Eighth Army on November 26; with so much on his plate, Ritchie had little attention to spare for the grim details of a single failed operation. Auchinleck believed that Rommel's eastward countermove had left German supply lines along the coast fully extended and vulnerable to attack—exactly the sort of task for which L Detachment had been formed. But if the SAS was to attack by land, rather than by air, it would need a forward base from which to launch operations. The ideal spot had become available: an oasis refuge deep in the Libyan desert, but within striking distance of the coast.

Jalo Oasis lies about 150 miles southeast of the Gulf of Sirte and west of the Great Sand Sea, the undulating ocean of dunes that makes up about a quarter of the greater Libyan desert. With its white wooden fort, mud houses, fringe of palm trees, and glittering azure waters, Jalo is exactly what a mirage of an oasis might look like in a fairy story. In fact, it is anything but a paradise: roastingly hot and whipped by an unceasing wind that can drive a man mad, it was home to a handful of Berbers, a few ill-tempered camels, and a colossal population of flies. The oasis water is almost undrinkably salty and thick with minerals, but as the only water source for hundreds of miles, Jalo was of vital strategic importance. It would change hands several times in the course of the war.

On November 18, 1941, in support of Operation Crusader, Brigadier Denys Reid had set out from Jaghbub Oasis, on the Egyptian border, with E Force, a mixed unit of Indian, South African, and British troops, intent on capturing Jalo, three hundred miles to the west, from the Italians. It was a sign of his determination that Reid took armored cars, but only enough petrol to travel one way. Six days later, Reid's force reached Jalo and, after a daylong battle with its surprised Italian defenders, seized it. Reid's orders were to continue north with a flying column and attack the extended Axis supply lines along the coast, while the Eighth Army launched another counteroffensive against Rommel's Afrika Korps. The LRDG were ordered to mount a series of raids on the airfields at Sirte, Agheila, and Agedabia on the Gulf of Sirte, in order to put out of action enemy planes that could otherwise inflict carnage on Reid's troops approaching from the south. It was Guy Prendergast, probably as a result of his conversation with Stirling, who suggested that L Detachment might be better equipped for this task: "As LRDG not trained for demolitions, suggest pct [parachutists] used for blowing dromes."

Here was an opportunity for the SAS, or what remained of it, to prove its worth. Stirling quietly gave orders to Jock Lewes to head to Jalo in the deep desert with the remaining men and as much weaponry, ammunition, and explosives as he could lay his hands on. Lieutenant Bill Fraser, his wrist now healed, was back on active duty, along with his dog, Withers. Jim Almonds was also back in the ranks, although still anxiously awaiting word on the health of his baby son.

The SAS took up residence in its new forward base on December 5. Johnny Cooper thought Jalo looked like a "Foreign Legion outpost, straight out of *Beau Geste*." Brigadier Reid warmly welcomed the new arrivals, as well he might: he was under orders to advance north to the area of Agedabia, near the coast, by December 22; if the SAS could inflict serious damage on the enemy air forces in the fortnight before that date, it would make Reid's task considerably easier.

Stirling established his headquarters in a disused storehouse, gathered his officers, and began to make plans for the next SAS operation—in the knowledge that, if it failed again, this would also be the last.

Chapter 6

DEVIL COUNTRY

THE AIRFIELDS OF THE GULF OF SIRTE WERE STRUNG OUT along the Mediterranean coast like buoys on a rope: Sirte, Tamet, Nofilia, Agheila, Agedabia. Once these had been sleepy little tuna-fishing villages; now they were home to the German and Italian air forces in North Africa, vital aerodromes from which Axis fighters and bombers harried the British lines, attacked the convoys sailing to and from Malta, and provided the air support so vital to the Afrika Korps. Auchinleck's counteroffensive had pushed Rommel back as far as Gazala, but the front line was still so distant that a direct attack on the airfields seemed laughably unlikely to those living and working on them. The air bases were linked by the coastal highway. Most were lightly defended, according to intelligence reports, with only a perimeter fence, a handful of sentries, and perhaps a few land mines; some were hardly guarded at all. These were juicy targets indeed: the long, frustrating wait for action was about to come to an end, in spectacular fashion.

Stirling laid out a three-pronged plan of attack. The first assault team, led by Stirling himself and Paddy Mayne, would be transported across the desert to within striking distance of Sirte on the western gulf coast. Sirte was believed to be the largest of the airfields. They would carry out surveillance and attack on December 14. The same night, a force under Jock Lewes would strike Agheila, the southernmost gulf airfield and the nearest to

Jalo. Finally, on December 21, just before Brigadier Reid struck north with his ground troops, Bill Fraser's section would attack Agedabia, on the eastern side of the gulf.

Two days after arriving in Jalo, Stirling's force of fourteen men climbed into the trucks of the Rhodesian patrol of the LRDG, and set off on the 250-mile journey to Sirte. The SAS team included Reg Seekings and Johnny Cooper, whose mutual antipathy had been sharpened by a fierce argument at the oasis just before departure. A sleeping blanket belonging to Seekings had gone missing. He stormed around the camp, angrily demanding its return and threatening to beat up whoever had stolen it. "Oh, bloody well lie down," said Cooper, who was trying to sleep. Seekings saw red, his habitual visual color: "You get on your feet, you bastard, and I'll knock your bloody block off. Big bloody mouth. I've had enough of you." The fight was defused, but it left a simmering residue. Seekings and Cooper were dismayed to find that they were both deployed in Stirling's task force; they would have to spend the next six days side by side, bouncing around in the back of a truck and then going into action together. "We were unhappy. We didn't speak. Looked daggers at each other all the way up on the job."

There are few experiences more uncomfortable than a long desert journey in a lorry with little suspension and wooden seats: the jolting and rattling made sleep impossible; the heat and monotony induced a state of sweaty semi-consciousness. For three days they rumbled and jounced northwest, the oceans of sand and rock broken by the occasional gully and unexpected escarpment. The trucks broke down or got bogged down, and had to be mended or laboriously dug out using sand mats. Tires burst, frequently but unpredictably. It was freezing at night, broiling by day, with no intermediate moment when the temperature felt bearable. Already, the men of L Detachment were calling it "Devil Country."

The navigator of the LRDG's Rhodesian unit was Mike Sadler, a quiet, unassuming, and exceptionally intelligent twenty-one-year-old. Born in Gloucestershire, Sadler was working on a farm in Rhodesia when war broke out. He immediately downed tools and signed up with an artillery unit, which was later deployed to North Africa. "I didn't want to miss anything. Some people are like that at that age. I certainly was." He transferred to the LRDG after encountering some members of the unit in a Cairo bar. Sadler had a naturally geometric mind. On his first cross-desert expedition, he watched the navigator steering with compass and chart, and decided that this was far more interesting and challenging than anything the army had so far offered. Trained in celestial and solar navigation by a former merchant seaman, he swiftly emerged as one of the LRDG's best guides. The desert, despite appearances, is neither flat nor featureless, but in 1941 large areas were still unmapped, blank spaces on the map. Desert navigation, like its equivalent at sea, is largely a matter of mathematics and observation, but the good navigator also relies on art, hunch, and instinct. The uneven ground caused the shadow on the sun compass to tilt this way or that, requiring the navigator to compensate. Sadler had an uncanny, almost unerring ability to know where he was, where he was going, and when he would get there.

On the third evening, Sadler announced that the little convoy was now seventy miles south of Sirte, and within range of enemy aircraft. The trucks had been painted a fetching if unlikely combination of camouflage colors: pale green and rose pink. In any other surroundings, they would have stuck out comically, like "something from the fairground," but when stationary they blended into the flat, pale colors of the desert. On the move, however, they were ominously easy to spot from the air. Sure enough, at around midday the next day, as the convoy crawled across a boulder-strewn plain, an Italian Ghibli reconnaissance plane appeared overhead, dropped two bombs, which fell wide by a considerable distance, and wheeled back toward the coast. The drivers gunned their engines and scrambled to take cover in a patch of low camel-thorn scrub to the south, perhaps half a mile in length. Camouflage nets were thrown over the vehicles, and the men spread out to take what cover they could find beneath the spiny bushes. Minutes later, two more Italian planes appeared. Their pilots deduced that the convoy must be hiding in the scrawny undergrowth, and so for the next fifteen minutes they blasted and bombed the patch of dry greenery. "Lightly and inefficiently strafed by Italian air force," reported Paddy Mayne, who spent the time calmly reading a paperback. Eventually, having run out of patience or ammunition, the Italian planes departed. It was a most unpleasant foretaste of an experience that would soon become routine: being hunted and attacked from the air in open desert. No lives or vehicles had been lost, but the unit had forfeited the element of surprise. "They'll report our presence all right," the LRDG veterans predicted.

The trucks rumbled on through the darkness, now driving without lights and reliant entirely on Sadler's compass and sense of direction. The route took them close to the village of Qasr Abu Hadi, little more than a cluster of tents and low buildings some fifteen miles south of Sirte. In one of those goatskin tents slept a pregnant woman, the wife of a local goat herder: six months after the SAS raiders had passed in the night, on June 7, 1942, she would give birth to Muammar Gadhafi, the future dictator of Libya.

At 9:00 p.m. on December 14, Sadler called a halt and announced that they were now just four miles from Sirte airfield. Since the Italian pilots had surely given warning of the approaching raiders, Stirling announced a change of plan: they would split the force in two. He and a couple of men would push on that evening, assess the chances of getting onto Sirte airfield, and, if it seemed feasible, attack the following night. Paddy Mayne, meanwhile, would drive some twenty-eight miles west to Tamet airfield with the rest of the troop, and launch a simultaneous assault there. "If one of us fails, the other may be lucky," said Stirling.

At around midnight, Stirling's men slowly groped their way toward Sirte airfield, looking particularly "villainous," as one recalled, "carrying large rucksacks and sub-machine guns and wearing stocking caps." The silhouette of a parked plane loomed up ahead, and then another. They were gingerly working their way around the aircraft, when a loud scream erupted from beneath their feet. Stirling had trodden on a sleeping Italian soldier. A gun went off in the dark. The three intruders turned and ran. Behind them they heard an antiaircraft gun start up, apparently shooting out to sea. The defenders, it seemed, were under the impression that they were facing a seaborne invasion. "The Italians were getting extremely excited and shouting," recalled Cooper. That evening, British intelligence intercepted and decoded a peculiar message from the mayor of Sirte, claiming that his town was under attack.

Stirling's team was safely back behind a low ridge about a mile to the south when the firing subsided. As dawn rose, he peered over the crest and his heart warmed. The little whitewashed town of Sirte was clearly visible now, and so was its airfield, with rows of neatly parked Italian military aircraft, predominantly Caproni bombers. Stirling counted at least thirty. In the course of the morning, more planes arrived, and others took off. The men dug in to wait for nightfall, when they would attack. But as the hot day wore on, they observed that something odd was happening on the airfield: more planes were taking off than were landing. By afternoon, there were only a handful left. And by evening, none at all. The events of the previous day had spooked the Italians into a full-scale evacuation of the airfield.

Deeply disconsolate, Stirling waited for nightfall, and then headed back to the rendezvous point near the coast road, where he had arranged to be picked up by the LRDG.

Paddy Mayne was busy burning.

Half an hour earlier, the Irishman and his team of ten had slipped onto Tamet airfield, single file, without being detected. Dozens of planes were lined up along the runway. Instead of planting their bombs immediately, however, Mayne pointed toward a large hut on the edge of the field; light shone from beneath the door and there were sounds of merriment within, a mixture of Italian and German voices. "Some sort of party must have been going on." Mayne, Reg Seekings, and one other man crept up to the door, guns drawn. Mayne described what ensued.

> I kicked open the door and stood there with my Colt
> .45, the others at my side with a Tommy gun and
> another automatic. The Germans stared at us. We
> were a peculiar and frightening sight, bearded and
> with unkempt hair. For what seemed like an age we just
> stood there looking at each other in complete silence. I
> said: "Good evening." At that, a young German arose
> and moved slowly backwards. I shot him . . . I turned
> and fired at another some six feet away.

Then the two submachine gunners opened up. "The room was by now in pandemonium."

As the attackers withdrew, the survivors began to return fire. Mayne ordered four men to keep the Germans and Italians pinned down inside the mess hut, and set off with the remaining six to attack the stationary planes. In the space of fifteen minutes, they planted Lewes bombs with thirty-minute time fuses on fourteen planes, and then climbed into the cockpits of ten more and shot up the dashboard controls. Mayne is said to have torn out one cockpit panel with his hands. Bombs were also swiftly planted on the petrol tankers, a line of telephone poles, and an ammunition dump.

A final volley of gunfire and grenades seemed to silence the last of the resistance from inside the hut. Mayne gave the signal to fall back to the rendezvous. "We had not gone 50 yards, when the first plane went up. We stopped to look but the second one went up near us and we began to run." Seekings turned back to see Tamet airfield aflame as planes exploded in quick succession and the petrol dump blew up with a shattering roar. From the desert, Mike Sadler observed the devastation: "It was a dramatic sight. The sky lit up by flashes. I had never seen anything like it." A few minutes later, Mayne and his men arrived at the rendezvous, panting and elated. The truck drivers started their engines, Sadler set his course and the convoy steered south through the darkness, the sky shivering and shimmering behind them.

As Stirling and his two men waited to be picked up, the sky to the west took on a livid glow, the air seemed to shudder for a moment, and the boom of rolling thunder rippled across the wind. "A succession of flashes" lit up the darkness, one observer recalled, followed by the eerie pink of fire reflected on nighttime clouds. The spectacle, said one of the LRDG officers, was like the northern lights, the great particle painting that splashes across the sky in the high latitudes of the Arctic and Antarctic. "What lovely work," murmured one of the men.

Mayne's assault on the officers' mess had been daring, brutal, and quite reckless. It alerted the enemy to the attack before the first bomb had been planted. Killing highly trained pilots was, arguably, an even more effective way of crippling enemy airpower than destroying the planes themselves, but it veered away from sabotage and close to assassination. It seems quite possible that Mayne, faced with the opportunity to kill at close quarters, had been unable to stop himself. "No prisoners taken," Almonds noted in his diary, without further comment. Stirling was shocked when the scale of the carnage was reported back to him. "It was necessary to be ruthless," he later wrote, "but Paddy had overstepped the mark. . . . I was obliged to rebuke him for over-callous execution in cold blood of the enemy."

In an official report on the Tamet raid, Mayne made only the briefest mention of the assault on the officers' mess: "Hut [was] attacked by sub machine gun and pistol fire and bombs were placed on and around it. There appeared to be roughly 30 inhabitants. Damage inflicted unknown."

Mayne's laconic report was very different from a British newspaper account that appeared soon afterward, apparently the result of a briefing from a highly imaginative press officer. Headlined "Raid on Tamet Landing Ground," it read:

> In the officers' mess of an Axis aerodrome just beyond Cirte [*sic*], 30 German and Italian pilots sat one night drinking, laughing and talking. The campaign wasn't

going too well for them. Rommel was retreating. But still they were a long way from the fighting line. The mess was snugly blacked out, a bright fire was burning. Some of them were playing cards.

Suddenly the door flew open . . . A British lieutenant, a famous international sporting figure before the war, walked into the mess with one man.

A burst from a Tommy-gun swept the card players and drinkers at the bar. German drinking songs turned to shouts of horror. Those who weren't killed or wounded tried to make for the doors or windows. They were mown down before they had gone a yard. They were 500 miles behind the front line, but a British patrol was in their midst.

The contrast between the studied understatement of those involved and the imaginative accounts written afterward by those who were not is a good example of the tension between reality and mythology that has dogged the SAS ever since.

Sadler expertly led the convoy back to Jalo Oasis, where the salty waters seemed the height of luxury after more than a week in the parched desert. Success had subtly altered the chemistry within the unit. Reg Seekings and Johnny Cooper, chalk and cheese in class, education, and temperament, had found a bond. In the adrenaline rush of danger, their former antagonism seemed to evaporate. As Seekings put it: "He'd got guts. I'd got guts. And we just clicked. We'd seen a bit of action and as dawn came up we got talking about that night, how exciting it was." As they chatted, the middle-class, thoughtful youngster and the bellicose working-class fist-fighter discovered that they had more in common than had ever separated them. Cooper had shown a level of pluck that Seekings had not expected, but that he respected. In turn Cooper seems to have sensed a way to measure himself against the older man's brutal fearlessness. "I was perhaps more scared than he was," he later acknowledged, "but I would never let myself down in front of him." Seekings recognized that, whatever the situation, Cooper would not turn tail. "We had complete understanding of each other, we were very confident in each other. It's a great thing to have a man alongside you who you know you can trust, and whatever happens he's not going to beat it." Stirling noticed the way the two men had suddenly connected: "Cooper was quick witted and high spirited. Seekings was slow and steady and shrewd. They were perfect complements to each other."

Henceforth, Cooper and Seekings would be inseparable, on the battlefield and off, forging an enduring, fighting partnership that would last for as long as they lived.

Jock Lewes and his team had gone out to strike Agheila airfield the same night, and arrived back at Jalo Oasis a few hours after the Stirling-Mayne party, with a story to rival theirs for adventure, if not in results. They had reached the target, 160 miles to the north, without incident, only to discover that the airfield, described in intelligence reports as a teeming air hub, contained not a single aircraft. Lewes blew up a line of telegraph poles and two trucks, and then ran into a patrol of native soldiers, attached to one of the Italian colonial regiments, which immediately surrendered. The corporal was taken prisoner. Never one to miss a racial tag, Lewes immediately nicknamed him "Sambo." Determined that the journey should not be entirely wasted, he hit on an alternative plan: the LRDG convoy included a single captured Lancia truck. "Having studied the enemy's convoy procedure," Lewes decreed that the Italian lorry could be used as a simple form of disguise. A few miles along the coast road, beside a small fort known as Mersa Brega, was a military truck stop and staging post, with a roadhouse canteen said to be frequented by senior German and Italian officers. Dozens of lorries, petrol tankers, and other inviting targets would be parked up around the building.

Lewes waited until the coast road was empty before he swung the Italian truck onto the tarmac, followed by the two British lorries. The Germans had captured a number of vehicles during earlier fighting, and with luck the British trucks would not attract undue attention. Lewes ordered the men to smoke, and appear as relaxed as possible. They drove for nine miles, and counted forty-seven enemy vehicles passing in the opposite direction. No one paid any attention to the troop of men wearing the same dusty khaki clothing as everyone else.

The sun was going down as the convoy pulled into the truck park and stopped. Lewes climbed out and covertly assessed the possibilities. He counted twenty-seven vehicles. Several drivers were dozing in the shade beneath their trucks. Others were eating inside the roadhouse. The new arrivals elicited no interest whatever. At this moment, an Italian driver appeared and asked Lewes for a match.

"*Italiano?*" asked the friendly Italian.

"*Inglese,*" said Lewes.

The Italian laughed politely, apparently assuming that this must be a German exercising that country's famously opaque sense of humor. He stopped laughing when Lewes pressed a revolver into his back and said, "Get on the truck." The Italian prisoner was bundled into the back, where he promptly burst into tears and had to be gagged.

A surreal scene now took place at the Mersa Brega roadhouse. Lewes's men moved quietly around the parking lot, planting bombs with short time fuses on each vehicle, including a three-ton Italian truck containing incendiaries. It was a matter of only a few minutes before someone spotted what was afoot.

Dave Kershaw opened the door of a truck, preparatory to tossing in a bomb, and was blinded by the flash of a gun fired by the driver inside. The bullet missed him by inches. "I just held up the .45 and pulled the trigger. I must have caught him right on the bridge of the nose because his face opened up." Kershaw could never expunge the memory of "what the inside of a man's face looked like" when shot at point-blank range. "It wasn't pleasant."

Suddenly the air was fizzing with bullets, though the enemy fire was "poor and erratic." Jim Almonds, manning the 20mm Breda antiaircraft gun mounted on the back of the Lancia, took aim at the roadhouse, and pulled the trigger. Nothing happened. The oil in the firing mechanism had thickened with the drop in temperature. "So we used the small guns we had. Shot the place up." The firing lasted twenty minutes, in "a hectic scrap fought at about 30 yards' range."

On a signal from Lewes, the men piled into the LRDG trucks, leaving behind the Lancia and between fifteen and twenty enemy dead or wounded. Lewes calculated that they had exploded thirty-eight bombs on the various vehicles and around the roadhouse. On the road, they passed a peculiar-looking, brightly painted vehicle with blacked-out windows, and emptied a blast of machine-gun fire into it as they sped past. Only later did it emerge that they had shot up a mobile Italian military brothel. After a few more miles, Lewes instructed the drivers to turn off the road, and head south for Jalo. The Italian prisoner, who now seemed only too happy to be in captivity, got extremely drunk on rum and sang loudly most of the way back to the oasis.

The participants would later describe what had happened at Mersa Brega as a "bash out," a "shoot out," and a "bit of fun." None described it as what it really was: a ferocious, close-quarters gun battle, at once thrilling, petrifying, and exceptionally bloody.

Bill Fraser and his team had already set off for Agedabia by the time the other three patrols got back to Jalo. In a way, Fraser's was the most crucial of the raiding parties. Brigadier Reid, the commander of E Force, was supposed to reach the area and link up with another flying column on December 22; if Fraser failed to inflict serious damage on the air squadron at Agedabia, the fighters and bombers could intercept Reid's force in the open and cut it to pieces. Reid's flying column set out in high spirits; only he and a handful of his officers knew that success, and survival, might well depend on five men trundling north in a lorry filled with explosives, just a few hours ahead of them.

Fraser and his team, armed with a total of forty Lewes bombs, were dropped by the LRDG sixteen miles short of the target;

from a safe observation point, they counted thirty-nine planes on the airfield, including a number of Italian fighters parked wingtip to wingtip. At 9:15 p.m., in pitch-darkness, they reached the airfield perimeter and slipped through the fence, carefully stepping over some tripwire booby traps. Over the next thirty minutes they planted thirty-seven bombs on planes, with staggered timers to ensure that all exploded at roughly the same moment; one bomb was found to have a damaged detonator and the two remaining bombs were planted in the middle of a sandbagged building filled with shells, ammunition, and incendiaries. The first bomb went off at forty-two minutes past midnight, followed by three more in quick succession, as the attackers scrambled off the airfield. Marching at speed for the rendezvous point, they tried to count the explosions. Then the bomb dump went up "with a blood-curdling roar" that sucked the air out of their lungs from half a mile away. The little team "yelled with joy and excitement."

The next morning, the LRDG trucks carrying Fraser and his men encountered the vanguard of Reid's flying column, heading north. Fraser was summoned to report to the brigadier. "Sorry, Sir, I had to leave two aircraft on the ground as I ran out of explosives, but we destroyed thirty-seven," he told the delighted Reid, who thumped him on the back and exclaimed, "There's nothing to stop us now." It later transpired that Rommel himself had been in the town of Agedabia that night. "He must have had a bit of a headache," wrote Reid. Fraser, the most inscrutable and distant of the officers, had succeeded beyond all expectations and established an important principle: a team of just five men could wreck an entire airfield in a matter of minutes.

On December 23, Fraser's team reached Jalo. An early Christmas celebration took place that night, with roasted gazelle, shot on the return journey, tinned Christmas pudding, and hot lime juice with rum. The Italian prisoner captured at the Mersa Brega roadhouse did a lot more singing. It was, wrote the cockney Bennett, "a very, very nice Christmas."

In the space of just one week, starting with Mayne's raid on Tamet and ending with Fraser's attack on Agedabia, L Detachment had racked up an astonishing tally of destruction: more than sixty planes, at least fifty enemy killed or wounded, including a number of pilots, dozens of vehicles, several miles of telephone line, petrol dumps, a bomb depot, and a brothel. Two LRDG men escorting Fraser's group had been accidentally killed by a British bomber, but the SAS unit had not suffered a single casualty. Total losses amounted to one secondhand Italian lorry. Cooper wrote that at last the founding theory of L Detachment had been "magnificently vindicated."

Stirling had no intention of resting. Rommel was falling back and growing more dependent on air support than ever. The SAS would strike again.

Chapter 7

A PARTY OF GHOSTS

FRASER HAD BEEN BACK IN CAMP FOR ONLY A FEW HOURS when Stirling asked him, with unanswerable politeness, whether he "would mind" heading back out again to mount another raid, "if he was not too tired." It would be "fun," Stirling said, and might even lead to "the grand slam: fifty planes in one night." It was an order, of course, disguised as an invitation, which encouraged the recipient to feel as if he was actually volunteering. Stirling somehow managed to make a perilous and daunting mission behind the lines sound like a day at the races, a spot of competitive excitement with convivial company. Stirling suggested that, after his first success, Fraser might like to attack the airfield at the Arco dei Fileni, the pompous stone arch erected near the coastal highway by Mussolini to mark the border between Tripolitania and Cyrenaica. A triumph of fascist kitsch and a monument to Italy's colonization of Libya, the British derisively referred to it as "Marble Arch." It never occurred to Fraser to turn down Stirling's courteous call to arms: no one ever did.

At the same time, Jock Lewes was detailed to attack the airfield at Nofilia, to the west, equidistant between Sirte and Marble Arch. Stirling and Mayne would launch a second attack on Tamet and Sirte: they knew the ground now, the enemy would not expect a repeat raid so soon, and, even if they did, they would have had little time to erect more robust defenses.

On Christmas Eve, Stirling, Mayne, and their men set off in a six-truck convoy, heading back to the coast. This time, the navigator Mike Sadler made for the Wadi Tamet, a long, deep ravine that ran into the desert from the town of Tamet. Entry to the ravine required a tricky drive down its steep sides but, once at the bottom, the trucks could drive at speed on a relatively flat surface with less danger of being spotted and attacked from the air. Three days later, at 9:00 p.m., some six miles from Tamet, the group split again: Mayne's team set off for the airfield where he had inflicted such carnage two weeks earlier, while Stirling and his men climbed back into the trucks to drive to Sirte, along the coastal road. Both teams would attack at 1:00 a.m. The experience of the first raid seemed to suggest that they could simply drive along the road without attracting attention; but first they had to get onto it. Stirling and his team heard the traffic before they reached the road: an entire German armored division, tanks on trailers, lorries and armored cars, was rumbling down the road toward the front at Agheila, where Rommel was digging in. It was impossible to get onto the road without being spotted. For four hours, the long German convoy continued. In the early hours, exactly on schedule, the sky lit up over Tamet. "Paddy's lit another bonfire," said Cooper. Finally, at around 3:30 in the morning, the last vehicle in the German convoy passed, and the three LRDG trucks slipped warily onto the road. Stirling insisted on being dropped near the airfield, but time was running out. New fencing had been erected around the base. The LRDG would wait at the rendezvous until no later than 5:00 a.m. "There was no hope of cutting through the wire and destroying the planes within so short a time." Once again, seething with frustration, Stirling called off the attack.

As a consolation, the LRDG agreed to drive along the road and, in the same manner as Lewes a few days earlier, "do a bit of shooting." A few miles down the road, they came across twelve supply trucks parked up, their drivers asleep in tents nearby. The team quietly planted Lewes bombs and drove on. A little farther ahead stood a line of lorries and other vehicles, beside a larger tented encampment. As dawn was breaking, the three trucks screeched past, firing tommy guns and rifles and hurling grenades, before veering off into the desert. This action certainly terrified a lot of sleepy Germans, but how much real damage the drive-by shooting inflicted is debatable. Cooper described leaving behind a "total confusion of blazing vehicles," but there was no disguising that Stirling's second raid had also failed. Back at the Wadi Tamet they were reunited with Mayne and his team, which had destroyed another twenty-four aircraft at Tamet, many of them newly arrived from Italy to replace the planes wrecked the week before. Stirling tried to make light of his own failure. "I'll have to pull my socks up," he said. "The competition is too hot." The remark was only half in jest. Like fighter pilots, the men were keeping a tally of their kills, which brought out "the spirit of personal competition." Of the officers, only Stirling had so far failed to inflict any serious damage on the enemy.

Jock Lewes set out for Nofilia airfield on Christmas Day, in convoy with Fraser and his band. Lofty martial sentiments still burned brightly in Lewes's heart, reminiscent of an earlier age of knightly valor and saintly sacrifice. "I feel my strength, and fear is far away," he wrote. "I will not seek to save my life but will choose the most difficult and dangerous work . . . If I am to die it matters only to those who live on and whom by living I might have helped." The news that he was likely to be decorated for his actions in Tobruk before joining the SAS only intensified his sense of glorious destiny. In October, he had written to Miriam Barford, asking for her hand in marriage. On Christmas Eve, he sent a telegram to his family, wishing them a happy Christmas and reporting that he now had a "Pullable Beard and Possible Medal." Jim Almonds was in Lewes's team. His thoughts also turned to home, to his sick son and the wife from whom he had concealed his activities. "What a Christmas," he wrote in the diary addressed to his wife. "You think I am in a training job somewhere. I feel a terrible cad to be hoodwinking you like this, but if I told you the truth, well, you would only worry."

Fraser and his team were dropped off for the attack on Marble

Arch on December 27, with rations and water for three days. Lewes pushed on, telling Fraser he would pick him up on the way back.

The following day, the LRDG deposited Lewes's team about eighteen miles from Nofilia aerodrome. A swift march and a dawn reconnaissance revealed potentially rich pickings. The airfield was covered in Stukas, the formidable German dive-bombers, brand-new to judge from their bright paintwork. Jim Almonds counted forty-three in all. "It must be glorious to soar over the desert on a morning like this," he wrote in his diary. They would attack that night.

About a mile outside the airfield perimeter was a disused water cistern, or *ber*, an ancient storage tank hollowed out of the rock to collect the rare desert rainfall. It was dry, sheltered, and a convenient place to hide out and wait for night to fall. But it was not empty. In one corner lay the parchment-dry, skin-covered skeleton of a desert fox that must have fallen into the old well and found it impossible to escape. For all his ferocity, Almonds was a man of sensitivity. As they waited for darkness to fall, he found himself imagining the last struggles of the doomed fox. "It made quite an impression on me. It would obviously carry on, until it was too weak to jump any more. I felt deepest sympathy for the animal. The desire to live. The desire to see things through."

At around 2:00 a.m, the men gathered their rucksacks and guns and crept onto the airfield. Lewes clamped a bomb on the first plane they found, and then a second. But as they pushed deeper onto the field, it rapidly became clear that all the other planes had gone. While the men had been in their snug underground cave, they had not heard the aircraft departing. Once again, a mission that had seemed so promising had come to nothing, or very little: even the two planes left on the airfield failed to explode properly, since they were almost empty of fuel.

The twenty-five-mile trudge back to the rendezvous point took all day. In darkness, the LRDG trucks turned and headed back to where Fraser and his team should have been waiting.

It was ten in the morning when the twin-engined Messerschmitt appeared above the horizon, making directly for the five-truck convoy. The drivers slammed on the brakes, in the hope that the pilot might not see them in the shimmering morning heat. The Messerschmitt flew overhead and seemed to be continuing on its way. "Everyone was breathing a sigh of relief," wrote Almonds, when the fighter suddenly banked, performed a tight descending circle, and then roared in low, no more than thirty feet off the ground. "He's coming back," yelled Almonds. The convoy scattered. The Messerschmitt 110 was one of the most lethal fighters in the Luftwaffe, armed with four machine guns and two 20mm cannon capable of firing 650 rounds a minute. As one bore down on the truck with Lewes and Almonds, Almonds seized a Bren gun and scrambled out of the back. Another man grabbed the box of magazines as bullets thudded into the truck, tearing out the center of the floor and blowing off two of the wheels. Lewes, in the front seat, seemed to be fiddling with some papers, no doubt removing the operational orders in case the truck had to be abandoned. Almonds had spotted a rocky knoll nearby, about head-height, that might provide at least some cover. He and the man with the magazines ran for it, joined by three New Zealanders of the LRDG. The German plane had turned and was coming in again. Almonds set up the Bren behind the outcrop and started firing. There now ensued a "deadly game of 'ring a roses' around the rock"; the German plane was fast, but slow to turn; once it had made a strafing pass, the men would scramble around to the other side of the knoll and then blast away at the plane from behind.

"I reckon you got him," shouted one of the New Zealanders. Almonds had indeed hit the rear gunner. The Messerschmitt peeled away, and the attack ended as suddenly as it had started. The respite was brief, for within minutes a pair of Stukas had taken over the battle; they dived in to attack the empty trucks. The men scattered, plunging into some low scrub, and then lying flat and still in the hope they would not be spotted. Some scooped sand over themselves to try to blend into the ground. Some hid under bushes, while others curled up and played dead. "There is no lesson which improves camouflage as well as a low level machine-gunning attack," one man drily remarked.

The first pair of attacking Stukas was replaced by another; for eight hours the onslaught continued, unsystematic but terrifying. In a brief lull, Almonds looked up, and saw oily black smoke rising in the distance: the Stukas had located at least some of the dispersed convoy. In midafternoon, a German reconnaissance plane flew over to assess the damage; the men lay still. Satisfied, the plane wheeled away. The one-sided battle was over. "They thought they'd got everyone," Almonds later wrote. But slowly the remnants of the team emerged from hiding, dusty and exhausted. Only now did Almonds realize that Lewes was missing. "Jock was sat in the truck. I don't know why he didn't get off. Just don't know why." Lewes had, it seemed, obeyed his own injunction: never run away.

A 22mm cannon shell had smashed through Lewes's thigh and severed the femoral artery. Another may have hit him in the back. He bled to death in a matter of minutes.

Jock Lewes was buried in a shallow grave in the sand. Someone said a prayer. A rifle, with his name scratched on it, was planted upright, with a helmet on top, as a temporary marker, "hoping someone would go that way again."

The truck had been badly shot up, but miraculously the petrol tanks remained intact. With something close to engineering genius, one of the LRDG mechanics managed to get it working again. Almonds, two other SAS men, and the LRDG survivors clambered aboard and headed south once more. No other trucks were intact, and the survivors from the rest of the party had already set off on foot for Jalo. Almonds headed first to the rendezvous near Marble Arch, "to let Bill Fraser know we hadn't forgotten him and we would send other trucks out for him." The meeting point was deserted. Almonds was more than eight hours late for the rendezvous, unavoidably detained by an aerial bombardment. Bill Fraser and his team had already moved on. "There was no sign of him or any of the party." They waited a few hours, and then pushed on for Jalo.

The single truck limped dejectedly into Jalo just before midnight on December 31. Stirling was furious that Lewes's body had been left behind, although it was Lewes himself who had insisted during training that collecting the dead was a dangerous waste of time.

Stirling tried not to show it, but the loss of Lewes was a devastating blow. The New Year's Eve gathering was a frugal and melancholy one: some jam, a pot of tea, and a tin of condensed milk. "We'd lost one of our best officers, our best men," said Cooper. "Everybody was upset." Even Seekings, who prided himself on disguising all emotion, was secretly grieving: "In some ways Jock's loss was worse than the 40 men in the abortive raid in November 1941."

In Lewes's empty tent lay an unopened letter from Miriam Barford, written the previous October, joyfully accepting his proposal of marriage.

That night, Almonds wrote in his diary: "I thought of Jock, one of the bravest men I have ever met, an officer and a gentleman, lying out in the desert barely covered in sand. No one will ever stop by his grave or pay homage to a brave heart that has ceased to beat. Not even a stone marks the spot."

The grave of Jock Lewes was never found. This austere warrior from another age was buried where he fell, and was absorbed into the battlefield without leaving a trace.

BILL FRASER AND his four-man team were quite unaware of the fate of Lewes. They knew only that they had failed to link up with the LRDG and Lewes's team and were now stranded in the desert, two hundred miles from Jalo Oasis, with roughly half a pint of water each and enough sardines, bully beef, and biscuits to last two days at most. The landing strip at Marble Arch had seemed impregnable, with freshly dug trench defenses and dozens of alert-looking German guards. The two SAS groups managed to miss each other at the rendezvous site. Finally concluding that the rest of the troop was not coming, Fraser and his men set off on foot, heading southwest.

The last of the water soon ran out. On the third day, they came across a rank pool of brackish salt water. This had to be distilled, a laborious process that produced far too little liquid to combat the dehydration brought on by heat, forced marching, and diarrhea. They resorted to drinking their own urine, and eating berries, snails, and tiny lizards found under rocks.

On January 6, 1942, ten days after being dropped near Marble Arch, the team nearly bumped into a squad of Italian engineers laying telephone lines. They hid until nightfall, and then launched an ambush: the Italians were held at gunpoint while rusty water was siphoned from their truck radiator. The team then escaped back into the desert with two jerry cans of water, some inde-terminate jam, one tin of pears, and another of fishy spaghetti. Despite this gastronomic windfall, some of the men were deterio-rating fast. Fraser decided, as he later put it, to "get a lift." That night, they worked their way back to the coast road, lay in wait, and then flagged down a Mercedes-Benz carrying two German wireless operators. The frightened occupants were disarmed and ordered to drive while the five British soldiers all crammed into the back and Fraser held a revolver to the driver's neck: "We were not going to leave the Jerries behind to raise the alarm." After an hour, Fraser ordered the driver to turn off the road and steer south into the desert, in what he hoped was the direction of the front line. Some fifteen miles later, trying to cross a salt marsh, the car became irretrievably stuck. The Germans were pointed northward and told to start walking. The British Eighth Army, Fraser esti-mated, should be about fifty miles to the east. The next forty-eight hours were eventful; they were shot at by Italian sentries, walked through a minefield, and ate the last of the food: a mouthful of sardines with jam. Some friendly Bedouin nomads supplied a few dates. A burned-out German vehicle, a casualty of earlier fighting, was found to contain several blackened tins of meat roasted by the heat, which were devoured with relish. A sandstorm erupted. Dimly, through the swirling grit, troops could be glimpsed in the distance; whether Fraser and his team would be shot or captured before they starved seemed an open question.

Then came the sound of an English voice. The British soldiers advancing from Agedabia were highly suspicious of the hirsute, ravenous figures staggering toward them out of the storm. "They must have thought we were a band of savages," said one survivor. "With our long matted hair and beards. Faces and hands caked in dirt, and torn ragged clothes." The men, wrote Fraser, had "behaved admirably," displaying undimmed "cheerfulness" throughout the ordeal. "Particularly noticeable was their determination not to be captured under any circumstances."

A few days later, they were on their way back to SAS headquarters at Kabrit, where the rest of the detachment had now returned from Jalo for some well-deserved recuperation. The scattered Lewes party had also made it across the desert on foot, with the loss of only one man who had been unable to walk any farther and opted to wait and be captured. The survival of so many was greeted with astonished delight by their comrades, as if "a party of ghosts" had come back from the dead.

The odyssey had a permanent effect on Bill Fraser's appetite: having come so close to starvation, whenever he caught "the smell of cooking food . . . he had to eat something immediately to satisfy his lust." In the space of a fortnight, Fraser had almost died of thirst, drunk his own urine, crawled across a minefield, dodged bullets, hijacked a German car, eaten a tin of semi-cremated beef, crossed the front line, and trudged for nine days across 150 miles of desert. Reunited with his dog, Withers, and utterly exhausted, he made his way to the tent he had vacated six weeks earlier and was understandably surprised to find that, since it was assumed he was dead, his bed was now occupied by someone else: specifically, the Conservative MP for Lancaster.

Chapter 8

BLITZ BUGGY

Fitzroy Hew Royle Maclean, diplomat, linguist, and explorer, was the latest addition to the SAS ranks, one of the bravest men in the British Army, and one of the funniest. Like Stirling, he was the scion of an ancient and warlike Scottish clan; unlike Stirling, he was an intellectual and a scholar, fluent in Italian, Russian, and German (as well as Greek and Latin). Tall, erect, with an angular face and dimpled chin, Maclean looked like a Roman senator who has just heard a very funny joke. After joining the Foreign Office in 1933, he served in Paris and Moscow with distinction, and was tipped as "one to watch" in the diplomatic service. He was determined to join the armed forces and go to war, but under wartime rules the diplomatic service was classed as a "reserved occupation," which meant that, to his intense frustration, he was forbidden to leave his official post on the Russia desk.

Having tried, and failed, to persuade the Foreign Office to let him go, Maclean hit on a solution that appealed to his finely honed sense of the ridiculous. The fine print of Foreign Office regulations stated that officials must resign if elected to Parliament. To his own astonishment and the fury of his superiors, in October 1941, Maclean managed to win a by-election in Lancaster, after one of the shortest political campaigns on record. He immediately quit the diplomatic service, enlisted with the Cameron Highlanders as a private, and was deployed to North Africa. One night in Cairo late in 1941, at a dinner party, Maclean fell into conversation with a "tall, dark, strongly built young man with a manner that was usually vague, but sometimes extremely alert."

"Why not join the SAS?" said David Stirling, who had briefly met Fitzroy Maclean before the war.

"What is it?" asked Maclean.

"A good thing to be in," came the enigmatic answer.

"It sounded promising," Maclean later wrote. "I said I should be delighted to join."

Fitzroy Maclean, now commissioned as a lieutenant, arrived in Kabrit in mid-January 1942, and was shown to an empty tent by a large guardsman from Aberdeen, who informed him that its previous occupant had been Bill Fraser, adding lugubriously: "The poor gentleman will not be requiring it any more." Maclean had barely settled in when a "wild looking figure with a beard" appeared through the tent flap carrying a small dog and demanded his bed back. Maclean was deeply impressed by the tale of Fraser's epic trek across the desert, "keeping himself alive by drinking rusty water from the radiators of derelict trucks."

Despite the death of Jock Lewes, the experience of the previous weeks had imbued the detachment, in Stirling's words, with "enormous self-confidence and a feeling of exhilaration." More than ninety planes had been destroyed; Fraser and the others had survived against the odds, and the unit had made a dramatic and demonstrable contribution to the war. Stirling paid a visit to Middle East Headquarters in Cairo, and found General Auchinleck in a genial and receptive mood.

The war, suddenly, seemed to be progressing well, as seen from Middle East Headquarters: Rommel had been driven back, Tobruk relieved, and Benghazi captured. The Auk congratulated Stirling on his involvement in attacking enemy airfields "up front," and authorized him to recruit an additional six officers and forty men. Stirling was promoted to major; Paddy Mayne was made a captain. Both were recommended for the Distinguished Service Order (DSO). Fraser would be awarded the Military Cross. Auchinleck was content to allow Stirling extraordinary latitude, in both the planning and execution of operations. Contact with headquarters was maintained by radio, but there is no evidence that the commanding officer either demanded, or expected, to be told exactly what Stirling was doing until after he had done it. Which was exactly the way Stirling wanted it.

With promotions, medals, and battle honors came a new sense of permanence, an increasingly sturdy collective identity. The unit began to refer to itself as "the SAS," and not just L Detachment.

The unit still had its detractors back at base. One critic carped: "Some unit commanders such as Stirling want to be absolutely independent . . . our experience in the past has proven this very unsatisfactory." The newly appointed deputy chief of the general staff, A. F. Smith, wrote: "I agree. It is of course quite wrong to have a number of little private armies." Among the traditionalists within Middle East HQ, there remained a deep suspicion, not entirely unfounded, that Stirling was fighting his own war, by self-made rules. But at least in the short term, with Auchinleck in command, the survival of the SAS was no longer in question. Reinforcing this sense of stability came new insignia, a motto, "operational wings" to distinguish trained parachutists from novices, and a distinctive white beret. The color proved a problem: worn on leave in Cairo's bars, the beret attracted wolf whistles from other soldiers, which inevitably led to fights, despite Stirling's prohibition on brawling. Eventually the white beret would be swapped for a slightly less obtrusive sand-colored version.

Back in October, Stirling had asked the men to come up with ideas for insignia designs. Bob Tait, the sergeant who had accompanied him on the first raid at Sirte, produced the winning entry: a cap badge depicting a flaming sword of Excalibur, the legendary weapon of King Arthur. This motif would later be interpreted, wrongly but permanently, as a "winged dagger." The motto "Strike and Destroy" was rejected as too blunt; "Descend to Ascend" seemed inapt since parachuting was no longer the primary method of transport. Finally Stirling settled on "Who Dares Wins," which seemed to strike the right balance of valor and confidence. The operational wings had been designed by Jock Lewes: the wings of a scarab beetle, with a parachute. Any soldier who completed parachute training could wear the wings on his shoulder; after three missions, they could be sewn above the breast pocket. Such marks and distinctions may mean little to the layman, but within a small unit like the SAS they were held in almost spiritual reverence, the emblems of a private brotherhood. The wings, Stirling noted, were treated as "medals in their own right." Technically, as a mere detachment, the unit was not entitled to such insignia; this was precisely the sort of rule Stirling liked to flout.

STIRLING HAD A NEW PLAN: the detachment's first amphibious operation. With Benghazi in Allied hands, he calculated, Rommel would be forced to ship increasing quantities of supplies through the Mediterranean port of Bouerat, some 350 miles to the west. If the SAS could get inside the harbor, with portable boats and a supply of limpet mines, they could paddle out to Axis shipping lying at anchor, probably including some large petrol tankers, and inflict substantial damage. He proposed taking with him two members of the Special Boat Section, a specialized marine raiding unit that had been attached to Layforce. The SBS men would handle the "folboats," folding kayaks made of wood and canvas.

The operation was scheduled for the moonless night of January 23. Air reconnaissance would supply information on the ships in the harbor immediately before the raid. A recruiting poster was printed up, and Pat Riley, the most charismatic of the NCOs, was dispatched to the various military camps around the Middle East in search of suitable men.

While recruiting troops, planning the Bouerat attack, and generally preparing the SAS for major expansion, Stirling based himself in his brother's Cairo flat, partly because it was more comfortable than Middle East HQ, but mostly because he was less likely to be interfered with by bureaucratic busybodies. Stirling's idea of a planning meeting was most people's idea of a party. Peter

Stirling's three-bedroom apartment became a scene of merry chaos, cluttered with maps, guns, papers, empty bottles, and full ashtrays, presided over by a resourceful Egyptian butler named Mohamed Aboudi who acted as majordomo, barman, unofficial quartermaster, and first line of defense against authority. "Mo" possessed an uncanny talent for simultaneously mixing pink gins, obtaining ammunition and vehicle spare parts, and answering the telephone. He was also adept at patching up the walls and calming the neighbors, after Stirling and his officers had staged late-night revolver-shooting competitions in the dining room.

A sudden influx of troops arrived from an unexpected quarter in early spring: a contingent of fifty-two Free French paratroopers under the command of Colonel Georges Bergé. These paratroopers were "tough cases," in Stirling's words, intensely patriotic Frenchmen who had escaped Nazi-occupied France and trained as parachutists in Britain. They were keen for any opportunity to take the fight to the Germans, and happy to do so under British command. Most of the British officers had at least a smattering of French, and a few of the French parachutists spoke English; even so, to avoid linguistic confusion, it was agreed that the smaller fighting units would usually be composed of one nationality or the other, while operating under Stirling's overall command. Mixing French and British soldiers might have been a recipe for tension; in fact, though the forces teased each other endlessly, relations were almost uniformly peaceful. French troops would play a vital part in the evolution of the SAS.

Bergé was a regular army officer who had escaped to Britain after the fall of France. In March 1941, he had parachuted into occupied France on a mission to ambush a bus carrying Luftwaffe navigators coordinating the Blitz, but the operation failed because the bus, not untypically of French buses, failed to turn up. Bergé was picked up by submarine and made his way back to Britain, where Charles de Gaulle appointed him to command the parachute unit of the Free French forces. His deputy was Lieutenant

Augustin Jordan, a former colonial civil servant, highly educated, impeccably attired, and courtly in manner, who had escaped to Britain from North Africa. Jordan's finesse was slightly misleading; he was as ruthless as he was polite.

Of all the new French arrivals, the most remarkable was Germain Guerpillon, a former consular official who was probably the least soldierly man in the detachment. Guerpillon was tubby, diminutive, disorganized, and infinitely enthusiastic. "He couldn't run, and he couldn't jump, and he was terrified of heights," one of his compatriots recalled. Initially, the other soldiers laughed at him, particularly the British, who nicknamed him "the duffer"; in time, they came to love him, and eventually to respect him deeply. For Guerpillon was indomitable.

The new men required training in explosives, desert warfare, and night operations. Parachute instruction continued because Stirling considered jumping out of planes to be "a good basis for judgment of character of the new volunteers." With Jock Lewes gone, Stirling had lost a superb trainer; to replace him as training officer, Stirling chose the man who was living proof of the effectiveness of Lewes's methods: Paddy Mayne. While Stirling, Seekings, Cooper, and a dozen others would head to Bouerat to sink ships, Mayne was instructed to remain in the Kabrit camp and train up the new recruits.

To say that Mayne was upset by this order does not quite do justice to the depths of his rage. His manner, on receiving the news, was "icy cold," just one shade short of openly insubordinate. "I could see he was exasperated," wrote Stirling, who nonetheless insisted that he had "no one else capable of this assignment." Mayne, however, sensed that he was being left behind by Stirling because of the unstated but intense personal rivalry between them. Mayne had destroyed dozens of planes, whereas Stirling had yet to record a single "kill"; the more junior officer was convinced (perhaps with reason) that this was a ploy to enable Stirling to even up the score, and perhaps even "overtake his 'bag' of aircraft."

Mayne managed to control his temper, but as he accepted the order Stirling noted that his tone of voice was "somewhat ominous."

The Bouerat raid did not quite go according to plan. The convoy of seven trucks, led by Mike Sadler, had almost reached the safety of the Wadi Tamet when it was spotted by an Italian reconnaissance plane. The convoy scattered to take cover in the ravine. Minutes later, six enemy planes appeared; for an hour, they strafed and bombed blindly, up and down the wadi, before disappearing over the horizon as darkness fell. Emerging from hiding, Stirling was relieved to discover there were no casualties, but the wireless truck and its three operators had vanished. (They had in fact been captured and would spend the rest of the war in captivity.) There was now no way to contact headquarters to obtain the latest intelligence and reconnaissance reports.

That night, twenty men crammed into the back of a single truck, along with several dozen bombs and a collapsible canoe. Five miles from Bouerat, the lorry hit a pothole, sending men and equipment flying; the delicate folbot was smashed beyond repair. "We will have to reorganize a little," said Stirling, displaying a nonchalance he surely did not feel. "There are plenty of targets waiting for us in Bouerat." With luck, they might find a rowboat that would serve. Soon after midnight, Sadler dropped the men in fields on the edge of the town. The raiding party split into three groups: one headed off to disable the wireless station, while the other two, led by Stirling and Riley, crept down toward the sea.

Bouerat was little more than a cluster of houses around a small bay, with two quays on either side, lined with large warehouses. The place seemed eerily quiet, with no sign of any sentries. It was one thing to plant bombs on an airfield, but now they were five hundred miles behind the lines, stealing silently through an enemy-held town. Stirling and his men tiptoed down the pier. The only sound was the lapping of the water. The air smelled strongly of petrol. Through the gloom they could make out the shape, of some fishing boats; otherwise, the harbor was empty. Tankers had clearly been in port very recently, but now they were gone.

Over the next twenty minutes, bombs were laid in the harbor workshops and warehouses, which appeared to be packed with machinery, plane parts, and stockpiled food. In the darkness, the two parties bumped into each other and very nearly opened fire. Both Stirling and Riley had to stifle giggles. "I'm glad you've learned the art of moving quietly, Sergeant Riley," whispered Stirling. With twenty minutes to go before the bombs exploded, the men headed back uphill, staying close to the road and pausing only to plant bombs on eighteen full petrol carriers assembled in a large lorry park. As they drove south in the LRDG trucks, the sky above Bouerat turned "a pale grey-pink." The plan to destroy Rommel's shipping had come to nothing, but for the first time Stirling felt he had "struck a real blow," knocking out the wireless station, disabling the harbor, and wrecking a fleet of valuable petrol carriers, all within a few feet of the sleeping enemy.

On the return journey, they ran into an ambush and came under fire from mortars and heavy machine guns. A dust storm earlier in the day had rendered all their tommy guns inoperable. A Vickers antiaircraft gun was deployed from the back of the truck, which had the required "demoralizing effect" on the attackers, and the party managed to escape. To have set off without their weapons in working order, however, was the sort of oversight of which Stirling was too often guilty; Paddy Mayne would never have made the same mistake.

Stirling may have wondered on the drive back why he and his men had found the harbor empty. The answer came from the BBC. As the jubilant party neared Jalo, a radio bulletin relayed some disturbing news: the pendulum of the wider war had swung again. Rommel had counterattacked, retaking Benghazi and pushing the British back across Libya as far as Gazala, reconquering the territory he had so recently lost. Deprived of wireless contact, Stirling had been completely unaware of the battle. With the recapture of Benghazi, Bouerat was no longer Rommel's major port. The LRDG had already pulled out of Jalo, which would also soon be back in enemy hands as Rommel continued his advance. Stirling finally got back to Kabrit on February 7; after just two weeks away, the war looked very different.

Stirling found Paddy Mayne in his tent, morosely drunk and reading a book in bed—a place, and a state, he had been in ever since the raiding party departed without him. Instead of training the new recruits, as instructed, he had pushed two beds together and climbed in, together with a stock of paperbacks ("mostly poetry") and a large supply of whiskey.

Stirling seldom lost his temper; Mayne lost his frequently. On the few occasions when both events occurred simultaneously, the effect was spectacular. The sight of his best soldier sulking in bed and "surrounded by bottles" triggered what Stirling, with typically delicate euphemism, called "a very heavy storm": a ferocious shouting match erupted, clearly audible to the rest of the camp, that lasted more than an hour. When the hurricane finally subsided, another bottle was opened, and the two men settled down to the only intimate conversation they would ever have together. For perhaps the first time, Mayne spoke of Eoin McGonigal, his closest friend, who had perished in the first raid. "I don't think I had realized until then just how close Paddy had been to Eoin McGonigal or what the relationship had been," Stirling later wrote, a little cryptically. "Paddy was able to relax totally with him . . . Eoin was able to communicate with Paddy on a different level." Stirling, in turn, opened up about the "bitter disappointment" and sense of failure he had felt on being told he would never be an artist. "The frustration was so great," he told Mayne, "that it drove me to compensate by tackling the most exacting physical goal I could set myself—the climbing of Mount Everest." That admission of frailty seemed to touch a chord in Paddy Mayne.

"It was the look in Paddy's eyes in response to this conversation rather than what he said (which was incoherent) that convinced me he was himself suffering from extreme frustration," Stirling later wrote. "The only thing he wanted to do, he said, was write."

Stirling felt he had discovered something about the demons that drove Paddy Mayne. "As there was no outlet for his creative energy, it got bottled up to an intolerable level . . . this led to some of his heavy drinking bouts, some of his violent acts and his black moods." The unfulfilled writer inside Mayne, Stirling believed, had gone completely unrecognized, "except by his mother and perhaps by Eoin McGonigal," explaining his mood swings and his aggression, but also his "astonishing intuition and inspiration on the field of battle." During that long, drunken exchange of confidences, Mayne had hinted at his own internal frustrations, artistic and literary, but perhaps also psychological and sexual. Stirling never forgot the conversation that took place following their most bitter confrontation. He would be "haunted" by the enigma of Mayne's contradictory character for the rest of his life: his "capacity for love and devotion on an almost spiritual level" combined with "sexual indifference to females (and males) and his social avoidance of women." The parentheses are Stirling's. "His compassion and gentleness in his day to day life," thought Stirling, contrasted with the "bursts of extreme violence, sometimes even against those who were close to him."

At the end of the evening, the two men shook hands and parted amicably. Mayne seemed immune to hangovers, either alcoholic or emotional, and "by next morning, he was back functioning with redoubled vigour." Stirling was honest enough to admit that forcing Mayne to take on a training role had been a "dreadful mistake." Pat Riley, now sergeant major, was appointed training officer in his place. Paddy Mayne would return to fighting on the front line or, more accurately, beyond it.

WITH JALO NOW back in enemy hands, the SAS and LRDG needed a new forward base from which to continue desert operations. The most logical was the oasis at Siwa, thirty miles inside Egypt from the Libyan border in the eastern part of the Great Sand Sea, on the edge of the Qattara Depression. A former fortress of the Senussi tribe, built around the ancient Greek temple of Ammon, Siwa Oasis was a far cry from the mosquito-ridden discomfort of Jalo. Clear natural springs frothed out of the ground, creating a vivid splash of greenery in the desert, with towering date palms and neatly tended olive groves. Cleopatra herself was said to have swum in the natural stone pool fed by a hot spring. There were a few European houses, as well as a sprawl of traditional villagers' huts. Fitzroy Maclean was enchanted by Cleopatra's Pool and immediately jumped into it: "Under palm trees were pools of clear water bubbling up from great depth . . . it was like bathing in soda water."

Stirling's attention had turned to Benghazi. For more than 2,500 years, competing forces had fought over the ancient Mediterranean seaport: Greeks, Spartans, Persians, Egyptians, Romans, Vandals, Arabs, and Turks. The Italians had invaded in 1912, ruthlessly oppressing the locals and building a charming seafront of Italianate villas. Benghazi flourished as a showcase for Mussolini's imperialist vision, and by 1939 some twenty thousand Italians were living in this thriving colony with shops, restaurants, and a cinema. In February 1941, it had been captured from the Italians by British and Commonwealth forces in the first major Allied military action of the Western Desert campaign. Two months later it was recaptured by Rommel's Afrika Korps. The port was seized back by the Allies on Christmas Eve, only to change hands once again barely a month later as Rommel's forces swept eastward. A vital target in the see-saw war, Benghazi and its surrounding airfields had taken on strong symbolic, as well as strategic, significance. With Tobruk back in Allied hands, Benghazi was the essential supply port for the Afrika Korps, while the nearby airfields—Berka, Benina, Barce, Slonta, and Regima—were vital to the Axis air forces in the battle for air supremacy over the Mediterranean.

The primary focus of that battle was Malta, now under intense

siege from the Axis air forces. As the only Allied base between
Gibraltar and Alexandria, the island was regarded, by both sides,
as militarily essential, a key to victory. Between 1940 and 1942, the
Luftwaffe and the Italian air force would launch some three thousand bombing raids, many from the airfields around Benghazi, in
an effort to batter and starve Malta into submission, by attacking its ports, towns, and cities, as well as Allied shipping supply-
ing the island. Churchill believed that, if Malta surrendered, the
German hold on the Mediterranean would be absolute, its supply
lines invulnerable, and Egypt would be next to fall. Rommel was
equally convinced that, if Malta withstood the onslaught, the war
would eventually swing in favor of the Allies. In May 1941, the
German commander observed: "Without Malta the Axis will end
by losing control of North Africa." If the Benghazi airfields and
harbor could be neutralized, or at least seriously impeded, then
Malta might hold out.

BENGHAZI WAS A bustling town, filled with men in the uniforms
of many nations. Recent experience suggested that the more
crowded a target, the less conspicuous would be a team of saboteurs. After two occupations, the British Army had a clear idea of
the layout of the town; there was even an elaborate and detailed
scale model of Benghazi in the intelligence headquarters at Alexandria. The large harbor on the Gulf of Sirte was usually packed
with enemy vessels. Once again, Stirling planned to use portable boats in order to mount an assault on the vessels at anchor,
which would demonstrate to HQ that L Detachment was capable
of destroying ships as well as planes, petrol tankers, and warehouses. Just a few weeks earlier, the plan would have been rejected
as harebrained, but with the two armies hunkered down across the
Gazala Line, and Churchill demanding a counterattack, Auchinleck was keen to show that offensive operations were continuing.
Here was a double opportunity: to disrupt Axis supply lines and
relieve the pressure on Malta. Stirling was authorized to mount an

attack on Benghazi—or at least ascertain whether such an operation was feasible—during the next moonless period, starting after March 10, 1942. Three other SAS raiding parties would mount simultaneous attacks on the nearby airfields.

This time, the raiders would not go by parachute, LRDG truck, or even on foot. Instead, Stirling planned to drive into the middle of Benghazi in his own customized car.

In one of those canny acts of larceny for which the SAS had a natural aptitude, the unit "obtained" a Ford V-8 station wagon, with a powerful engine, two rows of three seats, and a top speed of seventy miles per hour. Painted Wehrmacht gray, and with the roof and windows removed, it looked, from the air, like a German staff car. The Germans painted a "recognition signal," which changed every month, on the hoods of military vehicles to prevent attack from their own planes. British intelligence supplied the relevant signal. Machine guns could be mounted fore and aft, but unclipped and laid on the floor when necessary, to give the vehicle a "more innocent appearance." The attacking convoy set off from Siwa on March 15, with Stirling in the lead, proudly driving his "Blitz Buggy."

The Jebel mountain range rises about forty miles south of Benghazi. The hills enjoyed sufficient rainfall to sustain abundant plant life; the shrubs and small trees made it ideal terrain in which to hide up and prepare for the attack. Verdant foothills ran down some twenty-five miles to an escarpment overlooking the coastal plain, beyond which, some fifteen miles distant, lay Benghazi. The landscape reminded Paddy Mayne of the South Downs. "Low hills and valleys, lots of wild flowers and long grass," he wrote to his brother. "It's like a picnic." The area was sparsely inhabited by the Senussi (both a tribe and religious order), many of whom felt a passionate hatred of their Italian colonial overlords, little admiration for the Germans, and a corresponding affinity for the British.

The Jebel was also home to many spies. The Middle East branch of the British intelligence service, working under the vague title of the Inter-Services Liaison Department, had arranged for the LRDG to transport its agents behind the lines. Some of these had been living among the tribespeople for months, disguised as Arabs, recruiting local informants, gathering intelligence on what was happening in Benghazi and the surrounding areas, and sending this back by wireless. Shortly before Stirling's arrival, the LRDG had bused in the latest team of British spies, led by agent 52901, "a Jewish academic in his 60s" who spoke fluent Arabic, to link up with "friendly sheiks and report troop movements around Benghazi." The Germans and Italians, however, had their own undercover agents in the Jebel, where a small but intense espionage battle was under way. Whenever British troops appeared, small groups of Senussi would emerge, magically, out of the undergrowth, to trade eggs, cigarettes, and information. Most seemed friendly. Some were certainly working for the other side. And a few, undoubtedly, were working for both. The tricky task for the British agents in the Jebel was to sort out which was which.

In the Jebel foothills, the raiding parties split up: Mayne headed toward Berka, which had both a main aerodrome and a satellite airfield, while Fraser set out for Barce, in the northeast, an administrative center built around an old Turkish fort. Another team targeted Slonta airfield, away to the east.

Stirling's first foray into Benghazi was a complete failure. The rubber boats refused to inflate, and a high wind would have made launching them impossible anyway. The mission was aborted, but not before Stirling had made a thorough inspection of the harbor.

The others had not fared much better. Slonta was too heavily guarded to risk an attack. Fraser found only one plane to destroy at Barce. The team attacking Berka had not been able to locate the main airfield. Only Paddy Mayne met with success, blowing up fifteen planes on the satellite airfield at Berka, before hiding out with a friendly group of Bedouin encamped a few miles from the target. The next morning, by sheer fluke, one of the men from the LRDG turned up, looking to buy a chicken from the Arabs, and led the SAS men back to the rendezvous. "Never disbelieve in luck again, or coincidence," Mayne wrote to his brother. Bravery and ingenuity were vital to Mayne's success and survival; what is less often noted, though it was arguably a greater factor than all the others, was his astonishing good fortune. "I'd rather have a lucky general than a smart general. They win battles," Eisenhower once said, echoing Napoleon. Mayne's willingness to take chances no one else would contemplate was balanced by his extraordinary good luck.

An impromptu party was held the next night in the desert, "with rum and lime, rum and tea, rum omelette, and just plain rum." Paddy Mayne was the most enthusiastic participant. Once drunk, according to a report on the operation, "Capt. Mayne went through the weird rites of demonstrating how one should not fire at night: machine guns, light machine guns, tommy guns, pistols, and God knows what other intricate pieces of mechanism." The desert exploded with noise as Mayne loosed off every gun he could find into the night sky, and then fell asleep in the sand. The War Diary report concludes: "Casualties: Incredible as it may seem, nil."

Stirling was not downhearted by his own failure to destroy anything. This had been more of a reconnaissance operation than a full-scale raid, an opportunity "to spy out the land for an eventual large scale operation." The nighttime visit to Benghazi had proved that the Axis forces were unprepared for the kind of tactics adopted by Stirling: with enough chutzpah, and the right weather conditions, one could drive into the middle of the town and wreak havoc. This Stirling now proposed to do, in one of the most audacious (and hilarious) operations of the war. This time he would be taking with him additional bombs, inflatable boats, and the son of Winston Churchill.

Chapter 9

BENGHAZI BED-AND-BREAKFAST

T HE FIVE ITALIAN SOLDIERS MANNING THE ROADBLOCK into Benghazi were surprised when a German staff car with half a dozen passengers pulled up at the barrier at 11:15 in the evening of May 21, 1942. The car and its occupants did not seem particularly worthy of attention—the Germans were always rushing around at odd hours—but the noise it was making most certainly was: a strange, high-pitched metallic scream, audible from a distance of half a mile, that died away as the car came to a stop. Something had knocked the wheels out of alignment, and the bearings were protesting at maximum volume. The car was being driven with full-beam headlights, even though German regulations stated that all cars driven at night should have dimmed lights to reduce the danger of aerial attack. The man in the front passenger seat spoke with a strong foreign accent.

"*Militari,*" said Fitzroy Maclean, who had not spoken Italian for about three years.

The Italian sentry, armed with a machine gun, looked vaguely quizzical. "Staff officers, *di stato maggiore,*" added Maclean. "*Di fretto.* In a hurry."

Another Italian soldier was standing off some thirty yards to the right. Three more, carrying rifles, observed proceedings from beside the guard hut. All had bayonets fixed. Behind him, Maclean heard the ominous click of a safety catch being eased off the tommy gun in the hands of the man behind him. Cooper had drawn his knife in the darkness. In Maclean's left hand he held a half-eaten bar of chocolate; in his right, out of sight, he clutched a large wrench with which he planned, if necessary, to brain this Italian sentry.

The soldier lifted the bar and waved the car through. "You ought to get those dimmed," he said, pointing at the headlights. As the wail of the wheels rose once more, David Stirling accelerated into the night toward Benghazi.

The Italian sentry would have been astonished to discover how close he had come to being clubbed senseless by a British member of Parliament. He would have been still more stunned to learn that a pair of heavy-caliber machine guns had been hidden on the floor, and that the vehicle contained two inflatable rubber boats and enough explosives to demolish half of Benghazi. But he would surely have been utterly flabbergasted by the revelation that the tubby man seated in the middle of the back seat was one of the most prized potential prisoners of the war: Captain Randolph Frederick Edward Spencer-Churchill, the son of Britain's wartime prime minister.

Randolph Churchill was a tricky personality and a divisive figure, a frustrated son who had spent most of his life trying, and largely failing, to impress a celebrated father. He was opinionated, bad-mannered, and often very drunk. At moments of frustration, he tended to burst into tears. As the heir to a great name, he was cruelly nicknamed "Randolph Hope and Glory." But he was also clever, generous, and astonishingly courageous. He had come out to the Middle East with Layforce, and when the commando unit was disbanded he took over the propaganda section of Middle East HQ. Jock Lewes, who admired few people, had liked him: "Much too outspoken and militant in his convictions to be popular . . . but he puts heart into me by his robust and healthy character."

Stirling was also fond of Churchill, though not without reservations. "A likeable chap, but dear me he could talk. He just couldn't resist holding forth about how the war should be handled . . . But he was certainly brave enough." Stirling had allowed Churchill to join L Detachment, though he was hardly cut out for the rigors of desert warfare. On his first parachute jump, Randolph hit the ground hard because, in Stirling's uncompromising assessment, "he was just too bloody fat." Churchill wrote to his father in glowing terms about the new unit and its commander. "I am extremely happy where I am. My Commanding Officer David Stirling is a very great friend of mine. He is only 25 and recently got the DSO for his attacks on German airfields. At the moment the unit have 121 enemy aircraft to their credit. Apart from Bob Laycock, he is the most original and enterprising soldier I have come across. Not being a regular soldier, he is more interested in war than in the army. He is one of the few people who think of war in three-dimensional terms."

This was a most perceptive observation, and one that cut to the essence of Stirling's approach. Unlike most officers, who thought in linear terms, and cared about promotion, medals, and the steady progression of the battlefront, Stirling approached warfare sideways, and from an amateur perspective. Killing the enemy was only one aspect of the process. If, using surprise and guile, the enemy could be disorientated, alarmed, and embarrassed, then the three-dimensional impact could be far greater than traditional tactics.

After much badgering, Stirling reluctantly agreed to allow Churchill to come on the Benghazi raid, on the understanding that he would not take part in the action but remain with the vehicles at the LRDG rendezvous. There was more than a little calculation in this: Churchill was invited along as an observer, "to see the fun." A journalist by training, he was certain to report back to his father on the daring qualities of the SAS, and the more support Stirling could get from the top, the better he would be able to circumvent the obstructive elements in the middle of the military machine.

After the first, failed foray to the harbor, Stirling had refined the Benghazi plan. If two large ships could be mined and sunk at the harbor entrance, this would block the port, temporarily paralyzing Axis seaborne supply lines. If Rommel could be starved of food, fuel, and ammunition, then the deadlock might be broken. Even if the impact was only temporary, the effect on German and Italian morale might be significant. More troops would have to be deployed to defend the ports. Rommel could be made to look backward defensively, rather than east toward Cairo. A single, spectacular raid on Benghazi might change the course of the war.

Aerial photographs and intelligence reports confirmed a small strip of shingle, between the jetty and the harbor wall, ideal for launching small craft. It was agreed that the RAF would launch a bombing raid on the harbor the night before the attack, to divert enemy attention. Fitzroy Maclean was detailed to find boats that could be relied upon, unlike the fickle folboats. The only requirement, as Stirling put it, was that they "had to bloody well work." Maclean obtained two rubber dinghies, "small and black and handy," that could be swiftly inflated with a pair of bellows. The bellows emitted a loud asthmatic wheeze, but otherwise the boats appeared to be ideal. To test them, Stirling carried out a dummy night raid against the Allied shipping in Suez harbor, which proved to be almost as inadequately defended as Benghazi. When a passing British soldier spotted three men inflating a boat in the middle of the night beside the harbor and asked them what they were doing, he received the following response: "Never you fucking mind. Fuck off." Which he did. The raiders planned to employ exactly this tactic if challenged in Benghazi.

The party would consist of Stirling and Maclean, Seekings and Cooper, Gordon Alston, an intelligence officer who had spent three weeks in Benghazi during the latest British occupation, and Sergeant Johnny Rose, a former manager of a branch of Woolworths and an expert mechanic, who would keep the Blitz Buggy running. Churchill would come along in the capacity of official observer.

The four-hundred-mile drive to the Benghazi escarpment

took five days. Maclean marveled at the beauties of the changing desert, "sometimes flat, sometimes broken and undulating, sometimes sandy, sometimes hard and stony, a mixture of greys, browns, yellows and reds, all bleached by the sun and merging into each other." The wilderness was dotted with patches of scrub and low grass, from which dashed frightened gazelles, "hardly bigger than hares," as the convoy rumbled past. In the cold of the morning, the men drove huddled in greatcoats, but as the sun rose they gradually stripped down to shorts and the Arab headscarves adopted as an unofficial part of the SAS uniform. "Apart from their romantic appearance they were extremely practical," wrote Maclean, as a sun shield, dish cloth, and face mask to keep off the flies and sand. Crossing the ancient caravan route, the Trig al Abd, Maclean noted the desiccated bones of camels "and no doubt men, who in the course of centuries had fallen by the way and been left to die." Farther on, they passed the charred shells of tanks and trucks, some still containing corpses, victims of the winter fighting. Somewhere to the north lay the bones of Jock Lewes.

Stirling insisted on driving the Blitz Buggy himself, though he was an exceptionally inattentive and dangerous driver: "One hand on the wheel, puffing away quietly at his pipe, and looking at the scenery all around, and all the time doing a cool sixty, for all the world as if he's out for a run down the Great North Road." Maclean wondered what motivated soldiers to follow such a man, and found himself reaching back to the words of another desert warrior, Lawrence of Arabia. In *Seven Pillars of Wisdom*, T. E. Lawrence described the elusive essence of military leadership: "Nine-tenths of tactics are certain, and taught in books: but the irrational tenth is like the kingfisher flashing across the pool, and that is the test of generals." Stirling, it seemed to Maclean, was a perfect illustration of that irrational tenth, with his "never-failing audacity, a gift of daring improvisation."

On the morning of May 20, the team made camp in the safety of the Jebel. As always, curious Senussi goatherds appeared almost immediately, offering eggs in exchange for cigarettes: tea was brewed and shared, followed by a ritual in which the locals were shown photographs of their tribal and religious chief, Sayed Idris, now living in exile under British protection in Egypt. Grandson of the Grand Senussi, founder of the order, the future King Idris I of Libya was held in reverential awe by his tribe. His photograph symbolized the informal alliance between the Senussi and the British. "They fingered it admiringly . . . grinning," wrote Maclean.

That night, after a fortifying dinner of hot bully stew and tea, followed by a tot of rum, Maclean lay in his sleeping bag in the sand, watching the flashes over Benghazi as the RAF carried out the bombing raid on cue. The next morning, while Seekings and Cooper were preparing explosives and Maclean was testing his inflatable boats, another Senussi appeared in the camp, wearing a trilby and carrying a furled umbrella. Maclean immediately nicknamed him the "City Slicker." The man "spoke fluent Italian and showed more interest in our affairs than we liked." A whispered conversation took place, in which it was discussed whether this man might be a spy, and whether to take him captive as a precaution. When they looked around, the City Slicker had vanished. Before they could reflect further on this episode there was a loud bang, followed by a torrent of oaths. A faulty detonator had exploded in the hand of Reg Seekings: the injury was not severe, but enough to put him out of action. Seekings was furious; Randolph Churchill, on the other hand, was jubilant, for now he would take the place of the injured man. Within moments, Churchill was "oiling his tommy gun and polishing his pistol in preparation for the night's work."

It took five hours to maneuver the Blitz Buggy down the escarpment through boulder-strewn gullies; on the concrete road east of Benghazi, at around 10:00 p.m., the resulting damage to the suspension became apparent, and loudly audible. As Stirling accelerated, the squealing racket grew worse. Sergeant Rose spent five minutes hammering beneath the car in an effort to silence it, to no effect. Their approach to Benghazi would be less than stealthy.

TOP: David Stirling, founder of the SAS.

BOTTOM: Before a desert raid. Stirling standing at right.

Leaping from the back of a vehicle driving at
thirty miles per hour was, Stirling believed,
a good way to simulate a parachute landing.

The desert wind made controlling the parachute
after landing a tricky task.

Recruits were
required to
practice
jumping from
a rickety
thirty-foot
platform.

Jock Lewes
(right)
preparing
to jump from
a Bristol
Bombay
transport
plane.

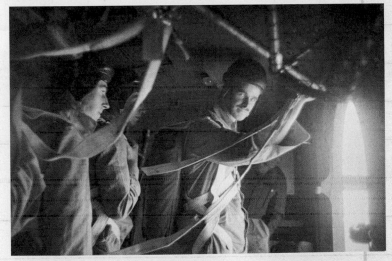

A recruit to
L Detachment
SAS jumps
into the
desert during
parachute
training.

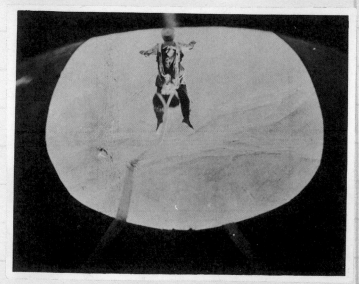

Eoin McGonigal

Blair "Paddy" Mayne

Fitzroy Maclean

George Jellicoe

Johnny Cooper

Malcolm Pleydell

Bill Fraser

Fraser McLuskey

Jim Almonds

Randolph Churchill

Reg Seekings

Pat Riley

Jock Lewes with Bren gun at Sandown Racecourse,
painted by Rex Whistler, 1940.

David Stirling and Jock Lewes
preparing a desert raid.

TOP: Paddy Mayne driving with Withers,
the dog adopted by the SAS.

BOTTOM: Mayne recuperating from injuries
sustained during an airfield attack.

TOP: General Bernard Montgomery in the North African desert.

BOTTOM: General Erwin Rommel, commander of the Afrika Korps, in Benghazi.

The Blitz Buggy.
Left to right:
Seekings, Johnny
Rose, Stirling,
Cooper.

Seekings (center)
and Cooper
(right), with
others of L
Detachment SAS.

The two lads who have
put their signatures
on here have just been
awarded the M.M for
the job before the last
one and believe me they
earned it.

Egypt 1942.

The back of the
photograph above,
inscribed:
"The two lads
who have put
their signatures
[initials] on
here have just
been awarded
the M.M.
[Military Medal]
for the job
before the last
one and believe
me they earned
it. Egypt 1942."

Christmas Night 1942, around the desert campfire.

A group returning from a raid displaying two dead gazelles,
shot for Christmas dinner.

Baron Markus von Lutterotti di Gazzolis und Langenthal, the aristocratic German doctor captured by the SAS.

In the desert. Left to right: Bob Lilley, Malcolm Pleydell (with paperback in hand), and Johnny Wiseman.

ABOVE: Preparing
for action in
the desert camp
at Bir el Quseir,
summer 1942.
Graham Rose and
Jimmy Storie,
two of the early
recruits to
L Detachment.

Chris O'Dowd, the
twenty-three-year-
old Irish recruit:
piratical,
irrepressible, and
indestructibly
cheerful.

Jack Sillito after his solo 180-mile foot-slog
across the desert from Tobruk to the SAS camp
in the Great Sand Sea.

ABOVE LEFT: Mike Sadler, the SAS desert navigator with an unerring ability to know where he was, where he was going, and when he would get there.

ABOVE RIGHT: Sadler after his 100-mile, five-day trek from Gabès to the oasis at Tozeur.

RIGHT: Winston Churchill in the garden of the British embassy in Cairo with Field Marshal Jan Smuts, South Africa's prime minister and a member of the Imperial War Cabinet (seated), and (standing, left to right) Air Chief Marshal Sir Arthur Tedder and Chief of the Imperial Staff Sir Alan Brooke.

MOST SECRET

MAJOR DAVID STIRLING.

      I have been asked by my chief to ask you to let me have, for him, without further delay the short note for which he called on what you would advise should be done to concentrate and co-ordinate the work you are doing.

      I have been asked to make sure that this in my hands to-day. I can be got at the Embassy.

9.8.42

ABOVE: Note from Sir Leslie Rowan, Churchill's private secretary, passing on the prime minister's request for David Stirling to outline his plans for the SAS.

RIGHT: Stirling's reply, laying out his ambitious ideas for expanding the SAS and placing all "Special Service Units" under his sole command.

MOST SECRET.

PM(0) Put away

PRIME MINISTER.

1.   I venture to submit the following proposals in connection with the re-organization of Special Service in the Middle East. ("Special Service" may be defined as any military action ranging between, but not including, the work of the single agent on the one hand, and on the other the full-scale Combined Operation.)

    (i) That the scope of "L" Detachment should be extended so as to cover the functions of all existing Special Service Units in the Middle East as well as any other Special Service tasks which may require carrying out.

    (ii) Arising out of this, that all other Special Service Units be disbanded and selected personnel absorbed, as required, by "L" Detachment.

    (iii) Control to rest with the Officer Commanding "L" Detachment and not with any outside body superimposed for purposes of co-ordination, the need for which will not arise if effect be given to the present proposals.

    (iv) "L" Detachment to remain as hitherto at the disposal of the D.M.O. for allocation to Eighth, Ninth and Tenth Armies for specific tasks. The planning of Operations to be carried out by "L" Detachment to remain as hitherto the prerogative of "L" Detachment.

2.   I suggest that the proposed scheme would have the following advantages:

    (i) Unified Control would eliminate any danger of overlapping, of which there has already been more than one unfortunate instance.

    (ii) The allocation to "L" Detachment of all the roles undertaken by Special Service Units would greatly increase the scope of the Units' training, and thereby augment its value to all ranks, who will inevitably greatly gain in versatility and resourcefulness.

    (iii) The planning of Operations by those who are to carry them out obviates the delay and misunderstanding apt to be caused by intermediary stages and makes for speed of execution which/in any Operations of this kind is an incalculable asset. It also has obvious advantages from the point of view of security.

D. Stirling.

9. 8. 42

-3-

Three miles out of town they reached the checkpoint (which ought not to have been there, according to the latest intelligence reports), making a din that echoed around the desert. "We could hardly have made more noise if we had been a fire engine with bell clanging," Maclean later wrote. His combination of swagger and bad Italian somehow got them through the first encounter without a fight, but on the other side of the barrier another threat appeared. Two German cars passed in the opposite direction, then stopped, turned around, and began to follow them into town. Stirling slowed down, inviting the cars to overtake them; they also decelerated. He drove faster; they did so too. He stopped. They braked. Stirling hit the accelerator, the Ford V-8 engine roared, and the Blitz Buggy tore through the night and hurtled into Benghazi at seventy miles per hour, screaming like a banshee. By Churchill's account, as they reached the native quarter, Stirling "crammed on the brakes and shot round a corner into a narrow side street." To add to the cacophony, the air-raid sirens now started up, accompanied by police whistles and shouting. Alston yelled out directions: "Second on the right, that's right. No you've passed it. Blast. Go on. Go on, take the next turning instead." In the back, the men clung on as they slewed from side to side: "We were simply scorching along, whipping around corners on two wheels, and all the time making enough noise to raise the dead."

Reaching what appeared to be a bombed-out cul-de-sac, Stirling turned in, braked, and switched off the engine. The pursuers had been shaken off. Since there was to be no RAF attack that night, the wail of sirens must surely have indicated that their own raid had been detected. "It very much looked as if the alert was being given in our honour," wrote Maclean. "They were onto us." Had they walked into a trap? Had the City Slicker given them away? The Blitz Buggy, with its telltale screech, was now a liability; it would have to be abandoned and destroyed to prevent it falling into enemy hands. To save time they would use only one of the boats. This was unloaded in its large kit bag, along with the explosives and machine guns; a Lewes bomb with a half-hour time fuse was placed inside the car beside the petrol tank. They would be leaving Benghazi—if they ever left it—on foot. Randolph Churchill was in a state of raging overexcitement, intoxicated by a combination of pure adrenaline and the neat rum in his water bottle. It was, he later wrote to his father, "the most exciting half hour of my life."

The six men set off in single file for the docks, led by Alston. Rounding a side street, they ran straight into an Italian policeman standing under a streetlight. Maclean retrieved his best Italian.

"What is all this noise?"

"Just another of those damned English air raids," said the bored cop.

"Might it be that enemy forces are raiding the town?"

This was considered to be quite a good joke.

"No, there is no need to be nervous about that," said the laughing policeman. "Not with the British almost back on the Egyptian frontier."

"Thanks. Good night."

"Good night."

This conversation, surreal as it was, put a different slant on matters. The sirens, it seemed, were simply responding to a false alarm, rather than warning of their arrival, and the pursuing cars had probably just been air-raid wardens trying to get them to dim the car lights. The destruction of the Blitz Buggy was therefore unnecessary. Moreover, the sirens had now fallen silent. Cooper was sent running back to defuse the bomb, with roughly five minutes left before it exploded. Fingers trembling, he stuck the safety pin back into the time pencil, extracted the detonator, and threw it over a wall. "I have never been so scared in my life," he later admitted.

Churchill and Rose were left to find somewhere to conceal the car. The remaining men set off again for the docks. Having passed through the European quarter of white-stuccoed buildings, they cut a hole in the perimeter wire surrounding the port and slipped down to the water's edge. Stirling headed off to reconnoiter the harbor; Alston did the same, in the opposite direction, and Maclean and Cooper set to work inflating the rubber dinghy on the sliver of beach. Through the gloom Maclean could make out several large ships at anchor, "no more than a stone's throw away." The equipment that night seemed determined to be both treacherous and loud. The wheezing of the bellows attracted the attention of a nightwatchman aboard one of the ships, and a voice floated across the water. "*Chi va là?*"

"*Militari,*" replied Maclean.

A short silence.

"What are you up to over there?"

"None of your business."

That seemed to do the trick.

After several minutes of pumping, the boat showed no sign of inflating. Somehow, on the journey to Benghazi, it had developed a puncture. They went back to get the other boat, and found Rose and Churchill maneuvering the car into a tiny, half-derelict garage. The operation now threatened to dissolve into dangerous farce: Stirling returned to the shingle and, finding it deserted, went off to look for the others; they, on returning to the same spot, were alarmed to find that Stirling and Alston had not returned, so Maclean went to look for them. Almost the entire unit was now wandering around in the dark. Cooper began pumping up the second boat, only to discover that this too was punctured: "It was heart-rending." One by one, the team reassembled. The last to appear was Stirling, who explained that he had run into a sentry but had got past him by "mumbling incoherently and pushing him aside." All the coming and going on shore had attracted yet more attention from the night sentries aboard the boats, who again quizzed the party, through the darkness, as to what, exactly, they were doing. Maclean replied testily that he was "very bored with being challenged and they were to shut up." It was now growing light, and the sound of "metal doors slamming and excited shouting" from the ships indicated that their crews were now thoroughly suspicious. Clearly, the mission would have to be abandoned, yet again. The men packed up the infuriating dinghies and headed back toward the perimeter. Maclean was nearing the fence when he found himself face-to-face with a very large African soldier from Italian Somaliland. The sentry grunted, and by way of inquiry prodded Maclean in the stomach with his bayonet. Maclean launched into a flood of Italian, of which the sentry plainly understood not one word. "It seemed," he wrote with fine understatement, "a more intractable problem than we had hitherto encountered." But Maclean had a very simple, and very British, solution. "I have always found that in dealing with foreigners whose language one does not speak, it is best to shout." This he now did, while gesticulating extravagantly, in a first-class impersonation of an irate and pompous officer who has been interrupted in the performance of important duties by an insolent underling. The sentry, browbeaten, eventually lowered his bayonet and backed off with "an expression of injured dignity." But as they filed off into the darkness Maclean realized that the party had miraculously expanded; two more Italian sentries, alerted by the commotion and apparently thinking some sort of drill was under way, had joined the line of men and fallen in at the back—one of the very few occasions, perhaps the only one, when Axis and Allied soldiers had marched together.

Maclean now opted for an act of brazen bluff. Leading his little Anglo-Italian troop, he marched up to the gatehouse, accosted the lone sentry, and indignantly demanded to see the guard commander. A sleepy Italian sergeant emerged a few moments later, pulling on his trousers. The two Italian hangers-on, sensing trouble, melted back into the darkness. Maclean now launched into a virtuoso harangue. Most of his Italian had been learned from studying art, and the use of obscure baroque terms may have added to the force of his speech. As later reconstructed by Randolph Churchill, it went something like this: "We are German officers and have come here to test your security arrangements. They are appalling. We have been past this sentry four or five times. He has not asked once for our identity cards. For all he knows, we might be English. We have brought great bags into the dock. How is he to know they are not full of explosives? It is a very bad show indeed. We have brought all this stuff in here, and now we are going to take it out."

Maclean then turned stiffly on his heel and stalked out, with the others following. The bemused Italian sergeant saluted. "As we passed him, the sentry on the gate made a stupendous effort and presented arms, almost falling over backwards in the process."

Dawn was breaking by the time the party had reassembled at the cul-de-sac. The car was now thoroughly camouflaged with rubble and planks inside the garage of a half-bombed house. Above it, up a rickety wooden outside staircase, Churchill and Rose had found a small, decrepit flat, plainly long abandoned, shuttered and "reassuringly derelict," and an ideal daytime hiding place: Churchill christened it "10 Downing Street." The six men fell asleep on the floor, drained by the night's alarms and excursions. They awoke as the town was stirring, "in very high spirits and feeling there was nothing we could not get away with inside Benghazi."

Any attempt to return to the Jebel would have to take place in the dark; waiting for nightfall was both boring and nerve-racking. Their hiding place, it transpired, was not quite as secluded as it had seemed in the dark. Through a crack in the wall they watched as an elderly Arab couple emerged from the flat next door and began cooking their breakfast over a fire in the courtyard at the back of the house. A hubbub of German, Italian, and Arabic rose from the street in front. The building opposite, it seemed, was some kind of German area headquarters, with "dispatch riders dashing in and out on motorbikes and busy-looking officers arriving and leaving." The men took turns to act as lookout through the window shutters. The heat rose. Since their stay in Benghazi had not been planned, no one had thought to bring any food or water. Randolph Churchill passed the time by reading F. S. Oliver's biography of Alexander Hamilton, one of the Founding Fathers of the United States. The sun threw a patch of light into the room; Rose watched it slowly creep across the floor and invented a game with himself to pass the time. "How long will it be before it reaches the plank with the crack in it? What's the betting that I'm still here by the time it reaches the far corner?" At midday, someone crawled noisily over the roof. Planes droned overhead. They could only talk in whispers, something that the voluble Randolph Churchill found almost impossible.

By early afternoon, Stirling declared he could stand the tension no longer: he was going for a swim in the harbor and would carry out a reconnaissance for possible sabotage targets at the same time. Dressed in corduroy slacks, desert boots, and a polo-necked pullover, with a bushy black beard and a towel draped around his neck, he looked, to Cooper's eyes, unmistakably English. "We thought: that's the last we'd ever see of him."

A few moments later, the fugitives tensed as heavy footfalls were heard coming up the wooden stairs, accompanied by labored breathing. Randolph Churchill cocked his tommy gun and took up a position behind the door. All eyes were fixed on the door handle. "We all seemed mesmerized," said Rose. The handle turned, and an Italian sailor, obviously drunk, lurched into the room. He took one look at the piratical figure brandishing a submachine gun, uttered a yelp, and fled. Churchill later wrote to his father: "Terrified by my appearance (I had quite a long beard which I am sure you would not have liked) he fell headlong down the stairs and bolted out." From the window, Cooper watched nervously to see if he would run into the German headquarters and was relieved to spot the man heading off at high speed in the opposite direction. The sailor was probably a looter, but the encounter did nothing to alleviate the anxiety of waiting. The men spent the next two hours with guns and grenades in hand, ready "to give any visitors a warm reception." Stirling finally returned, announcing that on his walk around town he had spotted two German torpedo boats tied up at the dock; these could easily be bombed that evening on their way out of town.

Rose had been working on the suspension and believed he had

finally silenced the squealing Blitz Buggy. At nightfall, they set off, but after a few hundred yards the noise started up once more. Stirling parked at the roadside, and Rose slipped back underneath with his tools. Passersby barely spared them a glance. "Nothing arouses less sensation than people working on a car," wrote Churchill. "No one said a word to us." Rose declared that the problem could not be fixed without a major overhaul. Stirling insisted they would continue as planned. Near the waterfront, he parked, Rose and Cooper picked up two bombs each, and the little party headed toward the dock, "walking down the middle of the street, arm in arm, whistling and doing our best to give the impression that we had every right to be there." To Stirling's annoyance, a sentry had now been posted on the dockside, and as they approached the moored torpedo boats four Germans stood up inside them and looked inquiringly at the approaching group. "We were holding the bombs, and trying to look as if we weren't," Cooper recalled. The team sauntered back to the car as nonchalantly as possible and drove off. After a few hundred yards, the jittery comedy of the situation became too much: "All we could do was giggle."

They passed through the checkpoint, in the opposite direction, in much the same way, and making much the same noise.

"*Militari*," declared Maclean.

"What sort of *militari*?" asked the sentry, a little more inquisitive than his compatriot of the previous night.

"German staff officers."

"*Molto bene.*"

The Blitz Buggy and its exhausted occupants reached the rendezvous in the Jebel at 6:00 in the morning, exactly twenty-four hours late. The LRDG, assuming that the party had been captured or killed, were preparing to pull out.

It was, wrote Randolph Churchill, "the longest day I've ever known."

• • •

COMEDY AND TRAGEDY are brothers. Men and women are prepared to die in war, for a cause, but death can be as meaningless and fickle in wartime as it can be at all other times. One of the grimmer ironies of conflict is that so many are claimed, not in the heat of battle, but by cold, capricious accident, often far from the battlefield.

Four days later at around midnight, Stirling was at the wheel of the Blitz Buggy, on the road between Alexandria and Cairo. Beside him sat Sergeant Rose. In the rear seat, dozing, lolled Maclean and Churchill, along with a celebrated journalist: Arthur Merton, the correspondent of the *Daily Telegraph*, one of the most distinguished reporters covering the war, a veteran who had famously reported the discovery of Tutankhamen's tomb in 1922. Stirling knew him slightly, and when Merton met him at dinner in Alexandria and asked for a lift back to Cairo, he had been happy to agree. Clementine Churchill, Randolph's mother, described how the party set off "at night with a good moon." Everyone was exhausted and half asleep. Stirling, as usual, was driving much too fast.

Taking a sharp bend at around seventy miles per hour, with horror he saw a truck directly in their path, the tail end of a slow-moving convoy. Stirling braked a fraction too late, and swerved into a sand bank; the Blitz Buggy spun off the road and rolled twice down the embankment.

Arthur Merton was killed. Trapped under the open-top car, he suffered fatal head injuries and died before reaching the hospital in Alexandria. Maclean regained consciousness in the hospital three days later, with a broken arm and collarbone and a badly fractured skull. "The others were all thrown clear." Randolph Churchill had three crushed vertebrae, and Rose had broken his arm in three places. Stirling fractured a wrist. He never spoke about the crash, but was said to be suffering from "shock" for some time afterward. They had cheated death in Benghazi, only to find it on the road home, in a banal traffic accident. Maclean later remarked that "David Stirling's driving was the most dangerous thing in World

War Two." They might have made light of the incident, but it had been a horrifying end to a mission that had achieved nothing. Stirling's refusal to discuss what had happened on the road to Cairo was a sign, perhaps, of just how deeply it had affected him.

War is not a science: it frequently fails to achieve the intended result, or finds success by chance; it kills the wrong people and spares those fully ready to die. Stirling was prepared to destroy any number of enemies in uniform; the first person he had killed, by mistake, was a civilian on his own side.

Stirling had now visited Benghazi twice without being caught, yet the operations had inflicted no damage on Axis shipping, no dent in enemy morale. Rommel's vital supply lines were undamaged, and the threat to Malta undiminished.

Yet one aspect of Stirling's plan worked flawlessly.

Convalescing from the car crash, clad in an iron brace for his back, Randolph Churchill requested permission to write a "secret and personal" report on the raid for his father, which Stirling was only too happy to grant. On June 24, Randolph wrote a private ten-page account of the episode for Winston Churchill. Exaggerated and boastful in parts but largely accurate, it gave a vivid account of events, stressed the daring and strategic value of L Detachment, SAS, and lavished praise on both Stirling and Maclean. "Fitzroy is worth his weight in gold . . . with him at my side I would be perfectly happy to spend a week in Rome," he wrote. Stirling's leadership of the successful foray into and out of Benghazi had "filled us with confidence for future operations."

This was just the sort of tale Winston Churchill adored, and liked to repeat after dinner, replete with secret missions, fast cars, brushes with death, narrow escapes, and British derring-do. That the mission had failed was neither here nor there. The story was also proof of his son's mettle, which was, of course, the main reason Randolph had written it. The fruitless raid in Benghazi would be Randolph Churchill's first and last foray with the SAS. His back injury was sufficiently severe for him to be invalided home. But he made a vital, albeit indirect, contribution to the SAS—not with his gun, but by his pen.

Winston Churchill may well have been unaware of L Detachment's existence before he read Randolph's breathless account. The story left a profound impression on the prime minister.

Chapter 10

SEVEN AIRFIELDS

T HE TWO MIGHTY ARMIES STILL CROUCHED, SNARLING, ON
either side of a front line that ran from Gazala, thirty miles
west of Tobruk, to the old Ottoman fortress of Bir Hakeim,
fifty miles to the south. Since February 1942, both sides had been
gathering strength for the next round of battle in the Western
Desert; with each passing day, the plight of besieged Malta grew
more ominous. Churchill repeatedly urged Auchinleck to launch
a counterattack, seize the airfields in Cyrenaica, and relieve the
pressure on the island, "the loss of which would be a disaster of
the first magnitude to the British Empire, and probably fatal in
the long run to the defence of the Nile delta." But the general
refused to be rushed, insisting he needed more time to build up
his reserves. Finally, he was presented with an ultimatum. In the
moonless period of mid-June, two convoys would set out from
Alexandria and Gibraltar, to try to reach Malta with vital supplies;
Auchinleck must attack by then, or stand down from his command. The Auk began to make his move.

Stirling was summoned to the office of the director of military
operations and asked how L Detachment could contribute to the
coming offensive. A day later, he presented his most sweeping plan
to date: SAS units would simultaneously raid six airfields around
Benghazi on the night of June 13; a seventh party would be taken
to Crete by submarine to attack the airfield at Heraklion.

Planning and equipping multiple missions was a daunting

logistical task. Much of the administrative work was left to Cooper and Seekings, both of whom had been promoted to the rank of sergeant. "Paddy Mayne and I would decide our next jolly and then we'd hand over all the details to the pair of them," Stirling said. "They were utterly dependable and there was an almost intuitive rapport between them." While Cooper and Seekings assembled the necessary rations, weapons, camouflage, and ammunition, Mike Sadler calculated distances and petrol requirements.

The strain of operations and the rigors of desert life were beginning to tell on Stirling. His wrist was not healing quickly, and he had developed chronic "desert sores," skin ulcers caused by the heat and chafing sand for which there was no very effective treatment. If these became septic, the infected tissue could be scoured out with a toothbrush, an exquisitely painful operation that frequently made them worse. Stirling simply taped a plaster over his sores and ignored them. He appeared as insouciant as ever, but may also have been suffering from the delayed trauma of the car crash. Most worrying of all, he had begun to experience migraines, the legacy from his first botched parachute jump, unpredictable and crushing headaches that left him immobilized and blinded with pain. Though largely indifferent to his own health, Stirling had come to realize that he needed a medical officer, both to tend the injured on operations and to maintain the health of the men at base camp.

Dr. Malcolm James Pleydell of the Royal Army Medical Corps had absolutely no idea what he was letting himself in for when he arrived at Kabrit in early June 1942. He had been told only that he would be attached to a unit operating in the desert, commanded by a young daredevil officer. "Everything is very hush hush down there," the officer arranging his transfer had said. "We never get to know anything at all really. They are always dashing in and out on raids." Pleydell was directed to a tent, surrounded by sandbags. A "tall and slender" figure rose to greet him. The handshake was firm, though the hand was wrapped in dirty bandages.

"Ah, you're Pleydell. By Jove, this is marvellous, having our own doctor. This is real luxury! By the way, have you had any lunch? No? Well, what about going over to the mess and having a drink, and then we can talk things over." As they strolled across the camp, Pleydell could hear explosions in the distance. Most of the men, Stirling explained, would shortly be "going out on a party," and "all those horrible bangs over on the beach" were in preparation for a series of night attacks on the coastal airfields. "Paddy and myself have to go off at the end of the week. I know it must seem awfully rude of us to push off like this just as you arrive." Pleydell had been expecting a man of blood and steel, a ruthless trained killer; instead he had been made to feel as if he had just joined a particularly jolly beachfront house party, with bombs. These men were "risking their lives in particularly daring and spectacular fashion," but acting as if "the whole thing was a glorious rag." Pleydell decided he was going to enjoy being part of L Detachment, SAS.

Born in Lewisham, in southeast London, some twenty-seven years earlier, Pleydell was a gentle soul, earnest, sensitive, and a little solemn. The experience of treating the wounded during the retreat from Dunkirk had been "traumatic," but at least it was more interesting than his next posting to a military hospital in Cairo, where the medical challenge was negligible, the officer class pretentious, and the endless paperwork stultifying. Like many men in uniform, Pleydell sought "to prove himself and satisfy any little doubts of the conscience," yet he was no fighting doctor, and "as a rule was very cautious of danger." He was determined to get something out of the experience of war, but uncertain what that something was. This mysterious unit might offer an opportunity to test his medical skills, his courage, and the authenticity of his own feelings. The simplicity of the desert was a long way away from the refined artificiality of Lewisham and the affectations of wartime Cairo. "I wondered if I should find sincerity there; for, rightly or wrongly, it seemed to me that sincerity was the thing that mattered most: the stamp which gave the coin its true value."

Like all the best doctors, Pleydell was a keen student of human nature. As a medic, he stood slightly apart from the fighting men, who came to regard him as a sort of resident shaman, different, slightly odd, but useful. He would emerge as the most astute observer and chronicler of the SAS.

Pleydell arrived as Stirling was parceling out the Benghazi targets. Paddy Mayne would attack the satellite airfield at Berka, which he had so successfully raided in March. Stirling, with Cooper and Seekings, intended to hit Benina, believed to be the principal aircraft-repair base. French units would strike at the airfields in Barce, Derna, Martuba, and the main aerodrome at Berka. The assault on Heraklion in Nazi-occupied Crete would be led by Georges Bergé, the French paratroop commander.

It did not take Malcolm Pleydell long to realize that he had joined a most peculiar fighting unit. From the outside, this was a "ruffianly, bearded, unkempt and ill-clothed mob." There was none of the spit and polish he had encountered (and resented) in regular army units. The men treated their officers with a respect very different from the rote obedience required under traditional military discipline. "These men were seldom impressed by what an officer said, or the way he spoke; it was what he did that counted." Stirling treated all his men with the same courtesy, never raising his voice or pulling rank. His authority seemed to stem from the quiet certainty of one who always got what he wanted, and knew how to ask for it. "There was about him a charm which it would be impossible to describe and this, together with his personal modesty and his flattery of others, made him very difficult to deny."

In the mess, seated on bar stools made from parachute container cylinders, Stirling's officers combined camaraderie with a "spirit of personal competition," frequently expressed in physical roughhousing: "If someone's trousers were not removed before the bar had closed you could be sure that there was something wrong." Bill Fraser alone held back from the horseplay, and was teased mercilessly for it. He seemed most relaxed in the company of his dog, Withers, who wore a naval coat and followed Fraser everywhere with "deep and very soulful eyes."

Stirling himself was a "baffling character," whose "flowery form of expression" seemed to disguise a hidden shyness. To Pleydell's trained eye, he looked "far from strong," with worsening migraines and infected sores. He had cut off the plaster cast from his injured wrist with a pair of scissors ("It was such a nuisance"), and flatly refused to wear another. Stirling was clearly going to be "a tricky case to treat."

The other ranks were as hard to categorize as their officers: Dave Kershaw, with his "lean look and eyes, bloodshot from the desert strain, giving him a piratical appearance"; Pat Riley, "huge and burly, who kept a rough law and order over all." The man who most intrigued the young doctor was Germain Guerpillon, the pint-sized Frenchman, so singularly ill-suited to the life of an SAS soldier, but adamant in his determination to become one. "The very fact that he had come to be in such a unit was just one more of those strange peculiarities that you met in the war," reflected Pleydell, who followed the progress of "the duffer" with affectionate fascination. One morning he watched Guerpillon hesitating at the top of the parachute training frame, desperate to jump but unable to do so, while "everyone laughed at him." Finally, Guerpillon leaped, hit the ground, pitched forward, and landed on his face, breaking his nose. Pleydell rushed forward, as Guerpillon staggered groggily to his feet. "*C'est rien, docteur*," he insisted, smiling broadly as blood cascaded down his face.

Of his new comrades, only Paddy Mayne gave Pleydell pause. A hulking figure, "dwarfing the very chair on which he sat," he spent hour after hour at the bar, smoking continuously, saying little. When he did speak, he seemed determined to provoke: he told Pleydell he disapproved of the Red Cross, and described how, for every SAS man killed, he would kill a given number of the enemy in revenge, thus "wiping off the debt." Pleydell was left in no doubt that Mayne was "out to kill when the opportunity presented itself. There was no question of sparing the enemy. No quarter was asked, and none given . . . to him there were no rules." There should be "some good killing" at the Berka satellite,

Mayne remarked airily. The young doctor pondered that phrase, and never forgot it: "I wondered if I could ever think of 'good killing' and felt rather weak-minded and unwarlike in my inability to do so." A man whose every instinct was to save life wondered whether, in extremis, he might be capable of taking it too. "I know I would have regretted it soon afterwards." Mayne seemed to take pleasure in slaughter: "Fighting was in his blood: he thrived on it."

In the two months leading up to the great offensive, the men were granted some much needed leave. Most spent it in the bars and fleshpots of Cairo. Paddy Mayne, however, did not join them. Instead, in mid-April, he vanished for several days. It was assumed that he must have been off on a solo bender. In fact, Mayne had gone on a private pilgrimage: to try to find the grave of his friend Eoin McGonigal. Gazala, where McGonigal had perished in the first disastrous mission, now marked the northernmost point of the British line. No-man's-land stretched away to the west. Mayne hitched a lift to Gazala with the RAF, and then spent several days "making enquiries and searching." McGonigal had died from his injuries six months earlier; since the men under his command were all either dead or in captivity, no one knew for sure where in the wide desert he had been buried. Mayne's quest was romantic, quixotic, and, as he probably knew before setting out, wildly unrealistic. On his return to Kabrit, he wrote to McGonigal's mother, explaining what he had done. Margaret McGonigal replied: "It was good of you to have gone to Gazala and taken so much trouble to try to find Eoin's grave. I know he did not have an identity disc—I think he just wanted to be an unknown soldier . . . so it is perhaps better as it is—just as he wanted." Mayne never told anyone else about his secret attempt to find the remains of his beloved friend, for that would have revealed the other, gentler side to Paddy Mayne, and a hidden broken heart.

THE THIRTEENTH OF June, 1942, was the most frenetic and furious day in the short history of the SAS, as the small units mounted simultaneous operations against enemy airfields from Benghazi to Crete. Most military operations involve a single, identifiable objective; Stirling's miniature army was about to attack seven different targets, with units under seven distinct leaders, over land and sea, with multiple vehicles, various weapons, and variable success. But the ultimate aim was the same: to smash as much of the enemy airpower as possible in a single day, and help ensure the Allied convoys got through to embattled Malta.

The French patrols, under the overall command of the soigné former civil servant Augustin Jordan, now promoted to captain, faced a particularly steep challenge. Unlike the Benghazi airstrips, reaching the targets in Derna and Martuba would mean driving long distances through numerous roadblocks and across territory swarming with enemy soldiers. The area roughly a hundred miles west of Tobruk was used as a staging post for German and Italian troops heading to and from the front. Some additional form of disguise would be necessary.

Captain Herbert Buck had been wounded and captured by the Germans at Gazala the year before. A fluent German-speaker, he contrived to escape by acquiring an Afrika Korps uniform, strolling out of the front gate of his POW camp, and walking to the British lines. Buck's escape had given him an idea, which he put to the planners in military intelligence: a unit of German-speakers, dressed in genuine German uniforms, could penetrate undetected behind the lines, circulate among enemy troops, and gain valuable intelligence. Buck set about recruiting German Jews from Palestine, several of whom had found their way into the recently disbanded No. 51 Middle East Commando, as well as German-speaking Frenchmen and Czechs. These extraordinary men, who often nursed a deep hatred for the Nazis, signed up with Buck's outfit in the certain knowledge that if they were caught behind the lines wearing German uniform, they would be shot as spies. The force, with a total strength of between twenty and thirty men, was given a deliberately misleading and meaningless name: the Special Interrogation Group, or SIG. Buck housed his men in an isolated camp on the edge of the Middle East commando base in Geneifa and put them through rigorous training: they spoke only German and were drilled with German military commands; each man was issued with German identification papers, pay books, and even love letters, written in German, from fictional German sweethearts. Two of the most important recruits were German prisoners of war, Herbert Brückner and Walter Essner, both of whom had served in the French Foreign Legion before being drafted into the Afrika Korps on the outbreak of war. Captured in November 1941, the pair professed to be committed anti-Nazis, and after careful vetting by military intelligence they were pronounced "wholly trustworthy." Some of the Jewish recruits were unhappy at having Germans in their midst, but Brückner ("big, brash and fair-haired") and Essner ("quiet and good-natured") swiftly blended in, for "both were light-hearted companions." The Germans brought an important additional element to Buck's training program: having recently been part of the German army, they were able to pass on the latest military slang, gossip, songs, and obscenities. The men of SIG not only dressed, marched, and spoke like real German soldiers, they swore like them.

Stirling contacted Buck in late May and laid out a proposal: the SIG, in their German uniforms, would transport the French forces, posing as prisoners, in captured German vehicles through the enemy-occupied zone and onto the airfields. Buck was delighted to accept a mission he believed to be "well within the capabilities of his small unit." Augustin Jordan, the commander of the French forces, also embraced the idea, which seemed to reflect a certain flamboyant French élan.

LYING UP IN the foothills of the Jebel, with an hour to spare before the attack on Benina, David Stirling gave an impromptu lecture on the art of deerstalking. The key, he told Seekings and Cooper, was to stay downwind of the stag at all times, use all available camouflage, and move with sufficient stealth that the quarry never saw you coming. Above all, the stalker should never take a shot unless certain of a kill, for anything else was unsporting. "Absorbed in his Highland exploits, we could forget the job in hand [and] time passed very quickly," wrote Cooper. For that hour, Stirling was back in Keir. "Right," he said at last, glancing at his watch, "ready to go."

The stalkers stole onto Benina airfield. Each man carried twenty Lewes bombs. For the next half-hour, they crept from one hangar to another: the first two sheds contained a Messerschmitt, two Junkers transport planes, and a pair of Stukas. Seekings stood guard by the door with a tommy gun, while Cooper and Stirling planted the bombs. The third hangar was packed with spare parts, technical equipment, and at least thirty new aircraft engines. Here the last of the bombs were planted.

As the trio prepared to retreat, Stirling spotted a small guard-house set apart from the hangars, with a faint light gleaming under the door. Perhaps it was the memory of Mayne's actions at Tamet, or perhaps it was simply a rush of battle blood, but Stirling now did something that, he later admitted, was "out of character." Turning to the other two, he suggested they give the Germans "something to remember us by."

Taking the pin out of at least one grenade (the official report refers to "grenades"), he opened the door of the guardhouse. Inside were some twenty German soldiers, and an officer apparently writing a report at a small table. "Share this among you," Stirling shouted, threw in the explosives, slammed the door, and ran. According to Seekings, the horrified German officer may actually have caught one of the grenades just before it detonated. "The explosion shattered the guardhouse," wrote Cooper. Moments later, the Lewes bombs began to go off inside the hangars. The three men slipped back into the darkness.

An hour earlier, Stirling had been giving a lecture on the ethics of stalking deer. Now he had just killed and injured at least a dozen people in an attack that may have been justifiable as an act of war but was hardly sporting. He could never fully explain what had motivated him in "wiping out the guard," and the episode haunted him for the rest of his life. "It was a silly show of bravado, I suppose," he told his biographer. "In a fight I would shoot to kill with the same enthusiasm as the next man, but I was not at ease with that action. It seemed close to murder."

The three were climbing back up the escarpment when Stirling suffered a sudden and crippling migraine, brought on by the stress of what had just taken place, and collapsed. Below them, a "fantastic fireworks display" erupted on Benina airfield. "The whole thing just boiled up, because there was so much petrol, oil and lubricants." The heat from the fire set off the Messerschmitt's 20mm cannon, sending brightly colored tracers (ammunition with built-in pyrotechnic charges that enabled more accurate fire, particularly at night) shooting across the runways. In the darkness, Cooper and Seekings dragged Stirling, "staggering and half blind," up the hill. Soon after dawn they were picked up by the LRDG.

AT THE SAME moment, forty miles to the east, a French team had successfully ignited the fuel dumps on Barce airfield, while another, under Lieutenant André Zirnheld, was fighting a pitched battle with German troops on the main airfield at Berka.

Zirnheld was a character straight out of French central casting: intellectual, poetic, handsome, and unfeasibly brave. Before the war he had been a professor of philosophy in Tunis, but with the fall of France he immediately took up arms and volunteered as a paratrooper under Georges Bergé. Of all the French recruits, none had adapted so completely to the SAS way of life. In an article for a French magazine, Zirnheld wrote: "I need not complain about the war. Because of it, I have had to learn to live through anything . . . After the war, the problem will be to discover a similar peace."

Zirnheld and his team had managed to plant explosives on six German bombers, before being spotted by the guards. In the running firefight that followed, several sentries were killed or

wounded, but the French team miraculously battled their way off
the airfield without casualties, and returned intact to the rendezvous.

THE SUBMARINE *TRITON* of the Greek navy surfaced in the Gulf
of Malia in the dead of night. Two rubber boats paddled slowly
toward the coast of Crete, towing a third boat weighed down by a
cargo of Lewes bombs, rations, and water. Aboard were Georges
Bergé, three French SAS men, and a single officer of the Royal Hel-
lenic Army, a native Cretan. They were accompanied by another
new recruit to L Detachment: Captain George Jellicoe, the 2nd
Earl Jellicoe, possessor of one of the most famous names in warfare.

Admiral John Jellicoe had commanded the British fleet at the
Battle of Jutland in 1916. The admiral had a bust in Trafalgar
Square, a grave in St. Paul's Cathedral, and a string of honors and
titles; he died in 1935, leaving his seventeen-year-old only son an
earldom, George V as a godfather, and a lot to live up to.

In 1939, Jellicoe signed up for the commandos, and sailed out
to the Middle East with Layforce. With his taste for danger, his
intelligence, and a "thick cloak of self-deprecation" lightly worn,
he was a man in Stirling's mold. They met in the long bar of Shep-
heard's Hotel in Cairo; on April 30, 1942, Jellicoe was posted to
L Detachment as Stirling's second in command, and immediately
volunteered for the Heraklion assault.

All six men were disguised as Cretan peasants, and heavily
armed with Beretta submachine guns and Colt .45 revolvers. The
only common language was French.

On the night of June 13, they cut through the perimeter barbed
wire around Heraklion airfield and planted bombs on the fleet of
parked Junkers 88 bombers. As the first bombs went off, pandemonium erupted. A German patrol rushed out of the front gate; the
SAS team fell in behind them and then "peeled off into the darkness." Bergé paused after half an hour and formally announced
that they would all be awarded the Croix de Guerre for the night's

work. He then led the party south. Or rather north, because in the excitement he had been reading the map upside down. "All right, you take the lead if you're so clever," he said resentfully when this was pointed out. Having sorted out their bearings, they again set off, heading for the beach near Krotos on the south coast, where a British caique, the *Porcupine*, should be waiting to pick them up. At dawn on June 19, they took refuge in the hills. A few hours later, a Cretan stumbled across the men in their hiding place. He seemed friendly and offered to bring food and drink, but Bergé later said he "did not like the cut of his jib." That afternoon, a few hours before the rendezvous, Jellicoe and the Greek officer walked down to Krotos to link up with the local partisans and check that all was ready for the pickup. At 7:00 that evening, Bergé ordered the three Frenchmen to pack up and prepare to head to the beach to join the other two. A few minutes later, he shouted: "Look out! We're surrounded." A brief, intense gun battle followed. The youngest of the Frenchmen, seventeen-year-old Pierre Léostic, was shot dead. Outgunned and encircled by German troops, the only option was surrender.

The sounds of battle from the hills alerted Jellicoe and the Greek officer to the betrayal of their party; they were picked up by rowboat and ferried to the waiting caique. Halfway across, they were hailed, in upper-class English, by the occupant of a boat heading the other way. This was Paddy Leigh Fermor, writer, intelligence agent, and one of the great adventurers of the Second World War, who was on a mission to link up with the Cretan partisans. He and Jellicoe "exchanged shadowy greetings" in the twilight, and paddled on.

The raid had destroyed at least twenty-one planes, two trucks, a dozen aircraft engines, several fuel dumps, and a bomb depot. The following day, in reprisal for suspected collaboration by the local Cretans, the Germans shot fifty inhabitants of Heraklion.

• • •

ON JUNE 12, a small convoy rumbled along the road toward Derna. It consisted of one Kübelwagen (the military Volkswagen), one Opel car, a German lorry, and a British lorry painted with the Nazi swastika, indicating that it had been captured. Nothing about the convoy was as it seemed. The British truck had not been captured by the Germans, but all the German vehicles had been captured by the British. The driver of the first lorry, in the uniform of a German private, was Captain Herbert Buck of the Scots Guards and chief of SIG. The men alongside him were Herbert Brückner and Walter Essner, former soldiers of the Afrika Korps, now working for the other side. The French prisoners in the back were Free French paratroopers, led by Augustin Jordan. Hidden carefully out of sight were the machine guns, grenades, and Lewes bombs with which they intended to lay waste to the airfields. The men standing guard over them, armed with machine guns and Luger pistols, were Jews.

At the first Italian checkpoint, a major demanded the weekly password: Brückner, playing his part to perfection, threatened to have the Italian reported to his superiors for delaying an important convoy of prisoners. The barrier was lifted. The convoy was similarly ushered through at the next checkpoint by an overweight German corporal who advised Buck to park at the nearby transit camp for the night, as there were "British commandos about." At the camp, the French sat around trying to look like disconsolate captives while the soldiers of SIG mingled with the Germans, purchased some provisions, and refueled the lorries at German expense. Corporal Adolf Schubert (real name: Ariyeh Shai, of Jerusalem) queued up for a plate of lentils and dumplings at the canteen.

The next morning, Brückner drove the French commander to reconnoiter the airfields at Derna. Jordan was encouraged by what he saw: a squadron of Messerschmitt 110s sitting on the western airstrip and at least a dozen Stukas on the eastern airstrip. Buck would remain at the rendezvous to coordinate operations: a small team of French SAS men would attack nearby Martuba, while Jordan would lead a larger team of nine SAS and three SIG men, including Brückner, to raid the Derna airfields.

Something was wrong with the truck driven by Brückner. The engine stalled repeatedly. They set off at around 9:00 a.m., but an hour later the vehicle had still not covered the six miles to the airfields. Each time it stopped, Brückner jumped down, swearing, and after tinkering under the hood, got it moving. Then it would stop again. Jordan, sweltering under a tarpaulin with the other men in the back, was becoming increasingly exasperated. Near the Derna airstrip cinema, the German driver jumped out once more and stomped off toward the nearby guard post, saying he had lost the key to the toolbox. "It's OK," whispered Peter Haas, one of the SIG men, "he's going to ask the Germans for a spanner." Jordan and the others waited tensely as the minutes ticked by.

Inside the guardhouse, the following scene (pieced together from the testimony of two captured Luftwaffe pilots) was taking place.

Brückner was a turncoat. He saluted the commanding officer of Derna garrison and explained that he was a captured German prisoner of war, driving a lorry filled with enemy saboteurs intent on blowing up aircraft. The officer was suspicious. Brückner became increasingly agitated, urging the officer to "organize as many men as possible with all speed and as heavily armed as possible to disarm the raiding party." He went on to explain that he had been captured back in November, and that the British had offered him money to drive them behind the lines. Initially he had refused. "However the sum increased and he accepted as he felt it was the best way of getting back his freedom." The garrison commander was now convinced. He summoned his men. Quietly, several dozen heavily armed German sentries surrounded the truck.

Jordan, unable to bear the suspense any longer, emerged from beneath the tarpaulin and peered through the back flap. He was immediately dragged out and held. "All Frenchmen out now!" What happened next is disputed. Some of the French may have surrendered. Some may have opened fire. The next moment the truck exploded. According to Jordan, Peter Haas was the last man left aboard. Knowing that as a Jew he would soon be tortured and murdered, Haas fired his machine gun into the stack of explosives, blowing it, and himself, to fragments. "He decided to try and save us by sacrificing himself," said Jordan. In the smoke and chaos, Jordan wrenched free of his captors and ran.

Brückner was later flown to Germany, and awarded the Deutsches Kreuz, the German Cross, for his brave action in exposing the team of French assassins. Something about the companionship of life in the desert had concealed the traitor. If a man shared the hunger, thirst, and heat, it was easy to imagine that he must be a friend. Brückner had sung around the campfire as lustily as any. But the German had always intended to lead the SAS into a trap. Brückner was the first quisling to use the unit's esprit de corps to conceal his real intentions, and he would not be the last.

For once, Paddy Mayne was out of luck. The Berka satellite airfield was not the sitting duck it had been a few weeks earlier. Guards had been posted on each aircraft, and by attacking the main airfield ahead of schedule, it was later claimed, the Zirnheld-led French, who tended to disdain timetables, had alerted the defenders. As Jellicoe remarked of the Free French forces: "They were very, very free; and very, very French." Approaching the airfield, Mayne and his team were spotted by sentries, who immediately opened fire. After a short and vicious firefight, the SAS men withdrew without injuries, pausing only to plant bombs on a petrol dump. A "desperate game of hide and seek" followed in the dark, as enemy patrols fanned out and combed the area. Before dawn, the unit split into two groups of two men each. Mayne and his companion eventually reached a Senussi encampment, where, after a meal of goat stew, they remained for the night. The next morning they awoke to see another member of their party pedaling across the desert toward them on a bicycle.

Bob Lilley had been one of the first to sign up with L Detachment. Nearing forty, he was one of the oldest men in the unit, and one of the toughest, with dark curly hair and black eyes. "Never hilarious and never downhearted," wrote Pleydell. "He always maintained a steady level of good humour as if life could not spring any surprises on him." The previous twenty-four hours had tested even Lilley's prodigious reserves of phlegm.

On separating from Mayne, he and a companion had come across a house near the airfield with a garden surrounded by a thick, well-tended hedge. With dawn breaking, concealment seemed the best option. Lilley climbed under the hedge and, with a composure that seems scarcely human, fell asleep. When he awoke, he was alone. The other man was never seen again. His fate has never been established. A friendly Alsatian dog appeared, and insisted on licking Lilley's face, until he punched the animal on the nose and it shot off whimpering. Italian voices could be heard on all sides. Concluding that capture was all but certain if he remained under the hedge, and even more likely if he tried to run away, Lilley opted for a tactic of extreme nonchalance. "I got out of the bush, stood up, and started to saunter off." He continued walking, through an enemy camp in the process of waking up. On all sides, Italian and German soldiers were shaving, washing, and lining up for breakfast. They paid no attention whatever to another man in shirtsleeves and shorts trudging through the encampment. Eventually, he found himself on a deserted road, running parallel to a railway line, and began to walk in what he hoped was an easterly direction.

A dot appeared on the road up ahead, which gradually resolved itself into an Italian soldier on a bicycle. The Italian slowed as he reached Lilley, staring hard. Then he stopped and dismounted. Lilley reckoned the cyclist was probably about twenty years old. Lilley understood no Italian, but by the man's gestures, which were not friendly, he plainly indicated that Lilley was now a prisoner and should accompany back him to the camp. "This I had no intention of doing," Lilley later recalled. "So we got to wrestling." Beside a railway line in the desert, two soldiers on opposite sides of the war, entirely without animus, now engaged in a hand-to-hand fight in the sand that was short, fierce, and lethal. The young Italian was fitter, but Lilley fought with the desperation of a man who believes he has no choice. "I got my hands around his throat and strangled him."

Bob Lilley later described the episode to Malcolm Pleydell. "Funny, killing a chap with your own hands, doc. I can still see his white face and dark brown eyes quite clearly. I left him lying there, sprawled out and looking up at the sun." Lilley picked up the dead man's cap and placed it over his face, as if he was sleeping. Then he climbed on the bike and began pedaling toward the tribal camp on the horizon.

DAVID STIRLING PRIDED himself on being "non-swanks," never boasting of his own or his unit's achievements. But back at the rendezvous in the Jebel, having at last taken part in a successful raid, he could not resist showing off: "It's a bit of a change to see my fires lighting up the sky instead of yours," he said to Paddy Mayne.

The rivalry between these two men was childish in the extreme, yet for Stirling it also served a purpose. Years later, the SAS founder admitted that while he had done his best to appear intrepid at all times, he had often struggled with his own fear. "I was afraid, on many occasions. I've little doubt we all were, but the secret—and perhaps the hardest thing of all—is to control that fear." Mayne, however, seemed entirely immune to anxiety. Stirling's terror of being found fearful in front of Mayne was greater than the fear itself. "With someone like Paddy in competition, and we were competitive, there was little danger of fear taking over."

"Half-joking" (but only half), Stirling inquired whether Mayne would care to come and inspect his handiwork: "It might be fun to go and see if the bits and pieces are still burning."

"I was being a little pomposo," he later admitted. Mayne immediately accepted what was, in effect, a challenge. "I want to make
sure you're not exaggerating," he said, with a glinting grin.

And so they set off the next morning, in a brand-new Chevro-
let truck borrowed from the LRDG, on a secondary raid that was
unscheduled, unnecessary, and dangerous, prompted solely by a
schoolboy rivalry between grown men. "It was foolish of course,"
Stirling acknowledged. "But that's how we were." Mayne drove.
Alongside him sat Stirling and Karl Kahane, an Austrian Jew from
Buck's SIG unit who had spent twenty years in the German army
before emigrating to Palestine. In the back sat Seekings, Cooper,
and Lilley, the desert strangler, with a Lewis machine gun concealed under a tarpaulin.

On the Benina road, about ten miles from the airfield, they hit a
roadblock. Not a flimsy Italian barrier, but a newly built construction of concrete and barbed wire, which could be neither rammed
nor skirted. As Mayne came to a stop, a German sergeant major
emerged from the guardhouse, carrying a "potato-masher" hand
grenade in one hand and a torch in the other. At least a dozen German sentries stood in a semicircle, with automatic weapons ready.
Karl Kahane did not wait for the sentry to speak: "We're coming
from the front. We haven't had a bath for weeks, and we're hungry.
So cut out the formalities and let us through."

The sergeant major seemed unimpressed.

"Password," he grunted.

Kahane did not know the password. He did, however, know how
to deliver a dressing down in fluent German military argot. Paddy
Mayne paraphrased the speech that followed: "How the fuck do
we know what the fucking password is, and don't ask for our fucking identity cards either. They're lost and we've been fighting for
the past seventy hours against these fucking Tommies. Our car
was destroyed and we were lucky to capture this British truck and
get back at all. So hurry up and get that fucking gate open."

Still unconvinced, the German moved around to the driver's
side, until he stood just three feet from the window.

At this moment Paddy Mayne did something very foolish, or very brave, but certainly effective. He cocked the Colt revolver held in his lap, with a loud click. The sergeant major heard the noise and knew exactly what it meant: he was a hair trigger away from a gun battle, in which he would be the first victim. Everyone remained "perfectly still for a few seconds" and then, as Mayne later wrote, the man made a sensible calculation: "If anyone was going to be hurt, he was going to be a sick man very early on." The German signaled his men to raise the barrier, and the truck trundled through.

The sergeant major was certain to radio ahead that enemy forces were approaching. Sure enough, four miles farther on stood another guard post with half a dozen Italian soldiers drawn up across the road "waving rifles." Mayne accelerated; the Italians scattered. As the truck stormed through, Seekings opened up with the Lewis machine gun. The enemy was now fully alerted, yet Stirling insisted they could not depart without leaving "a calling card." In the next half-hour, they blew up an unguarded transport filling station and fuel depot, set Lewes bombs on a small fleet of heavy lorries in a car park, and opened fire on the roadhouse beside it, where a number of Germans and Italians were drinking. "Short, snappy and exhilarating" was how Mayne described the engagement.

A five-mile dash across the rocky plain, with a German armored car in pursuit, was ended when the truck reached the safety of a deep ravine. The German pursuers fell back, fearful of an ambush. Maneuvering the truck up the other side of the steep gully took several more hours. "In the end we practically carried it up," grumbled Seekings.

It was a long drive back to the rendezvous. The men lolled drowsily against the sides of the truck. Suddenly Lilley shouted: "Burning fuse! Get out, quick." Mayne did not even have time to brake. The men scrambled out with the vehicle still moving, moments before a deafening explosion threw them all to the ground. According to the SAS War Diary, "Lilley just cleared the truck as it blew up." The jolting ride had set off a time pencil, and Lilley had picked up the smell of a burning fuse seconds before detonation. What remained of the brand-new truck, observed Lilley, "could have been put in a haversack." They set off again on foot, snorting with laughter.

As the teams reassembled in the Jebel on June 14 and 15, Stirling assessed the results and counted the cost. Augustin Jordan, who would take over from the captured Bergé as leader of the French contingent, was the lone survivor of his squad, and distraught. But dozens of planes had been destroyed in the combined raids, the Axis airfields had been distracted at a key moment, and large numbers of enemy troops had been tied down dealing with the threat. Of the seventeen Allied ships that had steamed off to relieve Malta, just two made it through to the island with desperately needed supplies, yet Stirling looked back with satisfaction on the operation. Had the SAS not been so successful in disrupting the airfields and wrecking planes, he believed, none of the convoy would have gotten through. With an untypical degree of "swanks," he later insisted: "We regard what we did as saving Malta."

Not until the unit returned to Siwa Oasis on June 21, to find the LRDG hastily evacuating the base, did Stirling discover how radically the war picture had been redrawn, once again, in his absence. That afternoon, the BBC announced that Tobruk was once more in German hands. On May 26, before Auchinleck's offensive, Rommel had launched his own attack, a brilliant lightning strike that would send the Allies reeling back 150 miles. The Afrika Korps was pushing into Egypt, while the British fell back, fighting hard, to a new defensive line running between El Alamein and the Qattara Depression. The Royal Navy was pulling out of Alexandria, bonfires of secret papers were being lit in Cairo, and the surging Axis powers scented victory in North Africa. Hitler promoted Rommel to the rank of field marshal, and told Mussolini that the decisive blow would be delivered without delay. "The Goddess of battles visits warriors only once," he declared, in the sort of pompous tosh favored by dictators down the ages.

Churchill was blunter: "Egypt must be held at all costs."

Chapter 11

MASS SABOTAGE AT SIDI HANEISH

A S THE CONVOY RUMBLED INTO THE DESERT, MALCOLM Pleydell was elated, excited, and slightly bemused. For the second time in as many months, he had absolutely no idea where he was going, or what he might be called on to do when he got there. He knew he was part of a substantial raiding party, but beyond that the operation had been "surrounded by an atmosphere of delightful vagueness." Stirling had promised only that they would "have some fun." The uncertainty was deliberate, for Cairo was riddled with spies. The men seemed "light-hearted and carefree," singing lustily as they headed off on a mission from which some would surely not return. That probability was never discussed. "To suggest a person was worried, in the slightest degree, was equivalent to the vilest form of abuse," wrote Pleydell. The doctor had spent the previous week issuing emergency first-aid kits. No one ever asked for instruction on how to use them, or even admitted that they might be necessary. Pleydell found this refusal to acknowledge the risks of what they were doing bizarre, and rather wonderful. He expected to be away from camp for just a few days; he would spend the next five weeks in the desert.

With the Afrika Korps just forty miles from Alexandria, the military equation had altered once again. Rommel's extended supply lines offered inviting new targets, including several additional airfields along the Egyptian coast. Instead of launching piecemeal attacks on moonless nights, Stirling now intended to deploy almost his entire force, numbering more than a hundred men, to an advance camp in the desert. From Qaret Tartura, a remote patch of scrub on the edge of the Qattara Depression, in the northwest of Egypt, they could harry and raid for weeks at a time without returning to base. To transport the men and supplies to the forward base Stirling obtained a fleet of three-ton trucks and, crucially, twelve brand-new four-wheel-drive American jeeps. These latter vehicles would transform SAS tactics. With the addition of a bulletproof windscreen from a Hurricane fighter, a water condenser to prevent overboiling, an armor-plated radiator, camouflage paint, reinforced suspension, and extra fuel tanks, these little cars became the most nimble desert vehicles. "The astonishing agility of the jeep enabled us to approach a target at night over almost any country," said Stirling, who added one more crucial modification. The Vickers K machine gun, capable of firing up to 1,200 rounds a minute, was originally intended for use on bombers to defend against fighter aircraft. A cache of these powerful guns was found in an Alexandria warehouse, and fitted to three jeeps as an experiment: two had twin guns bolted to the front, and the third carried four guns on two mountings, fore and aft. When the Vickers guns were fired simultaneously, the recoil caused the vehicle to shudder and buck like a spooked horse, but the destructive effect was dramatic and terrifying, laying down a solid curtain of fire. L Detachment engineers transformed the jeeps into heavily armed, all-terrain combat vehicles: light, sturdy, versatile, and lethal.

The hugely valuable partnership with the LRDG was nearing an end. After more than six months of operations the desert had become familiar terrain, and the SAS was now sufficiently expert in navigation to be able to operate without its "taxi service." "By the end of June [1942], L Detachment had raided all the more important German and Italian aerodromes within 300 miles of the forward area, at least once or twice, and some of them even three or four times." Mike Sadler was invited to join the unit as its senior navigator; he needed little persuading. Stirling decided to promote him. "You had better go down to the bazaar and get yourself some 'pips,'" he told the twenty-two-year-old Sadler, who did as he was told and transformed himself, sartorially, into a lieutenant. No one got around to informing the authorities of his promotion.

With its own transport and navigators, and the ability to attack at will from a forward base, L Detachment was fast becoming what Stirling had always intended it to be: a small, independent army, capable of fighting a different sort of war. "We were now self-supporting," Stirling later recalled, and from this point on "we really began to exercise our muscularity."

The convoy passed through the lines of the Eighth Army and into the no-man's-land beyond. "How frail and thin the line looked to be holding Rommel in check before the very gates of Alexandria," Pleydell reflected. To the south, the great Qattara Depression stretched away, a wilderness of salt pans and sand dunes covering seven thousand square miles, the second lowest point in Africa, and one of the most desolate. Ralph Bagnold, founder of the LRDG, had skirted the northern edge of the depression in 1927, believing the area to be impassable. It now formed a natural barrier blocking the southern end of the front line, the edge of what would be the El Alamein battlefield. A lone German outpost was deployed in the emptiness, with the thankless task of watching for enemy movements. Every day the wireless operator sent the same message, "Nothing to report," a statement so monotonous and predictable that it helped the code breakers of Bletchley Park to crack the Enigma code.

To Pleydell's eyes, this was "a stricken landscape . . . with only the old Arab track to show that man had travelled this way before, and here and there the smooth bleached skeleton of a camel, so old that the bone crumbled in the hand." The overladen convoy repeatedly got bogged down in the fine, light sand beneath the desert crust known in Arabic as *fech fech*. Through the haze, Pleydell's driver pointed out a man in the far distance, standing on an outcrop, watching them. A Bedouin? A German scout? A spotter for an LRDG patrol? No one seemed unduly worried, but Pleydell never forgot "the memory of that lone figure, and the uncanny sensation of having been watched in that bleak wilderness." That night they camped in a small wadi. Exhausted, Pleydell lay down in the sand and wrapped himself in his blanket: "I fell asleep wondering if I should ever be able to grow a decent beard like some of the other chaps."

The next night, the attacking forces moved some sixty miles north of the forward patrol base at Qaret Tartura, and then split into raiding parties. George Jellicoe and André Zirnheld, the French philosopher, set off to reconnoiter the coast road and strafe any targets that happened to appear. Stirling and Mayne headed for Bagush, the airfield from which the disastrous Operation Squatter had set off, now in German hands. The French commander, Augustin Jordan, and Bill Fraser were slated to attack two airfields at Fuka; Pleydell would accompany them in a noncombat role. The doctor watched Fraser's preparations with misgivings. "Poor Bill. God, I hope they don't get him," he reflected. "He seemed almost too young and boyish for this sort of thing." Pleydell and two drivers remained with the vehicles, as Fraser slipped into the darkness.

Two hours later he reappeared, alive but exceedingly grumpy, complaining that the French party attacking the other Fuka airfield had started a firefight, which had alerted the sentries and rendered his own attack impossible. (In fact, Jordan and his French team had destroyed eight Messerschmitts, with only one minor injury.) On the way back, Fraser told Pleydell a revealing story. Crawling through the darkness at the airstrip perimeter, he had heard Italian voices and realized that a small band of sentries was standing not more than ten yards away. Quietly, Fraser extracted a hand grenade and was about to pull the pin "when he thought better of it," stowed the grenade, and slipped away. Fraser never explained this act of mercy. "Perhaps he thought they were too childlike to be killed in cold blood," reflected Pleydell. "But for a kind thought . . . three or four Italians would now be buried under the sand of Fuka, three or four families would have been bereaved." Fraser was no less brave than Mayne and Stirling, and perfectly capable of killing when necessary; he just could not kill when it was not.

Back at the rendezvous, Stirling greeted the returning parties and totted up the scores, "welcoming us as if we had just come back from a game of golf." Jellicoe and Zirnheld had blown up a truck, gathered useful intelligence on the nearby Al Daba airfield, and taken three German prisoners. The most successful round was completed by Stirling's own party, which had destroyed thirty-seven planes.

In the course of the attack on Bagush, Stirling had discovered a new way to play the game, with jeeps.

Bombs had been planted on more than thirty planes in Bagush, but at least a dozen of these failed to detonate, due to damp fuses. Stirling suggested they return, immediately, and complete the job with the jeep-mounted machine guns. "After all," he pointed out, "they were designed to shoot up aircraft." Stirling led the way in the Blitz Buggy; Cooper manned the single Lewis gun alongside him; another gunner sat behind the twin guns in the rear; Mayne followed in one armed jeep, with another behind. The gunners were instructed to fire low, aiming for the petrol tanks. Still reeling from the initial assault, the defenders of Bagush were not expecting another, let alone the bristling little procession that now drove on to the airfield. At a stately fifteen miles per hour, the cars, with ten yards between them, drove around the remaining planes, pouring out a devastating broadside, at a combined rate of something close to 10,000 rounds a minute. As each plane exploded, the fire illuminated the next. Cooper had emptied a third magazine when his gun jammed. "The Vickers was designed for use in aircraft and therefore air-cooled. It would only accept a certain amount of ammunition down its throat before demanding a rest." The convoy left a scene of "complete confusion." Pleydell could see the conflagration from eighteen miles away, as repeated explosions "lit up the skyline like summer lightning." At dawn, nearing the rendezvous, they came under attack from Italian fighters, which had probably followed their tracks across the desert. Stirling and

Cooper leaped out as a plane swooped in. Seconds later there was an explosion, bringing the short but remarkable career of the Blitz Buggy to a fiery end. They walked the rest of the way.

Worried that Italian reconnaissance planes might have identified the encampment at Qaret Tartura, Stirling gave orders to relocate the forward base twenty-five miles west, to a spot known as Bir el Quseir, a long, low escarpment with numerous fissures and gullies ideal for concealing the vehicles. For the next month, this would be the SAS's desert home. The raids continued: on the night of July 11, a party under Mayne destroyed at least fourteen planes at Al Daba. Jordan wrecked eight more at Fuka. But while the tally mounted, so did the toll. The day after Mayne's raid, a patrol led by a dashing LRDG officer named Robin Gurdon (identified by Stirling as a possible second in command) came under attack from Italian fighters; Gurdon was shot through the stomach and chest, and died before Pleydell could reach him. The doctor had come to know Gurdon well and felt his loss keenly. The men almost never talked about their dead comrades. "You could never show your true feelings on the subject," Pleydell noted. But when no one was looking, he wept. "How strange the desert war seemed," he wrote. "The way we travelled over vast tracts of wilderness in order to search out and kill one another."

IN THE DESERT camp, an oddly peaceful, almost domestic routine developed. The doctor set up a makeshift surgery in a small cave, where the men came to be treated for desert sores and other ailments. To while away the hours, he made a study of the local fauna, such as it was: snakes, scorpions, and the occasional howling jackal at night. Paddy Mayne wore a "sleepy grin as he lay in the shadow of his jeep reading a Penguin and flicking away the occasional fly." Pleydell saw he was reading *The Spanish Farm* trilogy by Ralph Hale Mottram, First World War novels depicting an oasis of calm in the midst of a brutal war. Stirling spent the quiet hours happily reliving the recent raids and planning the next ones, "lying beneath the belly of a three-ton lorry, on his back, with one leg crossed languidly over the other, sucking peacefully on his empty pipe . . . for all the world, as if he was discussing the form of a point to point." Stirling never relaxed his dress code: whether going into battle or unwinding after it, he always wore a tie. The men chatted idly in the heat, using a shared jargon, weighted with euphemism, black humor, and profanity, a private language unintelligible to a stranger: heading into the desert was "going up the blue"; a raid was "a party" or "jolly"; grumbling was "ticking"; sinking into sand was "crash diving" or "periscope work."

One night, around the campfire after a dinner of bully-beef stew, someone opened an extra bottle of rum. "As it grew darker, the men began to sing, at first slightly self-conscious and shy, but picking up confidence as the song spread." Their songs were not the martial chants of warriors, but the schmaltzy romantic popular tunes of the time: "I'll Never Smile Again," "My Melancholy Baby," "I'm Dancing with Tears in My Eyes." The bigger and burlier the singer, Pleydell noted, the more passionate and heartfelt the singing. Now the French contingent struck up, with a warbling rendition of "Madeleine," the bittersweet song of a man whose lilacs for his lover have been left to wilt in the rain. Then it was the turn of the German prisoners who, after some debate, belted out "Lili Marleen," the unofficial anthem of the Afrika Korps, complete with harmonies: *Vor der Kaserne / Vor dem grossen Tor / Stand eine Laterne / Und steht sie noch davor . . .*" (Usually rendered in English as: Underneath the lantern, / by the barrack gate, / darling, I remember, / how you used to wait.) As the last verse died away, the audience broke into loud whistles and applause.

To his own astonishment, Pleydell was profoundly moved. "There was something special about that night," he wrote years later. "We had formed a small solitary island of voices; voices which faded and were caught up in the wilderness. A little cluster of men singing in the desert. An expression of feeling that defied the vastness of its surroundings . . . a strange body of men thrown together for a few days by the fortunes of war."

The doctor from Lewisham had come in search of authenticity, and he had found it deep in the desert, among hard soldiers singing sentimental songs to imaginary sweethearts in three languages.

NAVIGATING ACROSS THE desert is not easy at any time. Crossing seventy miles of desert, in the middle of the night, followed by seventeen heavily armed jeeps, with no headlights, an ancient map, and an increasingly impatient commanding officer was the sort of task only a navigator who was either supremely gifted, or mad, would have considered undertaking.

"Where are we?" demanded David Stirling, peering into the gloom.

"By my reckoning we're less than a mile short of the field," said Mike Sadler. "It's right in front of us."

At that instant the desert ahead exploded in a flood of artificial light. The landing-strip lights had been switched on at Sidi Haneish airstrip, 235 miles west-northwest of Cairo on the Egyptian coast. A Luftwaffe night bomber was coming in to land. The date was July 26, 1942. Sadler had brought them directly onto the target, on time, on the nose.

"That," said Sadler many years later, with thumping understatement, "was a bit of a relief."

At Stirling's signal, eighteen jeeps rolled forward, each armed with four Vickers machine guns, enough firepower to destroy an entire air force: which was exactly what he had in mind.

A few days earlier, lolling under the truck and sucking on his pipe, Stirling had come up with a new plan, and a change of tactics: a massed jeep attack. At the First Battle of Alamein during July, Allied forces had stalled a second German advance into Egypt. The Eighth Army had taken more than thirteen thousand casualties, and the North African war was again reduced to stalemate; but Rommel's eastward thrust toward Alexandria and Cairo had been halted. According to air reconnaissance reports, Sidi Haneish—or Fuka Landing Ground 12—was the main German

staging area for planes going to and from the front, principally
Junkers 52s, the transport aircraft on which Rommel was known
to rely. L Detachment had been founded on concepts of stealth
and economy, small groups of men achieving disproportionate
results; the very success of those techniques now necessitated a
noisier and blunter approach.

Tales of the British commandos able to slip behind the lines
and inflict devastating damage before flitting back into the desert
had begun to spread on both sides of the front line. German radio,
it was said, had even bestowed a nickname on the shadowy commander of this band of marauding rogues: "The Phantom Major."
The nickname was probably an invention of British propaganda,
but it stuck. Stirling's activities certainly came to the attention of
Rommel, who wrote in his diary: "These commandos, working
from Kufra [an oasis near the Egyptian border] and the Qattara
Depression, sometimes operated right up into Cyrenaica, where
they caused considerable havoc and seriously disquieted the Italians." British censorship (and good sense) precluded reporting on
SAS operations, but in the ranks of the Eighth Army, stories of
the unit's derring-do became a staple of barroom chat, and a most
effective recruiting tool. The men of L Detachment were under
orders never to brag of their achievements; they did not need to.
Others boasted for them. In the words of Vladimir Peniakoff, the
adventurer known as "Popski" who led a separate detachment of
desert raiders, Stirling swiftly emerged as "the romantic figure of
war in the Middle East," while his exploits, part legend, became a
mainstay of British military morale.

The dramatic narrative of war is as important a weapon as
guns and bullets, and at a time when the war in North Africa was
going badly, Stirling and his men demonstrated a willingness and
a capacity to fight back against the German advance. "This sort
of war possessed a definite flavour of romance," wrote Pleydell.
The men of L Detachment were mindful of their own drama, for
they looked and dressed like, and to some extent played the part
of, swashbuckling desert fighters. Some, thought Pleydell, came

in pursuit of glory, to perform "daring deeds which might become famous overnight." Regular irregulars, they carried a variety of guns. "If a chappie liked a weapon—a Luger, a Beretta or just the .45—he carried that." Some adopted Arab headdresses or bandanas; few wore regulation uniform; almost all, including Stirling, sported bushy beards. At the most grinding, boring, colorless, and perilous period of the desert war, Stirling's raiders added a dash of exotic adventure, a reputation for indomitability at a moment when Rommel threatened to dominate the battlefield. Few in the unit were conscious of it, but theirs was a psychological, even a theatrical role, as well as a military one.

Stirling professed to be baffled by all the barroom "nonsense" being talked about him and his unit; in truth, he reveled in the attention.

But notoriety came with a price. The Axis forces had been bitten hard, and were now taking countermeasures: erecting wire perimeter fences with lights, digging trenches around aerodromes, mounting additional guards, sometimes as many as one to each plane, and on some airfields stationing armored cars at the gates with powerful floodlights. Since it was increasingly difficult to slip undetected onto an airfield, L Detachment would instead go in with all guns blazing.

Twenty more jeeps arrived from Cairo, each one fitted with four Vickers machine guns, double-mounted and bolted to the front and rear. With the new vehicles came additional supplies of water, rations, petrol, ammunition, explosives, spare parts, and a few welcome luxuries: rum, tobacco, new pipes, sticky Turkish delight, and a pint of eau de Cologne—in place of soap. The men might be unable to wash, but they would go into battle highly perfumed. The peaceful desert hideout at Bir el Quseir was transformed into a busy transport hub, with jeeps swarming all over the escarpment. The place was beginning to "look like Piccadilly," Pleydell grumbled happily.

The next night, "a long line of vicious looking jeeps" formed up for a full dress rehearsal. As if organizing a Scottish reel, Stirling explained the plan: the jeeps, manned by both French and English troops, would form up abreast in two lines of seven, with five yards between each vehicle, shooting outward. Stirling would lead the way, firing forward, with two more jeeps flanking him a few yards behind, in an arrowhead formation. Each gun was loaded with a combination of red and white tracer ammunition, and both armor-piercing and incendiary bullets. Stirling fired a green Verey light flare into the sky to commence proceedings, bathing the scene in a "garishly green electrical sort of relief," and cacophony erupted. The drivers in the left-hand column faced particular peril. The forward gun was mounted on the right, which meant that one stream of bullets passed directly in front of the driver's face, while the rear gunner blasted away from behind his head. If he braked suddenly, or leaned backward inadvertently, he would be decapitated. "The noise was deafening," wrote Pleydell, "the tracer flying and bouncing along the ground on every side." Johnny Cooper considered this exercise, firing thousands of rounds into the empty desert behind enemy lines, to be "one of the more bizarre moments of the war."

Twenty-four hours later, the double line of jeeps formed up again in the darkness. Sidi Haneish airfield lay bathed in floodlight a few hundred yards ahead. Stirling fired the Verey light. The night turned green, and then exploded.

As the convoy smashed through the perimeter, the fusillade erupted, sending the airfield's defenders scrambling for cover. Forming up on the runway tarmac between two long rows of parked aircraft, the double line rumbled forward at walking pace, laying down a brutal blanket of strafing fire to left and right as sixty-eight guns opened up from a range of fifty feet. The noise was infernal, a terrible symphony of "roaring, belching fire" merging with the boom of igniting fuel and the crack of exploding ammunition. For Stirling, it was the sound of victory, a "tremendous feu de joie." The first aircraft detonated with such force that the men on the nearside felt their eyebrows and eyelashes singeing. Some planes did not just explode in the inferno, but seemed to "crumble and disintegrate as the bullets ploughed into them." A bomber, coming in to land, was hit by a volley from the leading jeeps just as it touched down; the plane burst into flames and slewed to a stop. "It was like a duck shoot," said Johnny Cooper, Stirling's front gunner. "I really couldn't miss." In the rear, Seekings blasted away in concert through the smoke. From somewhere, a mortar started up, followed by the steady rap of a Breda gun and a rattle of small-arms fire. The defenders were fighting back.

Stirling's jeep shuddered to a halt.

"Why won't it go?" shouted Stirling.

"We haven't got an engine," Seekings shouted back. A 15mm Breda shell had passed through the cylinder head, missing Stirling's knee by inches.

They scrambled on the jeep behind, where a figure sat motionless in the rear seat, "back curiously straight and head and shoulders resting on the guns." John Robson, a twenty-one-year-old artilleryman, had been shot through the head.

The column made another pass around the perimeter, picking off planes parked away from the main runway. A second Verey light, this one red, soared upward, Stirling's signal to withdraw. One officer recalled a small but typical coda: "As we moved off the aerodrome Paddy Mayne spotted an untouched bomber and, jumping from his jeep with a bomb in his hand, ran up to it and, placing the bomb in its engine, ran back and caught us up."

The jeeps, no longer in formation, hurtled for the gap in the fence and out into the open desert. Mike Sadler lingered at the southwest corner of the field, watching for any stragglers and photographing the devastation. Some of the wrecks were still burning when the Germans began towing them away. Within an hour, the airfield was functioning again. They had kicked a "hornets' nest," reflected Sadler. Soon the hornets would be flying, and in angry pursuit. Once in the open, a mile outside the perimeter, the jeeps split into groups of three or four and scattered south, with orders to find somewhere to lie up for the day, under camouflage, and then head for the rendezvous under cover of darkness. Official estimates put the destruction at thirty-seven aircraft, mostly bombers and heavy transport planes.

At dawn, Stirling took refuge in a bowl-shaped depression, with four jeeps, fourteen men, and one dead soldier. Robson's body was placed under a blanket. It was 5:30 in the morning. The light revealed "a ragged looking bunch. Faces, hair and beards were covered in a thick yellow grey film of dust." The man who had been sitting beside Robson scraped with a stick at the sand-crusted bloodstains on his trousers. The conflagration of the previous night had left many with thumping headaches, saliva that tasted of fuel, and inflamed eyes. Seekings brewed tea over a fire made from pouring petrol into a sand-filled tin. Two men set to work digging a grave. An hour later, the little party gathered around the "pathetic little heap of sand and stones" covering John Robson, beneath a cross fashioned from an old ration box. "We stood bareheaded, looking at the grave, each with our own thoughts," recalled one of the officers. "Most of us did not even know this man, who was one of the more recent arrivals; he was just a name to us, or perhaps a cheery red face and shock of black hair. It was indeed a curious burial, just a two minutes' silence with a handful of tired, dirty comrades. Yet for this short fraction of time, lost in the middle of nowhere, there was dignity."

A similarly bleak and simple ceremony took place, in French, a few hours later, about twenty miles to the east.

André Zirnheld's team of three jeeps had been slowed by punctures, and when the morning mist lifted they found themselves dangerously exposed in open desert. A low ridge with a fringe of scrub offered at least a modicum of camouflage. Four Stukas discovered them at midday and swarmed down. Zirnheld was hit in the shoulder and abdomen on the second pass. One of his comrades dragged him under cover. After nine attacks, the dive-bombers ran out of ammunition and departed. The jeeps were "riddled," but one was still functioning. Zirnheld was loaded aboard, con-

scious but fading, and they set off for the rendezvous in the hope
of reaching Dr. Pleydell in time. Zirnheld was too badly injured to
withstand the jolting, and after a few hours the French team holed
up in a small wadi. Soon after midnight, Zirnheld turned to Fran-
çois Martin, his second in command, and said: "*Je vais vous quitter.
Tout est en ordre en moi*" (I am going to leave you. Everything is in
order within me). Moments later, he was dead. The twenty-nine-
year-old French philosopher was buried under a cross made from
a packing case, marked with the words: "*Aspirant André Zirnheld
Mort au champs d'honneur 27 Juillet 1942.*"

Going through his belongings back at the camp, Martin came
across a notebook, in which Zirnheld had written a poem. It
has since become known as the "paratroopers' prayer," and was
adopted as the official poem of French airborne forces.

> *I ask you, O Lord, to give me*
> *What I cannot obtain for myself.*
> *Give me, my Lord, what you have left.*
> *Give me what no one asks of you.*
> *I do not ask for repose*
> *Nor for tranquillity*
> *Of body or soul.*
> *I ask not for riches,*
> *Nor success, nor even health.*
> *My Lord, you are asked for such things so much*
> *That you cannot have any more of them.*
> *Give me, my God, what you have left.*
> *Give me what others don't want.*
> *I want uncertainty and doubt.*
> *I want torment and battle.*
> *And give them to me absolutely, O Lord,*
> *So that I can be sure of having them always.*
> *For I will not always have the courage*
> *To ask for them from you.*
> *Give me, my God, what you have left.*

Give me what others do not want.
But give me also the bravery,
And the strength and the faith.
For these are the things, O Lord,
That only you can give.

Chapter 12

DESERT DOCTORS

SURGEON CAPTAIN MARKUS LUTTEROTTI—OR BARON Markus von Lutterotti di Gazzolis und Langenthal, to give him his full civilian title—was enjoying the joyride over the desert. The plane trip was a welcome break from the monotony of treating the desert sores and other ailments of the German troops. From the passenger seat of a Fieseler Storch reconnaissance plane, the young doctor looked down on a flat wasteland that seemed to stretch away into infinite emptiness. He had never seen anywhere so utterly devoid of life. Lutterotti wanted to inspect the desert at close quarters and stretch his legs, so he ordered the pilot to land. The Luftwaffe sergeant, Rommel's personal pilot, did not disguise his irritation. For an hour he had been flying aimlessly around the desert for no purpose other than to entertain this young officer. He began the descent, barely bothering to see what might be below, since it all looked exactly the same to him. Neither man spotted the camouflaged vehicles lurking beneath a low escarpment.

Captain Lutterotti wore German uniform, but he would have been offended to be described as German, and even more put out by any suggestion that he was a Nazi. The Lutterottis were Catholic aristocrats from South Tyrol, the German-speaking region of northern Italy, once part of the Austro-Hungarian Empire and annexed by the Italians after the First World War. Italy's German-speaking minority was distrusted by Mussolini, and Markus's outspoken father had fallen foul of the fascist authorities. The oldest of eight children, Markus had been obliged to complete Italian military service after his medical exams, and was briefly deployed to the Horn of Africa following Mussolini's invasion and occupation of Abyssinia. His time in Africa sparked an interest in tropical medicine, and on returning to Europe he studied at the Hamburg Tropical Institute. The war put a halt to his career in academic medicine. Signing up with the Afrika Korps seemed the best way to escape having to join the Nazi Party.

Deployed to North Africa at the beginning of 1941, Lutterotti took part in the May offensive, and then ran a small tented hospital at Bardia, behind the German lines. Perfectly bilingual, his language skills made him sought after as a translator for both Italian and German officers. He had even translated for Rommel and deeply admired the Afrika Korps commander. A man of liberal convictions and professional dedication, he insisted on treating North Africans, Allied prisoners, and his own comrades with precisely the same level of care. Gentle, inquisitive, and scholarly, Markus Lutterotti was not made for the blunt brutalities of war. During the advance, he had come across a mortally wounded soldier screaming in a trench, beyond help. He put him out of his pain with a massive dose of morphine. The incident would mark him forever.

Germany would win the war, Lutterotti was sure of that, but the prospect did not fill him with particular elation. He was twenty-nine. He wanted the fighting to end, he wanted to resume his study of tropical medicine, and he wanted to return to the mountains of South Tyrol. But first he wanted to see the open desert. It had been easy to persuade his commanding officer to lend him a reconnaissance plane and a pilot for the afternoon.

The Fieseler Storch touched down gently in the sand, a few hundred yards from two burned-out trucks, relics from the British retreat. Lutterotti and the pilot climbed down, lit cigarettes, and set off "laughing and talking," to inspect the wrecks. At that moment a vehicle suddenly hurtled into view, painted a peculiar combination of pink and green and manned by bearded, shouting men wearing Arab headdresses. Assuming this must be a German patrol, albeit an odd one, Lutterotti stepped forward to greet them, only to be stopped dead by a deafening burst of gunfire. The bearded gunners were strafing the stationary plane. The "look of astonishment" on Lutterotti's face was comical to behold. He whipped a red-cross armband out of his pocket and waved it above his head. "You can't shoot me," he shouted in English. "I'm a doctor."

Lieutenant Nick Wilder of the LRDG had been returning from a diversionary raid on Bagush airfield, timed to coincide with the massed jeep attack, when this unexpected prize dropped from the sky. Wilder's men planted bombs on the riddled Fieseler Storch, as the two amazed prisoners were bundled into the back of the truck. Lutterotti watched the plane explode as they sped away.

THE TWO DOCTORS lounged in the cooling sand after supper, discussing medicine, the war, and luck. "It was a joy cruise," Markus Lutterotti explained to an amused Malcolm Pleydell. "I went up for pleasure, and it ended unhappily . . . *C'est la guerre.*" This earnest, bespectacled German doctor was "a good chap," Pleydell decided.

Captives were not part of the SAS remit. "Generally we didn't take prisoners," Seekings later recalled. "I don't mean by that we shot them out of hand." Usually they were disarmed, briefly held, and then released; but out in the deep desert, simply abandoning prisoners would have been tantamount to killing them. Instead, Stirling had offered Lutterotti "parole," the ancient military convention under which a captive would be left unguarded in return for a solemn promise not to escape.

Lutterotti had smiled at this quaint suggestion. "What would you do in my position?" he asked.

Stirling laughed: "I certainly wouldn't accept parole."

"Then nor will I."

Lutterotti was handed over to Pleydell, with orders to keep the prisoners under close guard at all times. The two captain-doctors discovered they had much in common. Lutterotti had spent several childhood holidays in Clacton-on-Sea, spoke excellent English, and seemed more intrigued than alarmed to find himself in an enemy camp so far behind the lines. At one point during supper, the Tyrolean aristocrat overheard the name Jellicoe, and piped up: "Not Lord Jellicoe?" George Jellicoe nodded. "I think you know my wife," said Lutterotti. It is a small world, even in the vast desert. The Earl Jellicoe and Baroness Lutterotti, it transpired, had become acquainted at a formal luncheon in Hamburg in 1936. Jellicoe was an energetic ladies' man, and word swiftly spread around camp that the earl had done rather more than just lunch with the baron's wife.

The camp at Bir el Quseir was becoming too comfortable for comfort. The heavy traffic of vehicles had left deep tracks in the sand around the wadi, visible to enemy spotter planes. Wireless reports from Cairo appeared to indicate that the Germans, in response to the Sidi Haneish raid, were sending out scouting patrols to try to intercept the raiding parties. After nearly five weeks, the buildup of human waste in the latrine hole had attracted disgusting swarms of flies. Stirling announced that they would be shifting camp again, thirty miles to the west, before launching another intensive series of raids on the German supply lines. The targets, Stirling promised, would be "very enticing."

The German doctor and his pilot were model prisoners. "If you require any medical assistance, you have only to let me know," Lutterotti told Pleydell. "I will be only too happy to be of some use." The German-Italian doctor was amused at the way tea was drunk, with British regularity, at exactly four o'clock every day; he never missed teatime, and insisted on clearing away the mugs.

As they settled into the new camp, the doctors' unlikely friendship deepened. They talked of tropical diseases, the problem of flies, the role of the Red Cross, and the BBC, which Lutterotti had often listened to, in secret, back in Bardia. They even began to pool medical expertise on the subject of desert sores. Only when the conversation shifted to the future of the conflict did the atmosphere turn chilly.

"Do you think you are going to win the war?" asked Pleydell.

"Yes, I think so."

"Soon?"

"In about two years."

Lutterotti's bland certainty was unsettling, and nettling. The possibility of defeat had never been broached during Pleydell's time with the SAS.

"Well, how about Egypt, now? Do you think you will conquer us here?"

"Yes. I think we will take Egypt in two months." Lutterotti was not aggressive, merely confident. "It was said quite quietly," Pleydell noted, "without a hint of swagger."

The embarrassed silence was eventually broken by Lutterotti. "And you say you will win the war?"

"Yes," said Pleydell defensively.

"Then how are you going to beat Germany?"

Pleydell was about to launch into a passionate prediction of inevitable Allied victory, but then stopped himself.

"When I thought of our present situation—of the way we were just hanging on for our dear lives to a little strip of desert in front of Alexandria; of how we seemed to have our backs to the wall everywhere—I became aware that I had not got the vaguest notion as to how we would win the war."

The thought was somehow very funny. Pleydell snorted with laughter. Suddenly, both men were rolling around in the sand, giggling helplessly.

"I do not think he really understood what I was laughing about," Pleydell later wrote. "And for the life of me I could not have explained it."

• • •

Stirling had hoped to remain in the desert indefinitely, on permanent offensive. But the military planners in Cairo had other ideas—rather ambitious ones. At the beginning of August, a wireless message from Middle East Headquarters instructed the unit to return to Kabrit. Stirling was told to report to Cairo for further orders. He responded with a vigorous objection, and a request to be left to continue operations that were proving most effective. During the last month, the unit had destroyed at least eighty-six planes and several dozen enemy vehicles. The reply was immediate and insistent: L Detachment must return to base at once. Stirling later claimed to have been infuriated by the order, but the tone left him in no doubt that something important was afoot.

After loading up the trucks, the men were told to get a few hours' sleep and to be ready to depart at around 1:00 a.m., in order to drive in the darkest phase of the night. The two doctors and Jim Almonds lay on their backs, smoking cigarettes before turning in. The night was clear, and the sky flooded with stars. Lutterotti's Jesuit education had included astronomy and as a boy in the Tyrol, he explained, he had enjoyed "walks across the country by starlight." He ticked off the constellations in German—Grosser Bär, Schwan—and the Milchstrasse galaxy.

Pointing north, he picked out the brightest star in Ursa Minor: "The little pole star, very small but very important."

The astronomical conversation dwindled into silence, and the men turned in.

"Good night," said Lutterotti, as he and the pilot headed off to their sleeping patch beside a truck, accompanied by the guard.

"Good night," called the English doctor over his shoulder.

"Good night indeed," thought Pleydell. "A fine time to be saying good night when in three hours' time we would be bumping and jolting back on one of the ghastly night drives." But Lutterotti was not saying good night; he was saying good-bye.

Pleydell had laid out his blanket and was about to stretch out when Almonds reappeared, breathless. "The Germans . . . they've vanished."

The two prisoners had executed a simple ruse. The Luftwaffe pilot told the guard he was going to fetch his blanket from the back of the truck. A minute passed, and when the man did not return, the guard went to investigate. The pilot was nowhere to be seen. The guard rushed back to where Lutterotti had been lying, apparently asleep. By now, the doctor had also disappeared.

Lutterotti had planned carefully. Once the trucks were on the move, he knew, there would be no chance of escape. The nearest German troops must be at least sixty miles to the north. He had been surreptitiously gathering tea for days, pouring the dregs from the cups into a water bottle he had found and hidden under a truck. By the night of his escape, he had more than a pint of liquid and a bar of chocolate. He and the pilot agreed to split up, to increase the chances that at least one of them might get away. The British would expect him to head north; instead, he walked to the western side of the camp, before sprinting away. He had run perhaps three hundred yards when the first flare went up behind him, bathing the ground in light, including a patch of scrub to his right. Lutterotti dived into the bushes and lay still, panting.

Back at camp, the entire force had been woken and mobilized to hunt for the escaping Germans. Pleydell loaded his revolver, wondering if he would be able to shoot his new friend. "I sent up a little prayer that someone else might catch them," he wrote.

The search party fanned out and began scouring the surrounding area. But, as the SAS knew from experience, hiding in the desert was easier than it might seem, and in the darkness the advantage lay with the fugitives. Two hours later, with extreme reluctance, Stirling called off the search. They could not afford any more delay; two escaped prisoners were not worth the risk of driving in daylight. "Cheer up, David," said Paddy Mayne, with an attempt at levity. "The Jerries will [soon] have a full description of us. It's just as well we're leaving."

Lutterotti heard the convoy depart. Then he gingerly emerged from the undergrowth, took a sip of cold, stale tea, and began walking toward the North Star.

"You were incredibly stupid," Field Marshal Rommel told the exhausted, sun-blistered doctor four days later. Then the Desert Fox grinned: "But the fact that you managed to get back is pretty impressive, *sehr anständig.*"

Lutterotti reckoned that on the first night he had covered no more than ten miles before dawn came up and the stars disappeared. He lay up all day, in the scanty shade of a camel thorn. The desert stretched away relentlessly on every side. He ate a small piece of chocolate, but lacked the saliva to swallow it without a precious gulp of tea. Around midnight, the North Star reappeared, and Lutterotti set off once more. He began to lose track of time. The second day was the worst. The heat was brutal, and Lutterotti began to experience the first symptoms of heatstroke as he lay waiting for nightfall. The third night of walking, he knew, must be the last, one way or the other. He had no more tea, and the chocolate was long gone. Around dawn, he heard an animal, somewhere out in the darkness. "If that is a dog," he reflected, "then humans must be close too." He headed toward the noise. Three hours later, he was back in the German lines, and undergoing the first of multiple debriefings.

In later life, Pleydell often wondered what had happened to Dr. Lutterotti, whether he had survived the desert and returned to South Tyrol. What was he doing now, the Englishman wondered, as the trucks jolted back toward Kabrit? "Working in a tented ward? Drinking with his colonel? Had he been interviewed by the high officials? Anyhow, I bet he gave us a good write-up."

Pleydell would have won that bet. Lutterotti (and the pilot, who had encountered a German patrol and returned to camp in comparative comfort) gave a detailed and extremely favorable description of the British desert raiders, their courteous commander, and their rigorous adherence to the tradition of afternoon tea. For Rommel and his officers, the hitherto shadowy British commandos were coming into sharper focus. Lutterotti reported that Stirling commanded a mixed force of "British, New Zealand, Free French and Free German troops"; he described the vehicles, weapons, and camps. RAF reconnaissance duly reported that German armored cars were "scouring the desert" in the area the SAS had just vacated.

WINSTON CHURCHILL, frustrated by the stasis in the Middle East, decided to ring the changes, as he usually did when advised to be patient. General Auchinleck was sacked, and replaced as commander in chief of the Middle East by General Harold Alexander. Command of the Eighth Army would soon be handed to a bristling, sharp-faced martinet, General Bernard Montgomery. A new air of anticipation and urgency gripped Middle East Headquarters. The reinforced Alamein line was expected to withstand whatever Rommel hurled at it; a mighty new Allied offensive was planned for October. But in the meantime Axis forces continued to rely on sea convoys from Italy for supplies of food and matériel. Stirling's plan to launch an all-out assault on the ports of Cyrenaica may have had its origin in his hitherto fruitless efforts to blow up shipping in Benghazi—but in his absence the idea had been inflated and stretched into something far more radical. Stirling was ordered to attack Benghazi once more, but this time, instead of slipping in at night with a tiny force, he would be leading an army of more than two hundred men, over half of whom were not SAS-trained, in a convoy of eighty vehicles across a thousand miles of desert. He was even allocated a pair of Honey tanks. Once inside Benghazi, his orders were to "destroy everything in sight." A simultaneous seaborne raid would be launched against Tobruk by commandos and infantry, while the Sudan Defence Force, the British Army unit originally created to maintain the borders of

Sudan, would attempt to retake Jalo Oasis from the Italians, and the LRDG would attack the airfield at Barce, sixty miles northwest of Benghazi. The Benghazi raid, code-named Bigamy, was a classic combined-operations commando raid: naval personnel would take part in order to commandeer whatever ships were in the harbor, and would sink some to block the entrance; Allied POWs in the town would be liberated and armed.

This was all a long way from Stirling's concept of small, highly mobile attack units operating by stealth. It is not easy to maintain surprise with a couple of tanks in tow. Stirling claimed to have had deep misgivings about the operation from the start, but he made no official objection; indeed, he was not in a position to do so. An added inducement to go along with the plan may have been the promise (again, unofficial and unrecorded) that success would lead to further expansion of the SAS. The unit still had its detractors—a memo from the chief of staff to Auchinleck in July disparagingly referred to the SAS as one of several "small raiding parties of the thug variety." There was talk of downgrading L Detachment to a "minor role." A large-scale assault on Benghazi might not be what the unit had been invented for, but success could ensure its continuation.

Stirling needed to fight for the future of the SAS: his first sortie in this campaign would be across a formal dinner table.

On the evening of August 8, David Stirling shaved, bathed, climbed into his brother's dinner jacket, and prepared to launch a charm offensive against Winston Churchill.

The invitation to a private dinner with the prime minister at the British embassy in Cairo was almost certainly the result of Randolph Churchill's enthusiastic letters to his father, describing the exploits of L Detachment and its fearless young leader. Stirling certainly believed that "Randolph had been talking to his father in much the manner in which I had hoped." Fitzroy Maclean, now fully recovered from the car crash, also received an invitation.

The other guests included General Alexander, the newly arrived commander in chief, and Field Marshal Jan Smuts, South Africa's prime minister and a member of the Imperial War Cabinet. In the space of a few days, Stirling went from blowing up planes with machine guns to dining with prime ministers and generals in evening dress. It was a strange war.

Churchill was stopping off in Cairo on the way to Moscow for his first face-to-face meeting with Stalin, an encounter that his wife, Clementine, characterized as "a visit to the ogre in his den." The prime minister was in ebullient form, wearing a bow tie and his velvet "siren suit"—a military-style one-piece boiler suit that would not become fashionable again for another seventy years, until the invention of the "onesie." From the head of the table, Churchill held forth, "pink-faced and beaming." A great deal was eaten, and a great deal more was drunk. "It was a little unreal," Stirling later recalled. "A table set with the best of silver and served with the best food, with the British Prime Minister at the head of the feast, just 40 miles or so from the Allied front line." At one point, Churchill challenged Smuts to a game: who could recite more Shakespeare without stopping? After fifteen minutes the South African leader, a brilliant scholar with a prodigious memory, ran out of quotations, but Churchill continued, unstoppably. It took several minutes before Smuts realized that Churchill was not reciting genuine verse at all, but a sort of mock-Shakespeare of his own extempore invention.

After dinner, cigars were lit, brandy was poured, and Stirling and Maclean were summoned over to accompany the prime minister as he strolled around the elegant embassy gardens. The two young men were the type of adventurers Churchill adored, swashbucklers, daredevils, and, above all, amateurs. He was well aware that Maclean had used his election to the House of Commons as a ruse to get into the war, and he thoroughly approved.

"Here," he said, turning to Smuts, "is the young man who has used the Mother of Parliaments as a public convenience."

Stirling and Maclean had been warned that they should on no

account discuss the impending attack on Benghazi with Churchill. (The prime minister was regarded by some of his staff as an inveterate gossip and a major security risk, with a habit of turning top-secret information into amusing after-dinner entertainment.) They ignored this injunction. For the next few minutes, Churchill listened intently as the two young officers described L Detachment, its methods, successes, and plans for the future. Insisting that this was "a new form of warfare we were developing" with "awesome potential," Stirling suggested that the unit might have an important role to play behind the lines in Europe at a later stage in the war.

Churchill was "bowled over" by Stirling, intrigued by "the contrast between the young man's gentle demeanour and his ferocious pursuit of the enemy." When the prime minister rejoined Smuts in the embassy drawing room, he described to him Stirling's record of destruction and quoted the famous lines from Byron's *Don Juan*: "He was the mildest-mannered man / That ever scuttled ship or cut a throat." The continuation of that quotation also fitted Stirling's character: "With such true breeding of a gentleman, / You never could divine his real thought."

Before leaving, Stirling asked Churchill, Smuts, and Alexander to sign a piece of paper, as a souvenir of the evening.

The next morning Stirling was still nursing his hangover when a note arrived at Peter's flat. From Sir Leslie Rowan, Churchill's private secretary, it read: "I have been asked by my chief to ask you to let me have, for him, without further delay, the short note for which he called on what you would advise should be done to concentrate and coordinate the work you are doing. I have been asked to make sure that this is in my hands today. I can be got at the embassy." Leaving aside the civil service circumlocution, the import was clear: Churchill was intrigued and wanted to hear more, now.

Stirling immediately set to work on his brother's typewriter, and bashed out a two-page memo, headed "Top Secret," written so fast it included several spelling mistakes and missing words: "All existing Special Service Units in the Middle East be disbanded and selected personnel absorbed, as required, by L Detachment . . . Control to rest with the officer commanding L Detachment and not with any outside body . . . The planning of operations to remain as hitherto the prerogative of L Detachment." In other words, Stirling proposed to take over all special forces, extract anyone he wanted for his own team, and then run operations exactly as he saw fit. This scheme, he said, would increase "versatility and resourcefulness [with] obvious advantages from the point of view of security." But it would also leave him free from interference, with the unstated implication that the bureaucrats at headquarters were incompetent, interfering gossips. It was a power grab, pure and simple, and it worked.

That evening, Stirling was summoned back to the embassy for further discussions. Running up the embassy staircase, he cannoned into the bulky form of the prime minister himself. "The irresistible force meets the immovable object," grunted Churchill. This is known, in philosophy, as the "sword and shield paradox," a conundrum in which two absolute forms of power are pitted against each other. But it also captured something of Churchill's wartime philosophy: immovability would bring victory ("We shall never surrender"), but it must be combined with overwhelming and dramatic force. War was not just a matter of bombs and bullets, but of capturing imaginations. Stirling displayed just the right combination of daring and romance. Henceforth, Churchill would allude to him as the "Scarlet Pimpernel"—a reference to the hero of Baroness Orczy's novel, Sir Percy Blakeney, a wealthy, foppish Englishman on the outside, but in reality a master of the secret, undercover war. Stirling was just the sort of figure Churchill had been seeking to inject some panache into the North African war.

The encounter with Churchill would ensure the future of the SAS; it was also of immediate practical use. Stirling took the "souvenir" signed by two prime ministers and the commander in chief of the Middle East, and typed above the signatures: "Please give the bearer of this note every possible assistance." Seekings and

Cooper, the unofficial SAS quartermasters, now found that supplies, vehicles, weapons, and ammunition, hitherto so tricky to secure, could be obtained simply by flourishing this note. Stirling had no qualms whatever about this blatant forgery: Churchill had become a staunch supporter of the unit and so, he insisted, "in a sense it was authentic."

Chapter 13

QUITE, QUITE MAD

ROBERT MARIE EMANUEL MELOT WAS BELGIAN BY BIRTH, a cotton merchant by trade, a fluent Arabic speaker by dint of his many years in North Africa, and a brilliant spy by intuition and inclination. During the First World War he had been a pilot in the Belgian air force. When the second broke out, he was living in Alexandria with his wife and children, and immediately volunteered to join the British Army. Melot had traveled widely in the region, and few outsiders better understood the complex, malleable loyalties of the Libyan tribes, and the value of bribery.

Early in 1942, Melot offered his services to L Detachment as an intelligence officer, and swiftly proved his worth, liaising with other British agents in the Jebel and reporting back information gleaned from his numerous informants. Already forty-seven, portly and cheerful, Melot could not have been less like a Bedouin or Senussi tribesman in appearance and demeanor, yet he had a knack for melting invisibly into the local population. He spent months behind the lines, moving from one hiding place to another to "avoid the search parties which the enemy sent out after him" and living on food and water left at prearranged sites by the LRDG. Melot looked like a prosperous bank manager, but he was as tough as mahogany. His SAS colleagues found his name hard to pronounce, and so called him "Bob Mellor," thus elevating him to the status of honorary Englishman.

Fitzroy Maclean was in the first party to arrive at the rendez-vous point in the Jebel Mountains on September 9, 1942, five days before the scheduled attack on Benghazi. Melot emerged from the cave he had been living in for three weeks, smiling, welcoming, and ravenously hungry. Maclean fried some bully-beef rissoles in oatmeal, which Melot devoured as if they had been served up by the finest chef in Brussels. The intelligence officer had been keep-ing his ear to the ground, and what he had heard was not reassur-ing. Enemy patrols and guard points on the border of the Jebel appeared to have been reinforced, and suspicious troop movements had been seen in and around Benghazi. Some locals had started to move out. Maclean was alarmed, but not entirely surprised. Only a handful of those taking part in Operation Bigamy knew the objec-tive, yet before leaving Cairo Maclean had seen "signs that too many people knew too much." Melot suggested sending one of his agents, a Libyan deserter from the Italian army, down to Benghazi to investigate. Maclean watched the man depart, thinking how "singularly unreliable he looked." The spy returned after twenty-four hours with a most disturbing report. The town was awash with rumors of an imminent attack, the civilian population had begun to decamp, and a German machine-gun detachment had arrived along with as many as five thousand Italian troops. Even more worrying, the date of the attack, September 14, was "being freely mentioned."

By this time, the rest of the assault force had arrived in the Jebel, considerably the worse for a harrowing journey. The party, largely composed of SAS men but with an admixture of comman-dos and naval personnel, had set out in a mood of high optimism. Pleydell was told that he and his three newly recruited medical orderlies could expect to be running Benghazi hospital before the week was out. One of the sergeants claimed, fancifully, that he intended to hijack a German destroyer and sail back to England on it. But the expedition had run into problems almost immediately. One of the tanks became inextricably bogged down in a salt marsh just fifty miles from Kufra Oasis, and the other broke down and had to be abandoned. The trucks and jeeps repeatedly sank up to their axles in the Great Sand Sea, and had to be laboriously dug out. A lorry hit a hummock and overturned, fracturing the leg of one of the sergeants. Pleydell splinted the femur and filled the man with Pentothal, a fast-acting general anesthetic, and the convoy crawled on.

The Italians had mined the southern approaches to the hill country with Thermos bombs, air-dropped antipersonnel mines resembling vacuum flasks that were all but invisible in the sand. About sixty miles south of the Jebel, a jeep ran over one of these deadly little contraptions and burst into flames as its fuel canisters ignited. Lieutenant Commander Richard Ardley, one of several naval officers in the group, was badly burned. The driver, a man named Marlow, attempted to pull him from the vehicle and trod on another bomb, which exploded and shattered his right leg. Pleydell inspected the wound and concluded he would have to amputate. Ardley was in even worse shape, delirious with pain, slipping in and out of consciousness. Pleydell knelt in the sand, and set about removing Marlow's leg below the knee. An anxious Stirling appeared at his shoulder and asked if the men were likely to survive. Pleydell made no promises. "How long will you be?" The doctor replied that he should be able to move the wounded men in an hour. Stirling left him a three-ton truck and a jeep to guide them to the rendezvous. "That's the best I can do I'm afraid." The drive was slow and hellish, with the men tied down to the floor to reduce the jolting and the naval officer bellowing in pain with every bump. Marlow lay gray and silent, in deep shock. They arrived at the rendezvous as the sun was setting. Pleydell made the wounded men as comfortable as possible. Paddy Mayne arrived with hot, sweet tea, which he gently fed to the men, holding them upright to drink, quietly reassuring.

Pleydell was woken at 3:00 a.m. by one of the orderlies, a bespectacled Londoner named Johnson who had earned the nickname "Razor Blade" on account of his skill with the scalpel. "The officer's just died, sir," Johnson reported. Ardley had expired quietly in a deep morphine-sleep. As for Marlow, "he was hanging on, just doing that, and no more." At dawn, Ardley was buried "with no ceremony, in a small hollow, where the soil lay deep."

The mission had suffered serious casualties before it had even begun. Stirling debated whether to abort the operation, given the discouraging report from Melot's spy.

"This Arab is quite reliable?" he asked the Belgian.

Even so, Stirling sent a wireless message to headquarters warning that the operation might be compromised. The reply blandly ordered: "Disregard bazaar gossip." Therein lies one of the problems with secret intelligence: its recipients tend to believe it implicitly when it chimes with their own preconceptions, and reject it with equal firmness when it does not.

Maclean felt "reassured" by the response from headquarters. Pleydell did not. "We had lost our most powerful card: that of surprise." Paddy Mayne merely remarked that there was likely to be "some hard scrapping" in the next few hours. "Looks as though you're going to be kept busy, doc," said Almonds.

An advance party of a dozen men set off in the early afternoon of September 13, led by Bob Melot and Chris Bailey, a new recruit to the SAS. Their mission was to knock out an Italian wireless post on the edge of the Jebel escarpment. Once that had been done, the way would be clear to attack Benghazi. The main body of troops followed about two hours later: French, British, trained SAS men, new recruits, and a handful of navy personnel. There were many familiar faces in the party: Mayne, Fraser, Seekings, Cooper, Almonds, and the little Frenchman Germain Guerpillon, "the duffer." Stirling drove the lead jeep, with Sadler alongside him. Pleydell and his team established a medical post and advance rendezvous site on the edge of the escarpment, to await the returning troops and treat any wounded. Maclean noticed that the doctor was already "busy preparing bandages, splints and blood plasma" as the raiding party, led by Melot's Arab spy, set off down the steep escarpment.

Pleydell remained behind, waiting in the dark. The "completeness of the silence" was suddenly shattered by the "shrill laughter" of a jackal, setting hair on end and teeth on edge. The doctor tried to read *The Forsyte Saga* by torchlight. At around 2:00 came the sound of a motor, and a jeep careened into view. "Mr. Melot's been wounded, sir, in the stomach and legs. He's lost a good bit of blood . . . Mr. Bailey's caught it too."

It took twenty minutes to reach the point where Melot lay, covered in a greatcoat, almost ridiculously nonchalant about his wounds: "There's nothing much the matter with me. Hand grenade wounds, you know," he said, in his slightly antique English. Melot had led the successful attack on the Italian guard post, but in the short and vicious battle that followed, a grenade had exploded beside him, sending shrapnel into his abdomen, lower leg, and thigh. He had destroyed the wireless equipment, taken two prisoners, and managed to walk most of the way to the rendezvous with a fractured femur, before collapsing. He initially refused anesthetic—"I've never taken any medicine in my life"—but finally submitted to Pleydell's morphine injection, and declared it "the best thing I have had for a long time."

Bailey was brought in on a stretcher a few minutes later, with a single bullet hole above the heart and a collapsed lung. Pleydell returned to his jeep to get more supplies and was astonished to see a complete stranger rise up out of the darkness, a man dressed in the costume of a rural gentleman out for a ramble in the English countryside.

The figure was wearing a checked tweed jacket and plus fours, and carrying a knobbly walking stick. His face was adorned with a magnificent jutting beard and a pair of extravagant mustaches.

"Oh . . . I say . . . er, excuse me!" said the tweedy apparition, in "a very superior Oxford voice." "Do you happen to have seen David Stirling or Bob Melot around here recently?"

Pleydell was momentarily stunned by the sheer weirdness of the situation. They were standing on the edge of a desert cliff, in the middle of the night, with a major battle about to take place a few miles away, and a man who looked uncannily like George

Bernard Shaw and spoke like George VI had suddenly materialized from nowhere.

"Who are you?" he finally demanded.

"Me? My name is Farmer. I work around here, you know. But
look, old chap, *have* you seen Stirling recently? I want to speak to
him."

Pleydell pointed to where Melot lay under the greatcoat.

"Really! I *am* sorry," said the man, who then wandered over to
speak to Melot, who was now thoroughly addled with morphine.
They exchanged a few words, and then Farmer, swinging his walking stick, disappeared back into the darkness.

It had been, Pleydell later reflected, "a rather odd little incident."

Farmer's real name was Alan Samuel Lyle-Smythe, alias "Caillou," policeman, actor, writer, and, at that moment, secret agent of
the British Intelligence Corps. He was responsible for gathering
information behind the enemy lines, but made no effort whatever
to disguise himself, apparently believing that the more brazen his
approach and the more obvious his Englishness, the more likely he
was to be offered interesting titbits of information. Lyle-Smythe
was remarkably fearless, and wildly eccentric. A few months after
bumping into Pleydell in the desert, he would be captured and
incarcerated in a POW camp, from which he then escaped.

On the evening of September 13, 1942, he had set out in his
tweeds to warn Stirling that he had received a reliable report from
an informant in Benghazi: the attack was fatally compromised,
and the enemy was lying in wait. But he was too late.

Led by Melot's Arab spy, the main raiding party of two hundred men in forty jeeps descended the escarpment and trundled
along the road into Benghazi in the darkness. A cantilevered gate
barred the way on the outskirts of the town, with barbed wire
double-strung along either side of the road and signs of a newly laid
minefield. Another roadblock could be seen through the gloom,
150 yards ahead. This had not been there before. Bill Cumper, an
explosives expert and irrepressible joker, jumped down to inspect,

and swung the barrier up. "Let battle commence!" he said, snapping off a Nazi salute. Then battle indeed commenced.

From either side of the road, a brutal volley of machine-gun fire erupted, followed by Breda 20mm and mortar fire. They had driven straight into a trap. The lead jeep, with Jim Almonds at the wheel, charged forward, as the gunner in the rear opened up with his Vickers gun, strafing wildly in the direction of the gunfire. That seemed to dampen the enthusiasm of the attackers, although sporadic fire continued. Stirling made a swift calculation: they might be able to fight through this ambush and the next roadblock, but the town's defenders were plainly alerted and awaiting them. "Get the convoy turned round and we'll have a go another day," he told his driver. The jeep drivers performed laborious three-point turns, as the bullets continued to spatter around them, the air "alive with strings of tracer." Almonds was "last seen vigorously returning enemy fire"; moments later his jeep took a direct hit in the petrol tank from an incendiary bullet and burst into flames. The jeep convoy charged back toward the escarpment, no longer an orderly procession but a chaotic scramble, "racing to reach cover before the sun rose." Stirling assumed that Almonds and the two other men in his vehicle had perished; in fact, they had jumped clear just before their jeep exploded. Almonds and a Irish guardsman named Fletcher hid in a ditch by the road. As the sun rose, they saw a squad of twenty Italian soldiers advancing, bayonets fixed, searching for survivors. "Our best chance is to stand up and give ourselves up," Almonds whispered.

The two SAS men were taken into captivity in the Benghazi barracks, shackled, and interrogated. When Almonds refused to divulge any information, he was chained kneeling in the back of a truck, and paraded around the town to be spat and jeered at by the inhabitants. Back at Benghazi prison, Almonds found he was now sharing a cell with another prisoner, who introduced himself as Captain John Richards, an intelligence officer with the Inter-Services Liaison Department. Richards explained that he had been captured near Benghazi, but had then escaped and started to walk back toward the British lines. He had almost reached Tobruk before being recaptured and brought back to Benghazi. Garrulous and friendly, the officer spoke with a pronounced cockney accent, and seemed only too happy to talk about his adventures in the desert. Yet there was something about Richards that struck Almonds as odd: he claimed to have walked almost eighty miles, but he "looked unfatigued, did not limp and was wearing new Italian boots." He also asked a lot of questions. One morning, an officer appeared at the cell door and Richards was taken away. Two days later, Almonds was shipped to Italy and incarcerated in POW Camp 51 at Altamura.

Gentleman Jim's captivity, and his separation from the SAS, would turn out to be short-lived.

THE SUN WAS up by the time the vanguard of the main party reached the escarpment. Fitzroy Maclean looked back toward the Benghazi airfields, to see dozens of enemy planes "rising like angry wasps." The troops dispersed, taking cover among the ravines and hastily camouflaging their vehicles; minutes later the planes were upon them. Pleydell was tending to the injured Melot, who was "snoring blissfully, with his false teeth laid out beside him," when the first plane clattered overhead, spraying machine-gun fire. The attacking pilots knew that their quarry was holed up on the escarpment, but could not see exactly where: their tactics were therefore to pour as much metal and explosive onto the area as possible, in the hope that they would hit something. Working in relays, they bombed and strafed the ravines. Seekings estimated that at times some twenty planes were in action overhead. The fugitives could only hide and hope. "During the long, hot hours of that morning we could hear the shuddering, breaking noise of exploding bombs, interrupted by the brisk staccato of machinegun fire." From time to time a louder explosion indicated a direct hit on one of the concealed trucks or jeeps. During a lull, several wounded men, some seriously so, were brought to Pleydell to patch up as best he could. At dusk the planes departed, and the remnants of the troop climbed into the surviving vehicles and drove the remaining twenty-five miles to the Jebel. "That night drive was a wretched affair," wrote Pleydell, with the injured groaning in the back of the trucks, amid the stench of blood, burned flesh, and singed clothing. The rendezvous point was reached at 3:00 a.m. "Home sweet fucking home," someone grunted in the darkness.

The ordeal was not over. In midmorning, enemy planes located them in the Jebel, and swooped down once more. Several of the wounded were hit by machine-gun fire where they lay. A young corporal was brought in, horrifically injured by a bullet that had passed through his hips. Pleydell's medical transport took a direct hit and burst into flames. A few minutes later, a figure was carried in on a blanket and gently lowered in front of the doctor. Pleydell immediately recognized Germain Guerpillon, the former consular official, the least martial and most determined of the early French recruits. His face was drained of color, and his breath came in shallow gasps. The doctor knew at once that the Frenchman was close to death, and "far beyond any crude help that I could give." Pleydell had always liked and admired Guerpillon, not because he was a natural soldier, but because he was not: a civilian utterly determined to fight. He looked oddly at peace, although his hands clenched and unclenched "with mechanical lifelessness," reminding Pleydell of how he had once seen "a bird open and close its claws as it died." In a few moments Guerpillon was dead. The little Frenchman had successfully fought to vanquish his own fears, and died in the attempt, an end as noble as any more orthodox battlefield hero. Guerpillon had "no more obstacles or trials to overcome," Pleydell reflected, as he covered his body with a blanket.

Stirling called Pleydell over. "Hello, Malcolm," he said. "You *have* had a busy time. You must be absolutely exhausted." Even in the thick of battle, pleasantries were to be observed.

Stirling broke the bleak news. "We're moving off in two hours' time." Their hiding place in the Jebel had been exposed, and the planes would soon be back, perhaps with ground troops, to root out and exterminate what remained of the attacking force. With every passing minute their chances of escape dwindled. But much of their transport had already been destroyed. "We simply haven't enough room to take the wounded with us," said Stirling. "Stretchers are out of the question. I'm terribly sorry."

To Pleydell fell the grim task of choosing which of his patients were still fit enough to travel back in the packed trucks, and who must remain behind to face captivity. Six of the wounded required continuous medical attention: of these, Melot and another man with a shattered arm could probably travel suspended in camouflage nets. The remaining four, including Marlow, the amputee, and Bailey, whose chest wound remained critical, seemed likely to die unless they got to a hospital soon. Reg Seekings took a typically brutal line when one of the wounded men protested at being left. "I'm sorry, you've had it. You're just numbers," he said, and pointed to the rest of the troop, now preparing to leave the hills. "They're fit, they're ready to fight another day. You can't. I'm sorry." He would later describe this as "the hardest little speech I'd ever made in my life." It is highly unlikely he actually made it, since the responsibility for the decision was not his, but it certainly reflected his philosophy: "You've got to make yourself callous . . . After all, what's it all about? Winning a war, isn't it? So you've got to do these sorts of things." The men were exhausted. Some were in a state of shock, staring into space. Seekings bullied them into order, shoving them into the trucks, shouting and swearing: "I kicked men to their feet, belting them. It was crude and cruel, but the only way to do it." Seekings was a brute, but a lifesaver.

One of the medical team would have to stay behind with the wounded, to drive to Benghazi, surrender, and ensure they were given proper medical treatment. Pleydell volunteered without hesitation, but was ordered by Stirling to remain with the fighting force, since further casualties were likely. The orderlies drew straws to select who would perform a task that would certainly mean captivity, or worse. Ritchie, a regimental medical orderly with the commandos, drew the short straw. "He did not seem unduly upset."

"Goodbye," said Pleydell. "I'm sorry about all this. It's very bad luck."

"Well, someone had to stay, sir."

"Yes."

There was a pause in this stilted, oddly moving exchange, as they watched the trucks lining up to leave.

"You are quite sure about what you have to do?" said Pleydell.

"Yes, sir."

"You have the morphia and syringe?"

"Yes, sir. Thank you."

"Well. Goodbye. All the best."

"Goodbye, sir."

Pleydell and Ritchie shook hands.

The next day, the little troop of wounded men and the lone orderly were taken into captivity by Italian forces and transported to the Benghazi military hospital. All would die in captivity. Ritchie died eighteen months later, of unknown causes, in a prison camp.

Operation Bigamy had been a disaster. It had departed from Stirling's concept of small, highly mobile units operating with stealth, with most unhappy results. "We were too big," admitted Johnny Cooper. "They knew we were coming." The plan had required "complete surprise, good planning and rapid action," said Stirling, and achieved none of them. Over a quarter of his force had been killed, wounded, or captured, and more than half his vehicles destroyed; apart from diverting a number of enemy troops to defend Benghazi, its impact was negligible. The simultaneous raid on Tobruk had proved even more costly and ineffective. When the SAS limped back into Cairo, they were mistaken for a "grubby looking batch of German prisoners."

Armies are fickle organisms. A few months earlier, such a failure might have spelled doom for the SAS. Yet, instead of recrimination,

Stirling was rewarded. On his return to Cairo, while his bedraggled force licked its wounds, he was promoted to the rank of lieutenant colonel and told that the unit was being granted full regimental status. A unit that had started with a fictitious name was now a formal element in the British order of battle: on September 21, the SAS was ordered to undergo a major expansion, to 29 officers and 572 other ranks. A combination of Churchill's enthusiasm, the reputation of the SAS, and its track record of destruction (when properly deployed), and perhaps a desire to appease Stirling for the debacle of Operation Bigamy, had conspired to turn an abject failure into a most unlikely triumph. The unit, noted Order 14521 promoting L Detachment to regimental status, "has had conspicuous success and its morale is high."

The new force would be divided into four squadrons: A Squadron, under the command of Paddy Mayne; B, commanded by Stirling himself; C, the French squadron; and D, the Special Boat Section (this would hive off from the SAS in April 1943, as the Special Boat Squadron, under the command of George Jellicoe). At the age of twenty-six, Stirling had become the first man to create his own new regiment since the Boer War. He was understandably proud, and completely stunned. Yet if he thought that this meant he now had a free hand, he had not reckoned with the prickly new commander of the Eighth Army: General Bernard Montgomery.

The previous commander had looked with an indulgent eye on Stirling's unconventional approach to warfare. Monty was a quite different sort of general. He had not been grouse shooting on the Stirlings' Scottish estate, was not a natural gambler, did not drink, and did not like being told what to do by anyone, least of all by a young Turk with a taste for extreme adventure. Their first encounter was not a happy one.

Soon after his return to Cairo, Stirling made an appointment to see Montgomery in his trailer. The general resembled an "underweight fighting bantam cock," thought Stirling, all sinew and strut. He asked, sharply, what Stirling wanted. Wrong-footed by the absence of polite preliminaries, Stirling explained that his force could offer important support to the coming offensive by raiding Rommel's overextended supply lines and knocking out fuel dumps, ammunition depots, and airfields: for this he would need to recruit at least 150 first-class fighters from other regiments. Monty fixed him with a bayonet stare.

"If I understand you correctly, you want to take some of my men from me. Indeed my best men; my most desert-worthy, my most dependable, my most experienced men. I am proud of my men. I expect great things of them. What makes you think, Colonel Stirling, that you can handle my men to greater advantage than I can handle them myself?"

Stirling, shocked and stung, launched into a defensive speech, insisting that there was no time to train up raw recruits for the sort of offensive actions he had in mind. But the general was not listening.

"I'm sorry, Colonel, but the answer is no. A flat no. Frankly your request strikes me as slightly arrogant. I am under the impression that you feel you know my business better than I do. You come here after a failure at Benghazi demanding the best I can give. In all honesty, Colonel Stirling, I am not inclined to associate myself with failure. And now I must be on my way. I'm sorry to disappoint you, Colonel Stirling, but I prefer to keep my best men for my own use."

Stirling was livid. Hitherto, he had always achieved his ends through a combination of charm and argument. Here was a general immune to both, and even more determined to get his own way than Stirling himself. Instead of cherry-picking recruits from Middle East forces, he would have to build up the expanded SAS with men from the infantry base depot, most of whom were without desert or combat experience. This, in turn, meant restructuring the force: most of the L Detachment veterans would fight under Mayne in A Squadron, while Stirling's B Squadron, largely made up of new recruits, would have to undergo training in Kabrit before going into action.

Stirling did not know it—and Montgomery was careful to

conceal it—but the younger man had made a profound impression on the new commander of the Eighth Army. Monty was touchy and rude, but he was also brilliant, a fine judge of character, and a master of warfare. At a dinner, soon after their first ill-tempered meeting, Monty remarked: "The Boy Stirling is mad. Quite, quite mad. However, in war there is often a place for mad people. Now take this scheme of his. Penetrating miles behind the enemy lines. Attacking the coastal road on a four-hundred-mile front. Who but the Boy Stirling could think up such a plan?"

Chapter 14

ALAMEIN

Paddy Mayne lay in the sand, in the cool of the October evening, totting up the booty from his latest raid: two cameras, including a Rolleiflex with viewfinder, some German automatic weapons, a shotgun, and a handful of Italian prisoners. "The loot has looked up. We were like a lot of pirates," he wrote to his brother. "We are in the Sand Sea, about 200 miles from the nearest oasis, and just going out and acting the fool from here." Mayne's base camp lay in the dunes on the edge of the Great Sand Sea, some 150 miles south of the coast road and beyond the range of enemy planes. From here, the buccaneers of A Squadron sailed out on nightly raids. "Acting the fool" was a euphemism for piracy of the most ruthless and profitable sort: sabotaging the railway line, ambushing convoys, destroying communication lines, mining the road between Tobruk and Mersa Matruh, and generally causing mayhem in the German rear ahead of Montgomery's imminent westward surge. In the space of just twenty days, the railway link to Tobruk was severed thirteen times. The threat of night raids forced the German and Italian convoys to travel the road by day, where they were vulnerable to air attack by the RAF.

Mayne's force of eighty men included most of the L Detachment veterans, including Lilley, Cooper, and Fraser. Reg Seekings was not among them; to his chagrin, he was detailed to lick the rookies of B Squadron into shape. Among those under Mayne's command was a twenty-three-year-old Irishman named Chris

O'Dowd, irrepressible and indestructibly cheerful, who had taken part in the failed Benghazi operation. There is a photograph of O'Dowd cleaning his revolver in the desert camp before a raid: his hair is wild and matted, beard untrimmed; he wears shorts, a tattered jersey, and a broad grin; he looks filthy, happy, and extremely dangerous. At the other end of the social and sartorial scale came Lieutenant Harry Wall Poat, a former tomato farmer from the Channel Islands, who spoke in a refined upper-middle-class accent, sported a neat mustache, and was never less than immaculately attired, even after weeks of desert living.

The official reports of this period are rigorously matter-of-fact, a dry litany of violence, deliberately underplayed, austerely factual: "Fired on by heavy machine gun, rifle and 20mm fire . . . unable to get through on radio . . . had to chase [a] convoy which speeded up when it spotted us . . . owing to shortage of petrol and water, party split . . . all jeeps opened up with K guns . . . hid for three days . . . ran into minefield . . . mined road, blew telegraph poles, cratered road . . ." And so on. The only allusion to danger is heavily ironic. "Much frightened by a cheetah, with whom we shared our lying up wadi." There is more detail about the cuisine than the killing: "Chased a gazelle for ten minutes, wounded it with K's and finished it off with a pistol. Made very good eating."

Traditional warfare tends to follow straight lines: advances, retreats, fields of fire, front lines, vanguards, rear guards, and points of engagement. The SAS was pioneering a new sort of war, so asymmetrical as to be almost lopsided. Increasingly confident in their tactics and terrain, the independent jeep units selected targets as they appeared, with little deliberate planning. This was war on the hoof, invented ad hoc, unpredictable, highly effective, and often chaotic.

Corporal John William Sillito, known as "Jack," was navigating a jeep party to blow up a section of the railway near Tobruk in mid-October 1942 when his unit came under attack from a German night patrol. In the ensuing confusion, Sillito became separated from the rest of the men: "Suddenly he found himself completely alone." He carried only a revolver, a compass, and a small flask containing enough water for twenty-four hours. Sillito was a straightforward man, a farmer in civilian life. Having reflected for a while, he concluded that he had three options: he could go north and surrender; he could strike out east, in the hope of evading the Axis troops and reaching the British lines at Alamein; or he could head south, and try to cross the 180 miles to Mayne's desert camp. He chose the third option, despite knowing that there was "next to no chance of meeting any form of life or water, and where a mistake in direction meant certain and unpleasant death."

At first, the trek was not unpleasant, though it was lonely. Recent rain had left puddles of drinkable water. But as Sillito trudged on, the moisture dried up and the skies became "pitilessly blue and unchanging." He ran out of water on the second day, and began to store and drink his urine, which steadily grew more concentrated and disgusting. He walked at night and lay up during the day, under whatever shade he could find. On the fourth day, his feet blistered and cracked; by the fifth, his tongue had swelled up and his limbs began to cramp. Still he trudged south, while "the flat landscape stretched on and on in front of him." On the seventh day, now pitifully weak and starting to hallucinate, he spotted a convoy of jeeps in the far distance. Sillito jumped up and down, shouting, but the vehicles seemed to be heading away. Fumbling with his box of matches, he stripped off his shirt and set fire to it and then waved the burning garment above his head, but the smoke seemed to evaporate in the heat. The jeeps vanished over the horizon. "He was alone once more, with the heat, the sweat, and his thoughts." And no shirt. On day eight, close to death, he spotted the white dunes that mark the edge of the Sand Sea. Somewhere, about forty miles inside the sandy ocean, was the camp. If he could find the spot where the jeeps drove in and out of the Sand Sea, he might be saved; he knew he could not walk another forty miles.

A three-jeep SAS raiding party had made an unscheduled stop

for repairs when a "skeleton, with sore and bleeding feet," staggered out of the heat. Back at camp, Malcolm Pleydell bathed and bandaged Sillito's tattered body, and listened to his story in stunned admiration. Then the corporal stood painfully to attention for some souvenir photographs. Stirling reckoned that a fortnight after his astonishing desert trek, the man had "recovered completely." Pleydell knew Jack Sillito would never fully recover: "A hesitancy of manner and an expression in the eyes told their own story of mental strain and physical hardship."

ON OCTOBER 23, Montgomery struck, hurling his Eighth Army's nearly 200,000 men and more than a thousand tanks at Rommel's panzer army. By November 4, the Germans were in retreat; four days later, a vast Anglo-American invasion force landed in Morocco and Algeria and began heading east. The Second Battle of Alamein marked a turning point in the war: the first decisive Allied victory since the start of the war, raising morale and lifting the threat to Egypt and the Suez Canal. As Montgomery's victorious army pushed west, the First Army, formed of British and American land forces under General Kenneth Anderson, advanced east through Tunisia: Rommel was trapped in an enormous vice that would soon close, with crushing force. Despite his initial hostility toward Stirling, Montgomery had predicted that the SAS "could have a really decisive effect on my forthcoming offensive." The precise impact of the SAS on the military situation is, of course, impossible to measure, but Monty himself was convinced that the unit had played a pivotal role in the weeks before and after Alamein. The string of raids behind the lines had disrupted communications, sown confusion, and further sapped German morale.

At the end of November, the two SAS squadrons met up with Stirling at Bir Zelten, a new desert base farther west: from there, Paddy Mayne's men then set out to harass the retreating German forces around Sirte, inflicting further mayhem and taking remarkably few casualties.

But B Squadron, marauding to the west around Tripoli, suffered badly in the December raids. The squadron was operating in a more densely populated area, where many of the local Arabs were distinctly unfriendly and much more likely to tip off the enemy. The Germans, alert to the threat of raids, were now actively hunting down the SAS. In his diary, Rommel noted that his troops were "combing through the district hoping to stumble on a Tommy." By the end of December, B Squadron had lost more than a dozen men, and three of its six officers had been captured or killed. Reg Seekings narrowly escaped after his unit ran into an enemy patrol. With characteristic bluntness, he put the high casualty rate down to inexperience on the part of B Squadron, whose men had not been "trained up to the proper standards." But there was another, rather less obvious reason for the series of reverses suffered by B Squadron: an English fascist spy who went by the name of Captain John Richards.

Jim Almonds had run into Richards in the POW camp at Benghazi, and immediately spotted him as a stool pigeon, one of the oldest and nastiest species of spy. The word derives from the practice of tying a single pigeon to a stool in order to lure others: the stool pigeon (also known as a stooge) is a decoy, an informer who infiltrates a group by appearing to be the same as them, while secretly collecting information for the enemy. The prisoners captured in the desert war offered considerable scope for espionage of this sort: a spy introduced among prisoners of war, appearing to be a fellow captive, could extract vital information simply by eavesdropping, asking apparently innocuous questions, and gaining the trust of his compatriots.

For months, Lieutenant Colonel Mario Revetria, the chief of Italian military intelligence in North Africa, had been trying to find out more about the mysterious British raiders who emerged from the desert, often hundreds of miles behind the front lines, to attack airfields and ambush convoys. Rumors abounded about this unit, but there was very little in the way of hard intelligence. Revetria was a canny and experienced intelligence officer who knew that the only way to combat such a force was to discover its secrets. He needed to know who led the SAS, its size, training, and tactics; he needed an informant, an expert stool pigeon. And in Captain John Richards, he found one—a weapon that was far more effective in combating the SAS than any number of soldiers with guns.

Richards's real name was Theodore John William Schurch: an accountant by trade, a private in the British Army, and a committed fascist. Born in London in 1918 to an English mother and Swiss father who worked as a night porter at the Savoy, Schurch left school at sixteen but possessed what was later described as "innate intelligence and natural shrewdness." He also had an acute persecution complex. "Ever since I can remember I have been looked at askance on account of my foreign name," he later said, by way of exculpation. "The result was that my mind became warped and distorted at an early age." Working as a junior accountant for Lancegaye Safety Glass in Wembley, he met Irene Page, the company's twenty-three-year-old telephone operator, a young woman with a "large well formed bust" and extreme right-wing views. Every Saturday, she dressed in fascist uniform—black shirt, gray flannel skirt, tie, and beret—to meet up with fellow right-wing fanatics. Irene introduced Schurch to a network of suburban English fascists. Although initially he had been chiefly interested in Irene Page's bust, he was instantly attracted to the ideology of fascism. At one of the meetings he met Oswald Mosley, the leader of the British Union of Fascists. At another clandestine party gathering in Willesden, he was introduced to an Italian Blackshirt named Bianchi, owner of a Cardiff export firm, who spoke perfect English. Bianchi told Schurch that the Italian fascists had their own secret service, and suggested that he might make an ideal recruit.

The idea of becoming a secret agent took root. In 1936, at the behest of Bianchi, he enlisted in the Royal Army Service Corps and trained as an army driver; a year later, again at the suggestion of his fascist friends, he volunteered for deployment to Palestine. There he began to pass military information to a man named

Homis, the Arab owner of the General Motors concession in Palestine, who wore gold rings and a thin dark mustache. In return, Schurch was paid in cash—small amounts at first, but gradually more. As a driver at staff headquarters, he was in a position to glean all sorts of information of interest to both the Arab intelligence service and its Nazi allies: troop deployments, matériel shipments, and the travel plans of senior officers. "In my small way I was helping the fascist movement," he later said. He was also developing a "taste for expensive pleasure." Schurch's wartime comrades remember him as an easygoing character who liked to gossip and always seemed to have plenty of money. In 1941, Schurch's unit was deployed to Egypt. At the urging of Homis, he requested a frontline posting with the intention of crossing over to the Italian side at the first opportunity. He was finally sent to Tobruk; two days after his arrival the port fell to the Germans, and he was captured along with hundreds of other British soldiers. In the prisoner-of-war camp at Benghazi, he asked to see an officer of Italian military intelligence. The Italians made inquiries, and a few days later Schurch was brought before Colonel Mario Revetria. The Italian intelligence chief swiftly realized that the talkative little man chain-smoking in his tent might prove exceptionally useful, and took him to dinner in the officers' mess.

On September 13, Schurch was dressed in the uniform of a captain, supposedly in the Inter-Services Liaison Department, and sent back to Benghazi, where a large number of newly captured POWs were being held after the failed Tobruk and Benghazi raids in the preceding days. Schurch was an ugly man, with "a shrunken face and crooked, protruding teeth," but with his hair slicked back and his blond mustache neatly trimmed he could easily pass for an officer. In the confusion following the abortive raids, none of the prisoners—with the exception of Jim Almonds—paused to wonder whether the friendly Captain John Richards was really who he said he was. Schurch returned to Revetria with intriguing information: some of the POWs were members of "a special unit of the LRDG, later known as the SAS."

Revetria was "very much interested in the SAS," and Schurch was ordered to return to the POW camp and gather "all information respecting this kind of unit." The SAS had perfected the art of slipping behind the front line by driving around it; Schurch found he could slip back through British-held territory simply by being British and wearing an officer's uniform. Pretending to be an escaped prisoner of war, he crossed the lines at Alamein, gathered information for Revetria on Allied lines of communication, and then returned; he remained behind after Benghazi fell to the British, mixed with the town's new occupiers, and then once again crossed over to the Axis side. A delighted Revetria rewarded him with money, wine, the best Italian cigarettes, and his own villa.

With the Battle of Alamein, the advance of the Eighth Army, and the series of raids by the SAS, Captain John Richards was deployed once more, to infiltrate and extract information from the captured men of B Squadron. "During this time 2 or 3 patrols of the Special Air Service were captured," Schurch later explained. "Colonel Revetria made it my responsibility to get information from all prisoners of the SAS. I mixed with three officers and also other ranks of these captured patrols, and from information received in this manner, we found where other patrols were located, and also their strength. From the information received we were able to capture two other patrols, and acquired information as to the operations of other patrols in that area in the near future." The SAS had demonstrated that it could defend itself militarily in the harshest conditions; the greatest threat to the unit, however, had come from a spy who looked and behaved like an English officer.

THE FINAL CHAPTER of the desert war was about to open, and Stirling was determined to write himself into it, with a bold act of devilry that would demonstrate the prowess of his force once and for all, guarantee the future of the regiment, and ensure a major role for the SAS in the next phase of the war in Europe. He proposed to lead his forces west to harry the Germans and disrupt their communication lines as they retreated into Tunisia, while simultaneously gathering intelligence that might reveal whether Rommel intended to make a stand on the Mareth Line, the string of fortifications built originally by France to defend Tunisia against attacks from Libya. The elegant Lieutenant Harry Poat would lead one group to attack targets west of Tripoli—at the specific request of Montgomery, who was determined to prevent the retreating Germans from organizing an orderly destruction of the port—the French SAS would raid between Gabès and Sfax on the Tunisian coast, and Mayne would operate around the Mareth Line. But, for himself, Stirling had an even more dramatic goal in mind: he would drive northwest, pass *through* the retreating German lines, and then link up with the advancing First Army. In between the two Allied armies lay largely uncharted desert, a huge force of Axis troops, and an enormous, impassable salt marsh. Stirling told Pleydell that he intended to drive "straight across to the south of the fighting zone from one front to the other," adding that "the journey would give him a good idea of the nature of the country for future operations." It might establish the possibility of maneuvering an armored division behind the retreating Germans.

The mission might yield important intelligence. But it was also a stunt, a calculated feat of military theater: the opportunity to become the first unit of desert rats to greet approaching American forces was, Stirling later admitted, "irresistible." Success might lead to further expansion of the regiment, perhaps to brigade status; in Stirling's imagination the SAS might even swell to three separate regiments, operating in the eastern Mediterranean, Italy, and Nazi-occupied Europe.

Pleydell observed Stirling with a doctor's eye, and did not like what he saw. The SAS commander "was not looking too fit," he reflected. Stirling's desert sores had become so badly infected that he had been hospitalized in Cairo for several days. His migraines had returned, exacerbated by solar conjunctivitis, an eye infection caused by a combination of flying sand and blazing sun. Stirling had taken to wearing sunglasses to protect his eyes, which gave him an oddly gangsterish appearance. Pleydell's efforts to persuade Stirling to bathe his eyes were politely ignored. He seemed dangerously thin, worn down by his multiplying responsibilities, not least the creation of another, parallel SAS regiment.

For months, Stirling had been lobbying for a second SAS regiment to complement the first. At the end of 1942, approval was finally granted, and 2SAS came into being, under the command of David's brother Bill Stirling, a lieutenant colonel in the Scots Guards and former commando who shared his brother's vision for the unit. Bill Stirling had been in command of 62 Commando, also known as the Small Scale Raiding Force, formed to carry out raids in the English Channel. Late in 1942, after being sent to Algeria, 62 Commando was disbanded, and Bill began lobbying Allied Forces HQ for permission to raise a second SAS regiment. The second regiment was attached to the First Army in Algeria, and began recruiting and training at a new base in Philippeville, in northwest Algeria. What had begun as a single, small, semi-private army had spawned an ever-expanding family of special forces, including additional French troops, a unit of tough Greek fighters known as the Greek Sacred Squadron (after the Sacred Band of Thebes), and the Special Boat Squadron. The SAS idea was bearing more fruit than one man could easily carry. Stirling had always been a peculiar mixture of parts: a born organizer who disliked administration, a man of action with limited physical stamina, an officer of vaulting ambition who now saw his creation expanding in ways he had not anticipated and could not fully control. His determination to get back to the desert may have reflected, in part, a desire to escape the responsibilities mounting up on his desk.

To reach the First Army, Stirling's party would have to skirt the Great Eastern Sand Sea, stretching out from Algeria into Tunisia, and then pass though the Gabès Gap, a natural bottleneck between the Mediterranean and the vast and impenetrable salt marshes to the west. All traffic heading for the coast had to pass through the gap, which was still in German hands and only

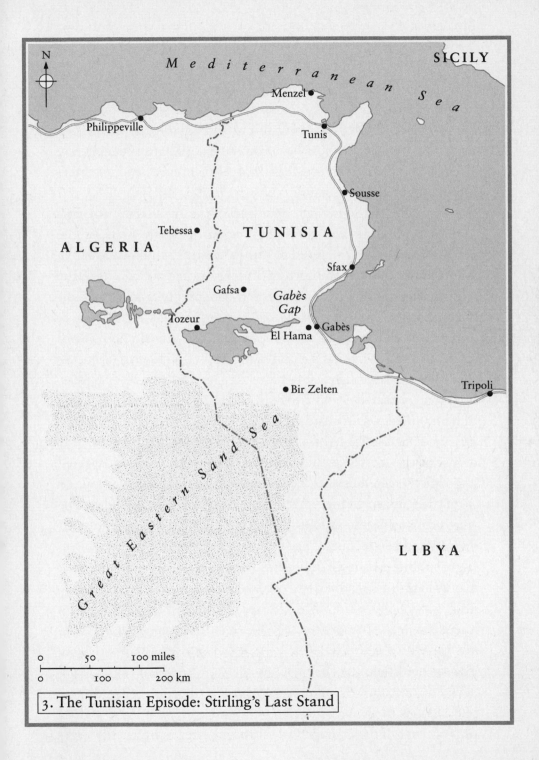

N

M e d i t e r r a n e a n   S e a

SICILY

Menzel

Philippeville

Tunis

Sousse

Tebessa

TUNISIA

ALGERIA

Sfax

Gafsa

Gabès Gap

Tozeur

El Hama

Gabès

Bir Zelten

Tripoli

Great Eastern Sand Sea

LIBYA

| 0 | 50 | 100 miles |

| 0 | 100 | 200 km |

3. The Tunisian Episode: Stirling's Last Stand

five miles wide at its narrowest point. Additional jeeps would be brought along simply to carry fuel, and then abandoned en route.

At sunrise on January 16, 1943, Stirling's column of five jeeps and fourteen men set off from Bir Zelten, preceded by a French unit under Augustin Jordan. Stirling's force included the navigator Mike Sadler, Johnny Cooper, and a thirty-one-year-old French sergeant, Freddie Taxis, who spoke Arabic. There was a strong possibility of encountering hostile local tribesmen, and an interpreter might prove essential.

The route to the forward positions of the First Army at Gafsa required a wide sweep south of Tripoli, through some of the harshest terrain encountered so far. Where the sands of the Great Sand Sea had taken the form of mighty ocean rollers, here the rutted desert waves were "short and choppy like a rough Mediterranean sea." As the convoy made its juddering way northwest, often reduced to driving at no more than one mile an hour, word came over the radio that Tripoli had fallen to the Eighth Army. As the convoy neared the Gabès Gap, the going became ever harder, with boggy marshes and furrowed dunes alternating with steep, boulder-filled ravines. At dusk on January 22, two German reconnaissance planes buzzed overhead. Stirling pressed on; in the early hours of the morning, they reached the tarmac road and passed through the gap "absolutely on tiptoe," as Stirling put it. A mile or so farther on, a German armored division was encamped by the roadside, and in the process of waking up. "We're going to bluff it," Stirling told Cooper. "Just look straight ahead." As they passed a group of German soldiers drinking coffee in the morning sun, Cooper gave a friendly nod: "Nobody challenged us . . . Nobody shot us. Nobody did anything." They now needed to get away from the coast road as quickly as possible, and find somewhere to hide for the day. Sadler headed for the foothills of the Jebel Tebaga, only to cross another dirt road that was not marked on his map. They turned into open country. A little farther on, Stirling spotted a long, narrow ravine dotted with bushes that "seemed to offer perfect cover." The troop was exhausted after more than thirty-six hours without rest, food, or sleep. The jeeps were hurriedly camouflaged, and the men settled down to sleep, spreading out in the nooks and corners up and down the gully, many too tired even to remove their boots. Before turning in, Cooper and Sadler climbed to the lip of the ravine to survey the road. Through binoculars, they saw a column of troops halt and climb down from their vehicles. "We assumed they were all getting out just to pee," Sadler later recalled.

Mike Sadler was woken by the crunch of boots on stones, and opened his eyes to see a pair of German paratroopers standing over him pointing Schmeisser submachine guns. Cooper, who had been asleep alongside Sadler, began to extricate himself from his sleeping bag and struggle to his feet. "Down!" ordered one of the Germans. Cooper and Sadler lay still. Their guns were thirty feet away, hidden in the camouflaged jeeps. The two paratroopers indicated that Sadler and Cooper should stay where they were, and dashed off down the ravine to help round up the rest of the British party. Cooper and Sadler did not need to formulate a plan: "The only thing to do was to leg it." The moment the Germans were out of sight, they started running up the steep side of the ravine. Moments later, they were joined by the Frenchman, Freddie Taxis. All three sprinted for the lip of the gully. Behind them they heard gunfire, and cries of *"Raus! Raus!"* (Out! Out!)

Stirling and the rest of the troop were captured without a fight. A tubby, red-faced German officer (who, to Stirling's indignation, turned out to be the unit dentist) pointed a Luger at the SAS leader and marched him out of the ravine. At the top, a grim sight awaited: a force of some five hundred German soldiers with guns trained, and an armored personnel carrier blocking the exit from the wadi. The captors were a special Luftwaffe paratroop force, Company z.b.V. 250, sent out to track down the raiders and alerted to the presence of the SAS following a skirmish with Jordan's troops the day before (the French party was captured a few days later). The eleven prisoners were searched, marched to the roadside, and then herded onto lorries under heavy guard as the sun was setting. After driving south for almost two hours, they were ordered into what appeared to be a large garage and locked inside. The jubilation of the guards suggested they had discovered the identity, and value, of their captives. Stirling estimated they must be somewhere in the vicinity of Medina. One of the buttons on his jacket concealed a compass: he was formulating an escape plan.

Sadler, Cooper, and Taxis, meanwhile, were heading in precisely the opposite direction. After their lung-bursting sprint to the top of the ravine, they had hurled themselves beneath bushes in a small gully. For several hours, they hid as the Germans combed the area. Sadler extracted a piece of paper from his pocket on which he had scribbled the latest signals from HQ and buried it in the sand. "It was the longest afternoon I have ever spent," he said. By good fortune an Arab arrived with a large herd of goats, which milled around their hiding place, helping to conceal them. "We never knew whether the herder did it on purpose, to hide us." As night fell, they heard the Germans withdraw.

All three had been sleeping fully dressed, but they had no weapons, map, compass, water, or food. Sadler had made a careful study of the geography. The First Army, he calculated, was still more than a hundred miles away to the northwest. If they walked, keeping the salt lakes to their west, they should eventually reach the oasis town of Tozeur. "With any luck, I reckoned this ought to be in the hands of the Allies by now," Sadler later recalled. "So we set off."

They walked all night, and at dawn encountered a group of friendly Berbers, who gave them some dates and a goatskin, which they sewed together with bootlaces to create a makeshift water container. They walked on, until the punishing heat forced them to halt. When night fell they walked again, and at first light fell asleep in the fissures of a large rock. A burly Arab brandishing a shotgun appeared a few hours later, looking not much more welcoming than the Germans who had woken them two days earlier. Within minutes, they were surrounded by tribesmen and boys carrying rocks. "Give them your jacket," Taxis instructed Cooper.

"They are saying we should give them our clothes because they are going to kill us anyway." A rock flew. Cooper was struck on the forehead above the left eye. Stunned and temporarily blinded by pouring blood, Cooper was seized by the other two and half dragged across a wide expanse of loose rock, which the barefoot Arabs could not easily cross. Then they ran.

On the fourth day, they were nearing collapse. In the distance, Sadler was sure he could see the faint green smudge of the oasis at Tozeur. But it seemed certain they would die of thirst, or go mad, before reaching it. Taxis had drunk salt water from the marsh, and was vomiting and hallucinating wildly. He could barely stand. To the surprise of his British companions, he turned out to have six toes on each foot, and after four days marching in ill-fitting boots he was all but crippled. The polydactyl Frenchman lay down and demanded to be left behind to die. With a combination of bullying, encouragement, and force, the others pulled him to his feet and they struggled on.

Sadler had himself entered the strange twilight of delirium, where reality and fantasy merge, when two very large black men wearing First World War helmets appeared out of the desert. Sadler wondered if this could be another mirage. The apparitions spoke in French, and pointed ancient rifles with fixed bayonets. Moments later, the ragged trio were being plied with wine and white rum, goat meat and potatoes, while Cooper's head wound was stitched by a French medical orderly: they had encountered Senegalese soldiers of the Foreign Legion, part of the Free French forces, the very tip of the advancing First Army.

The *New Yorker*'s celebrated war correspondent A. J. Liebling had been hanging around Gafsa for days in search of a scoop. The forward point of the American advance, he calculated, was the most likely place for the two Allied armies to connect, a moment he wanted to witness. The little desert town looked "like a set in an old Beau Geste movie," with a mixed population of Europeans, Jews, and Arabs, and a newly arrived battalion of American infantrymen, which had done wonders for trade at the local

brothel, whose girls Liebling described as "sort of French." Lieutenant Colonel Bowen had taken over the yellow stucco Hôtel de
Ville, which boasted a bath and running water, as his headquarters. Liebling was there, buttering up the signals officer in the
hope of sending a story by telegraph, when an officer of the French
Foreign Legion entered the building followed by a trio of tramps.

> Their shoes were wrapped in rags, and I deduced that
> their feet must be a mass of blisters. Two of the men
> wore long beards and one, whose head was wrapped in
> a blood-soaked bandage, looked as if he badly needed a
> shave. All three were wearing khaki battledress, from
> which great swatches of material were missing, torn
> off to make bandages. One of the men carried a goat-
> skin watersack, with the long hair outside; it reminded
> me of Robinson Crusoe. Their faces were sunken and
> their eyes seemed preternaturally large, and in one case
> really protuberant. The eyes of this fellow were round
> and sky blue and his hair and whiskers were very fair.
> His beard began well under his chin, giving him the
> air of an emaciated and slightly dotty Paul Verlaine.

"We've been walking for five nights and five days," said Mike
Sadler. "Have any of the others come in? Have you heard anything
about Big Dave?"

Liebling was incredulous: "Are you really from the Eighth
Army?"

Colonel Bowen was even more dubious. He took one look at
the hairy, ragged trio and ordered them to be placed under guard,
on the grounds that "they might be spies." For the three men,
whose sense of reality had already been loosened by a combination
of exhaustion, dehydration, and rough Algerian wine, the situation lurched into the surreal: they were now prisoners of their own
allies, and much too tired to argue. Waiting to be escorted under
guard to the American headquarters at Tebessa, Cooper fell into

conversation with the American journalist. His tumbling, half-delirious description of the work of the SAS was reproduced ver-batim by Liebling:

When we were first formed, we used to specialize in German airplanes on the ground. Get back behind their lines, get onto an airfield at night—do in a sentry, you know, or something of that sort; it's easy—and then attach pencil bombs to as many planes as we could get to. The bombs are timed to go off in a short time. We do a bunk, the bombs go off, and all the planes burn. Quite a good idea. Colonel Stirling, the one we call Big Dave, really thought of it first. Bright chap. Colonel Stirling thought of using jeeps. Wonderful things jeeps, absolutely fine. They go anywhere in desert country. Our fellows come in behind the enemy lines, and then simply live in the desert for weeks, annoying them. One chap in SAS has got a hundred and twenty planes with his own hands. Big Dave must have got nearly a hundred. But Jerry got onto that airport dodge. Now there are too many guards and booby traps. So on this last trip we just did mines, traffic disruption, and general confusion. Glorious fun, really. We went along for weeks without any trouble. We would always hide out in the daytime and sleep, and then do all our moves at night. We would find deep wadis or crevices to hide away in. We would come out onto the roads at night and shoot up enemy convoys. We made a shambles of the enemy's line of supply. One of our best tricks was to come onto a road and move along it toward the front, so they would never suspect us of being intruders . . . But we got to feel too safe. We had gone so long unobserved that we thought it would last forever. We were lying up in deep wadi about ten miles north of Gabès. Some Arabs must have spotted us going in there and told Jerry. There wasn't a chance to fight our way out of that position. We managed to climb up a cliff. We waited around to see if any of the others would get away, but nobody did. There was a lot of shooting in the wadi, and then silence.

Cooper's ebullience suddenly evaporated. "Big Dave must have been killed."

A. J. Liebling's report was published in the *New Yorker* on November 17, introducing American readers to a new sort of warfare, in which bearded, scruffy Brits fought behind the lines and found it all glorious fun.

David Stirling had not been killed, although he had come very close. At 10:00 p.m. on the evening after his capture, he demanded to be allowed outside in order to urinate. Two of the guards escorted him, smoking cigarettes. Some twenty yards from the building, Stirling simply started running. Shots rang out, but in the darkness the sentries fired blind. Stirling had decided to head south, an escape plan based almost entirely on wishful thinking: the area was densely populated, he had no idea where he was, and a single, exceptionally tall, unarmed foreigner was certain to be spotted. Even so, he covered some fifteen miles and then hid in a bush as dawn broke. The next day, he was discovered by an Arab herder who led him to a small ravine and indicated he would bring water. A few minutes later, he returned, accompanied by an Italian patrol. Stirling was back in captivity. This time he was bound and taken under heavy guard to the village of El Hama, and then on to the Italian headquarters at Menzel.

There he was interrogated by Colonel Mario Revetria of Italian military intelligence. Revetria was so excited to have captured the SAS leader that he could not resist showing off, and instead of pumping Stirling for information he described everything he knew about the SAS, although not how he knew it. Stirling was duly impressed: "You know as much as I do about my own organization," he said.

A few hours later, Stirling was marched onto a Junkers 52 and flown to Sicily. Here he was interrogated once more, in a cavalry barracks, first by the Italians, and then by a German staff officer. He gave only his name and rank.

On February 11, Stirling's mother was officially notified that he was missing in action. "I am hopeful that David may yet turn up," Randolph Churchill wrote to her. "At worst he is a prisoner." Rommel himself wrote to his wife, describing how the man who had made so much trouble for him, for so long, was finally in captivity: "The British lost the very able and adaptable commander of the desert group which has caused us more damage than any other British unit of equal size."

Stirling was moved to another POW camp, outside Rome. The Caserma Castro Pretorio was "well equipped and comfortable," but after so many months of frenetic activity, Stirling found the inertia boring beyond description. During the day, the prisoners remained in cells, but in the evening they were allowed out to eat together and socialize. There were kindred souls about. The man in the next cell, another officer awaiting interrogation, introduced himself as Captain John Richards of the Royal Army Service Corps and explained that he had been captured in Tobruk in November 1942.

Teddy Schurch had been flown to Rome shortly before Stirling's capture. When his new commanding officer, one Captain Morocco, told him that "a very important person had been captured," none other than the leader of the SAS, Schurch seems to have felt a surge of something like professional pride: "At last he was going to meet the commanding officer of the men and officers with whom he had spent all his time obtaining information." Morocco ordered Schurch to "obtain all possible information about Stirling and his organization," and in particular the name of the officer who would succeed him as leader of the SAS.

Quite how much Stirling inadvertently divulged to the stool pigeon over the next two weeks has never been revealed. In a witness statement made at Schurch's treason trial, Stirling claimed he had been warned by another officer that Captain Richards was working for the Italians, and that he had been on his guard from the start: "Such information as I passed was untrue and designed to deceive him . . . I cannot remember discussing the name of my successor in the SAS. In fact at that time I was unaware of my successor's identity." Schurch remembered their conversations differently. "As all the necessary information regarding the SAS had already been obtained, I was told only to obtain the name of Colonel Stirling's successor. This I found out to be a Captain Paddy Mayne." There was really only one person capable of taking over the regiment, and Stirling appears to have revealed as much to Schurch. This information was undoubtedly shared with Nazi intelligence. Bizarrely, the Germans knew he would be taking over the SAS before Mayne knew himself.

THE DESERT WAR was drawing to an end, and with victory in sight in North Africa the role, the location, and the very nature of the SAS would change once again. It had already been altered beyond all recognition from the handful of soldiers dropped into the desert in Operation Squatter. Many of the "Originals," as the first recruits described themselves, were gone. David Stirling was eventually transferred to Colditz, the notorious German POW camp, where he would be reunited with Georges Bergé and Augustin Jordan, the French SAS commanders captured earlier. Jim Almonds remained a prisoner. Fitzroy Maclean had been dispatched by Churchill to Yugoslavia, to link up with Tito's partisans. Jock Lewes was dead, along with Germain Guerpillon, André Zirnheld, and many others. American-born Pat Riley, the Irishman Chris O'Dowd, Bill Fraser, Reg Seekings, and Johnny Cooper had all survived, and would play key roles in the second great chapter of the SAS story. Mike Sadler, having finally persuaded the Americans that he was not a spy, helped to guide the advancing Eighth Army across the desert for the final act of the war in North Africa, and then rejoined the SAS. The force, now composed of two regiments, would plunge into the war in Europe under the leadership of a fiery, inspiring, occasionally violent Northern Irishman. The SAS under Paddy Mayne would be a very different force.

Malcolm Pleydell took a new posting in 64 General Hospital in Cairo. The young doctor left the SAS with a hymn of love to the desert.

> This was the end of our campaigning in Africa, and now we might bid farewell to the desert: the loneliness, the solace and the clean sterility. Here in these little cliffs and caves that had been our hiding places, we had left our mark. In a few weeks they would be erased by wind and sand. Here we had learned to navigate, to plot our course and mark our position; here we had grown wise, becoming self-reliant and tolerant of the humours of others; we had matured, we had known greater mental sufficiency, had discovered our fears and our reactions to danger, and had tried to overcome them. We had become familiar with hardship and with the submission of the body to rigid control. This was the bequest of the desert. Our time had not been wasted.

Part II

WAR IN EUROPE

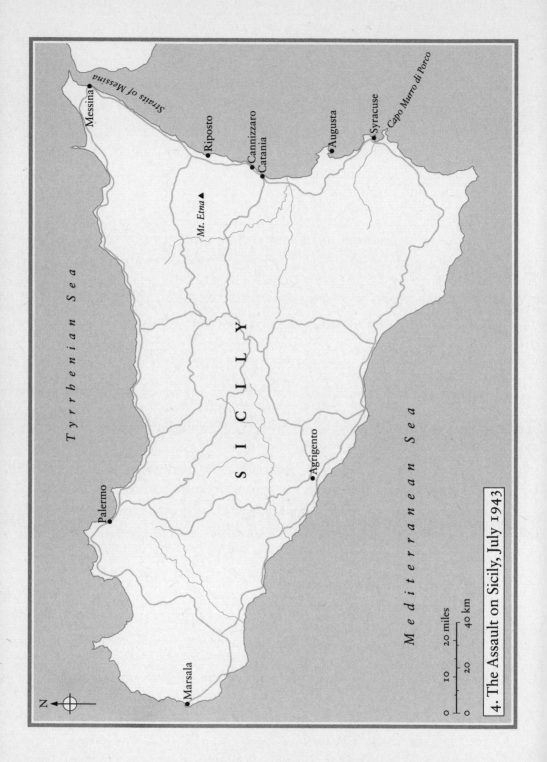

4. The Assault on Sicily, July 1943

Chapter 15

ITALY

"THE SHIP IS WITHOUT A RUDDER," MALCOLM PLEYDELL observed sadly as he took his leave of the SAS, two months after the capture of David Stirling. "There is no one with his flair." Paddy Mayne was a fighting commander, beloved and respected for it, but bravery is only one aspect of leadership. However much he might be admired for his battlefield panache, he was unexploded ordnance, and his subordinates trod warily around him. He was baffled and bored by paperwork. He lacked Stirling's polish and willingness to charm the top brass, many of whom felt that the SAS had "outlived its usefulness." He was also in trouble, again. In March, Mayne learned that his father had died. He requested three days' leave to return to Northern Ireland for the funeral; this was refused without explanation. Mayne smoldered with resentment, drank, and then went, as Seekings put it, "on the rampage." In the course of a few hours in Cairo, it was said, he smashed up several restaurants, got into a punch-up with half a dozen military policemen, and was flung into a cell.

There was widespread expectation in the ranks that, with Mayne out of control and Stirling in a POW camp, the regiment would soon be disbanded. But Mayne somehow managed to get himself released and argued fiercely that the regiment should be preserved; eventually a compromise was reached, involving considerable restructuring. The original unit, 1SAS, would be split into two parts: the Special Boat Squadron (SBS), under George

Jellicoe, to carry out amphibious operations, and the Special Raiding Squadron (SRS), under Mayne, to be used as assault troops in the coming invasion of Europe.

Jellicoe's SBS, 250-strong, moved to Haifa and began training for operations in the Aegean. The 2SAS, meanwhile, the new sister regiment formed under David Stirling's brother Bill, would continue training in northern Algeria before deployment in the Mediterranean and then in occupied Europe.

The story of the two SAS regiments would now evolve in parallel, sometimes in combination, and frequently in competition.

Mayne's newly named section, the SRS, though it included many SAS veterans, was a far cry from the muscular, mobile force Stirling had dreamed of before his capture: reduced in strength to between 300 and 350 men, it was now under the overall command of HQ Raiding Forces, to be used in straightforward attacking operations. The SRS was no longer the independent, agile, self-sustaining SAS of the desert, but the pointed tip of a much larger army, a tactical force. In all but spirit, the 1SAS had ceased to exist. It would soon return to its original shape and purpose, but for the moment, in order to survive, the SAS had to fall into line. Uncharacteristically, Mayne acquiesced in this uncomfortable new arrangement without resigning, getting excessively drunk, or hitting anyone.

IN THE LATE spring of 1943, the SRS began a fresh round of intensive training in Azzib, Palestine: endurance marches around Lake Tiberias in broiling heat, cliff scaling, weapons use, bayonet practice, wire cutting, beach landings, and the use of explosives. A new mortar section came into being under Alex Muirhead, a young officer who knew little about mortars but possessed the sort of mathematical mind necessary for the precise and devastating art of dropping shells onto enemy positions. "Soon he could put 12 rounds into the air before the first one had hit the ground," a contemporary noted admiringly.

For some of the veterans there was a sense of transition. Bill Fraser, now deprived of the company of his dog, Withers, seemed increasingly distant and elusive. Johnny Cooper had volunteered for officer training, leaving Reg Seekings without a restraining voice, and more prone to pick fights than ever. The Irishman Chris O'Dowd kept up a steady stream of jokes, but there was tension within the SRS: the old guard rubbed shoulders with a fresh batch of newcomers, not always comfortably. Men like Seekings considered themselves a battle-hardened, desert-baked elite and did not try to disguise it. No one had a clue what Mayne's training program was leading up to (including Mayne himself), save that it must involve heat, cliffs, hand-to-hand fighting, and lobbing mortar shells.

On June 28, the SRS headed for the port of Suez, and climbed aboard the *Ulster Monarch*, a bulky former passenger ferry that had once operated in the Irish Sea, to be delivered to its first mission in Italy. Before the ship set sail, General Montgomery arrived for an inspection and made his standard exhortatory speech. As with all relations between the general and the SAS, the event assumed an awkward aspect. Monty had expected his address to be met with loud adulatory applause, the sound he liked most, but for some reason it had been decided to hold back on cheering until he returned to shore. His words were greeted with total silence. Monty may have wondered if the truculent spirit of David Stirling was somehow aboard the ship. Even so, he was impressed by the sight of the fit troops, lined up in their beige berets. "Very smart," he muttered as he descended the gangplank and the cheers finally erupted. "I like their hats."

As the *Ulster Monarch* steamed out of Suez and headed north, the shape of what lay ahead began to emerge, not least in the form of the secret password with which the troops would identify one another on the forthcoming operation: the phrase "Desert Rats" would be met with the response "Kill the Italians."

The largest amphibious assault force ever assembled was already gathering for the invasion of Sicily: more than three thousand ships carrying 160,000 soldiers, the combined forces of Montgomery's Eighth Army and the US Seventh Army under General George Patton. D-Day in Sicily was set for the early hours of July 10, 1943. The task of the SRS was to knock out the artillery defenses at a key point on the Sicilian coast: Capo Murro di Porco—Cape of the Pig's Snout—a distinctly nasal promontory stretching into the sea south of Syracuse on the island's eastern side. The cape was a "veritable fortress," according to intelligence reports, perched atop a steep rock cliff and equipped with searchlights, a range of heavy guns, and Italian defenders who would outnumber the assault team "by 50 to one." If the SRS failed to knock out the Italian guns, the invasion fleet aiming for this section of the coast could be blasted to shreds long before they reached the shore.

At 1:00 on the morning of the invasion, 287 men of the Special Raiding Squadron, led by Mayne and including Seekings, Fraser, and many other desert veterans, climbed into landing craft and were lowered from the *Ulster Monarch* into a bucking sea. The wind had risen to the point where any kind of seaborne operation seemed barely possible, let alone a full-scale invasion. As the landing craft plowed through the rising chop, many of the men were sick into cardboard buckets, which promptly fell apart. No one spoke. Less than a mile from shore, the wind abruptly dropped and voices could be heard drifting across the waves. Shapes bobbed on the surface through the gloom, accompanied by urgent cries for help, in English. Up ahead, dozens of Allied paratroopers were drowning. Dispatched in gliders to land in the Sicilian interior and wreak mayhem ahead of the main force, many had been blown off course by the high wind and crash-landed in the sea. One group perched on a downed glider was picked up by an SAS launch, but most were left behind. The landing craft plowed ahead. "The poor devils were shouting for help but we didn't stop," remembered Reg Seekings. For some of the SAS men, the decision to press on brought back memories of the moment, so many months earlier, when the men injured during Operation Squatter had been left to perish in the desert. As ever, Seekings expressed the reality of war in the bleakest terms: "We shouted to them to hang on, but we couldn't stop to pick them up . . . We'd got a job to do. We couldn't stop and mess that up."

The flat-bottomed craft hit the beach under cover of darkness and the men poured ashore, cut their way through the barbed wire, and reached the foot of the cliff. It was not until the bamboo scaling ladders were up against the cliff and the first men were ascending that the Italian defenders woke up to what was happening. Two machine guns opened fire, shooting blindly into the darkness while the searchlights swept the sea. Alex Muirhead's mortar section opened up, and moments later the cordite dump behind the gun emplacements exploded with a roar. It was all over quite quickly. One section simply climbed up the hill path. Another, led by Johnny Wiseman, cut through the perimeter wire around the battery and then opened fire on the concrete emplacement. The Italians surrendered with indecorous haste. "They gave up very easily," said Wiseman. A Cambridge graduate and former spectacles salesman, Wiseman lost his false teeth but won a Military Cross that day. Instead of the "tough, experienced and fanatically patriotic defenders we had expected," these Italians were "fawning, friendly, smiling little creatures," pathetically eager to get away from the war. In one bunker crouched a group of terrified women and children.

But nasty little pockets of resistance remained, including a number of snipers. One team of SRS men spotted a group of Italians taking potshots from the cliff edge, as if for sport, at the paratroopers still struggling in the water. What happened next is not recorded in official reports, but one of the SRS men later noted: "They didn't see their families again." While the coastal guns were being put out of action with explosives, the rest of the assault team headed inland to disable a second battery that had now opened up. As Reg Seekings pushed forward, his troop was approached by a group of Italians waving a white flag. At the last moment they flung themselves down and a blast of machine-gun fire from an unseen pillbox raked the British unit, killing one man and wounding two others. Seekings stormed the machine-gun post, hurled in a grenade, and then killed the occupants with a revolver as they staggered out, one after the other. A shell splinter passed through his nose, but Seekings was elated. "To a certain extent I enjoyed it, but it's not everyone's cup of tea," he said. "I enjoyed the killing. I was scared, but I would have gone into action every day if I could."

At 5:20 a.m., Mayne fired a green Verey light into the gray dawn sky, to indicate that the coastal batteries were safely in Allied hands. The rest of the invasion fleet was now approaching the beaches, a flotilla of Homeric proportions. "We looked in amazement at the armada of ships which filled the sea to the horizon," one of the officers recalled.

The SAS attack had been a complete success: eighteen large guns captured or destroyed, including four mortars, two hundred enemy killed or wounded, and more than five hundred taken prisoner, including the brigadier commanding the battery. Several captured Allied paratroopers had been released. The SRS had lost one dead, two wounded, two berets, and a single water bottle. The assault would later be described by the general in command as "a brilliant operation, brilliantly planned and brilliantly carried out."

Yet it had been a brutal introduction to a new form of conflict: a war of terrified civilians, unseen snipers, and false flags of surrender blurring the line between a fair fight and an execution. The clarity and gentlemanliness of war behind the lines in the desert seemed suddenly distant.

Just two days later, the SRS was thrown back into action, to clear the Italian naval port of Augusta, eleven miles north of Syracuse, a vital launchpad for the Eighth Army's drive northward. Despite rumors that the port had been abandoned, it was clearly still occupied by the enemy, and these were not second-rate, war-weary Italian forces but crack German troops of the Hermann Göring Division, camped in the hills above the town.

With the sun going down, the landing craft approached a harbor lined with white cottages. "All was very quiet and peaceful." Then machine-gun fire spattered across the bay, and shells began to land around the launches. The men tumbled pell-mell onto the sand and over the seawall, with Mayne in the lead, as a pair of Royal Navy destroyers began pummeling the German firing positions. One pillbox was pulverized by the naval guns. "We simply flew across the beach and into the streets beyond," wrote Cooper. While the men adopted house-to-house fighting tactics, Mayne could be seen strolling down the street, hands in pockets. Two medical orderlies were killed, brought down by machine-gun fire. But then the German resistance seemed to evaporate. By nightfall the section was headquartered in a fourteenth-century citadel, with lookouts posted around the town to await the expected counterattack. At about 4:00 a.m. came the sound of heavy tracked vehicles moving above the town, the unmistakable rumble of tanks. The SRS braced for battle, but the sound gradually faded. The Germans had withdrawn.

With Augusta secured and empty, the SRS threw a spontaneous, spectacular, and extremely boisterous looting party. The port had previously served as a headquarters for Italian naval officers and was copiously stocked with food and drink. Within hours the men could be seen staggering drunkenly around the town in a variety of bizarre costumes "liberated" from the local shops and houses: some wore straw boaters or Italian military headgear, but a few went further and dressed entirely in drag, having appropriated the finery of the ladies of Augusta. Paddy Mayne was seen pushing a baby's pram down the street, filled with bottles; he then used a grenade to blow open a safe in the bank, but was disappointed to discover only a few silver spoons and an old brooch. A sing-along was held in the town square, using a trumpet, a tambourine, some cymbals, and a stolen pianola, which was then carried back in triumph as a gift for the captain of the *Ulster Monarch*.

The rest of July was spent encamped in Augusta. It was a strange time for the unit, a period of relaxation in the Mediterranean sun, interrupted by occasional Luftwaffe bombing attacks. Some recalled it as a "blissful" interlude, but for many it seemed an odd hiatus, a jolting sort of calm. Various operations were planned, and then called off. Mayne introduced a new, intensive physical-training program, though with what end in mind was never clear. The men marched up Mount Etna and down again. For some of the longest-serving SAS men, the stop-start nature of their existence was an unhappy reminder of the way the Layforce commandos had been used—or underused—in the earlier part of the war. In August, the squadron set up camp in Cannizzaro, twenty-five miles north of Augusta. Paddy Mayne prowled around, tense and troubled. Some of the officers avoided him, fearful that they would be compelled to go drinking with the commander, a ritual fraught with unpredictability and danger. When the boozing could not be avoided, Mayne forced the men to sing sentimental Irish songs, and observed them, as one participant put it, "like some emperor watching his gladiators." By mid-August, the last German troops had retreated across the Strait of Messina to the Italian mainland, and the Allies' long, slow, cruel slog up Italy began. The SRS, once again, was at the pointed end.

On September 4, 243 men landed at Bagnara, on the tip of Italy's toe, with orders to secure the port and prevent its demolition ahead of the main invasion force, twelve hours behind them. Mayne was the first on the beach and strode into town. (Luckily, the SAS had landed on the wrong part of the shore—had the unit landed on the intended beach, which was heavily mined, he would have been blown to pieces.)

The German defenders at Bagnara, described in the regimental War Diary as "of good physique and experienced," were already pulling out, but with rear-guard ferocity, fighting from the high ground above the port as they retreated. A tracer bullet tore through Harry Poat's trouser leg, setting fire to it and killing the man crouching behind him. Another group pulled too far ahead

SWITZERLAND

AUSTRIA

N

YUGOSLAVIA

A
p
Genoa
Bologna
e
La Spezia
Florence Fiesole
n
Incisa
Ancona

CORSICA

n

Pescara

i
Rome
Termoli
R. Bifurno
n
Campobasso

SARDINIA

e
Naples
s
Taranto

Bagnara

SICILY

PANTELLERIA

MALTA

LAMPEDUSA

5. The SAS Campaign in Italy

| 0 | 50 | 100 miles |
| 0 | 100 | 200 km |

and was pinned down in a farmhouse by enemy fire; when they tried to emerge, one man was shot dead. An unsuspecting team of German sappers was ambushed, and shot down too easily. "Like being at the funfair," one man queasily recalled. Behind the town they found caves crammed with civilians who emerged cheering. A few hours later, the main body of regular troops poured into the town, British cruisers battered the German positions in the hills, and the town was taken. The SRS had lost five killed, with sixteen wounded. Some thirty Germans were killed.

The Bagnara operation had been an average episode of war, unspectacularly successful, typically exciting, no more than averagely unpleasant. The SRS was fulfilling the requirements of HQ Raiding Forces, and doing the job well, but mounting frontal assaults on enemy positions was a task for commandos, not for the specialized forces under Mayne's command. The lateral-thinking war pioneered by the SAS was being shoehorned into the more traditional, one-dimensional demands of the Italian campaign— they were doing what any group of highly trained soldiers could do, suffering and succeeding in the normal way. That was not why the SAS had been formed. Stirling's unique idea was being eroded. The full consequences of that change, the loss of their singular advantage as a fighting squad, would become horribly apparent at Termoli, two hundred miles to the north, on the opposite side of Italy. Even granite-minded Reg Seekings could not recall the place without a shudder: "Termoli was terrible."

On September 8, six weeks after the removal of Mussolini as prime minister, the Italian government surrendered. Henceforth, the fight for Italy would be waged against German forces alone, and by the end of the month these were dug in along a line running east to southwest across Italy's calf. Capturing the port of Termoli, on the Adriatic coast, would open up the way for the US Fifth Army, under General Mark Clark, to march on Naples: "Success would turn the hinge-pin of the enemy line at a crucial point in the Allied advance."

At first Operation Devon went smoothly. The SRS landed at

Termoli with 207 men, accompanied by two units of commandos. The commandos would take the town, while the SRS secured the approaches. A twenty-strong squadron of SRS under a young lieutenant, John Tonkin, was ordered to press on through Termoli and capture the bridge over the Biferno River. Regular troops would then move in.

The German defenders of Termoli turned out to be few but tough, some wearing the arm flash that denoted veterans of the Cretan campaign. One group holed up in an outhouse until heavy mortar fire forced their surrender. A German major emerged dragging a horribly wounded comrade. He explained that the man was his brother and pleaded with the British forces to end his agony: a trooper stepped forward and put a bullet in the dying man's head. Tonkin's unit passed through the town and into the hills, but as they pushed on toward the bridge, Tonkin realized, too late, that they had overtaken the retreating Germans. A line of German paratroopers appeared on a ridge. A sharp skirmish ensued. "It was a perfect ambush [in] the middle of the German retreat." Tonkin ordered the unit to scatter: "Every man for himself." A few minutes later, Tonkin was surrounded and captured, with three of his men. Only six of the unit managed to dive into the undergrowth and scramble to safety.

By midday, Termoli was safely under British control, and the regular infantry was pouring into the town. The SRS set up billets in a deserted monastery.

At German headquarters in Rome, Field Marshal Albert Kesselring, commander of German forces in Italy, blew a gasket. The assault on Termoli had caught him, and its defenders, entirely by surprise. The 16th Panzer Division, part of the German reserve army in Naples, was ordered to move north and "recapture Termoli at all costs and drive the British into the sea."

For the SRS, the first indication of the German counterattack came at dawn on October 5, when two Tiger tanks were spotted on the high ground above the town. At least six more German tanks maneuvered into position, and by midday the counteroffensive was fully under way, a cascade of shot, shell, and machine-gun fire. Four Sherman tanks sent to repulse the attack were destroyed. The Allied perimeter line began to buckle. Under intense pressure some of the regular army units began to withdraw in disarray, to the disgust of the SRS, leaving them and the commandos "to hold for as long as possible until the army could regroup and attack in strength."

A local Italian fascist, sensing a reversal of the tide, opened fire from an upstairs window. Corporal "Jock" McDiarmid, a Scotsman with a reputation for raw violence, entered the house and re-emerged a few minutes later, grinning. "He'll fire that Beretta no more."

Paddy Mayne appeared quite unperturbed by the speed and effectiveness of the German retaliation. He wandered the perimeter, "encouraging, cajoling and instructing," and taking photographs. Bob Melot, the intelligence officer from North Africa, was wounded once again by flying shrapnel, but insisted there was "no time to wait for treatment and returned to the fighting." (Melot's transformation from Belgian cotton merchant to English officer was all but complete: he now displayed "all the qualities of a legendary English gentleman.")

The defense of Termoli was reinforced by a small team from Bill Stirling's 2SAS, which had already been bloodied on various operations elsewhere in Italy. This was the first time the two branches of the SAS had fought shoulder to shoulder. A line of Bren guns was set up on a ridge at the edge of town, and a steady stream of fire seemed to slow the German advance. But as mortar rounds began dropping into the town, and the Luftwaffe swooped low to bomb the harbor, the commander of the regular infantry urged Mayne to send "every available man to stem a fresh and powerful attack." A small flotilla of fishing boats was sequestered in case evacuation should become necessary. It seemed clear that Termoli was about to be overrun. Mayne ordered Johnny Wiseman, the former spectacles salesman, to load his troop into a truck in a side street and move as quickly as possible to shore up the left flank, where another counterattack was expected imminently.

As the seventeen men climbed into the truck, with seventy-eight grenades in their packs, a German spotter hidden in the town clock tower tapped out a message to the panzer gunners in the hills. The German shells landing on Termoli were being directed from within.

Reg Seekings fastened the tailgate on the truck. "Let's get moving," he said. Wiseman saw Mayne's messenger appear around the corner and jumped down from the front seat to see if there had been a change of plan. An Italian family, a man and wife with a teenage daughter and a son of about eight years old, watched the activity from the doorway of their home. They had taken in some washing for the troops, and had become friendly with the SAS soldiers.

Then the shells landed: five of them, targeted with precision by the spotter in the tower. What had been a scene of bustle seconds earlier dissolved into a series of hellish images.

The lorry and its human cargo seemed to disappear under a direct hit from a 105mm shell. Pieces of smoking human flesh lay scattered across the side street. "Here lay a man with half his head blown off, an arm lay there, and elsewhere an unrecognizable lump of flesh," one witness recalled. Bill Fraser sat dazed in the middle of the road, blood pouring from a shoulder wound. Reg Seekings had been standing by the tailboard. His tunic was splattered with blood and human pulp. By some fickle magic, he had lost only a fingernail. In the telegraph lines overhead hung a piece of Chris O'Dowd's skull. A torso was found blasted into the second floor of a building sixty yards away. The medical officer clambered among the dead and dying, with nothing he could do. One body lay still and burning in the street. Seekings decided, irrationally, that he must find a jug of water to put out the flames and headed for the nearest building. That was when he saw the little boy.

The Italian family lay in the doorway, the mother and father both dead, torn to pieces. The teenage girl had vanished. The boy lay amid the shambles, alive, but with his intestines spilling out.

"Suddenly he got up and ran around screaming," Seekings later recalled. "Terrible sight. There was absolutely no hope for him, and you couldn't let anybody suffer like that. So I caught him, and I shot him."

A few minutes later, Seekings spotted the boy's teenage sister, shell-shocked but uninjured, tending the wounded amid the rubble; she wore an expression of peculiar, dreadful calmness he would never forget.

The fight for Termoli raged for another twelve hours, but then the attack suddenly ceased and the panzers began to pull back. The German commander, Field Marshal Kesselring, later commended "the toughness of the enemy's defence," but no one was quite sure why the assault had ended so abruptly: "The Germans had ample forces and a heavy support to smash the light forces that were there [but they were] unable to do so. It seems as if their troops were without the morale to advance far (for fear of being cut off) and the attack was abandoned when the threat to the town was greatest." The target spotter was seen scrambling across the roofs away from the church tower and shot down with a Bren gun. His signaling equipment was discovered in the belfry.

The dead were buried in the monastery garden, overlooking the sea. Someone got a pole and knocked down the remains of smiling Chris O'Dowd from the overhead wire. It rained for a week, but still the stench of burning flesh hung over the town.

The top brass were delighted by the successful defense of the port. The SRS, the commandos, and some of the regular infantry had held up the entire 16th Panzer Division. The landing at Termoli had upset the balance of German forces by introducing a threat to the north of Rome, easing pressure on the US Fifth Army and forcing Kesselring to send his reserve panzers to the east coast in a fruitless attempt to dislodge the British forces. "I have never met a unit in which I had such confidence," General Miles Dempsey, the commander of XIII Corps, told the SRS.

The unit had lost twenty-one men killed, twenty-four wounded, and twenty-three taken prisoner. But there was another, invisible toll. The war in the desert had been harsh and dangerous, but exciting and memorable. After Termoli, most men just wanted to forget. The theatrical war pioneered by Stirling had given way to something far darker and dirtier. It took one sort of courage to attack an enemy airfield in the middle of the night, but quite another to kill a little boy with his insides blown out.

Mayne never spoke about Termoli. Some thought the horror had renewed his internal fury, manifested in an unnerving external calm. As Seekings observed: "He just grew colder and colder and colder."

Twenty-four-year-old Lieutenant John Tonkin, prisoner of war, was somewhat surprised to receive an invitation to dine with General Heidrich, the German divisional commander. A guard politely asked whether the British captive would prefer chicken or pork.

Cut off after advancing too far during the Termoli operation, Tonkin had been captured by the German 1st Parachute Regiment and taken to the divisional headquarters at Campobasso: there he was subjected to interrogation by a German officer with a limited grasp of English. "Goodbye," said the officer, by way of introduction, an opening gambit that gave Tonkin a fit of the giggles. "I defy anyone to carry on after that," he later wrote.

Born in Singapore to parents of French Huguenot descent, Tonkin had joined the SAS from the Royal Engineers during Stirling's last recruiting drive. He was a "classic English public schoolboy" in the eyes of his contemporaries, a keen sportsman, and an excellent shot. On the way to Italy he had taught the other ranks to play bridge. But there was more to Tonkin than the conventional tastes and attitudes of the English upper-middle class. Humor was an essential ingredient of the SAS ethos, but Tonkin's sense of the absurd went far beyond the banter and ragging of the mess. Englishmen use humor for all sorts of purposes: aggression, defense, as a cover for shyness or contempt. In Tonkin's case, it was both armor and weapon, a central constituent of his courage. "But who in war will not have his laugh amid the skulls?" wrote Churchill. Other men stiffen the sinews with exhortation, or comradeship, or through fear of exposing their own cowardice. Tonkin used jokes. He simply found the war very funny.

Escorted by two officers to the German officers' mess at Campobasso, Tonkin was struck by the extreme courtesy of his captors. He wondered if the "wings" on his uniform, denoting his status as a trained parachutist, explained the "excellent treatment" he seemed to be getting from the German 1st Parachute Regiment. He was offered a plate of delicious sandwiches, and chatted happily with some German doctors who spoke fluent English. Then came the dinner summons from General Heidrich. A decorated veteran of the First World War, a professional soldier, and a parachutist himself, Heidrich (not to be confused with war criminal Reinhard Heydrich) insisted on having a meal with every captured parachutist, whether or not they had arrived by parachute. The invitation, Tonkin wrote, "came as a bit of a shock as I wasn't at all sure of the etiquette between a junior British officer and a German general . . . Topics of conversation were obviously going to be tricky." But it was not the sort of invitation that could be declined. "So chicken it was."

The two men sat down and, far from being awkward, the conversation flowed comfortably for the next few hours, ranging over the full landscape of the war: the battles on the Eastern Front, the British withdrawal from Crete, and the landings at Termoli, which the German general described as "a beautiful stroke [that] had inconvenienced them a great deal and was perfectly timed." Cigars were produced. Like many old-fashioned German officers, Heidrich believed that in waging war against Britain Hitler had made a rash mistake. He told Tonkin that "it was madness for the two great western powers to be wasting their strength when in

50 years' time they would be fighting for their lives against the hordes of Asia." Tonkin could not help admiring the general with his old-world manners, though he sensed that the tubby, genial figure before him "could be very ruthless" if the occasion demanded. Heidrich handed Tonkin five more cigars as they parted and wished him good luck.

As Tonkin was being driven back to his cell at the Campobasso headquarters, the German major escorting him turned and said gravely, "It is my unfortunate duty to inform you that we have orders that we must obey, to hand you over to our special police. I must warn you that from now on the German army cannot guarantee your life."

Exactly a year earlier, Hitler had issued his infamous Commando Order, the *Kommandobefehl*, ordering the immediate summary execution, without trial, of any captured enemy soldiers found operating on Nazi-occupied soil:

> From now on all men operating against German troops in so-called Commando raids in Europe or in Africa, are to be annihilated to the last man. This is to be carried out whether they be soldiers in uniform, or saboteurs, with or without arms; and whether fighting or seeking to escape; and it is equally immaterial whether they come into action from ships and aircraft, or whether they land by parachute. Even if these individuals on discovery make obvious their intention of giving themselves up as prisoners, no pardon is on any account to be given.

Some German commanders, such as Rommel, had refused to relay this order to their troops, considering it dishonorable, illegal, and contrary to the accepted conventions of war (which it was). But as the conflict entered a more brutal and desperate phase, those rules had changed, and anyone operating behind enemy lines could expect no quarter. Captured commandos would no longer dine on chicken with their captors. Hitler had passed a death sentence on the SAS.

Tonkin realized that the major was sending him a coded warning. "When a man knows he is going to be shot, it sharpens his mind wonderfully," he later wrote. The next evening, he was taken by lorry up a frozen pass, northward into the hills. No one had said where they were going. He realized he "must escape, or die." When the lorry parked for a moment, Tonkin unclipped the canvas at the front, scrambled out and over the driver's cabin, and sprinted into the darkness. For the next two weeks he walked south until, by pure chance, he stumbled into an advancing British patrol. On October 18, barely a fortnight after his capture, Tonkin was back with the unit.

THE 2ND SAS REGIMENT had been formed by David Stirling's elder brother, but in many ways (and certainly in the eyes of Mayne's leathery veterans) it was a younger sibling, liable to be patronized and ignored. Bill Stirling is described in the SAS War Diary as a "man from the shadows," and compared to his younger brother he remains a distant and enigmatic figure, without David Stirling's eccentricity and flair. Yet they shared precisely the same approach to the SAS, insisting that it should operate behind the lines for strategic, not merely tactical, purposes. The best use of his regiment, Bill Stirling urged the bosses, was for it to be deployed in small units deep into Italy, where they would employ "any means available . . . for the disruption of Italian communications."

Initially based in Algeria, 2SAS was largely composed of new recruits with only a handful of L Detachment veterans. Their initial operations, a series of seaborne raids around the Mediterranean, were uniformly unsuccessful. At the end of May 1943 a raiding party attempted to land on Sardinia to seize a prisoner for intelligence purposes, and was forced to retire under heavy fire. A similar mission to the island of Pantelleria, west of Sicily, did result in the capture of a solitary sentry, but the poor man was dropped while the team were climbing back down the cliff and broke his neck. An attempt to destroy the radar station on Lampedusa failed to anticipate that the radar would pick up the raiding party on approach: the attackers were forced to withdraw as the garrison opened fire. An operation to parachute two teams into northern Sicily in July to attack a variety of targets also foundered when the unit's radio was damaged beyond use. One participant called it a "bloody balls-up."

There is some grim irony here. Mayne's raiding force, packed with veterans trained in the techniques of small-force penetration, was being used in a traditional commando role. But 2SAS, brave men with less experience behind the lines who might have been better employed as straightforward commandos, were being used as Stirling intended and were carrying out strategic raids, but with little impact.

The opportunity to demonstrate the mettle of 2SAS came in early September with Operation Speedwell, a plan to attack rail links across northern Italy in order to slow the German forces heading south to repel the Allied invaders. One of the most color-ful members of the team was Lieutenant Anthony Greville-Bell, an upper-class former tank commander with a swaggering, swash-buckling air and a tungsten constitution. The team parachuted into the Apennines on the evening of September 7, then split into smaller groups in order to attack different sections of the northern Italian rail network.

Greville-Bell broke two ribs after landing in a tree, and could find no trace of his commanding officer. He later recalled the "unpleasant grating noise" that came from his chest when he walked. Five days later, tanked up on morphine, he and two other men blew a train off the rails inside a tunnel on a stretch of the Bologna-to-Florence line. The feat was repeated twice more.

Despite frostbite, dysentery, intense hunger, and a 10,000-lira bounty on their heads put up by the Germans in active pursuit of the saboteurs, Greville-Bell and his two companions continued south through the mountains, occasionally cadging food and shelter from friendly local peasants. In Fiesole, outside Florence, the fugitives, now close to starvation, threw themselves on the mercy of a local Italian noble who was said to have been critical of Mussolini and might therefore prove sympathetic: the aristocratic Italian turned out to be married to an Englishwoman whose sister had been in the Pony Club with Greville-Bell back in Devon. They were sheltered "royally" for three days, before setting off south once more. Having linked up with a group of partisans and derailed another train near Incisa, the party finally reached the British advance line on November 14, after seventy-three days on the run. Greville-Bell had lost forty pounds.

The fate of another group of 2SAS men was very different. Sergeant Bill Foster and Corporal James Shortall landed safely and set out to attack a section of railway between Genoa and La Spezia. They never reached it. On September 25, they were captured by German troops and taken to the nearest infantry headquarters and interrogated. Both refused to reveal the name of their unit or the purpose of their mission. They were then locked in the local Italian police station. Three days later, the German military police brought the two prisoners back to headquarters, where a firing squad of ten was assembled "to shoot two men . . . Englishmen who had landed by parachute." The prisoners were driven to a disused pottery factory and marched to a rise above an old loading track, where stood a lone tree. A statement was read out proclaiming that the two men had been condemned to death for sabotage, "by order of the Führer."

Foster was tied to the tree. He refused to be blindfolded, but asked for a priest. "We have no time for that," he was told. With Shortall standing just a few feet away, the execution squad aimed and fired. One of the German witnesses recalled Shortall's "impassive attitude" as Foster's body was dragged away. Shortall was shot without his uttering another word. As he lay on the ground, a German officer administered a final bullet to the head with his revolver. The men were buried in an unmarked grave in the factory grounds. Two days later, two more men from 2SAS were executed, just twenty-four hours after being captured.

Hitler's revenge on the SAS had begun in earnest.

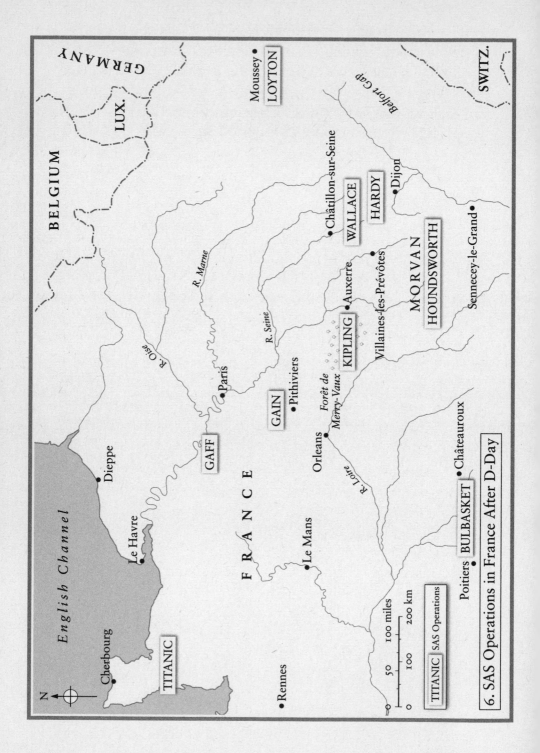

English Channel

Cherbourg

TITANIC

N

Dieppe

Le Havre

GERMANY

BELGIUM

LUX.

Moussey

LOYTON

R. Marne

R. Oise

Paris

R. Seine

Châtillon-sur-Seine

WALLACE

Belfort Gap

HARDY

Dijon

SWITZ.

GAFF

GAIN

Pithiviers

Forêt de
Merry-Vaux

KIPLING

Auxerre

Villaines-les-Prévôtes

MORVAN

HOUNDSWORTH

Sennecey-le-Grand

Orleans

R. Loire

F R A N C E

Le Mans

Rennes

BULBASKET

Poitiers

Châteauroux

100 miles

200 km

50

100

0

TITANIC   SAS Operations

6. SAS Operations in France After D-Day

Chapter 16

BULBASKET

On June 1, 1944, five days before D-Day, John Tonkin was summoned to a briefing at General Dwight Eisenhower's headquarters in London. Eight months earlier the SAS officer had escaped from German captivity after his bizarrely civilized chicken dinner with a senior German general. Now promoted to captain, Tonkin was told that he and his squadron from 1SAS would be parachuting into the west of France on D-Day on an operation code-named Bulbasket. Once the invasion was under way, German troops stationed in the south would undoubtedly begin heading north toward Normandy to repel the Allied invaders. Tonkin's task was to delay those reinforcements in any way he could.

The previous six months, leading up to the great invasion of Europe, had seen many changes to the SAS: the regiment had regained a name, lost its distinctive beret and a commanding officer, and attracted a huge influx of new recruits. The Special Raiding Squadron reverted to its original name, 1SAS. Along with 2SAS, two French SAS regiments, a Belgian contingent, and a signals squadron, the total strength of the new SAS Brigade swelled to a mighty 2,500 men. The brigade came under the command of a regular gunner, Brigadier Roderick McLeod, considered by some to be "out of his depth with SAS officers and men."

The Special Boat Squadron, under Jellicoe, had meanwhile achieved mixed success harassing Axis forces on the islands of the

Mediterranean. The first SBS operation on German-held Crete in June 1943 had landed a force of thirty soldiers by submarine, which then marched sixty miles over rugged terrain and successfully destroyed fuel dumps and aircraft. But another SBS operation on Sardinia a week later ended in disaster when the raiders were betrayed to the Italians by their interpreter.

There were many familiar faces in the ranks of 1SAS: Bill Fraser, recovered from his wound at Termoli, commanded a squadron; Seekings was reunited with Cooper, now a newly minted lieutenant; Mike Sadler, the skilled desert navigator, rejoined 1SAS as an intelligence officer, but not before touring the United States as a military poster boy to raise money for war bonds. 1SAS also recruited its first military chaplain, the Rev. Fraser McLuskey.

As part of the 21st Army Group—the British formation assigned to Operation Overlord, the Allied invasion of Europe in the west—SAS soldiers were required from 1944 onward to wear the conventional red beret of airborne troops. Paddy Mayne ignored this constraint and continued to sport the beige one.

1SAS had returned to Britain early in the new year of 1944. Each of the men was given a month's leave, a travel voucher, and £100. Some rushed off to see wives and sweethearts. Some returned to their families. Some rushed to the nearest pub. Paddy Mayne disappeared. Again, no one was quite sure where he had gone. By February, the men were encamped in two disused lace mills at Darvel, a village in East Ayrshire, undergoing a new round of grueling training in the damp surrounding hills. The mood was convivial, agitated, and anticipatory. The invasion of Fortress Europe was at hand, and everyone knew it. Mayne led a new recruitment drive. The Ulsterman exhibited no nerves whatever during military action, but addressing an audience reduced him to squeaky-voiced terror. Even so, his descriptions of SAS life prompted dozens of volunteers. At least 130 new men were drawn from the British Resistance Organization's Auxiliaries, a unit originally intended to resist the Nazi invasion of Britain that never materialized. Now they would be helping to invade Nazi-occupied Europe. While the troops continued training in Ayrshire—in explosives, parachuting, firearms, and unarmed combat—back in London the battle over how best to deploy the SAS erupted once more, and claimed a prominent casualty. When Bill Stirling discovered that the high command intended to drop SAS units thirty-six hours ahead of the main invasion, to act as a barrier of shock troops between the fighting front and the German reserves, he hit the roof: the SAS would be placed in maximum danger for minimal strategic advantage. Most SAS officers agreed, believing that the regiment should operate deep behind the front lines, not on them.

Bill Stirling penned a blistering letter to Supreme Headquarters Allied Expeditionary Force (SHAEF), explaining exactly how stupid this idea was (among the traits shared by the Stirling brothers was a talent for extreme epistolary rudeness). Refusing to retract his criticisms, he resigned, to be replaced as commander of 2SAS by his deputy, Major Brian Franks. David Stirling believed that his brother had saved the SAS: "He lost his battle, but the regiment won theirs." It had been a brave act, supported by many of the men, but it signaled the end of the Stirling brothers' leadership of the SAS.

Like many dramatic gestures, Bill Stirling's resignation proved premature, since his concerns were eventually given due consideration: the plan for deployment of the SAS was amended to something far closer to the role envisaged by the Stirling brothers. Only five three-man teams would be dropped immediately beyond the Normandy beaches on the eve of D-Day, to sow confusion by imitating a much larger paratroop force—an operation code-named Titanic. A large French force would be deployed in Brittany, again to confuse the Germans about Allied intentions. But the bulk of the SAS fighting units would be dropped far behind the lines after D-Day, to destroy communications, impede the movement of reinforcements, train up local resistance fighters, spot targets for Allied bombers, and generally foment havoc.

Two squadrons of 1SAS would be sent deep into France on D-Day itself: one, under Bill Fraser, would parachute in near Dijon;

the other, commanded by John Tonkin, would land farther west, near Poitiers. The two missions were code-named Houndsworth and Bulbasket, ideally meaningless names, although the latter may have derived from Tonkin's nickname "Bullshit Basket," bestowed on account of his penchant for amusing tall stories. Operation Overlord, the invasion of France, depended on establishing a secure foothold in Normandy, swiftly and with as little warning as possible. If the Germans were able to deploy reinforcements with sufficient speed and efficiency, the invaders might, as Hitler demanded, be hurled "back into the sea." Both Houndsworth and Bulbasket would aim to sabotage rail links, ambush convoys, and above all slow down the northward progress of the formidable 2nd SS Panzer Division—known as Das Reich, a brutally battle-hardened unit comprising twenty thousand men and ninety-nine heavy and sixty-four lighter tanks—as it rumbled toward the Normandy beachheads.

The days leading up to the jump were spent attending tutorials given by the Special Operations Executive (SOE), the secret unit formed by Churchill to "set Europe ablaze" by conducting sabotage, espionage, and resistance in countries under Nazi occupation. Tonkin and Fraser would be liaising on the ground with SOE agents, and the complex constellation of local partisan groups, collectively known as the "maquis" (derived from the dense shrubland of the Mediterranean, which was considered ideal for guerrilla fighting). One veteran agent warned Tonkin not to put too much faith in the French resistance, and to remember "the mutual ambition and jealousy that dog them." Tonkin spent the evening before D-Day doing jigsaw puzzles with Violette Szabo, the SOE agent whose subsequent actions would mark a high point of wartime heroism. The young agent knew what the stakes were: Hitler's infamous Commando Order, requiring the summary execution of any soldier found behind the lines whether in or out of uniform, meant that the "winning" part of the SAS motto now required an even greater degree of "daring." One French briefing officer was particularly blunt about the consequences: "Most German commanders would obey this order. And as to the SS, it didn't matter as they would have shot you even before Hitler's order . . . Don't get captured and if you're cornered, go down fighting."

Accompanied by Lieutenant Richard Crisp, Tonkin jumped out of a Halifax bomber shortly after 1:00 a.m. on June 6, 1944, floated gently down through bright moonlight, and made a perfect landing in the Brenne Marshes, between Poitiers and Châteauroux. "I doubt if I'd have broken an egg if I'd landed on it," wrote Tonkin, having lost much of his kit but none of his sense of humor. He attached a message to the foot of the homing pigeon he had carried to France in a rucksack—still one of the most reliable forms of communication in war—and then launched the bird "with more force than skill, for it circled twice and made straight for the nearest big tree, fifty yards away. I believe it may still be there."

Tonkin's task was to hide out in the woods, gather his force of around forty men, make contact with the SOE spy network and the local maquis, and then set about impeding the passage of German troops moving north, by any and every means possible—a mission far more challenging than it sounds. Some in SOE considered the SAS troops a liability, conspicuous in their uniforms and apt to "draw danger not only on themselves but on all the maquis in the region." Tonkin's force was not small enough to be easily concealed from local eyes, but not big enough to mount any serious and long-term impediment to the German advance. Roadblocks and small arms would not stop the mighty Das Reich tanks. "It was ridiculous to think that scattered parties of parachutists could do anything much to delay the arrival of panzer divisions," said one gloomy officer. Ridiculously difficult, perhaps—but not impossible.

Soon after dawn, a young maquisard arrived at the drop zone, carrying a Sten gun, the submachine gun much favored by resistance groups. A stilted exchange of passwords took place.

"Is there a house in the woods?" asked Tonkin, in wobbly French.

"Yes, but it is not very good," said Agent "Samuel," whose fantastical real name was Major René Amédée Louis Pierre Maingard de la Ville-ès-Offrans, an aristocratic twenty-five-year-old Mauritian and one of the pillars of SOE's French section.

Over the ensuing days, as Tonkin waited for the rest of his force to be dropped into the Vienne, in west-central France, the young French spy painstakingly explained the state of the local resistance. The region contained more than seven thousand maquis. These were enthusiastic and brave, but most were woefully underequipped and largely untrained. The situation was further complicated by the bitter antipathy between the communist and the Gaullist groups, who had violently clashing political agendas. The Vienne also contained its share of Nazi collaborators. Tonkin decided to put his trust in the maquis and rely on them to provide protection and support, and to keep a lookout for German forces: a risky strategy, but the only one available. Tonkin sent back an "enthusiastic message re relations with populace."

Having first set up camp in a wood near Pouillac, Tonkin's squadron settled down to await the airdrop of supplies, including four jeeps—to be mounted with Vickers guns in the approved desert manner.

French rural gossip is among the most contagious in the world, and the arrival of a large contingent of British soldiers did not stay secret for long. Just three days later, a visitor arrived in the woods: "A small, very frightened, and therefore very courageous French civilian." A railway employee, this minuscule hero brought the military equivalent of gold dust: in the railway siding southwest of Châtellerault he had spotted eleven petrol trains, loaded, guarded, and camouflaged. Petrol was an Allied priority target. Moving the Das Reich Division from Montauban to Normandy would require an astonishing 100,000 gallons of petrol; starved of fuel the panzers' advance could be slowed for days. While Tonkin set about calling in an airstrike, a team cut the railway south of Poitiers, immobilizing some one hundred trains for the next three days. At 8:00 p.m. on June 12, six hours after Tonkin had radioed in the coordinates, twenty-four Mosquito bombers swooped low over the sidings at Châtellerault, spraying the area with 20mm cannon fire and dropping ten tons of bombs. The resulting petrol explosion soared eight thousand feet into the sky, and the ensuing fire covered an area of six thousand square feet. From their forest hideout Tonkin and his men watched the livid glow in the sky. Their satisfaction would have been even greater had they known that two days earlier a battalion of the Das Reich Division had entered the village of Oradour-sur-Glane and, in reprisal for the sniper killing of a German company commander, rounded up and murdered 642 of its inhabitants, including more than 200 children.

On June 25, a message arrived by carrier pigeon in the military lofts and was swiftly conveyed to London: "Tonkin reports being chased from position by Germans who are looking for them." That day, the SAS team moved camp to a new site in the forest about a mile from the town of Verrières. The place was heavily wooded, with plentiful water from a stream, but it was barely fifteen miles from the nearest German troops stationed at Poitiers. A last-minute decision at headquarters had led to small units of SAS men being dropped to attack other targets, some a considerable distance from Verrières, before making their own way to the rendezvous point. It would take three weeks for the full complement of Bulbasket forces to gather at Tonkin's base camp.

Most military action involves extended periods of boredom and inactivity, interspersed with brief moments of extreme violence. The life of the SAS behind the lines was no different. The summer was hot and humid, and for much of the time the men were sedentary. In some ways, the atmosphere recalled the desert war, with the SAS hidden deep in enemy-held territory, sailing out from time to time to attack targets of opportunity. But in other respects life in the woods was very different. Several maquisards lived permanently in the camp alongside the SAS soldiers; sometimes dozens might arrive for training, and then disappear again. Among the British troops there was considerable admiration for the French resistance fighters, but also some suspicion. The SAS had never fought alongside civilians before: the maquisards were good company, dedicated to the liberation of France, but "singularly ill-disciplined" in Tonkin's view, militarily incompetent and savage toward anyone suspected of disloyalty. "The possibility of Gestapo agents was always a great source of worry to us," said Tonkin. One evening a girl was dragged into the camp, accused of fraternizing with the Germans. To the British, she seemed oblivious of having done anything wrong, and spent the evenings sewing shirts for the SAS men out of parachute silk. After a few days she and another alleged collaborator were marched to the edge of the forest by the maquisards. The girl asked that her ring be given to a friend in the village. Then she was shot and buried in an unmarked grave. The SAS men were hardly squeamish types, yet some were deeply shocked.

Tonkin grew worried, overworked by the administrative demands of running a substantial military camp inside enemy-held territory. From time to time, small parties sallied out to attack bridges and rail lines and to ambush convoys. As a result, the Germans appeared to be sticking to the main roads, but local intelligence indicated that a full-scale hunt for the British saboteurs was under way. Tonkin's messages to headquarters reflected his mounting anxiety: "lousy with enemy"; "troop movements through the area day and night"; "situation serious 400 Germans looking for [us]"; "area unhealthy." Parties were sent out to try to find a more isolated and obscure place to hide. The men were becoming jaded, incautious, lusty, and thirsty. "The local wine and cider is stronger than one thinks," Tonkin noted. On operations, passing through the friendly local villages, the soldiers' minds were not fully on the job in hand. "The girls looked very nice," wrote Tonkin. "There was a general tendency to relax. The highest discipline must be maintained to prevent them wandering away from camp." Two men even headed into Verrières and drank a glass of wine at the village café. Others slipped away to scrounge eggs, cheese, and other foodstuffs from local farms. Tonkin would later be criticized for security lapses, and for failing to understand

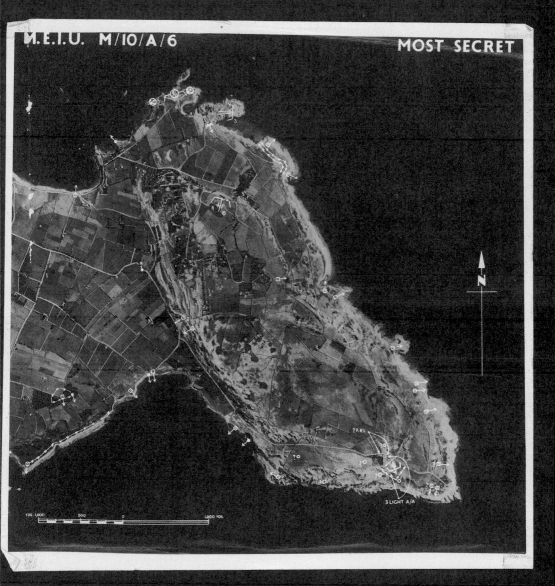

Aerial reconnaissance photograph of Capo Murro di Porco,
target of the unit's first landing in Sicily,
a few hours ahead of the invasion on July 10, 1943.

TOP: Bill Stirling instructing
trainee commandos outside Keir,
the family home in Scotland.

BOTTOM LEFT: John Tonkin and
Paddy Mayne relaxing during
the Italian campaign.

Bill Stirling (right), elder
brother of David (left),
the founder and first commander
of 2SAS.

ABOVE: Jock McDiarmid, a Scotsman with a reputation for raw violence, whose actions in Italy and France blurred the distinction between rough justice and cold-blooded killing.

John Tonkin, the young officer captured at Termoli who subsequently escaped after enjoying dinner with the German general in command.

TOP: Reconnaissance photographs of Termoli taken shortly before Paddy Mayne's men stormed and took the town, "the hinge-pin of the enemy line."

BOTTOM: Tragedy in Termoli. The chaotic and bloody aftermath of a direct hit by German shells on a truck carrying seventeen men.

TOP SECRET

APPENDIX 'C' to HQ AirTps/TS/2500/40/G(L)
dated 8 September, 1944

Map of France identifying by code name
the numerous SAS operations
behind enemy lines after D-Day.

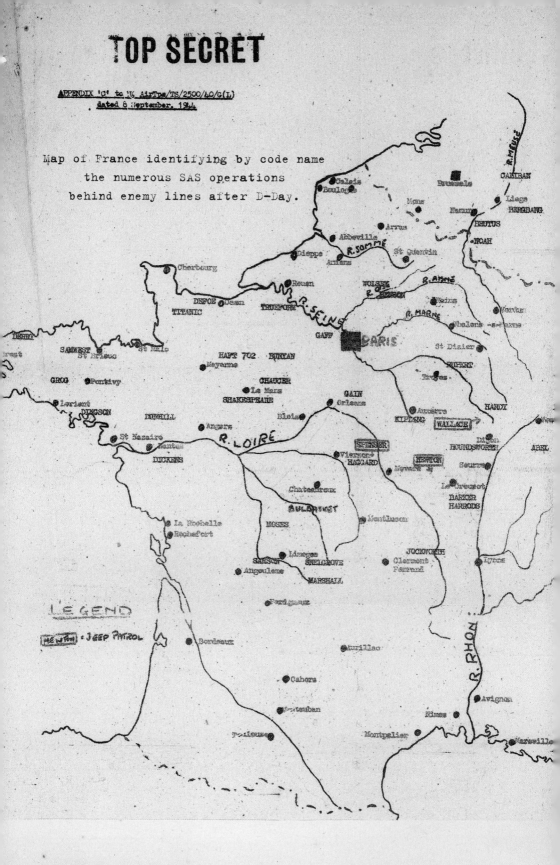

Roy Farran, alias "Paddy McGinty," the most celebrated officer in 2SAS: inspiring, unconventional, and entirely ruthless.

OPPOSITE: Operation Tombola. Sketch map for the assault on the Villa Rossi and Villa Calvi, headquarters of the German LI Corps at Albinea.

"Battaglione McGinty." Seated at center is the Italian woman partisan known as "Noris": "As brave and dangerous as a tigress and completely devoted to the British company."

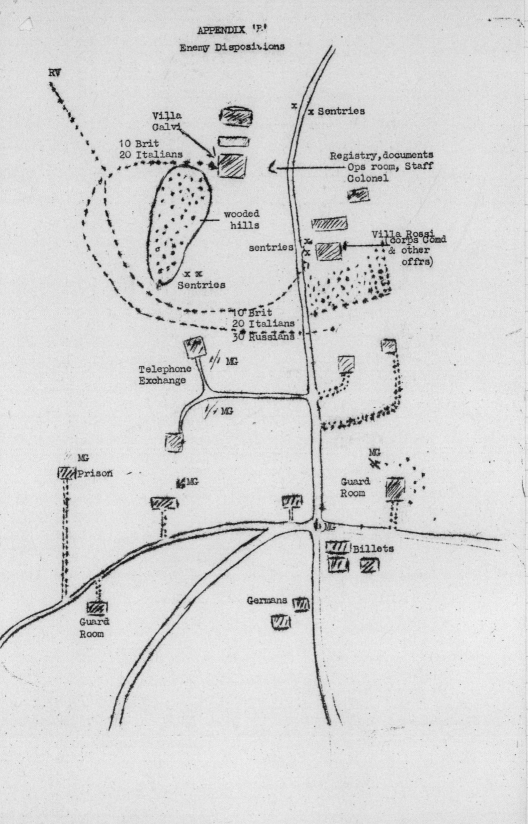

APPENDIX 'F.'

Enemy Dispositions

RV

Villa
Calvi

10 Brit
20 Italians

x   x Sentries

Registry, documents
Ops room, Staff
Colonel

wooded
hills

Villa Rossi
(Corps Comd
& other
offrs)

sentries

x
x

x x
Sentries

10 Brit
20 Italians
30 Russians

Telephone
Exchange

MG

MG

MG
Prison

MG

MG

Guard
Room

MG

MG

Billets

Guard
Room

Germans

Italian partisans in the foothills of the Apennines.

A photograph from the war diary of Italian soldiers
taken prisoner: "Fawning, friendly, smiling little
creatures," wrote one SAS officer.

TAC   HEADQUARTERS,

21 ARMY GROUP.

B.L.A.

7th September, 1944.

     I should like to thank you and the officers and men of First SAS very much indeed for your message of congratulations on my promotion. It is most kind of you all, and I appreciate your thought.

I would like to take this opportunity to tell you what splendid work you have all done.

B. L. Montgomery
Field-Marshal

The Commanding Officer,
First S.A.S.,
B.L.A.

Letter from Montgomery to the SAS, after
his promotion to field marshal.

The SAS under fire in Germany: while the two men at left are
taking cover under the jeep, Paddy Mayne, leaning up against a tree
with his back to the camera, appears to be reading a book.

ABOVE: Lincoln
Delmar Bundy,
the Arizona
cowboy turned
fighter pilot who
was shot down
over France and
then unofficially
enrolled in
the SAS.

Bill Fraser,
at the forefront
of battle in
Africa, Italy,
and France,
thrice wounded
and highly
decorated, but
also tortured by
"inner demons."

ABOVE:
Colditz
Castle, POW
camp. David
Stirling,
one of
its least
cooperative
inmates,
called it
"the Third
Reich's
most closely
guarded
hostelry."

German boy soldiers conscripted to fight in a
doomed cause in the grim final chapter of the war.

TOP: Liberation. SAS soldiers festooned with bouquets
by French villagers as they pressed east.

BOTTOM: Colonel Paddy Mayne, commander of 1SAS, decorated war hero
and a far cry from the bearded, volatile ruffian of the desert war.

Bergen–Belsen
concentration
camp, discovered
by SAS troops
in April 1945;
SS guards being
forced to bury
the dead in
mass graves.

Camp commandant Josef Kramer and Irma Grese,
the warden for women prisoners, known as the
"Beast of Belsen" and the "Beauty of Belsen."

Kenneth Seymour, the young signaler injured and captured in the Vosges Mountains, whose claims to heroism were hotly disputed by his comrades.

"LY HER...

"COUNTRY WANT PEACE"

S RUSSIA'S

Called In Defence Of Gestapo Chief

SERGEANT KENNETH SEYMOUR, of Sutton, Surrey, sole survivor of 34 parachutists captured by special German detachments in the Vosges in 1944, gave evidence at the War Crimes Trial at Wuppertal yesterday on behalf of Wilhelm Schneider, one of four Gestapo chiefs accused of responsibility for the murder of his comrades.

British authorities, at the request of one of the defendants, agreed to summon Seymour as a witness.

First of the party to land, Seymour broke his ankle and was captured. The others, taken later, were shot except one who committed suicide to keep parachute landing secrets.

HEATH: NIGHT ROAD CHECK

"HERALD" REPORTER

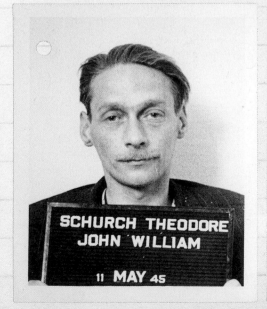

Theodore Schurch, former London accountant and secret fascist spy: the only British soldier executed for treachery in the Second World War.

SCHURCH THEODORE JOHN WILLIAM
11 MAY 45

SCHURCH THEODORE JOHN WILLIAM
11 MAY 45

TOP LEFT: Paddy Mayne's
sand-colored beret.

TOP RIGHT: Map on parachute silk.

CENTER RIGHT: SAS "operational
wings," worn by trained parachutists.

BOTTOM LEFT: SAS cap badge, featuring the flaming sword of
Excalibur and motto, "Who Dares Wins."

BOTTOM RIGHT: Bagnold's sun compass, essential for desert
navigation.

the complex local loyalties. But he had one attribute that arguably outweighed any failings: he knew how to keep up the spirits of his troops, when most men ought, by any objective standard, to have been paralyzed with fear.

By the end of June, the Verrières camp had expanded to include some forty SAS men, a dozen French resistance fighters, and a single American cowboy.

Lincoln Delmar Bundy was a rancher from the strip of Arizona on the edge of the Grand Canyon. The seventh of fourteen children, Bundy had grown up in Cactus Flat, attended school until the age of fourteen, and always planned, insofar as he troubled to think about the future at all, to become a cowboy like his grandfather, father, and brothers. A "dancing-eyed, square shouldered boy," in 1942, at the age of twenty-four, Bundy signed up for war, left Arizona for the first time in his life, and began training as a pilot in the US Army Air Corps at Napier Field, Alabama.

Soon after daybreak on June 10, Second Lieutenant Lincoln Bundy of the 486th Fighter Squadron took off in his P-51 Mustang, nicknamed "Rustler," from the airfield at Bodney in Norfolk, crossed the Channel, and headed deep into France. His task was to strike railways, junctions, bridges, airfields, crossroads, convoys, and any other targets that might slow the German advance to the front. Shortly before 10:00 a.m. he diverted from the rest of his formation and swooped down to strafe a convoy of German trucks, destroying one of them. Minutes later, his Mustang was hit by antiaircraft fire, and Bundy baled out, parachuting to earth beside a small wood. For the next four days, he was sheltered by the local villagers, before announcing that he intended to head south, on foot. His plan, inasmuch as he had one, was to make for neutral Spain and then somehow get back to England. After walking for nearly two weeks, living off the land and whatever he could steal or beg from friendly farmers, he encountered a group of maquis near the town of Verrières. On July 1, a ragged figure, footsore, hungry, and cheerful, was led into Tonkin's forest camp.

"Captain, I see no reason why the lack of an aircraft should stop me from fighting," Bundy told Tonkin. The young American was immediately and unofficially enrolled in the SAS.

The day after Lincoln Bundy joined the SAS troop, Tonkin ordered his men to shift camp. They packed up and set off for a new site in the nearby Bois des Cartes, taking the American with them. But within twenty-four hours they were back in Verrières again, having discovered that the new site lacked sufficient water to maintain such a large group. The same evening Tonkin set out on yet another reconnaissance expedition in search of a safer place to hide his men. He even considered dispersing the unit. His anxieties redoubled when two NCOs, Sergeant Eccles and Corporal Bateman, failed to return from a sabotage mission. If they had been captured, as seemed likely, they would be undergoing "hard interrogation," and it was only a matter of days or hours before they revealed the whereabouts of the camp. That the local maquis had known where to bring the downed American pilot was proof enough that the camp's location was common knowledge. According to one account, there was even some suspicion that the newest addition to the force might be an enemy agent, although it seems highly unlikely that the Germans would have sent an American cowboy to infiltrate the SAS when numerous French collaborators were available for the job. Tonkin radioed London for confirmation of the newcomer's identity, but received no reply.

In any case, the Germans had no need to spy on the camp: they knew exactly where it was.

At first light, the mortar shells came crashing through the forest canopy. Most of the men were still dozing in their sleeping bags when the air exploded. In the darkness, some four hundred German troops had stealthily taken up position around the woods: men of the SS Panzer Grenadiers, the SD (the intelligence agency of the SS), and a bicycle reconnaissance squadron engaged in antipartisan operations. Tonkin ran to the edge of the wood and saw a line of gray-uniformed soldiers advancing along the hedgerows, less than two hundred yards away. The heaviest weapons available to the SAS squadron were the Vickers guns mounted on the jeeps, but trying to fight their way out would have been tantamount to suicide. Tonkin planted a time pencil in the explosives cache and ordered the men to scatter. For the second time in a year he shouted: "It's every man for himself." Most of the Bulbasket troop, Lincoln Bundy among them, fled down the slope into the valley. Tonkin and a handful of others headed west, uphill, deeper into the woods. Then, realizing he had left behind his wireless and codebook, Tonkin doubled back alone, only to discover that the Germans were already ransacking the camp. He hid behind a rock. Bursts of gunfire could be heard from different parts of the wood: nine captured French resistance fighters were murdered on the spot. The explosives bin detonated with a roar. In the confusion, Tonkin crawled away through the undergrowth.

The men who had run into the valley were all captured. One SAS lieutenant, badly wounded, was beaten to death by a German rifle butt. Lieutenant Crisp was shot in the leg. In total, twenty-eight captive SAS men and the American pilot were bound, loaded on, trucks and driven to Poitiers.

A flurry of alarming wireless messages reached London from the various informants scattered through the region. "Tonkin attacked this morning Foret de Verriers [*sic*] 100 Maquis dispatched to assist him . . . unconfirmed Tonkin captured wounded . . . Reliable report from wine merchant 20 or 30 prisoners . . . Tonkin betrayed and surrounded by 400 Jerry, including SS and 2 field guns, ordered base to scatter, planted time pencils in explosives result 20 Boche dead, many wounded." Some of the British survivors believed they had been betrayed by a spy, but German sources suggest that the two captured SAS men, Eccles and Bateman, had been broken under interrogation by the SD three days before the attack and revealed the camp's location. The local SOE team, code-named Hugh, sent in the most laconic, but probably the most accurate, verdict: "Sorry about SAS, but not surprised. Too close to Poitiers."

Only eight men managed to evade capture, and they were eventually reunited at the fallback rendezvous, a farm east of Verrières

known as La Rocherie. "Thank God you got through," Tonkin
said, as he greeted the only other surviving officer. The rest of the
squadron, he reported, had been "rounded up and taken to Poitiers
for interrogation."

The irrepressible Tonkin fought on. "Tonkin and men in good
spirits," the official Bulbasket log recorded. Now a much leaner
group, far easier to conceal, they acted as radio liaison between
the local French resistance forces and SHAEF HQ in Britain. On
July 14, perhaps with revenge in mind, Tonkin called in an airstrike on the barracks of the SS Panzer Grenadiers who had taken
part in the attack on the camp at Verrières. Up to 150 enemy troops
were reportedly killed, and some fifty vehicles destroyed, in what
may have been the first operational use of napalm in the war. On
August 1, Tonkin reported a pitched battle between 1,800 Germans and 1,000 French fighters: "Maquis request immediate air
support cannot hold out much longer." RAF Mosquitoes attacked
once more, successfully dispersing the German troops.

The twenty-nine men captured in the attack on the Bulbasket
camp were driven to the stone-built military prison in Poitiers,
where they joined Eccles and Bateman. Held in groups of eight,
they were interrogated, one by one, but not ill treated. Three of
the most seriously injured captives were transferred to the Hôtel
de Dieu hospital, and held there under close guard.

In the German LXXX Corps headquarters in Poitiers, a particularly grim game of pass-the-buck was under way. Among the
Wehrmacht officers, there was little appetite for fulfilling Hitler's Commando Order to execute any and all captured SAS men.
In theory, carrying out the *Kommandobefehl* should have been the
responsibility of the SS security police, but the SS claimed they
lacked the men to do the job. The commander of the corps, General Gallenkamp, was out of town, perhaps deliberately, inspecting
troops on the Atlantic coast. That left his chief of staff, Colonel
Herbert Köstlin, and an intelligence officer, Dr. Erich Schönig,
to decide the fate of the captives. An attempt to palm them off on
the Luftwaffe as airborne troops failed; a military judge declined

to get involved, saying the Commando Order did not require any legal process; the pressure increased when an official German news report announced that the captured enemy commandos had already been liquidated. Köstlin and Schönig were in a bind: failure to comply with Hitler's express order could easily mean their own heads would be next on the block. And so they did what craven bosses always do when faced with an unpleasant task: they shoveled responsibility onto someone further down the chain of command.

Oberleutnant Vogt, a former clergyman who had led the bicycle troops in the Bulbasket assault, was detailed to carry out the execution. A little over a week earlier, Vogt and his men had been ambushed by the maquis in Saint-Sauvant Forest, some twenty miles south of Poitiers. Twenty-seven Germans and more than thirty Frenchmen had died in the ensuing battle. Apparently with symbolic reprisal in mind, Vogt chose Saint-Sauvant as the execution spot. On the evening of July 6, three long pits were dug beside the track running through the forest. The next morning, trucks carrying the twenty-seven SAS men and the American pilot drew up in the predawn darkness. Each prisoner, with hands bound, was accompanied by two German soldiers of Vogt's unit, and lined up in front of the pits. Richard Crisp was called out of the line, and limped forward to hear an interpreter read out the execution order.

A long burst of machine-gun fire was followed by a series of single shots. Schönig later reported that "the parachutists died in an exemplary, brave and calm manner." The three men still in the military hospital, too badly injured to be brought before the firing squad, were denied even the dignity of facing death with foreknowledge: six days after the executions at Saint-Sauvant, lying in their hospital beds, they were each injected with a lethal dose of morphine.

Lincoln Bundy was listed as "missing in action." The sum of $397.21 was sent by the air corps to his mother in Cactus Flat, along with two shirts, two pairs of trousers, a tie, and a carton of belongings, "in order that you may safely keep it on behalf of the owner pending his return."

In the village of Saint-Sauvant, word of the murders in the forest quickly spread.

On August 6, two RAF Hudsons touched down on a makeshift landing strip created by Tonkin and his men with "a jeep, a harrow and rake," and the help of three downed American pilots. The planes took off, bumpily, a few minutes later, with a team of "happy SAS and three delirious Americans."

Operation Bulbasket had succeeded in slowing down the advance of the panzers; it had inflicted extensive damage on rail and road networks, killed and injured large numbers of enemy troops, and substantially boosted the local French resistance. But at a terrible price. Quite how high that cost had been was hinted at in one of the last wireless messages sent to Tonkin: "Cases are preparing against war criminals [with a] mounting mass of evidence . . . forward to England by any secured means the names of enemy units and their responsible commanders who are guilty of atrocities."

Chapter 17

HOUNDSWORTH

THE MASSIF DE MORVAN, WEST OF DIJON, IS WILD COUNtry: six thousand square miles of densely forested hills, remote, rugged, and sparsely populated. On the wine-making plains of Burgundy below run the major roads and railways linking Paris and Lyons, but the high Morvan is traversed only by a few forestry tracks and small roads. The villages are few and far apart, the people resilient and independent-minded. It is good country for hunting, and hiding, and fighting unconventional war.

In the early hours of June 6, 1944, nineteen men parachuted into the Morvan, the advance reconnaissance party for Operation Houndsworth, the companion mission to Bulbasket. They were led by Major Bill Fraser, as much of an enigma as he had been in the desert: aloof, probably homosexual, indestructible, unknowable. While Fraser led one stick of parachutists, the other was commanded by another familiar figure, newly minted lieutenant Johnny Cooper. Here, too, was Reg Seekings, promoted to staff sergeant major, as blunt and belligerent as ever. Their promotions, and the change in their relative ranks, seem to have had no impact whatever on their friendship. Cooper treated Seekings like a fellow officer; Seekings treated his commander as if he was still an NCO.

The Morvan, with its thick woods and steep gullies, is a difficult place to parachute into at any time; high wind, dense cloud, and rain on June 6 made it even harder. "It was a black, miserable night," Cooper recalled. Seekings grumbled, in no particular order, about the weather, the pilot, and the kit bag he now had to jump with, attached to an ankle by a twelve-foot rope, which tended to get tangled. The pilot was unable to locate the drop zone through the clouds, so the parachutists were dropped blind, with orders to assemble at the rendezvous point as best they could. The jump was rough. The parachutists were "tossed around like feathers in a whirlpool," Seekings recalled. Cooper hit the wall of a farmhouse and was temporarily knocked out. When he came to, he buried his parachute and set off into the night with a luminescent ball under one arm as his recognition signal, hooting in what he hoped was approximately the sound of an owl, and occasionally calling "Reg!"—all of which would surely have attracted the attention of the Germans, had any been around. Fraser landed at least a dozen miles from the rendezvous point, spotted some German troops with guns, and opted to hide out in the woods. Several men landed in trees. In the kit bag attached to his leg, Seekings had packed a large amount of extra soap, which he had been told was in short supply and could be used for trading with the French. The bag burst open on impact with the ground, sending bars of soap flying everywhere in the rain. "You could smell Lifebuoy for miles," said Seekings. As instructed, Cooper attached a message to the leg of one of the two carrier pigeons he had brought along, and released it. The wretched bird simply sat on the ground, until it was chased across a field "to get it airborne." The recalcitrance of the first pigeon sealed the fate of its companion, which was swiftly killed, cooked, and eaten.

It took four days for the full reconnaissance team, with the help of sympathetic French farmers and the local resistance network, to reassemble in the forest at a spot known as Vieux Dun. Fraser had chosen to set up camp alongside the headquarters of the Maquis Camille (also known as Maquis Jean), one of several partisan groups operating in the woods.

French resistance to Nazi occupation had taken on a particularly aggressive and complex form in the Morvan. The German Forced Labor Draft of 1943, requiring every young Frenchman to register for compulsory war work, had prompted hundreds to take up arms and retreat into the woods. By 1944, there were an estimated ten thousand active resistance fighters in the region. As elsewhere in France the maquis were patriotic, frequently eager, and brave, but often amateurish and underequipped, their ranks riven by betrayal and political rivalry. Seekings was scathing of the way political ambition impeded their military effectiveness. The maquis, he sneered, were "really political parties who had run away into the woods," with leaders who shied away from fighting on their home turf "because they wanted to become local governor or mayor in that area." Accusations of betrayal and double-dealing were bandied about with lethal effect: "Anybody they didn't like was labelled a collaborator."

The growing strength of the maquis in the Morvan had created a strange situation: the Germans knew that large bands of "terrorists" were operating in the forests, but hesitated to attack, since they knew that local resistance networks would give advance warning of any major troop movements, allowing the maquis to prepare counterattacks, or melt away. When the Germans did attempt to take on the insurgents, much of the muscle was provided by the Milice, the fascist paramilitary French militia formed to root out resistance. The maquis considered the French Milice more dangerous and ruthless than the Gestapo; the SAS War Diary describes them as "the most hated men in France. Traitors, cowards and bullies." By 1944, the conflict in rural France had taken on many of the aspects of a civil war, with all the treachery and cruelty that this entails.

The rest of the SAS squadron for Operation Houndsworth, sixty-four men in total, climbed into three planes at Fairford airbase on June 17 and headed for the Morvan, the ideal territory from which to target the rail links and roads south of Dijon.

Fraser's advance party laid out flares at the drop zone, and waited. "In the early morning, planes were heard passing over in the mist and rain. They had not seen the flares and had turned back."

Only two of the planes returned to Fairford. The third, carrying a force of sixteen men led by Lieutenant Leslie George Cairns and a six-man aircrew, was never seen again. Its fate has never been fully ascertained, although a wreck in a Normandy field was identified in 2015 by amateur investigators as the missing aircraft and has since been designated a war grave by the French authorities. The disappearance of Cairns and his men was a hammer blow to SAS morale—reminiscent, for some, of the disastrous Operation Squatter.

Four days later, the two surviving planes returned to the Morvan and successfully dropped the remainder of the squadron. Their number included Johnny Wiseman, the decorated veteran who had lost his false teeth in the Murro di Porco raid, and Alex Muirhead, the mortar specialist. Here, too, came a less martial figure: the Rev. Fraser McLuskey, the first chaplain to 1SAS. Known as "the parachute padre," he crashed to earth through a tree and was found lying unconscious.

McLuskey was the thirty-year-old son of an Edinburgh laundryman, a cheerful, self-mocking Scot with a wide, open face and an unshakeable, deeply examined faith. He was also one of the few men in the ranks of the SAS to have witnessed prewar Nazism at first hand. In 1938, as a young divinity graduate, he toured Germany on a travel fellowship and became interested in the Confessional Church, a Protestant denomination set up to defy Nazi efforts to control the established church. There he met Irene Calaminus, the daughter of one of the church pastors; they married soon afterward. The start of the war saw McLuskey appointed chaplain to the University of Glasgow, but by 1942 he had become convinced that he could no longer stand aside from a conflict he knew to be righteous. "I realized I must take some share in the burdens," he wrote.

Save for the odd hasty prayer muttered over the grave of a dead comrade, religion had played little part in the early history of the SAS. Few of the men were devout, though with death all around them some were more prepared to give the Almighty a hearing. "I could not preach—in the bad sense of that word—to these men," said McLuskey. "I had to talk to them." Most of the squadron welcomed the smiling, calming Scottish padre. "He smoothed the feathers of fear," said Johnny Cooper. "Just his presence." The unfailingly truculent Reg Seekings, however, had no time for religion. "Parsons didn't particularly interest me," he said.

Officers like David Stirling and Paddy Mayne were assiduous in caring for the physical welfare of their men, but McLuskey provided something the SAS had never had before: someone prepared, without sentimentality, to tend to their spirits, even their hearts. Over the next two months he held regular open-air services in the woods, attended by all, whether or not they held any religious conviction. The men sang hymns, sotto voce: "The enemy were never close enough to keep us from singing, although their distance from the camp dictated the singing's strength." McLuskey helped the medical officer to tend the wounded, and treated "a fairly widespread outbreak of boils" caused by lack of fresh fruit; he ordered a stock of paperback thrillers to be dropped by parachute to keep the men occupied, and essential extra supplies: "In work of this character there can never be too many cigarettes or too much tea," he observed. Even morale-lifting letters from home got through to the forest camps, thanks to McLuskey. The men were not permitted to write back, and the rote letters sent to the families of SAS men were less than wholly reassuring: "You may take it for granted that he is safe unless you hear to the contrary from us." Paddy Mayne did his best to provide some comfort for the families, telling Alex Muirhead's pregnant wife, for example, that he was "in fine form [and] doing terrific work . . . try not to worry unduly."

McLuskey was seldom far from the action, hastening to the side of anyone whose confidence and courage might need reinforcement. In his backpack he carried an altar cloth and a large crucifix in sections, which could be assembled in seconds should the need for an impromptu service arise. He worried about the psychological health of some of the men, noting that prolonged tension interspersed with fierce fighting caused "carelessness, impatience, edginess, and depression."

The war behind the lines could be dirty, yet McLuskey joined it with a clean conscience. "I had no doubt the war was necessary . . . I didn't see any ethical problem." Only in one respect did the padre experience moral uncertainty: whether, and in what circumstances, he could, or should, take up arms himself. "Perhaps this is an academic question as there are many combatant jobs which do not involve shooting," he reflected. But if his comrades came under attack, would he pick up a gun and fight back? McLuskey knew how to fire his revolver but opted not to carry it. Speaking of himself in the third person, he wrote: "In this case, the chaplain did not carry arms, but whether rightly or wrongly, he was not always sure." The ordinary soldiers took particular care to protect the unarmed chaplain whenever the shooting started. "We were all unanimous that we would look after the padre," said one NCO. In time McLuskey came to believe that, as the lone noncombatant, his presence held additional significance for the SAS troops. "I think the men were glad to see the padre as a kind of symbol of the will of God for peace for all men." A man who fights with a gun can be brave, but a man who opts to take part in a shooting war without one may be braver still.

ON JUNE 24, local French informants reported that enemy troops were approaching the Bois de Montsauche, where Alex Muirhead was encamped with his section. The column consisted of German troops and Russian soldiers captured on the Eastern Front who had switched sides to fight for the Nazis. The British called them "Grey Russians," being neither Soviet Red nor fully White Russians, but somewhere in between, men of indeterminate loy-

alty serving alongside the field-gray Wehrmacht. The enemy column was on a training exercise, practicing ambushing techniques,
and wholly unaware that the woods were seething with SAS and
maquisards eager to give their own, practical lesson on how to
conduct an ambush. At 8:00 p.m. Muirhead, Seekings, Cooper,
and four more SAS troopers, along with a small posse of resistance
fighters, concealed several Bren guns alongside a straight stretch
of road leading to Château Chinon, primed a handful of bombs,
and settled down to wait. A thin steel wire was strung from two
trees at shoulder height.

At about 10:00 p.m., in fading light, two German motorcyclists
roared into view, the vanguard of the column heading back to
the barracks at Château Chinon; both outriders were spectacu-
larly decapitated, their motorcycles slewing across the road. The
convoy slammed to a standstill. Two plastic bombs thudded into
the lead truck, and the Bren guns opened fire. The German staff
officer in the first truck, who had "come down from Nevers to
instruct the 'grey Russians' in the art of laying ambushes," was
killed in the first burst. As the troops spilled out of the other three
vehicles, they were scythed down. "It was a massacre," said Cooper. The survivors dashed for the open fields.

When the smoke had cleared, Muirhead counted thirty-one
enemy dead; one Frenchman had been killed. All four trucks were
destroyed, and five French hostages were released. Only one light
vehicle, bringing up the rear, had managed to escape by means of
a desperate U-turn. A second officer, a seriously wounded Russian,
was captured. The French made it perfectly clear that if and when
they got their hands on the prisoner, he would be tortured into
revealing whatever he knew, and then killed. "The military maquis
were very, very strict," said Seekings, with a flicker of admiration.

The captive officer, interrogated by a Russian-speaking SAS
soldier, explained that he had been captured at Stalingrad by the
Germans, who had presented him with a very nasty choice: if he
agreed to fight for the Nazis in France, his life would be spared;

if not, then not. "What would you do?" he asked his captors. "If I go back to Russia, I'll be shot. If I go back to my German masters, I'll be shot. And now these Frenchmen want to shoot me too for what I've done here." According to Cooper, the wounded man "implored us to dispatch him rather than hand him over to the French." Seekings obliged. "Reg shot him through the back of the head."

German retaliation for the ambush was swift, merciless, and directed firstly at the innocent. The villages of Montsauche and nearby Planchez were burned to the ground; the villagers, knowing they would be the first target of German fury, had already fled. Surrounding farms were attacked, and any remaining inhabitants killed: a man fishing was shot dead with his fishing rod in his hand. Three civilians leaving church were gunned down. The French resistance swiftly struck back, with SAS help. As a German and Russian contingent traveled down the Château Chinon road to collect their dead from the first ambush, a second team of concealed maquis opened fire, with similar effect. Another eighteen enemy soldiers were killed.

The next day, Sergeant "Chalky" White, who had been injured in the parachute jump, was lying in a large bed in the makeshift maquis hospital at Château de Vermot, not far from the resistance camp in the Bois de Montsauche, when the headboard above him was "riddled by a burst of machine gun fire." The German counterattack had begun in earnest, with an all-out assault on the maquis camp by some 250 German and Russian troops, armed with mortars, grenades, and machine guns. White and the other injured men were swiftly evacuated into the surrounding forest. Instead of entering the woods, however, for the next hour the attackers contented themselves with pouring fire into the trees, which made plenty of noise but otherwise had little effect. In the meantime, an SOE agent alerted the SAS to another ambush opportunity: there was only one road into the woods, and the German-Russian retribution force had come up it; at some point, therefore, they must drive back down it again. News of the attack on the French camp arrived as Fraser McLuskey was conducting an open-air service. The hymn singing came to an abrupt halt, and in the pouring rain a force under Bill Fraser set out to attack one section of the vulnerable road, while Wiseman's unit, including Reg Seekings, headed for another.

Fraser had crawled to a point about two hundred yards from the road when he spotted two men in German uniforms on the roadside, idly smoking and chatting. "He held his fire and decided to await developments." In ones and twos, soldiers returning from the inconclusive assault on the Vermot woods drifted back to what was apparently a rendezvous point. When about fifty men had assembled, they formed into ranks, and began marching along the road: at that point, the two SAS Bren gunners, having had ample time to take aim, opened fire from just a few yards away. The gunners had "an absolute field day," wrote Fraser, who estimated that "not more than ten men escaped injury from the fracas."

A few minutes earlier, Wiseman's team had gingerly approached a section of the same road a little way to the north. The place seemed deserted, save for a line of empty trucks. Reg Seekings, as usual, took the lead and crawled through the undergrowth to get a better look. When he popped his head up, he found he was looking down the barrel of a machine gun manned by the lone German soldier who had been left behind to guard the vehicles. "I misjudged a bit," Seekings later said, the first and only time he admitted an error. Luckily, the German machine-gunner was as surprised as he was, and for a moment seemed paralyzed. Seekings turned to the rest of the men and shouted, "Look, enemy!" This statement of the obvious prompted Wiseman to remark in his official report: "The rest of the party, more sensibly, sank to the ground." At that exact moment the machine-gunner opened fire, loosing off a single burst before his gun jammed. He then tossed two hand grenades, which landed wide, on either side of Seekings, who tried to raise his own gun to fire back but found his left arm was hanging uselessly at his side. "I thought, Oh good God, my bloody arm's gone." A bullet had lodged in Seekings's neck, at the base of the skull.

As the attacking force retreated, pulling Seekings with them, the wounded man experienced a succession of disjointed memories, images of his home in Cambridgeshire, his family, and an early girlfriend. He felt he was "in an underground river with the water going faster and faster." It was a three-mile hike back to camp: Seekings recalled being forced to run at one point, wading through swamps, dropping his pipe and insisting on returning to pick it up. He continued to bark orders. When someone attempted to bind his neck wound, he shouted: "It's my arm, you stupid bastard, not my head." Fraser McLuskey carried his kit bag. A thunderstorm suddenly broke, and Seekings felt his head clear momentarily. Then "everything seized up." He was half dragged, half carried back into camp.

Naked and delirious, Seekings was laid out on a table under a tarpaulin to keep off the slashing rain and inspected by the maquis doctor. Fraser McLuskey acted as assistant surgeon, while the doctor (who was actually a dentist) probed around in the bloody hole between the injured man's skull and the top of his spine. "Under the tarpaulin, and with the somewhat uncertain light of a torch," McLuskey recalled, "we found that a bullet had entered the back of his neck and lodged itself deeply near the base of his skull." The doctor digging in half-darkness around Seekings's spinal cord could easily have caused greater injury than the wound itself. Finally the French medic announced that he could not reach the bullet: "So he decided to leave it where it was."

Seekings was made of some resilient substance that seemed capable of withstanding almost any kind of physical or psychological punishment. McLuskey nursed him and shaved him. Their conversation became friendly, and then almost spiritual. "The last few days, I've seen religion lived," McLuskey confided. "Men helping one another, no thought of reward." The neck wound healed with remarkable swiftness. Within weeks, Seekings was back on active duty, as cantankerous and cussed as before. Months later, the bullet would be removed in a British hospital, having apparently done him no lasting harm whatever. But it did change him in one respect. He would insist thereafter, and quite wrongly, that the regimental padre had saved his life. His view of religion remained unchanged, but he was now a committed convert to the Reverend McLuskey.

The SAS and maquis struck camp that night. In the village of Vermot itself, the German revenge was under way. Six village men were dragged from their homes and shot and a fourteen-year-old girl raped, a foretaste of what was to come. The next morning the Germans and Russians arrived with a much larger force, and murder in mind. Finding the Vermot woods deserted, they burned the château, wrecked the medical equipment abandoned by the maquis doctors, and then set off for the nearby village of Dun-les-Places. The SAS War Diary, not usually a document to shy away from graphic detail, records only that this small French village, guilty by association with the maquis, was "given over to rape and murder." The mayor was one of the first to die. The thirty-eight-year-old village priest, Curé Roland, was taken from the home he shared with his mother, frogmarched to the church and taken up into the bell tower. There a noose was tied around his neck, and he was flung off the building. Another seventeen of the village's "most prominent citizens" were lined up in front of the church and machine-gunned beneath the twisting corpse of the priest. According to Fraser McLuskey, the Russian troops were particularly brutal, and largely "responsible for bad treatment to women, including rape." Rage and lust sated, the attackers set fire to the village and marched away. In just three days the combined forces of the SAS and the maquis of the Morvan had killed at least eighty-five of the enemy, but the people of Montsauche, Planchez, Vermot, and Dun-les-Places had paid for that success with their blood and homes.

• • •

THE SAS ON Operation Houndsworth needed more jeeps, which were proving as useful in the dense Morvan forests as they had been in the open desert. An early radio message complained bitterly of "trying to service [a] 5,000 square mile area with two jeeps and unreliable civilian cars." The jeeps were parachuted in, partly dismantled, on large trays, with a parachute at each corner, and a large central parachute attached to a junction box in the middle. Dropping a 2,500-pound car out of the sky was an inexact art. And extracting a jeep from a tree is not an easy task. The couplings frequently sheered off with the weight of the vehicles or the parachute lines entangled, ensuring that the jeeps did not so much parachute into the Morvan as plummet. No fewer than seven jeeps were "pranged," a mild euphemism for the impressive moment when a lump of metal hurtled to earth and smashed into the ground, leaving a large crater and very little in the way of usable car.

But, once safely landed, the jeep was a formidable weapon. Equipped with four separate petrol tanks, each had a range of a thousand miles. When in the forests, the German troops tended to stick to the main arteries, leaving the jeeps to travel with relative impunity along the maze of back roads. As one officer put it, with the traditional twin Vickers guns mounted and fuel tanks full "we were then in a position to take some serious action."

This action took a variety of destructive shapes all across the region. Johnny Wiseman established a new camp near Dijon, from which he set out to reconnoiter vulnerable communication lines before calling in RAF airstrikes. A six-pounder anti-tank gun was dropped, principally intended for use against road vehicles—but the SAS found more imaginative uses. On August 14, a large German transport plane, a Junkers 52, passed overhead within range. Alex Muirhead took a shot, and reported that the aircraft was "definitely hit and believed brought down."

Just twenty-five miles from the SAS camp, at Autun, stood a large synthetic-oil factory, producing some 7,500 gallons a day, vital to the increasingly fuel-poor German forces. Lightly guarded and located in open ground, the factory was vulnerable to attack, but the timing of any assault would be tricky. The factory workers were French, and killing civilians was not part of the SAS remit. Local intelligence, however, revealed a gap of over an hour between the end of the night shift and the arrival of the day workers; in the early hours of the morning, the place was almost deserted. A preliminary attack using mortars was carried out on July 10.

Emboldened by this success, Muirhead, Seekings, and Cooper decided to launch an altogether more elaborate assault a month later. On August 10, an attack team composed of seven jeeps drove to within two hundred yards of the factory perimeter, and Muirhead set up his mortars. At 3:30 a.m., "in full moonlight," the first of forty mortar shells and incendiary bombs crashed down on the factory. The ensuing spectacle prompted Muirhead to lyricism. "The mortar bombs were plumping most satisfactorily into the factory area . . . then with a roar the seven Vickers Ks opened up at 200 yards, each pouring two full pans into the rising storm. The vivid flash of an electric discharge was plainly seen and bullets could be seen to ricochet off buildings." The defenders of the factory believed they must be under aerial attack, and flak began arcing into the night sky. "They had no inkling they had been mortared from less than a mile away." The oil plant burned continuously for four days.

MUCH OF THE SAS work on both Houndsworth and Bulbasket was covert reconnaissance, gathering intelligence, assessing the movement and strength of enemy troops, and reporting back to London. Cooper described their role as "an LRDG job in Europe," precise, secret observation, without ever being seen.

Intelligence gathered by the Houndsworth team correctly revealed that Erwin Rommel had made his new headquarters at Château de la Roche-Guyon, north of Paris. The charismatic and popular German field marshal was commander of the troops opposing the invasion, and the possibility of removing him at this vital juncture was enticing: "To kill Rommel would obviously be easier than to kidnap him, but if it should prove possible to bring him to this country, the propaganda value would be immense," wrote brigade commander Roderick McLeod. So Operation Gaff (a gaff being a hooked spike for landing large fish) was launched on July 25, when Captain Jack Lee and five other SAS men parachuted into Orleans, with orders "to kill, or kidnap and remove to England, Field Marshal Rommel, or any senior members of his staff." Lee's real name was Raymond Couraud. A former French Foreign Legionnaire and sometime gangster, Couraud had helped organize an escape route for artists in France fleeing the Nazis, before joining SOE and finally signing up with Bill Stirling's 2SAS. On landing in Orleans, Couraud's assassination team began making its way cross-country toward Rommel's headquarters, hiding out with various sympathizers along the route. His report for July 28 states: "Stayed for two days in a chateau . . . Ate plastic [explosive, presumably, though why remains unclear] and was extremely sick for two days: cured myself with six gallons of milk."

It was while recovering from this unlikely illness, and even less likely cure, that Couraud learned that Rommel had been seriously injured when his staff car came under air attack. Operation Gaff was abandoned, but Couraud went to take a covert look at the German headquarters anyway. "I am glad that I do not have to attack this place," he wrote after seeing the mighty fortified castle at Château de la Roche-Guyon. "I can see that it was very well protected." Nothing daunted, Couraud and his team went on to destroy two trains, seven trucks, and a staff car driven by a Gestapo major ("got his papers"). A few days later they attacked the German command post at Monts, and killed a dozen Germans. Couraud then slipped through German lines, disguised as a policeman, and joined Patton's advancing Third Army. "Extremely successful week," he wrote.

Cooper maintained that SAS intelligence gathering was of "far more value than the ambushing of roads." As if to prove the point, mid-August saw the arrival of Major Bob Melot, the irrepressible Belgian intelligence officer who had seamlessly transferred his skills from the Libyan desert to the French interior. Melot, at forty-nine the oldest but possibly also the toughest man in the SAS, dropped from the sky with two more jeeps, both of which "pranged."

Cooperation with the French resistance was invaluable but highly complex and often perilous. Local French sympathizers set up a signals system to warn the SAS when a village was occupied by the enemy: "If we ventured out of camp, before entering a hamlet, we would check the washing line in the garden of the first house. If a pair of blue trousers was hanging there we would know that there were Germans or French Milice in the area." The French resistance also gave advance warning of any attack on the camps, sometimes with spectacular results. On July 31, a pincer movement was attempted on Wiseman's camp at Urcy, nine miles southwest of Dijon: a force of French fascist Milice attacked from one side of the wood while the Germans attacked from the other, and a pitched battle ensued. Wiseman, however, had already slipped away. The Germans and their French collaborators had been shooting at each other in a storm of "friendly fire" that left twenty-two dead.

At the same time, the French resisters were fickle allies, riven by internecine disputes that frequently turned deadly. "The blood feud between the maquis was terrible," wrote Cooper. Fraser McLuskey considered even the most competent French fighters to be liabilities: "Cooperation with them in military operations is in most cases inadvisable and in many cases highly dangerous." Spies, real and imagined, were everywhere, and as the German occupation was rolled back the score-settling intensified. Seekings, who by now gloried in the nickname "Le Maquis Anglais," intervened after he saw a woman accused of collaborating with the Germans being dragged away by a French mob: "I threatened to shoot these people . . . they were after her because she spoke German." On another occasion, a young Belgian refugee attached himself to one of the combined maquis-SAS parties. Two nights later, he was shot. "He was a member of the Gestapo," the SAS officer in command reported blandly. But it is entirely possible that the Belgian refugee was perfectly innocent, just as the woman "saved" by Seekings may well have been guilty. In the murderously shifting loyalties of the war's final phase in France, it was impossible to tell where the truth, and therefore justice, really lay. The SAS could only stand by, as the tide of war turned in a welter of recrimination and bloodletting.

Chapter 18

AN EYE FOR AN EYE

ON THE AFTERNOON OF AUGUST 8, 1944, FRASER MCLUS-key was summoned to Bill Fraser's tent in the forest, a sturdy construction made from timber and draped over with a parachute. Inside, "lying lazily on a sleeping bag, chatting with Bill and with Mike Sadler," was an enormous, instantly recognizable figure, "larger than life, physically and in every other way." Paddy Mayne had dropped in to inspect the troops.

McLuskey had first met Mayne a few months earlier. The introduction took place in the officers' mess at around 9:00 a.m., just as the commander of 1SAS was coming to the end of an all-night boozing session. Mayne offered McLuskey a morning beer. When McLuskey accepted without hesitation, he won Mayne's immediate and enduring approval. Like most people meeting Mayne for the first time, the padre was initially wary, but soon came to recognize the other qualities that lay behind the alcoholic aggression. "He was quite unique in his ability to win the confidence of his men. . . . I conceived not only an enormous admiration for him, but a very great affection." Mayne had parachuted into France with a windup gramophone player strapped to his leg and a handful of his favorite records in his rucksack. While the strains of Percy French songs such as "The Mountains of Mourne" floated through the woods, Mayne wandered around the camp with unfeigned nonchalance, as if "on an afternoon stroll."

Mayne's visit to the forest was hardly routine. For six months he had been shuffling paper, organizing war for others. He was determined to see the battlefield for himself. Brigadier Roderick McLeod had taken some persuading to allow the commander of 1SAS to join his men on the ground. Knowing Mayne's insatiable thirst for combat, McLeod issued him with strict orders "to coordinate action, not lead attacks." Specifically, he was to prepare the troops for a planned offensive in which the SAS would act as reconnaissance units for an all-out Allied assault on German forces west of the Rhine (an operation subsequently rendered unnecessary by the American advance). Mayne and Sadler had originally intended to parachute into France east of Orleans, but at the last moment they had dropped instead into the Houndsworth area of operations in the Morvan.

Mayne stayed only two days with Fraser's squadron, long enough to learn of its successes, and some of its setbacks. A few days earlier, Captain Roy Bradford had been killed in a shootout after accidentally driving his jeep into the path of a German convoy. Undeveloped photographs in Bradford's camera of other SAS men were later used by the Germans on posters, offering large rewards for information about the "terrorists" in the woods. A day later, a jeep carrying three SAS men and a French maquisard encountered a staff car containing five Germans in the little village of Ouroux. After a vigorous but inconclusive exchange of fire, the occupants of both cars leaped out and a hand-to-hand battle ensued, short, brutal, and to the death. Shot through the shoulder, the SAS jeep driver, John Noble, kneed one of the Germans in the testicles and then clubbed him unconscious with the butt of his revolver. Another German came to the aid of the first, and he and Noble fell, fighting, into a ditch; the German was throttled into submission, and then finished off with a bullet to the head. A beefy German sergeant major, meanwhile, was grappling ferociously with another of the SAS party. Noble, still bleeding from the shoulder, brought the bout to an end by shooting the German dead. A fourth German took to his heels and was chased and killed by the French resistance fighter, while the fifth was taken prisoner and subsequently made to do chores around the camp. The obedient prisoner-servant was known as Hans, which may or may not have been his name. This was the sort of fighting tale Mayne relished: ruthless close-quarters combat, roadside shootouts, and wanted posters reminiscent of the Wild West.

On August 9, a two-jeep convoy threaded its way north along the back roads: Mayne drove the first vehicle, with Sadler navigating, while Bob Melot drove the second. Their destination was the Forêt d'Orléans in the Loire Valley, the biggest French state-owned forest, where D Squadron was engaged in Operation Gain, the third of the major SAS operations under way in occupied France. Mayne was anxious to find out what had happened to this mission, and with good reason. The story of Operation Gain was a grim one.

The aim of Operation Gain was to disrupt any and every rail link carrying supplies to the German forces in Normandy. The first elements of the squadron, led by Major Ian Fenwick, had landed in the Orleans area on June 14; over the next five days, a total of nine officers and forty-nine other ranks arrived by parachute. Allied bombing of the French railway system had created a bottleneck south of Paris, ensuring that trains heading north had to pass through the area between the capital and Orleans. The pickings were rich, but, being so close to Paris, the area was also teeming with German troops and their French collaborators.

Fenwick's team of parachutists included a familiar face: a man who had last seen action with the SAS outside Benghazi, when he blasted through a roadblock before being captured by the Italians and paraded through the streets in chains. Jim Almonds, "Gentleman Jim," was as resilient as before, but a little grayer and more reticent than he had been in the desert. He seldom spoke about the experiences of the previous eighteen months, even though what had happened to him was the sort of story another man might have dined out on for life.

After three months in the Altamura POW camp, starved, frozen, filthy, and lice-infested, Almonds had escaped by ambushing his guards and then tying them up with rope made from the entwined string of Red Cross parcels. He walked south for two weeks, living off the land, before he was recaptured, placed in solitary confinement, and then taken three hundred miles north to another POW camp at Ancona. His final escape was remarkably unspectacular. Following the armistice that formally ended Italy's war, the Italian camp commandant, now the soul of bonhomie and insisting that Britain and Italy were allies, asked Almonds to reconnoiter a nearby port and report on the strength of German forces there. Almonds agreed to do so, left the camp, and then immediately absconded. In the hope of encountering the advancing Allies, he began walking down the Apennines or, more accurately, running. Having covered some 230 miles in thirty-two days, he bumped into the American vanguard, and was finally reunited with the British Army in Naples, after thirteen months of brutal captivity, two escapes, and a long jog down the spine of Italy. He referred to it ever afterward as his "Italian picnic."

"What job would you like to do next?" Almonds was asked by the officer receiving escaped POWs.

"I would like to rejoin my regiment," he replied unhesitatingly.

Instead, bizarrely, he was first posted as head of security at Chequers, the prime minister's country residence, a wholly inappropriate job from which he was eventually extricated by the direct intervention of Paddy Mayne. "Pleased to see you back," said Mayne, as if Almonds were returning from holiday. "How did it go in Italy?"

Almonds, now squadron sergeant major, was in the first stick to jump on Operation Gain. He landed west of Pithiviers, with one leg in a ditch, and dislocated a knee. Half limping and half hopping, with the aid of the local resistance network, he was brought before a rustic maquis doctor, who administered anesthetic in the form of a pint of homemade brandy; this rendered Almonds so drunk that he barely noticed when his knee was wrenched back into its socket and roughly bandaged in place.

Word of Hitler's Commando Order had by now permeated the ranks of the SAS, and everyone on Operation Gain knew they would probably face execution if captured. Some, at least, must have wondered if it was worth the risk. But none tried to pull out. "I never heard of anyone refusing to go," said Almonds. "Some were frightened to back out on account of what other people might think of them." As in the desert, the combination of adrenaline, optimism, and peer pressure proved more than equal to the force of realistic fear.

At first Operation Gain lived up to its name, as the squadron launched a series of successful sabotage missions against rail lines and attacked a motorized patrol. Scouts who spoke French were sent out on bicycles in civilian clothes to explore and report back on German troop movements. Occasionally they got too close. One Lieutenant Anderson headed off for an evening ride through the French countryside:

> All went well and I was enjoying myself fine until just as I was passing three Jerry soldiers, who were out walking, the pump fell from my bike, engaged itself in the chain, and I went head over heels, hit the deck, and then the bike hit me. I let go one mouthful: "Fuck me you bastard." Suddenly I remembered the Jerries and when I saw them walking towards me, I immediately started to curse in French but all the time thinking I had had it. However, they just laughed, helped me pick up my bike, and off I went, pedalling like hell.

The commander of Operation Gain, Major Ian Fenwick, was a *preux chevalier* from another age, a figure more reminiscent of the First World War than the Second. A brilliant and handsome product of Winchester and Cambridge, he was a distinguished

cricketer and tennis player, a natural warrior descended from a
long line of soldiers, and a fine artist. In between raids Fenwick
sat happily in the Forêt d'Orléans, sketching and smoking. After
a successful attack on a night train carrying troops and ammunition, he sent a wireless message to headquarters: "We are happy
in our work."

After three weeks in the forest, that contentment suddenly
evaporated. On July 4, an additional twelve-man team, under
Captain Pat Garstin, was sent out to reinforce Fenwick's Operation Gain squadron. As the plane circled over the drop zone at
La Ferté-Alais, thirty miles south of Paris, the recognition signal
lights on the ground twinkled through the thin clouds, indicating that it was safe to jump. But the moment Garstin's men hit
the ground, shortly before 2:00 a.m., a force of thirty German
security police and a unit of French Milice surrounded them.
The commander of the ambush, one Obersturmführer Schubert,
ordered Garstin, who had fractured his leg, to assemble his men.
Garstin refused and was immediately shot in the neck and arm.
Four other men were wounded, one mortally. Just three, who had
dropped into trees outside the ambush cordon, managed to escape.
The rest were rounded up, loaded into trucks, driven to Gestapo
headquarters on the Avenue Foch in Paris, and subjected to "third
degree" interrogation as "terrorists." Serge Vaculik, a Czech-
born Frenchman attached to the squadron as an interpreter, was
beaten with particular viciousness. Then they were transferred to
a prison, stripped naked, and handcuffed. Some said a captured
French maquisard had been tortured into revealing the drop zone.

On August 8, the seven remaining captives were handed a pile
of civilian clothes and some shaving utensils and told to make
themselves presentable as they were being taken to Switzerland
to be exchanged for German prisoners. Garstin, crippled by his
wounds and barely able to stand upright, believed this was true.
Vaculik did not. At 1:00 a.m. the following day they were loaded
on to a lorry and driven northwest out of Paris. One of their guards
was Karl Haug, a fifty-year-old Wehrmacht timeserver who had

been taken prisoner by the British in the last war and spoke some English and French. Three hours later, in a deserted forest clearing near Beauvais in the Oise they were ordered to climb down.

"Are we going to be shot?" Vaculik asked Haug.

"Of course you are," Haug laughed.

Vaculik, who had loosened his handcuffs with a spring from his watch, whispered to the others, "They're going to shoot us—when I shout, all make a run for it, and perhaps some of us will survive."

With Garstin complaining furiously that there had been no trial, the men were lined up in front of a five-man firing squad.

Seconds later, Vaculik emitted a piercing yell and sprinted toward the woods. The Germans opened fire. Garstin was shot before he had hobbled a few yards, killed by a burst of machine-gun fire in the back. Three other men were gunned down on the spot. Vaculik and one other man made it to the tree line. Another lay pretending to be dead, and then escaped as the Germans searched the woods. The officer commanding the execution squad was so frustrated at losing three of his victims that he "had a hysterical crying fit from sheer anger." Sheltered by the maquis, Vaculik would eventually testify at the war crimes trial of his would-be executioners.

Shortly before the execution of Garstin's team, several hundred German troops, acting on another tip-off, surrounded the Gain operating base in the Forêt d'Orléans. Fenwick and Almonds were both absent from the camp, preparing the drop zone for the expected arrival of Paddy Mayne. The handful of remaining SAS men in the base camp managed to slip past the encircling troops. Fenwick, however, believing that Almonds and the others had been captured or killed, radioed Mayne to warn him of the drastic turn of events, and then headed back toward the camp to find out what had happened. Mayne and Sadler shifted their drop zone to the Morvan.

En route to the Forêt d'Orléans, a German reconnaissance plane spotted Fenwick's jeep and its four occupants, and alerted the SS troops on the ground. Outside Chambon-la-Forêt, Fenwick encountered an elderly Frenchwoman on a bicycle, fleeing the village as fast as she could pedal. She stopped just long enough to warn the SAS team that they were driving into a German ambush. Fenwick's response was polite, almost chivalric, and in keeping with the long British tradition of needless sacrifice: "Thank you, Madame, but I intend to attack them."

With Fenwick at the wheel, the jeep screeched into Chambon-la-Forêt with the twin Vickers guns blasting. The first German machine-gun nest was silenced. Then a 20mm cannon shell passed through Ian Fenwick's forehead and brought his charmed thirty-three-year-old life to a sudden and very messy end. Of Fenwick's demise, a fellow officer wrote with suitable grandiloquence, "Thus died a very gallant Englishman." Some of the other men were less impressed, regarding Fenwick's final act as "bloody stupid." Almonds believed that, had he been there, he could have prevented Fenwick's last, suicidal charge.

There were still more losses to be sustained in Operation Gain. Mayne arrived with Sadler after a long and circuitous jeep journey from the Morvan, and was consulting with Fenwick's successor, Jock Riding, when word came that two signalers, Privates Leslie Packman and John Ion, had failed to return from a patrol. News soon arrived from the resistance: the two men had been ambushed in their jeep by the SS and taken to the château at Chilleurs-aux-Bois. Twenty-four hours later, by the château moat, they were executed, each with a shot to the head. Some said their hands had been cut off. A week later, after the Germans had pulled back, Almonds was sent to investigate. Near the execution site, he found a tuft of Ion's blond hair.

The losses were mounting, in grisly fashion, but the SAS War Diary offered an encouraging tally of the unit's successes. Fraser's Houndsworth team blew the rail lines linking Paris, Dijon, Nevers, and Beaune twenty-one times, derailed six trains, destroyed sixty-seven vehicles of different sorts, shot down at least one plane, and blew up a goods yard, a petrol plant, and the synthetic-oil factory, twice. At least 220 of the enemy had been killed or wounded, and between 2,000 and 3,000 maquis had been armed, and trained after a fashion. Leaving aside the plane that had vanished with Cairns and his men, Houndsworth casualties amounted to just two dead and seven wounded. Operation Gain cut sixteen railway lines, hit forty-six enemy vehicles, and killed at least six Germans, while furnishing vital intelligence on troop movements south of Paris.

As in the desert, however, the real value of SAS operations lay in their unquantifiable impact on human confidence. Houndsworth had given a "considerable fillip to Maquis morale and corresponding decrease in German morale," the official SAS report noted. Local intelligence confirmed that the retreating German troops were, in some cases, close to despair. "Enemy morale throughout is extremely low, almost zero," one report observed. "This is a confirmed fact." The SS were the exception. The same report noted: "SS troops proud, with good morale, and well-clothed and transported." As the end approached, for some in the British ranks the war seemed to be reducing into a conflict between two ruthless military elites: the SS and the SAS.

Two MORE SAS operations were launched in mid-August, as the Allied advance into France and the German retreat created a fluid, fast-moving situation ideal for SAS hit-and-run tactics. Operation Haggard established a base between Bourges and Nevers, west of the Loire, with orders to spread "alarm and despondency" by attacking the German troops retreating east. In less than a month the squadron killed at least 120 Germans in ambushes and coordinated air attacks, destroyed twenty-five motor vehicles, and blew up two bridges. "This operation no doubt assisted in the general German collapse south of the Loire," wrote Brigadier Roderick McLeod, commander of the SAS Brigade. Operation Kipling, based in the Forêt de Merry-Vaux, carried out reconnaissance operations in central France, attacked roads and railways, and provided intelligence to the advancing US divisions under General George Patton.

Kipling was the coda to 1SAS operations in the wake of D-Day, and it provided one incident that may stand as emblematic of how far the SAS had traveled from the "war without hate," as Rommel had characterized the desert campaign. On August 22, two SAS jeeps drove toward the village of Les Ormes, looking for a garage to weld a broken Vickers mounting and intending to make contact with the local maquis. In an eerie echo of Ian Fenwick's last moments, an elderly Frenchwoman intercepted them outside the village and warned that the SS—"hundreds of them"—were still in occupation, and about to execute twenty French hostages in the main square. Smoke could be seen rising from burning buildings in the village.

Two hostages had already been killed when the lead jeep, driven by Lance Corporal "Curly" Hall, stormed into the village and opened fire at the assembled troops, roughly 250 in number. Some fifty or sixty Germans were killed or wounded, two staff cars destroyed, and several trucks burned. Among the dead was the commanding officer, an executioner killed midexecution. But the SS swiftly returned fire, killing Hall and disabling his jeep. In the confusion, the surviving French hostages fled to safety. Captain Harrison, the officer in Hall's jeep, scrambled onto the second vehicle, which had performed a calm three-point turn, and left the way it had come.

Back at the Kipling camp, one man took the death of Hall particularly hard. Sergeant James "Jock" McDiarmid was a veteran of the SRS; it was he who, on being fired on by an Italian civilian from an upper window in Termoli, had climbed the stairs and killed the sniper with his bare hands. He had won the Military Medal for his actions in Italy but there was also something dark about McDiarmid, something murderous. After the SS had withdrawn from Les Ormes, McDiarmid drove into the village and was shown Hall's body laid out in a coffin, with the two dead hostages on either side. The moment undoubtedly affected him deeply.

On September 22, McDiarmid's patrol encountered a car carrying two Germans in civilian clothing. The men jumped out with hands raised. They were found to be carrying a revolver each, and were shot dead. Four days later another car, carrying four more Germans, in naval uniform, was intercepted heading east. "They were very arrogant, and as they were attempting to return to Germany to carry on the war, and it was thought they might have something to do with the murder of Captain Garstin and his party, they were shot." The distinction between rough justice and murder was blurring. Paddy Mayne, though capable of cold-blooded killing, had given strict orders on the treatment of prisoners: "Before they surrender, the Germans must be subject to every known trick, stratagem, and explosive which will kill, threaten, frighten and unsettle them; but they must know they will be safe and unharmed if they surrender." As the war approached its finale, the rules were evaporating.

The regiment had played an important part in the success of D-Day, causing mayhem behind the lines, impeding the flow of reinforcements to Normandy, and bolstering the French resistance. But at a high cost. Dozens of SAS soldiers had been killed and injured, and dozens more had perished as a consequence of Hitler's Commando Order. In the grim accountancy of war, success had brought reprisal; every killing invited further vengeance. Before leaving France in the first week of September 1944, Bill Fraser presented an SAS flag to the people of Dun-les-Places, the tiny village where many of the inhabitants had been slaughtered in brutal German reprisals.

This new kind of war carried another, more intangible cost: an eye for an eye, brutality met by greater brutality. The gentlemanly, jovial, dangerous, and exciting warfare pioneered by Stirling was evolving into something harder and crueler under the pressure of a long and horrific conflict.

The SAS might be tough, and harsh when necessary, but they were human. The relentless fear, whether acknowledged or hidden, the waiting, the threat of betrayal, the uncertainty, the death of comrades, all began to fray the minds of even the most robust and spirited warriors. "Constant tension leaves its mark," wrote Fraser McLuskey, the padre.

Bill Fraser had seen more violence than any man in the regiment. His willingness to take on the most perilous assignments never wavered. He had been badly wounded twice, yet seemed to come back more determined than before. But something was crumbling within. Withdrawn, opaque, he never spoke of his fears but saturated them with alcohol. Mike Sadler had spotted these "internal demons." Before an operation, Fraser would drink himself into action; after the fighting, he drank himself into oblivion. Johnny Wiseman had led the attack at Capo Murro di Porco, seen seventeen of his men blown to pieces by shells at Termoli, and hidden out in the forests of the Morvan for weeks. But now he felt himself nearing the edge. Paddy Mayne, a man with enough internal demons himself to populate a small hell, summoned Wiseman and told him bluntly that he was no longer psychologically equipped for frontline action. "He was right," Wiseman said, many years later. "I'd reached the end of my tether." To overcome frailty is one definition of courage; to acknowledge it with honesty is another.

Paris was liberated on August 25. Mayne and Mike Sadler arrived a few days later, having driven up via Le Mans, through the advancing Allied armies. They proceeded to have a "splendid lunch" at a black-market restaurant off the Champs-Élysées, by way of celebration. The others guests at the table included several members of the French SAS and some senior French maquisards. The drink flowed in staggering quantities, with much back-slapping and singing. But as the meal wound down and coffee was served, Mayne reached into his pocket and pulled out a hand grenade. The table fell into horrified silence as he placed it on the table, and then extracted the pin. There was a puff of smoke. Some of the more quick-thinking diners dived under the table. Most, including Sadler, sat rooted to their seats. Sadler remembered thinking: "He can't be intending to blow himself to pieces, and us?" The grenade fizzled out. Mayne put it back in his pocket. "What are you all worried about?" he said.

It was a typical macho Mayne performance, but also a leitmotif for the war the SAS was now fighting: daring bravado, with cruelty not far below the surface.

WHILE MAYNE WAS celebrating the liberation of Paris, his predecessor, David Stirling, was settling into Germany's most notorious POW camp. Colditz Castle, the vast fortress near Leipzig in eastern Germany, was used by the Nazis to incarcerate the most important prisoners, and the most incorrigible escapees. Stirling qualified in both regards: his fame as a desert warrior continued to expand, and he had spent the previous seventeen months attempting to escape from every camp he was placed in, with a singular lack of success. Stirling was very good at escaping; but he was very bad at staying escaped. In the spring of 1943, imprisoned in Gavi, a fortress south of Turin, he tunneled through an outer wall with his friend Jack Pringle, but was overpowered before he reached the perimeter. When Italy dropped out of the war, he was taken by train to Innsbruck but broke out of the cattle truck transporting him and hid in a haystack. He was recaptured after two days and transferred to a camp in Austria called Markt Pongau. A few days later, he and Pringle threw a blanket over the perimeter fence, clambered over, and dived into the river Pongau, under fire from the watchtowers. Two days later they were captured again. "David is regarded with the gravest suspicion by the prison staff and they daren't leave him alone for a minute," one fellow prisoner wrote in a letter home.

Taken to Mährisch Trübau prison camp in Czechoslovakia, Stirling decided to go one better than simply trying to escape himself: he attempted to organize a mass breakout of all two hundred officers in the camp. After months of elaborate planning, the escape attempt was about to be put into action when the prisoners were all moved to Brunswick. Stirling barely had time to prepare another escape when, in August 1944, he and Pringle were moved to Colditz. Situated on an outcrop over the river Mulde, Colditz, or Oflag IV-C, was regarded by the Germans as escape-proof, a claim that Stirling, and just about every other inmate, was determined to prove incorrect. The mighty castle, Stirling observed, was "the Third Reich's most closely guarded hostelry."

Such an obsessive determination to escape was, in some ways, the same cast of mind that had created the SAS: Stirling was still behind the lines, breaking the rules and attempting to make as many problems as possible for the enemy by lateral thinking. In between failed escapes, he wondered what had happened to the unit he had created: "My thinking time revolved around what Paddy Mayne and the boys were up to—had the SAS survived, or had it been closed down?"

Chapter 19

PADDY MCGINTY'S GOAT

Roy Farran of 2SAS was the sort of individual for whom the SAS might have been invented: he was ruthless, inspiring, and unconventional, combining a conviction in the rectitude of his own decision making with an unwillingness to take orders from others if he disagreed with them. His extreme bravery was unsettling, for there was something unmoored about Farran; by the time he joined the younger branch of the SAS his military record was already the stuff of legend.

An Indian-born, devoutly Catholic Irishman, with ferrety features and a dry wit, Farran had fought with distinction as a tank commander in the desert war, where his capacity for doing things his own way swiftly emerged. Ordered to organize the burial of four Italian soldiers killed inside their tank, he simply immolated the vehicle by pouring diesel oil into the ammunition box inside and igniting it. "As I set fire to the trail of petrol, I prayed for forgiveness," he later wrote. During the battle for Crete in 1941, his squadron encountered a group of surrendering German soldiers: "Five parachutists came out of the olive trees with their hands up. I was not in any mood to be taken in by any German tricks. I ordered the gunner to fire." Soon afterward, he was wounded in the legs and arm, captured, and imprisoned in a POW hospital in Athens, where the gangrene in his thigh was dug out by an efficient German doctor. As soon as he was able to walk again, Farran escaped by scrambling under the perimeter wire, hiding in a ditch, and then linking up with the Greek resistance, from whom he borrowed enough money to buy a boat. At this point he adopted the name "Paddy McGinty" as a pseudonym, after the Irish song "Paddy McGinty's Goat" about a goat that goes to war in 1917 with the Irish Guards and swallows a stick of dynamite. With three other escaped POWs he set off across the Mediterranean, aiming for Egypt; after four days they ran out of fuel, so Farran rigged up a sail made out of blankets, and six days later, close to dying of thirst, they were picked up by a British destroyer off Alexandria. In the hospital, a doctor extracted a large piece of additional shrapnel from Farran's right heel.

In March 1943, Farran was in Algiers, lobbying to rejoin the Eighth Army, when he learned that a new SAS regiment was undergoing training. "I had heard vague stories of David Stirling's exploits in the desert," he wrote. He immediately signed up.

In September, Farran was part of a five-squadron detachment of 2SAS that landed at Taranto and began pushing north in a series of jeep raids behind the German lines: blowing bridges, attacking airfields, and releasing prisoners from concentration and internment camps. With the Italian army starting to desert in numbers, the pickings were plentiful. "Found Italian army supply train in station," recalled one report in the War Diary. "Took 40,000 military cigarettes and 100 lbs. macaroni. Enlisted Italian infantryman as cook, named Bruno." Another patrol captured an "office truck" belonging to the German 1st Parachute Regiment, "containing many valuable papers and plenty of loot."

Farran's Italian campaign involved organizing reconnaissance and ambush operations ahead of the Allied advance. In October, he arrived in Termoli with twenty men, just in time to aid Paddy Mayne's SRS in repelling the German counterattack. "It was the only pure infantry battle I fought in the war and I never want to fight another," said Farran, who had discovered he much preferred dirtier battles inside enemy territory. A few weeks later, he and four units of SAS men were landed by torpedo boat near Ancona, and proceeded to wreck seventeen sections of the railway linking the port to Pescara. Farran emerged from the first part of his war with a dazzling reputation, lots of scars, a Military Cross with two bars, a nom de guerre, and a Stirling-like determination to follow his own lead and obey orders "when it suited" him.

While 1SAS was deployed to France immediately after D-Day, 2SAS was left training in Scotland and waiting for action, to the intense irritation of fighting officers like Farran. Operations were repeatedly drawn up, promised, and then canceled. A plan to drop an SAS team east of Nancy was postponed after a local SOE agent warned that to do so would be "criminally sadistic" since the area was crawling with Germans. Of course, an area crawling with Germans was exactly what Farran craved. On July 19, twenty men were parachuted into southern Normandy to gather information, but achieved little. Instead of operating behind the lines, they found themselves entangled with the advancing British and American troops.

A second, larger contingent of fifty-nine men under Captain Tony Greville-Bell (the officer who had survived the regiment's Italian campaign by walking several hundred miles with three broken ribs) landed east of Rennes three weeks later, only to find themselves swiftly overtaken by the advancing US Third Army. Yet another squadron was deployed to attack road and rail lines between Paris and Rouen, but achieved only "moderate success." The SAS was hampered by lack of firm intelligence, and by interference from advancing Allied troops. A fluid battlefield allowed free movement and ad hoc actions, but also made it harder to plan what the SAS did best: sudden assaults on strategically important targets, firmly anchored on the element of surprise.

Farran's chance finally came with Operation Wallace, a mission to penetrate deep behind enemy lines and cause carnage. On August 19, a squadron of Dakota transport planes landed at Rennes airfield, each carrying a jeep mounted with twin Vickers guns. Farran, with sixty men (including the Frenchman Couraud, alias Captain Jack Lee, as his deputy), then set out for the Forêt de Châtillon, where an advance party had already established a forward base forty miles east of Auxerre and some two hundred miles inside enemy-held territory.

Farran split his fleet of jeeps into three groups, and headed east through a front line that was becoming more unstable and uncertain by the day as German resistance buckled. Initially, the route through the back roads seemed safe enough. At times, French civilians came forward to greet the Allied troops with gifts, even though the Germans were still in occupation: "Flowers, wine, butter and eggs, which were heaped high on the jeeps." On the fourth day, the first pair of Farran's extended fleet of jeeps reached the village of Villaines-les-Prévôtes, and drove directly into some old foes: a company of the Afrika Korps, recently returned from Italy and still wearing their khaki tropical battledress. The Germans immediately opened fire, destroying both vehicles and killing one man and capturing another. Farran and the rest of the squadron arrived soon afterward, to be greeted by a round fired from a 20mm gun at a range of about twenty yards. "The shell went high and the jeep crashed into a ditch and came to rest, less one of its wheels which continued down the road." Farran posted two men with a Bren gun on top of the roadside bank and ran back to warn the rest of the convoy. A pitched battle, with mortars and machine guns, erupted in the village streets. After an hour, Farran and his men withdrew, leaving behind an estimated fifty enemy dead. Farran pressed on to the camp at Châtillon, "winkling [our] way around pockets of Germans to the open country in the enemy rear," pausing only to shoot up a freight train and a radar station, which the Germans then evacuated and destroyed themselves, "apparently being under the impression that Major Farran's party was the American advance guard."

For the next month, Farran and his men harassed the retreating Germans from their forest hideout, mining roads, blowing rail lines, and launching ambushes on road transport—an activity known as "brewing up" in army parlance, an idiom more reminiscent of making afternoon tea than destroying enemy vehicles with Vickers guns and hurled explosives. With the promise of help from the local maquis (which never materialized), Farran laid siege to the German garrison at Châtillon and gloried in the cacophony: "All the sounds of war echoed in the streets—the rattle of the Brens, the rasp of the Vickers, the whine of bullets bouncing off the walls." In the midst of battle, Farran happened to glance up at one of the buildings: "A pretty girl with long black hair and wearing a bright red frock put her head out of the top window to give me the 'V' [for victory] sign. Her smile ridiculed the bullets." Farran estimated that more than a hundred Germans had perished in the battle for Châtillon.

Regular drops of supplies by the RAF enabled Farran to continue fighting without pause. Soon after the attack on Châtillon, cigarettes, clothes, ammunition, newspapers, mail, petrol, and whiskey dropped from the sky, along with twelve new jeeps. "It was like Christmas Day," wrote Farran.

Pressing on east toward the Belfort Gap, the corridor between the Vosges and Jura mountains into which the Germans were being squeezed by the advancing First French Army, Farran found his jeeps surrounded by happy French peasants, "girls kissing our cheeks, bereaved mothers shaking our hands and everybody dancing around us with joy." Occasionally, the elation of liberation proved excessive: "Major Farran found the enthusiasm of the locals, who heralded his arrival with the ringing of church bells, militarily inconvenient."

Farran and his men were not the only SAS forces harassing the retreating Germans. Although the actions of the French SAS regiments fall outside the scope of this history, one episode cannot go unrecorded for its sheer, Gallic guts. Since August, the jeep-borne troops of the French 3SAS had carried out a series of successful guerrilla actions in the area south of the Loire, disrupting communications and mounting ambushes in concert with the local resistance. On September 3, the force was ordered to block the retreat of a large German column reported to be forming up at Sennecey-le-Grand, a picturesque Burgundy village ten miles south of Chalon-sur-Saône. The following day, as some three thousand German troops were assembling, a column of four jeeps led by Captain Guy de Combaud Roquebrune charged up the main street, machine guns blasting. Up to five hundred German troops were believed to have been killed or injured in the first attack. Having reached the other side of the village, Combaud Roquebrune found his escape route blocked; he turned his jeep column around and attempted to fight his way out of Sennecey-le-Grand the same way he had fought his way in. But now the Germans were ready. One after another, three of the jeeps and their occupants, including Guy de Combaud Roquebrune, were destroyed. One jeep, with two of its crew surviving, somehow made it through the fusillade and were spirited to safety by the maquis. Forty years later to the day, a memorial was unveiled at Sennecey-le-Grand, which bears the names of all SAS wartime casualties: the British of 1 and 2SAS, the French of 3 and 4SAS, and the Belgians of 5SAS. It remains the only memorial to a British regiment and the war dead of all its component parts located outside the United Kingdom.

Some brief entries from Farran's report for the month of September give an idea of the breathless, continuous action, as the SAS engaged scattered German troops on a chaotic battlefield, dodging the artillery of the advancing Americans and the furious reprisals of the retreating Germans, until they finally found themselves encamped in the midst of a defeated but still powerful army:

> *4 September:* Sergeant Young brewed up two staff cars . . . Lieutenant Carpendale's party bagged one ten-ton troop carrier containing 30 Germans and one staff car.

> *5 September:* Lieutenant Mackie laid an ambush and after half an hour a motor cycle combination carrying seven Germans was allowed to approach within 50 yards. Only one German escaped.

6 September: Girls crowded round the jeeps with bouquets of flowers. Accordingly, when a German staff car mounting a machine gun appeared, the presence of so many girls made it impossible to give more than two bursts with a Vickers.

7 September: Landing party at drop zone attacked by 600 SS troops with four armoured cars. Major Farran moved the six jeeps out into a small field enclosed by woods and then noticed a gap in the south west corner through which jeeps crashed. Lieutenant [Hugh] Gurney [was sent] to attack enemy's immediate rear. He machine gunned the German infantry, especially some officers standing on a mound. Major Farran placed an ambush to attack enemy transport on the return journey . . . the Colonel and second in command of the attacking force were killed.

8 September: Party attacked enemy billets . . . 20 Germans killed whilst shaving in the farmyard, billets set on fire.

9 September: Truckloads of Germans have been inquiring at all the villages about British parachutists . . . the squadron felt a little uneasy. Some women from a village ran screaming into the wood . . . a large body of Germans who were beating the Foret-de-Darney were burning farms in their path.

10 September: Reports that the Germans still searching for the SAS . . . they were said to have burned the village of Hennezel and shot the curate.

11 September: Farran's party crossed the main road from Vaucelles. He considered it a pity to waste the opportunity of an ambush. Troop was told to lay mines. This had just been completed when two staff cars appeared at high speed. The first passed over the mines safely but the second blew up.

12 September: Lieutenant Gurney brewed up a staff car containing five brass hats. The death of these senior officers, including a General, was confirmed next day by civilians . . . also attacked and killed some Germans standing around a broken down 3-tonner. Major Farran organised the squadron to attack transport on the roads as he was determined to make the Germans pay for the miserable night he had just passed.

13 September: Lieutenant Gurney's troop shot at an ammunition truck. The truck exploded. Lieutenant Gurney was hit in the back and fell; he died shortly afterwards. The French later described how the Germans kicked the body of the English "terrorist," but eventually [they] were allowed to bury him in the village cemetery . . . German resistance had stiffened and the situation for Major Farran's squadron became very precarious.

14 September: Squadron remained in its base in the Bois de Fontaine. American shells were landing so close that slit trenches were dug. No one dared talk above a whisper, and every time somebody dropped something they expected a German to appear . . . another patrol was sent out to contact the Americans.

15 September: Considerable German shouting and movement.

16 September: By morning it was almost certain the Germans were withdrawing . . . at 12.00 an American

armoured car crew came into the wood. The squadron
nearly went mad with joy.

The SAS had finally linked up with advance units of the US
Seventh Army. "We were so overjoyed to see their grinning Yan-
kee faces that we danced a Highland reel on the spot." After a
campaign of "singular ferocity," Farran's men had inflicted more
than 500 enemy casualties, destroyed some 65 enemy vehicles and
more than 100,000 gallons of petrol, at a cost of 17 SAS troopers
and 16 jeeps. Farran hailed Operation Wallace as the purest vindi-
cation of Stirling's principles, "a text book for future SAS work,"
using small units to harass the enemy behind the lines for strategic
gain: "With correct timing and in suitable country, with or without the active help of the local population, a small specially trained
force can achieve results out of all proportion to its numbers." Farran was awarded a DSO to go with his other decorations, which he
accepted, oddly, in the name of Paddy McGinty, the owner of the
warlike Irish goat.

The SAS headquarters had by now moved to Hylands House,
near Chelmsford in Essex, an imposing neoclassical villa with col-
umned portico and surrounded by five hundred acres of estate.
The officers were billeted in grand style, while the men slept in
Nissen huts dotted around the park. Every evening, in the salon
that doubled as the officers' mess, the padre played the grand
piano, while the men belted out the regiment's favorite songs.
The drink flowed in torrents. On one occasion, it was said, Paddy
Mayne drove a jeep up the wide main staircase, possibly as a bet.
The indulgent owner, Christine Hanbury, merely asked the SAS
to dismantle and remove the vehicle when they had sobered up.
It seemed a far cry from flyblown Kabrit, where a handful of raw,
sunburned novices had once hammered out the same drinking
songs, under canvas, on a stolen piano.

Chapter 20

A PREDILECTION FOR RISK

S OLDIERS, IT IS OFTEN SAID, TEND TO FIGHT THE LAST war; that military truism also applies to the last battle, the last skirmish, the last ambush. The conflict in central France had seen an enemy in confused retreat, and the Allied armies advancing, ineluctably if not steadily. The SAS had fought, with remarkable impact, in the spaces that opened up in between the armies, and behind the German lines. As the summer of 1944 wore bloodily on, and the Germans were forced back ever closer to their own borders, military planners expected that pattern to continue, with the Nazis on the back foot and Allies on the front, until the Germans were finally forced out of France, across the Vosges Mountains, and back into the Reich. SAS tactics, it was assumed, would continue to bear fruit, as one army continued to move forward and the other moved back. Both assumptions were wrong.

From 1871 until the First World War, the Vosges Mountains had marked the border between France and the German empire. Alsace-Lorraine, wedged between the Vosges and the Rhine, is a half-German, half-French hybrid, and some of the most fought-over territory on the planet; the region was annexed by the French Republic in 1918, but then seized back by Hitler's troops in 1940. German-speaking inhabitants had been systematically deported in the twenty years before the war, but many who remained still considered themselves German, and were prepared to do whatever they could to stymie the Allied advance and help Germany to retain its hold on Alsace-Lorraine.

One evening in mid-August, a natty, multilingual, danger-seeking spy-turned-soldier parachuted into the Vosges looking for adventure and the local partisan chief, who fought under the splendid nom de guerre of "Colonel Maximum." Captain Henry Carey Druce of 2SAS landed near the village of Moussey, forty miles west of Strasbourg, in command of a small advance party. His primary task was to find a suitable drop zone where a far larger contingent could be brought in. With the help of the French resistance, the SAS would then attack the rail lines running into Germany, hold up the retreat by blockading the passes, ambush convoys, and generally continue doing what had been done so effectively farther west. Operation Loyton was expected to last three weeks, and inflict critical damage on an already enfeebled enemy in headlong flight. It did not work out that way.

By the time Druce landed on August 12, German troops were already pouring into the area to reinforce and hold the Vosges; the American advance would stall. With the benefit of hindsight, the commander of 2SAS, Colonel Brian Franks, observed: "The difficulties of the Vosges terrain, coupled with the sentimental consideration of the incorporation of Alsace Lorraine into the Reich, indicated that a considerable stiffening of German resistance would occur on the western slopes of the Vosges." The Germans were not running away, and Druce and his men, instead of stalking a fleeing enemy, would find themselves the quarry, chased and harried across the woods and ravines of the Vosges like hunted animals.

Born in Holland to a Dutch mother and an English army officer, the twenty-three-year-old Druce was a Sandhurst-trained professional soldier who had volunteered to be a glider pilot before being seconded to MI6 in 1942. His career as a spy in occupied Holland came to an end when he was betrayed by a double agent, and he was forced to escape through occupied France, disguised by his civilian clothes and fluent French. Druce was witty, insouciant, and flamboyant, an eccentric with a "predilection for risk" and a peculiar fashion sense who favored corduroy trousers and a top hat. He was told he would be commanding the advance party just twenty-four hours before he jumped, when the appointed team leader pulled out after suffering a bad attack of fear. He was accompanied by a French officer attached to SOE, Captain George Baraud.

Druce landed upside down, shortly before 2:00 a.m. Badly concussed, he "talked nonsense," by his own account, for the next two hours. The wireless operator, Sergeant Kenneth Seymour, had broken his left foot on landing: he could not put on his boot, and could walk only with extreme difficulty. Druce was still feeling "a bit muzzy in the head" when his group was greeted by partisans commanded by Colonel Maximum, real name Gilbert Grandval, who would go on to become labor minister under President Charles de Gaulle. The Frenchmen immediately helped themselves to all the guns brought by the SAS, and then escorted Druce and his men to their hilltop camp, containing about eighty French fighters armed with a handful of rusty rifles, fifteen escaped Russian POWs, and a downed Canadian pilot named Lou Fiddick, who had grown up on Vancouver Island and was perfectly at home in the wilds. In exchange for the weapons already expropriated by Maximum's men, "it was agreed that we were to be fed and housed and also defended by them . . . it seemed a fair bargain."

Druce had visited the Vosges before the war "and knew fairly well what to expect in the way of terrain." He behaved as if he was on holiday, taking "a stroll through the countryside" and enjoying the local cuisine. "We had an excellent meal and slept the clock round," he wrote. Druce awoke to discover that German troops were flooding into the valley below, but he declined to be rattled. "I was not unduly worried since the Germans might have been there for any reason at all." Had he known the real reason they were there even Druce's sangfroid might have gone up a few degrees: an informer had already reported the arrival of the SAS to the Germans, and the area was being combed.

All day and well into the evening, unarmed Frenchmen, fearing reprisals, poured into the camp. "This was a nuisance," wrote Druce. But not enough of a nuisance to interrupt his sleep. "We doubled the guard and went to bed." By the following morning, thousands of German troops, including elements of the SS 17th Panzer Grenadier Division, were swarming through the Celles Valley. Druce now had to admit that the Germans were "alive to the situation" and hunting for them in "unpleasantly large numbers." It would be safer, he concluded, to establish a new base higher up the mountains and put some distance between himself and the large crowds of loud and overenthusiastic Frenchmen. "The French were quite incapable of moving without a tremendous noise."

After two hours of marching, the fourteen SAS troops found a mountain path, and immediately ran into a forty-strong patrol of Germans, who "were busy eating" and initially failed to spot the approaching British. Druce tried to back quietly away, but "unfortunately one German saw the last man in our column and shouted 'Achtung,' whereupon he was shot by the man he had seen." Although tempted to launch an attack, Druce reluctantly decided to beat a hasty retreat: "My task was to bring in reinforcements and therefore I was not keen on risking our necks for a few Germans. Unfortunately this meant leaving Sergeant Seymour as a prisoner of war, for he still could not walk." The injured Seymour was exceptionally displeased to be abandoned.

For the next two weeks Druce and his band of men were on the run, forced to dodge around the Vosges, hiding in hay barns or camping in the open despite the increasing cold as autumn neared. "In all it seemed there were about 5,000 Germans chasing us," wrote Druce, who remained in contact with the maquis despite deteriorating relations with the fickle and demanding Colonel Maximum. The French resistance chief could not understand why

SAS troops were evading the enemy rather than launching immediate, albeit suicidal, attacks on the Germans. "I explained that my
task was to bring in more SAS and it helped if I was alive to do it,"
wrote Druce. The uncertainty and strain were compounded by
"horrible rumours of Sergeant Seymour having a) shot himself,
b) been shot and c) been bayoneted to death."

Food was running out. The Germans, in reprisal, had begun
rounding up the male inhabitants of Moussey and marching them
off to forced-labor camps. The stress was beginning to tell even on
Druce, who confessed to "feeling very depressed and helpless, and
with strong temptation of going off and shooting up what we could
find." Finally, Druce located a suitable drop zone, in a remote corner of the plateau. Ten SAS reinforcements were parachuted in
on August 26, followed by a wireless message to the effect that
the commander of 2SAS, Colonel Brian Franks himself, would
land with another twenty-five men in four days' time. Druce was
waiting for his commanding officer to arrive, accompanied by a
large contingent of maquis, including several Russians, when a
Frenchman named Fouch was found in the woods. He claimed to
be "looking for mushrooms." Highly suspicious, Druce ordered
that Fouch be interrogated.

At 3:00 a.m. on August 31, planes were heard overhead, and
moments later canisters of supplies and weapons began drifting
down to the drop zone, followed by Franks and his men. Then
pandemonium erupted. One canister filled with ammunition
exploded as it hit the ground. The maquis began looting the supplies before the SAS men had even landed. In the confusion, the
captive Fouch seized a Sten gun and rushed off. The Russians,
who spoke some German but no French, shouted "Achtung!"
The French, hearing German voices in the darkness, assumed
they must be under attack and began shooting wildly. The loot-
ers meanwhile were gorging themselves. "One Frenchman died
of over-eating," Druce recorded. Another of the maquis extracted
what he took to be a hunk of soft cheese from one of the contain-

ers and devoured it, only to discover that it was plastic explosive, which contains arsenic. He then "died noisily."

Over the next hour, Druce rounded up as many of the parachutists as he could find, including Colonel Franks, who had taken to the woods immediately on landing, convinced that the "unbelievable noise" must indicate an ambush. "The area was too hot for us to remain," wrote Druce. At that moment the maquis dragged in Fouch, who had been recaptured after a long pursuit through the woods. Druce was in no mood for clemency. "I ordered Fouch to be shot. Captain Baraud shot him through the heart at point blank range." The body of the presumed spy was left where it had fallen, but by the next morning the corpse had vanished. "Afterwards it was said that he had been wearing a bullet-proof waistcoat."

With the arrival of six jeeps over the next few days, the unit achieved some mobility and began to fight back, using now-familiar guerrilla tactics. Three German staff cars and a truck were destroyed on the road into Moussey. When an elderly car appeared moments later, it was attacked too and forced into a ditch. Later it was found to have contained the village mayor, a leader of the resistance who somehow emerged unharmed from the wreck of his ancient electric carriage and sent two bottles of champagne to Colonel Franks along with a cheerful message: "Thanks for the salvo fired in my honour this morning."

After six weeks of frustration, Druce got his chance to take the fight to the Germans. One morning he led a three-jeep convoy into Moussey just as an SS commander was assembling his men; he opened fire at forty yards, and, having expended several pans of ammunition, raced back into the mountains. In the chaos, the 250 German troops occupying Moussey withdrew, believing Druce's attack must be the herald of an assault by a far larger force. Two French Arabs, suspected of spying for the Milice, were intercepted by Druce and shot out of hand.

By the end of September, the advancing Americans—General

George Patton's Third Army—had outrun their supplies and temporarily ground to a halt. Colonel Maximum announced that his maquis did not intend to do any more fighting "until the arrival of the Americans." The Germans continued to scour the area for the SAS.

A strange stalemate set in. Food was running low, as was morale. At least twenty of Franks's men were missing, believed to have been killed or captured on operations. But at this moment an unexpected intelligence windfall arrived from one of the French resistance leaders: the detailed order of battle of the 21st Panzer Division. The 21st were old adversaries from the desert war, decimated in Normandy and now re-formed by amalgamation with two other panzer divisions. Quite how this secret document was obtained remains unclear, but in Allied headquarters a precise description of the strength of the 21st Panzer would be greeted as a pearl of great value. Franks detailed Druce to head west in civilian clothes, accompanied by the Canadian airman, Fiddick, link up with the Americans, and pass on this vital piece of information. Druce was also to "explain our position to the Americans and give them any information they might need."

Two days later, Franks received a radio message that Druce had safely reached the Third Army, after passing through the German lines three times. Druce was immediately flown to SAS headquarters at Hylands House to be debriefed. Just twenty-four hours later, he parachuted back into eastern France with a new radio, orders for Franks, some letters for the men and a case of whiskey. He then began retracing his steps back to the Vosges camp, where the situation was growing worse by the day.

Over the preceding weeks, German military intelligence had built up, from interrogated prisoners and local informers, an increasingly accurate picture of who and what they were fighting in the Vosges. A report by the intelligence section of the 2nd Panzer Division, labeled "secret" and headed "Appearance of SAS units," gave chapter and verse on the unit's mission, equipment, and strength. The British troops, it reported, specialized in "single combat, characterized by ambush, deception, utilization of the weapons in hand to hand fighting (brass knuckles, daggers etc)," and warned: "Experience gained in the campaign in Italy and France shows that members of the SAS are specially trained for this kind of work. Their activities are extremely dangerous. The presence of SAS troops is to be reported immediately." The Germans even had names, albeit misspelled, to go with the shadowy forces operating behind the lines: "The commander of the 1st SAS Regiment is Colonel Kaine [*sic*]. The Commander of the 2nd SAS Regiment is Colonel Fanks [*sic*]." The Germans were remarkably—even suspiciously—well informed about what the SAS was up to.

By the time Druce arrived back in the Vosges, Franks had already come to the conclusion that Operation Loyton, which was intended to run for three weeks and had so far lasted two months, would have to be abandoned. The Germans had reinforced along the Moselle, and the US Third Army was static. "We were really boxed in," admitted Druce. The SAS had tied up several thousand German troops, wrecked a number of rail lines, and put heart, albeit briefly, into Colonel Maximum and his maquis. But the idea of harrying the retreating German army had not worked for the simple reason that the German army had stopped retreating. By October 9, the men had only enough rations to last another twenty-four hours. "We had no explosives and the likelihood of having a resupply drop appeared negligible." The autumn weather was closing in, with a freezing wind whipping through the hills. "I decided to end the operation and instruct parties to make their way to the American lines as best they could," wrote Franks. The troop was split into parties of four and six, while a six-man rearguard was left behind to await a sabotage team that had failed to return. SS troops attacked the next day, led to the camp by a French informer, just hours after the departure of Franks and the others. After a ferocious hour-long resistance, the six SAS men and a lone maquisard surrendered, and were imprisoned at Saales. Six days later, the prisoners were driven into a pine wood alongside the road to Grande Fosse; the men were taken off the truck, led away in handcuffs, one by one, and shot.

Franks, Druce, and about two dozen others made it back to the American lines. A total of 210 male inhabitants of Moussey were marched into captivity in Germany, of whom only seventy returned.

Of the thirty-one SAS men captured during Operation Loyton, all were murdered save one. The unlikely survival of Sergeant Kenneth Roy Seymour, the wireless operator captured at the outset of the operation, has been the subject of speculation, and accusation, ever since.

Seymour was a twenty-two-year-old heating and lighting engineer from Sutton in south London. Nothing in his life had prepared the young signaler for capture, imprisonment, and Nazi interrogation. The account he gave of his ordeal after the war was extraordinary in its testimony to human resilience. On August 17, unable to walk due to his broken foot, Seymour was left by Druce to await capture on the twisting mountain path in the Vosges. Seymour described how, instead of meekly surrendering, he had crawled to a jutting rock just off the path and "dug himself in to fight a lone action against a large German force," armed with a Bren gun, a carbine, and his .45 revolver. For an hour he held off the attackers, who apparently believed they were facing a formidable force of men; when the Bren gun ran out of ammunition, he resorted to his carbine and then the revolver. Finally, some fifteen Germans attacked in a semicircle and forced him out by lobbing grenades. Seymour wrote that as he was dragged past a line of jeering German soldiers, "each one assisted me with a clout of his revolver." He was still carrying his left boot, and hobbling with one bare foot. A soldier grabbed the boot and tossed it into the undergrowth. When Seymour protested, "by signs they replied that I would not require it as I was to be shot."

"I was marched over to the nearest tree and put up against it. Two of the enemy were detailed as a firing party and were just taking aim when a senior officer came rushing up to them. He ordered the party not to fire and I was led away for interrogation."

Seymour's interrogator spoke good English with a faint American accent. This was Wilhelm Schneider of the Gestapo, a senior figure in the German intelligence hierarchy in Alsace-Lorraine. Seymour was left in no doubt about his options. "If I did not tell the truth it would be the worse for me." He gave his name, rank, and serial number, but nothing more; when pressed, he admitted that he was part of a "recce party," but refused to give any details of the mission. When Schneider pressed him to reveal the parachute drop zone, Seymour said he "gave convincing answers, but not true." Taken to the nearby prison camp at Natzweiler-Struthof (the only concentration camp on what is now French soil), Seymour was given black coffee and a lump of stale bread, and then subjected to further questioning. At one point, Schneider produced a captured British wireless set, along with a onetime pad (the key to the British system of cryptography) and codes written on a strip of silk. "I replied I knew nothing about wireless."

Over the next six months, Seymour was shipped from one German prison camp to another, and repeatedly interrogated. Often held in solitary confinement, he was forced to sleep on the floor with only a blanket for cover. His skin erupted with raging scabies and impetigo. After the first month in captivity, Seymour and a group of a dozen captured American airmen were loaded onto a cattle wagon and told they were being taken to Frankfurt for further questioning. The train was pulling into Karlsruhe when the city came under Allied air attack. The prisoners were swiftly offloaded and bundled into an underground shelter. An hour later, they emerged to find Karlsruhe "practically flattened and in flames," and a very angry local population, intent on extracting summary vengeance.

"They were ready to lynch us if they got hold of us," Seymour recalled. "Women were in hysterics. They had got the idea that we were part of the crews that had been shot down during the raid . . .

They threw stones at us and anything they could lay their hands on. I was hit on the head by a brick. Persons passing us on bicycles struck us, men on the pavement made rushes at us between the guards, one in particular putting his arm around an airman's neck and hammering his face with his fists. Had it not been for the action of the military personnel I am sure we would not have reached the station alive."

A further succession of camps followed, each more brutal than the last. In mid-February 1945, Seymour was incarcerated in Stalag Luft III, near Żagań in western Poland, the camp made famous by the film *The Great Escape*. One morning, at five o'clock, he and the other prisoners were rousted from their beds and told to prepare to ship out. The Russian guns could be heard in the distance. According to Seymour's account, the forced march to Stalag IX-B at Bad Orb, north of Frankfurt, would last forty-two days. He was now able to wear both boots, but still limping. The rations varied from appalling to nonexistent. For the first week, the prisoners "slept out in the snow with no blankets." Many died from cold and starvation. Finally, they reached the camp. "By this time every man was weak and suffering from malnutrition, the majority were also suffering from dysentery of which I was one, many also suffered from frost bite."

A fortnight later, a rumor swept the camp that the Americans were approaching, and two days after that the German commandant surrendered control to the senior British officer. "The German guards marched out, leaving the camp in our hands," Seymour wrote. Stalag IX-B was liberated on April 2, 1945. Seymour was flown back to Britain and was treated at a military hospital until he was well enough to return to Sutton, where he immediately became engaged to his long-term sweetheart, Pamela Vaughan.

Seymour's story was one of intense suffering, heroically borne. It was uplifting, even inspiring.

But it may have been quite untrue.

Seymour's claim to have fought a single-handed action against dozens of Germans in the Vosges Mountains is distinctly dubious. According to one account, his leg was so badly injured he was being carried on a stretcher by two maquisards when the troop encountered the German patrol. Since Seymour was certain to be captured, he would hardly have been left behind with a valuable Bren gun.

Seymour's commanding officer Henry Druce was emphatic: "He never fired a shot."

At his war crimes trial after the war, Gestapo officer Wilhelm Schneider testified that, far from refusing to talk, Seymour had been most cooperative, since he had not only divulged details of the operation but had also "shown how to work the wireless set and cipher." Another German officer, Julius Gehrum, confirmed that account: "The prisoner with the injured foot answered Schneider's questions, and Schneider said to me afterwards 'with this man we can begin something.'"

Schneider was cross-examined by Major Hunt, the chief prosecutor for the 21st Army Group.

"You interrogated Seymour, did you not?"

"Yes."

"And you thought you could get something out of Seymour, did you not?"

"Yes."

"And you have said that you did get something out of Seymour, have you not?"

"Yes."

"And unless you are lying, you got some very important information out of Seymour, did you not?"

"It was very important at the time."

"And it was military information, was it not?"

"Yes."

Schneider implied that far from being coerced and threatened, Seymour had been willing to talk from the moment of his capture. "He was very annoyed that they had left . . . they just left him lying there in his helpless state."

Hunt then cross-examined Seymour, pointing out repeatedly

that while other captured members of the SAS party had been executed within hours, his life had been spared. At times, it seemed as
if Seymour, and not Schneider, was in the dock.

"You cannot give me any reason why you were not shot, can
you?"

"None at all. My only thought about it is that I was the first to
be captured."

"I am a little puzzled. You gave false information, you say, to
the Germans?"

"Yes."

"What made you say anything at all? Was it because you had
been threatened, or why?"

"I do not really know."

"You could have said nothing of course, could you not?"

"Yes."

"Did you think it was a halfway house to give them false information, is that your idea?"

"Yes, I should say it was."

"And at any rate it would put off the shooting for some time, is
that the idea?"

"I was just trying to be optimistic."

Hunt picked away at Seymour's claim to have lied to the Germans, arguing that if the information he gave had failed to produce results and Schneider had suspected he was being fed false
information, then Seymour would surely have been killed.

"You say what you told the Germans was untrue about the
landing lights . . . did nobody come to you and tell you they had
tried the information that you had given and they had no luck in
capturing parachute troops?"

"No, nobody came to see me at all."

Hunt stopped just short of the outright accusation that Seymour had willingly and knowingly collaborated with the enemy
and saved his own skin by revealing everything to Schneider. "You
have given the picture of a man interrogating you who really is not
using threats to you at all," Hunt remarked darkly.

It would be morally obtuse to rely on the testimony of a Gestapo officer facing the hangman's noose. Schneider had every reason to divert guilt onto Seymour. Perhaps the young wireless operator really had fought the lone battle he described, and then cleverly passed false information to the Germans while keeping silent about the military details he knew. But the prosecutor plainly did not think so, and nor did Seymour's surviving comrades in arms. "His value as a witness was doubtful," said the intelligence officer investigating the deaths of SAS personnel after the war. Druce, as usual, was blunter: "We wrote Seymour off as a traitor."

Treachery is an accusation that comes easily to those looking back. Seymour had exhibited bravery of a high order by volunteering for Operation Loyton and parachuting into the Vosges. But when the moment came to choose between resistance and death, or collaboration and survival, he seems to have chosen the more human and less heroic path. Everyone likes to believe they would not have done the same, but very few will ever put themselves in the situation where such a choice might arise. Seymour did.

IN THEIR ABSENCE, the men of the SAS had become, suddenly and rather uncomfortably, famous. Hitherto, almost total secrecy had surrounded the brigade, in part for reasons of operational security, but also because SAS's unorthodox activities still carried, for some, a whiff of disrepute. In the summer of 1944, commanders were given formal permission to speak about their operations for the first time. The British press discovered the SAS, and had a field day: "Britain's most romantic, most daring, and most secret army"; "Hush-hush men at Rommel's back"; "Ghost Army paved the way for the Allies." Some of the more traditional military figures might still consider SAS operations unsporting, but the public most certainly did not. Languishing in Colditz, Stirling had no idea that back in Britain he was being hailed as the pioneer of "a kind of Robin Hood system of operations." The hints of roguish derring-do, combined with a distinct lack of hard detail, created a hunger for SAS stories that has never abated: "One day their exploits in France will be told, but for the moment they must remain secret."

On October 8, 1944, General Dwight Eisenhower wrote a letter to the commander of SAS troops, Brigadier McLeod, sending congratulations "to all ranks of the Special Air Service Brigade on the contribution which they have made to the success of the Allied Expeditionary Force."

> The ruthlessness with which the enemy have attacked Special Air Service troops has been an indication of the injury which you were able to cause to the German armed forces both by your own efforts and by the information which you gave of German dispositions and movements. Many Special Air Service troops are still behind enemy lines; others are being reformed for new tasks. To all of them I say "Well done, and good luck."

Those new tasks would include a return to Italy, taking the war on to German soil, and warfare on a scale of savagery the SAS had never encountered before, as Hitler's Reich entered its death throes in a welter of blood and cruelty.

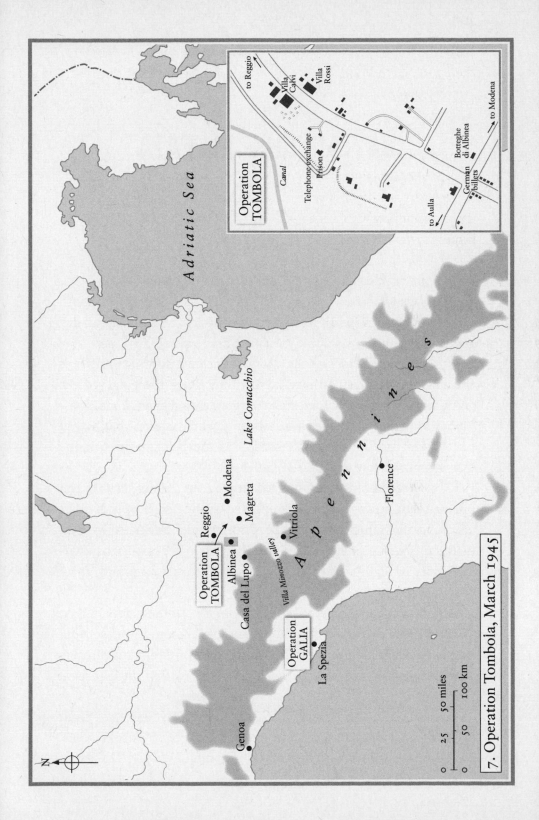

Operation
TOMBOLA

to Reggio

Villa Calvi

Villa Rossi

Canal

Telephone exchange

Prison

to Modena

to Aulla

Botteghe di Albinea

German billets

Adriatic Sea

Operation
TOMBOLA

Reggio

Modena

Magreta

Albinea

Casa del Lupo

Vitriola

Villa Minozzo valley

Lake Comacchio

A p e n n i n e s

Florence

Operation
GALIA

La Spezia

Genoa

N

0   25   50 miles
0   50   100 km

7. Operation Tombola, March 1945

Chapter 21

BATTAGLIONE ALLEATA

O N THE AFTERNOON OF MARCH 26, 1945, TWO YOUNG Italian women cycled into the little village of Albinea, south of Reggio. Usually a drowsy backwater, Albinea that day was a scene of considerable bustle. The German LI Corps had set up its headquarters in the town, some twenty miles north of the last line of German retreat running along the ridge of the Apennines. German officers had commandeered and taken up residence in Albinea's two largest buildings: the grander Villa Rossi, on the east side of the main road, was the headquarters of the corps commander, while Villa Calvi, on the opposite side of the road, surrounded by trees, housed the German chief of staff and bureaucracy. Four sentries were posted outside each of the villas, checking the papers of everyone who entered. Six machine-gun posts had been erected behind sandbag ramparts around the village, and an eight-strong German patrol marched up and down the main street. The LI Corps had dug in for a long stay.

The two women, dressed in Italian peasant clothes, attracted no attention whatever. After half an hour spent discreetly observing the activity surrounding the divisional headquarters and flirting with the sentries, they headed back down the road in the direction they had come.

An hour later they reached Casa del Lupo, a farm set back from the road with a large shed that usually housed oxen and now contained one of the oddest units ever assembled under SAS command: twenty British soldiers, forty Italian partisans, and some sixty Russians, deserters from the German army and escaped prisoners of war led by a swashbuckling Russian lieutenant. Their number also included a Scottish bagpiper, dressed in a kilt.

This bizarre little ragtag army was led by Major Roy Farran, still fighting under the nom de guerre Paddy McGinty.

Through an interpreter, the two women partisans reported on the disposition of German forces in Albinea. The town contained some five hundred troops, they reckoned, most of them housed in barracks to the south of the two villas. Farran issued his orders: the force would slip into the town after dark and attack at 2:00 a.m. It was a typically bold plan; but it had also been explicitly vetoed by the 15th Army Group, led by the American general Mark Clark, under whose command Farran was supposedly operating. No matter—Farran's orders were to spread alarm among the German forces by giving the impression that large numbers of British paratroopers were operating behind the lines. Blowing a German corps headquarters to pieces in the middle of the night with his "motley band of ruffians" seemed to him a good place to start.

Over the previous months, the SAS had been widely scattered through Europe. Two 1SAS squadrons had spent Christmas in Britain, where Paddy Mayne was planning the next stage of operations in northern Europe. The French 4SAS was deployed to the Ardennes, along with the Belgian SAS, and a squadron of 1SAS, to bolster defenses against the counteroffensive launched by the Germans on December 16, 1944.

Much to his satisfaction, Bob Melot, intelligence officer and desert veteran, had found himself stationed in Brussels, the city of his birth forty-nine years earlier. He moved in with his mother. Melot had cheated death in Libya, Italy, and occupied France; he had proved his hardiness so often, and survived so many wounds, that he had come to seem immortal and, to the younger recruits, almost impossibly old. On November 1, he was driving his jeep to a party in the suburbs of Brussels when he skidded off the road and into a ditch, striking his head on the bulletproof windscreen.

By the time rescuers reached the wrecked car, Melot had bled to death. He was buried in the Brussels town cemetery, his coffin carried by six SAS soldiers. Melot had become a beloved mascot for the brigade, though the gently ironic, Arabic-speaking Belgian seemed an unlikely recruit for a ruthless British special forces unit. But then courage, like death, seldom appears where it is expected.

Operations behind the lines in northern Italy were proving particularly demanding, due to the mountainous terrain and the fickle qualities of the local partisans. Six months before Farran crept up to Albinea, a team of thirty-two men from 2SAS had parachuted into the countryside north of La Spezia on Operation Galia, with orders to attack supply routes behind the shifting front line. The team was led by Captain Bob Walker-Brown, the son of a Scottish surgeon who had joined the SAS after successfully tunneling out of an Italian POW camp, crawling to liberty through the main sewer, and then walking to the Allied lines. He had an enormous mustache, a bluff sense of humor, an upper-class accent so fruity that the men barely understood his commands, and a habit of saying "what, what" after every sentence, thus earning himself the nickname "Captain What What." His principal task was to deceive the Germans into thinking that an entire parachute regiment had landed, and thus divert German forces from opposing the offensive by the US Fifth Army. His orders were to make "the presence of the SAS known to the enemy in the quickest possible time." This Walker-Brown did by attacking anything and everything between Genoa and La Spezia: he ambushed convoys on the Genoa road, mortared villages occupied by German and Italian fascist troops, shot up marching columns, and, in one particularly spectacular coup, attacked a staff car, which was afterward found to contain "a high fascist official," now dead, and about 125 million lire in a suitcase.

The Germans, now in no doubt whatever about the SAS presence among them, launched an intensive manhunt, believing, according to a German prisoner, that they were under attack from a force of at least four hundred parachutists. "Suitably flattered" by this tenfold inflation of his team, Walker-Brown was hiding out in a deserted village when he received word from the partisans that "a large force of Germans [had been] observed at 250 yards advancing in extended order." He decided to beat a retreat across some of the highest and coldest mountains in Europe.

Most of the unit's equipment had been either lost or stolen by the partisans, including rations, rucksacks, and sleeping bags. The radio was broken. The mule drivers had run away, along with their mules. The mountain tracks across Monte Gottero were "sheets of solid ice," wrote Walker-Brown. "Weather conditions were very severe. It was cold and there was heavy snow on the ground [that] made movement extremely difficult and tedious." After twenty-four hours of wading through snow at times waist deep, they crossed the summit, only to discover that a combined force of German ski troops and Mongolian soldiers were in close pursuit and barely an hour behind them. The large band of partisans holding Monte Gottero "immediately vanished into the mountains on hearing this intelligence." Walker-Brown paused briefly in the mountain village of Boschetto before pressing on. "By this time we had completed 59 hours continuous marching without rations or rest." An hour after the SAS had left Boschetto, the village was attacked by a force of two thousand Germans, its partisan defenders captured and then killed. The pursuers finally abandoned the chase, and Walker-Brown's weary force could get some respite, but by early February 1945 he judged that his men were too ill and exhausted to continue, and headed toward the front line. "Owing to the physical condition of the men it was not possible for them to carry much on the last stage of the march." Determined to "reach the Allied lines at all costs" and with only a single tin of bully beef left to eat, Walker-Brown led his men across the heights of 5,500-foot Monte Altissimo, waded the river Magra, and finally reached an American forward patrol. He was awarded the DSO for his "display of guerrilla skill and personal courage," but he deserved another medal for understatement above the call of duty: the trek, he said, had been "difficult and tiring [what, what]." Just six of Walker-Brown's team had been captured, but he estimated they had killed between 100 and 150 Germans, destroyed at least twenty-three vehicles, and kept hundreds of enemy soldiers scouring the mountains when they might have been fighting the Americans.

That operation was a foretaste of what Roy Farran was planning in Operation Tombola, the grand and savage finale to the SAS campaign in Italy.

"THE DETAILS OF this operation might well be from a book by Forester," wrote Farran, a reference to C. S. Forester, the creator of the popular Hornblower adventure novels. On March 6, 1945, an advance party of parachutists had landed safely south of Reggio, to be greeted by Italian partisans. Farran had been instructed by 15th Army Group headquarters that he should remain in Florence to coordinate operations; he could fly with the men to the drop zone and act as a dispatcher, but should on no account parachute in himself. He later claimed that he had "fallen out of the aeroplane by mistake." It would take more than a mere order to prevent Farran from leading his troops into battle.

Once on the ground, he set about fashioning a guerrilla unit out of some exceptionally unpromising ingredients: "140-odd Italians of mixed political affinities," about 100 Russians and only 40 trained SAS men. There were also some 15 women partisans, used as couriers ("staffettas") and intelligence gatherers. Farran's new force was clad in a bewildering variety of uniforms—Italian, American, British, and, confusingly, German—worn along with bushy beards, bandanas, and nonmilitary hats. "Many had only one eye," Farran noted, several lacked shoes, and all were "armed to the teeth with knives, pistols, tommy guns and rifles."

"I was very shaken indeed by the appearance of the raw material," wrote Farran after reviewing the troops under his command. They resembled, he decided, "a picture of Wat Tyler's rebellion."

Their military caliber was as varied as their dress. Some of the

Italian partisans were veteran mountain fighters, but "the rest were absolutely useless." A fierce enmity smoldered between the Italian communist partisans, the Christian Democrat "Green Flames" led by a handsome young priest named Don Carlo, and a newly formed right-wing group commanded by a piratical and corrupt former quartermaster, known only as "Barba Nera" (or Black Beard). The Russians were brave and enthusiastic, but unpredictable. The leader was Victor Pirogov, a former Red Army lieutenant who had escaped from a German POW camp and fought under the more Italianate name Victor Modena. "A big, blond Russian from Smolensk, with a charming smile and a great reputation as a partisan," he cut an extraordinary figure, clad in blue peaked sailor's cap and German jackboots, with a strip of blue parachute silk wound around his neck.

An initial series of raids, launched from Farran's mountain base, did little to reassure him that his recruits were up to the job: the Russians showed a "marked reduction in their offensive spirit after they had taken a few casualties," and without the SAS to prod them forward "the Italians were only just worth feeding." Still, with a mixture of "threats and persuasion," and resupplied by airdrops of food and ammunition, Farran was convinced he could instill some sort of military discipline into this "heterogeneous force." They took the name Battaglione Alleata (Allied Battalion) or, less formally, Battaglione McGinty.

Knowing that uniforms, however approximate, promote cohesion, Farran sent a message back to base requesting a consignment of berets, along with green and yellow feather hackles. The force also adopted woven badges with the SAS motto in Italian: "*Chi osa vince.*" The women staffettas had "McGinty" embroidered on their pockets and a badge consisting of a bow and arrow. In a final flourish, "to add character to this already colourful and composite force" (as if it needed any more), Farran summoned from headquarters a bagpiper from the Highland Light Infantry, David Kirkpatrick, who made his first parachute descent to join this strange crew. "Whether he jumped in a kilt has not been recorded," wrote

Farran, who later admitted that he had wanted Scottish musical accompaniment to the operation in order "to stir the romantic Italian mind and to gratify my own vanity." A somewhat more practical 75mm howitzer was dropped at the same time.

The battalion had been in training for two weeks when Michael Lees, the SOE officer liaising with the local partisans, planted a plan in Farran's mind. The German LI Corps had established its headquarters just twenty miles away at Albinea: a tempting though difficult target. "I had long toyed with the idea of a really large operation behind the centre of the front [and visualized] myself . . . at the head of a whole army of partisans." The top brass in Florence, however, had other ideas. After initially approving the attack on Albinea, and dropping a useful batch of air-reconnaissance photographs, 15th Army Group HQ received intelligence reports that the Germans were planning their own assault on partisan groups and unequivocally ordered Farran not to proceed. Once again Farran ignored the command, and later wrote, with ringing insincerity: "Unfortunately I had already left on the long march to the plains when the cancellation was received on my wireless set in the mountains. In any case, having once committed a partisan force to such an attack, any alteration in the plan would have been disastrous to guerrilla morale."

By the morning of March 26, the hundred-man-strong raiding party was safely installed in an ox shed at Casa del Lupo, ten miles from Albinea. Farran dispatched two of the Italian staffettas, Valda and Noris, to reconnoiter the target. "An attractive girl could pedal through a German-held village with impunity" and gather vital intelligence, reflected Farran. "How a woman can loosen a soldier's tongue." Noris was a particularly arresting figure, "a tall, raven-haired girl with Irish blue eyes, as brave and dangerous as a tigress and completely devoted to the British company." In camp, she wore a red beret, a battledress blouse, and a skirt sewn out of an army blanket with a pistol tucked into the waistband. Farran was not scared by much, but he was a little afraid of Noris, and more than slightly smitten. "Noris was worth ten male partisans."

She and her companion returned after five hours and reported: "Everything seemed normal in Albinea."

The raiding party emerged in small groups from the ox shed in the misty, predawn darkness of March 27 and headed for the town. Once in Albinea, the Russians formed a cordon across the road, "to cut off the objective from help." Several hundred Germans were asleep in billets about four hundred yards to the south. These would surely come pouring up the road as soon as the shooting started, and Victor Modena and his men would be waiting. The two assault teams, each composed of ten SAS men and twenty Italian partisans, crept toward the two villas: Farran and the remaining force would provide covering fire, and send up a flare after twenty minutes to signal the order to withdraw.

A few minutes after 2:00 a.m., an explosion of gunfire mixed with the eerie wail of bagpipes, as the piper added his own, surreal element to the assault with a loud rendition of "Highland Laddie." The sentries guarding the villas died "before they knew they were being attacked." The front door stood open at the Villa Rossi, where the general commanding the LI Corps, a divisional commander, and thirty-seven other officers and men had been peacefully sleeping a few moments earlier. The raiders stormed in, firing wildly and hurling grenades. A siren on the roof sounded the alarm, every light in the house seemed to blaze on at once, and the occupants, lurched from sleep, seized their weapons and responded with the desperate speed of cornered men. A frantic battle took place in the hallway, bullets screaming off the marble walls. "After fierce fighting the ground floor was taken but the Germans resisted furiously from the upper floors, firing and throwing grenades down the spiral staircase." An attempt to charge up the stairs was repulsed; a second attack was also beaten back, leaving two SAS men dead, one officer and an NCO. The surviving Germans then tried to fight their way out: six were gunned down on the stairs. Two surrendered. The Italian partisans "dealt" with them—Farran's code for summary execution. After twenty minutes, the attackers withdrew, leaving a fire burning in the ground-floor kitchen.

At the Villa Calvi, on the other side of the road, another vicious battle was still raging. Finding the door locked, the raiders used a bazooka and Bren gun to blow off the lock, then rammed open the door, tossed in a handful of grenades, and crashed inside. The delay had given the defenders more time to prepare, and another brutal close-quarters battle took place. "The din was deafening," said one of the SAS participants. After several minutes of "furious fighting," the Germans again withdrew up a spiral staircase to the upper floor leaving behind eight dead, including the chief of staff himself, Colonel Lemelsen. From the lawn, the raiders poured a torrent of Bren-gun and bazooka fire into the upper floors. Wooden furniture, files, and curtains were dragged into piles in the registry and map rooms downstairs, and then ignited with plastic explosive and a bottle of petrol. Farran was in his element: "Bullets were flying everywhere, and over it all, the defiant skirl of the pipes." As the raiders withdrew, the building was "burning furiously."

As expected, German troops had swiftly emerged from their barracks and rushed north in an attempt to relieve the besieged occupants of the villas, only to meet Victor Modena and his men spread out across the road. "The Russians returned fire very accurately and their ring was never broken during the attack," wrote Farran with somewhat surprised approval.

On Farran's signal, the raiders first headed west, then south, taking a wide circle back to the rendezvous at Casa del Lupo with dawn beginning to break. As the force pulled out, Villa Calvi exploded. "The sky was red from the blazing villas," wrote Farran.

Carrying their wounded on stretchers, fueled by Benzedrine tablets, pummeled by driving rain, the party made its way across country "buzzing with Germans" and back into the hills. They reached the base camp in the Villa Minozzo valley twenty-two and a half hours later, by which time Farran's old leg wounds had rendered him unable to walk, and he was brought in, much to his embarrassment, on the back of a pony. The partisans, "cheering over and over again for McGinty and Battaglione Alleata," immediately threw a party: "Fried eggs, bread and vino by the gallon." With the piper playing, the SAS men gave the partisans a demonstration of the eightsome reel, a traditional Scottish dance, a spectacle that Farran described as "one of the greatest moments" of the campaign.

Farran calculated that at least sixty Germans had been killed in the attack on Albinea. The LI Corps command center had been utterly destroyed, along with "the greater part of the headquarters' papers, files and maps." Villa Calvi had been demolished, and Villa Rossi damaged beyond repair. A joint force of British parachutists and partisans had successfully penetrated and then devastated a German base far behind the lines that had seemed, to its occupants, so heavily guarded and so far from the battlefield as to be invulnerable. The crushing effect of the raid on German morale was doubtless reinforced by the death of Lemelsen, a relative of the overall commander of the German Fourteenth Army in Italy. Gratifying reports reached the SAS camp of the raid's impact on the German troops. "The Germans in the whole area are now in a state of alarm."

For his troubles, Farran narrowly escaped a court-martial. He was given a "rocket" by 15th Army Group headquarters for launching a "premature attack disregarding orders," which he cheerfully disregarded.

Throughout the spring, as the 15th Army Group offensive got under way, Farran's mobile "guerrilla battalion," now reinforced by the arrival of several jeeps, fought a series of actions against the retreating Germans. Farran left a memorable description of his men preparing to go into action from their base in the little village of Vitriola.

> Long, greasy-haired pirates were sitting on the steps, cleaning their weapons in the streets. Jeeps dashed about everywhere with supplies. The night air was broken by the tap-tap-tap of Morse from our wireless sets and the Russians sang as they refilled their magazines.

At night one could hear Modena's tame accordionist and occasionally Kirkpatrick's pipes, which were now suffering from lack of treacle, an essential lubricant for the bag, I am told.

On April 22, he learned that an extended column of German lorries, carts, and tanks was slowly crossing the ford at Magreta, an ideal ambush site. The raiders hid in the foothills, and then opened fire at 2:30 in the afternoon: trucks exploded, horses stampeded, the convoy ground to an appalled halt, sitting ducks in the water. "The shooting was very good," wrote Farran grimly. "It was obvious the Germans were really on the run."

Farran's picaresque little army had inflicted damage out of all proportion to its size and his own expectations: at least three hundred Germans killed and fifteen trucks destroyed. "There is little doubt that the actions considerably accelerated the panic and rout of some three or four German divisions," wrote Farran. As in North Africa and France, the essential value of the operation lay in tying up enemy troops, fomenting fear and uncertainty, and the demoralizing "effect of the presence of so formidable and enterprising a force in the immediate rear of the enemy."

On May 2, Field Marshal Alexander sent out a "Special Order of the Day" to Allied forces in the Mediterranean theater:

> After nearly two years of hard and continuous fighting which started in Sicily in the summer of 1943, you stand today as victors of the Italian campaign. You have won a victory which has ended in the complete and utter rout of the German armed forces in the Mediterranean. By clearing Italy of the last Nazi aggressor, you have liberated a country of over 40,000,000 people. Today the remnants of a once proud army have laid down their arms to you—close to a million men with all their arms, equipment and impedimenta.

The second phase of war for the SAS, which had started almost two years earlier at the other end of Italy with the assault on Capo Murro di Porco, was over.

A month before Farran's attack on Albinea, Brigadier Mike Calvert became commander of the SAS Brigade. Calvert had fought with the British special forces known as the Chindits during the Burma campaign, and had seen ferocious action behind the lines. On his appointment "Mad Mike" Calvert sent a message to the men now under his command: "You are special troops and I expect you to do special things in this last heave against the Hun."

Chapter 22

INTO THE REICH

THE SAS HAD FOUGHT DESERT WAR, GUERRILLA WAR, AND conventional war, a war in forests, mountains, and fields, on freezing snow, clinging mud, and baking sand. It had fought Germans, Italians, French, and Russians, against uniformed troops, collaborators, spies, and irregulars. But as the war entered its final bloody chapter, the SAS found itself fighting against people defending their own land, staunchly and desperately, albeit in a heinous cause.

On March 25, 1945, the SAS crossed the Rhine at the tip of an army invading Germany itself. Hitherto, they had fought to liberate lands occupied by Hitler's armies; now they were themselves the occupiers. Some of the German forces, wrote Johnny Cooper, were "running like hell," but others were fighting for every inch of German soil: the fanatical SS and others implicated in the crimes of Nazism, but also ordinary men of the German home guard, the Volkssturm, young boys and older men between the ages of thirteen and sixty recruited to give their lives in one last, suicidal defense of the doomed Third Reich. The combination of the ardor of youth and the misguided patriotism of older age would ensure that the subjugation of Germany came in a last deluge of wasted blood, young and old.

The SAS, having launched so many devastating ambushes in France and Italy, now faced the prospect of being ambushed at any moment. "It was as if our Maquis role in France was reversed," said one member of 1SAS. This was a war fought from behind hedge-rows and in ditches, messy and unorganized, and nastier than any-thing the SAS had experienced hitherto.

The SS seemed "happy to fight and die," and the SAS often seemed happy to oblige them. "We never took prisoners on those occasions." The reactions of German civilians to this army of occupation varied widely: some were cowed, most were petri-fied, some rushed to surrender, and some remained defiant. One moment the SAS troops would be sharing their rations with half-starved German women and children; the next, a teenage boy would emerge from behind a wall and take aim with a Panzerfaust, the handheld, high-explosive, antitank weapon, an act of fanatical, self-destructive bravery so naive that only an adolescent could be persuaded to do it. Often these child-soldiers had no other weap-ons. The SAS had not signed up to kill teenagers. For many, the last ghastly episode of the war was the worst.

Frankforce, named after Brian Franks, commander of 2SAS, consisted of two reinforced squadrons, one each from the 1 and 2SAS regiments, numbering about three hundred men in all, mounted in seventy-five armed jeeps. Initially they would support the parachute landings across the Rhine, and then act in concert with armored divisions pushing into Germany. The jeeps were stiff with weaponry: in addition to the twin Vickers, each carried twelve spare drums of ammunition, with a bazooka and Bren gun in the rear; every third jeep was armed with a .50-caliber Brown-ing with a mounted searchlight. Some were armed with three-inch mortars. The SAS rode into Germany on small, mobile arsenals, bristling with highly concentrated killing power.

The end of the war was plainly in sight for the SAS, but that knowledge brought with it a flicker of superstitious dread, not fear exactly, but the intuition that having cheated the odds for so long, death might yet come at the very end. Reg Seekings was not easily unnerved, but as he lay under his jeep one night, he felt a stab of apprehension when his gunner, a tough Glaswegian named Mack-enzie who had served time for arson, remarked calmly: "I'm going to cop it. I want you to promise to write to the wife and tell her I went down shooting your guns." Like many soldiers, Seekings believed in a military sixth sense: "People have a premonition and pretty often it's bloody true," he said.

As a defense against identification, and execution under Hitler's Commando Order, the SAS were ordered to wear black berets, rather than the distinctive red beret of airborne forces, and to identify themselves as tank corps troops. All references to the SAS were to be excised from their pay books. In effect, they would be fighting under cover, camouflaged as ordinary soldiers. The disguise was appropriate enough, for the role assigned to the SAS had departed, once again, from the script laid down by David Stirling: they were to act as forward reconnaissance, assault troops to weed out pockets of resistance, draw enemy fire, clear the roads, and keep the tanks and ground troops rolling forward. "Our job was to speed up the attack," said Seekings. "To hit hard, drive through the German lines, turn back and shoot them up the rear, and make a gap for the ordinary army to come through. . . . We were just driving a wedge all the time."

After crossing the Rhine on the amphibious landing craft known as Buffaloes, the forces of the two regiments split up. The 1SAS unit would carry out reconnaissance patrols for the 6th Airborne Division northeast of Hamminkeln; 2SAS was attached to the 6th Independent Armoured Brigade to head east from Schermbeck.

Pat Riley, the American-born desert veteran, had spent the previous year recruiting and training troops for the various French operations, and now rejoined the regiment just before the Rhine crossing. He recalled the forward skirmishing as an erratic, piecemeal affair, "a scrap here and a scrap there," confused and overlapping engagements that never quite cohered into pitched battle. There was "nothing by way of a standup fight," wrote Cooper. The men recalled the slog into Germany in a series of bloody vignettes.

Two days after crossing the Rhine, 1SAS made its first contact with German forces. Bill Fraser's squadron was called forward to tackle a densely wooded area where the enemy was dug in. Canadian paratroopers had already lost eight men to accurate fire from a Spandau machine gun concealed among the trees. A force of twelve jeeps, with Fraser taking the lead, drove slowly up the left flank into a small clearing and crept forward to within thirty yards of the Germans before they were spotted. The Spandau opened up, sending bullets thudding into the leading jeep, which flipped over. Alex Muirhead's mortars took out the machine-gun position, and then the other nests were knocked out, one by one. The attack advanced the front by some two thousand yards, but Bill Fraser's war was over. A bullet had passed through his hand. It was hard to tell whether he was disappointed because he had "wanted to see it through," or whether he was pleased to have a Blighty wound that would take him out of battle and send him home. If anyone deserved some peace, it was Bill Fraser, but as ever he remained inscrutable, distant, lost.

A few days later, Seekings was passing through another wooded area when he felt the odd sensation of being watched. A moment later a boy, perhaps fourteen years old, emerged from nowhere holding two hand grenades, the long-handled variety known to the British as "spud-mashers." Seekings trained his gun on the teenager, preparing to shoot the second he moved. A long, slow second passed as the boy and the old soldier stood locked in eye contact. Slowly the German boy lowered the grenades and surrendered. Only later, from a surrendering colonel, did Seekings learn that throughout that wordless confrontation, a group of concealed German paratroopers had their guns trained on him. "If you'd shot him, we would have fought to the death."

"Some of the poor little blighters were only 13 or 14 years old," recalled Cooper. "They were crawling out of holes everywhere. The Germans put schoolboys in uniform and forced them to fight, when their chances of survival were minimal. It was inhumane." Yet the SAS was prepared to kill children if necessary. "If you shot one little bastard the others would start crying," a trooper grimly recalled. At one point, under sporadic fire, two captured teenage

Germans were made to sit on the hood of a jeep, as human shields. During a pause one of them leaped down and tried to run away; he was shot dead. The youngest German recruits displayed an arrogance that had, by and large, been crushed out of their elders. On April 10, Muirhead's squadron encircled a group of Germans that had opened fire from behind a ridge. They turned out to be twenty marine cadets attached to an SS unit. The NCO in command was twenty-four, the rest were all under twenty years old. "They were very cheeky," the War Diary reported. "One asked us to light his cigarette, another for chocolate and another for a comb. He had his hair parted with a .45." That could mean a revolver was fired over his head, or it could indicate that he was shot in the head for his insolence. The diary does not go into detail.

As the front advanced, Paddy Mayne toured the different squadrons, usually accompanied by the padre, Fraser McLuskey. A soldier in John Tonkin's squadron remembered how Mayne's arrival was greeted by the production of a tin bath, into which was poured every kind of alcohol available, mostly Schnapps, to create a vast and terrifying cocktail. McLuskey played the piano. Everyone got blind drunk, and Mayne the drunkest.

The 1SAS force was commanded by Harry Poat, the tomato grower from Guernsey, who left a vivid account of the days in late March and early April as the SAS advanced, field by field, village by village, hedgerow by hedgerow. "The fighting is very hard and we have 'mixed it' many times with the Hun. They are all SS and the real thing, and although they no longer have an organized defence, they are fighting cleverly in a guerrilla role, and I can assure you they are better at it than our friends the maquis . . . the chaps have fought magnificently, and killed many SS." On April 2, the Allies took Münster after some ferocious street fighting by the US 17th Airborne Division and the British 6th Guards Tank Brigade. More than 90 percent of the Old Town had already been destroyed by bombing. On Easter Day, Fraser McLuskey held an open-air service some fifteen miles north of the city.

Seekings, reunited once more with Cooper, played the role of grizzled, cranky veteran, terrorizing his superior officers as he had once tried to bully Cooper. "The young officers weren't prepared to argue the toss with me," he later bragged. "They were shit-scared of me." Yet the killing may have begun to affect even Seekings. East of Erle, driving slowly along a country track, he spotted a line of uniformed soldiers approaching on the other side of the hedgerow. Quickly backing the jeep into a culvert, Seekings cocked the Bren gun and waited. The soldiers came into view, a line of eleven German home guardsmen, trudging in single file, mostly middle-aged and wholly oblivious of what was about to happen. Seekings waited until the Germans were within a few feet of his hiding place. "I opened up with a whole magazine, chopped them down, riddled the bloody lot." Once he would have gloried in the butchery. Not now. "The slaughter was terrible."

The SAS were also frequently the targets of ambush, not the architects. For most of the war they had relied on concealment. Now they were usually advancing, and at the mercy of an invisible enemy. "The country up ahead is very woody and not our cup of tea at all," Poat wrote in a letter to headquarters on April 13. "Open country is the only place for us." But in the land they now traversed, open country was rare. Seekings and Cooper were leading a column of jeeps through a small copse when bullets started to fly around them. "Reg, we break!" shouted Cooper, as he gunned the engine and reversed at high speed. Seven men had been injured and one killed. "We belted out of there like shit off a shovel," wrote Cooper. "I don't think we saw a single German."

Two days earlier, 1SAS had experienced the full peril of this new terrain and this new form of combat. On the Nienburg-to-Neustadt road, one of the armored cars up ahead was suddenly hit by a Panzerfaust fired by a teenager who had leaped from a ditch. The next moment, heavy fire erupted from the woods to the left of the road. "We were at a terrible disadvantage standing high on the road firing our Vickers while the enemy were lying in the undergrowth," wrote Poat, who ordered the jeeps to form a defensive circle, firing outward. He swiftly realized they were in danger of being surrounded. "It was absolutely impossible to see the enemy as the woods were too thick. The chaps fought like devils, firing everything they had. After about ten minutes I saw we were out-numbered and out-positioned and the casualties were mounting rapidly, so I gave orders for us to form a body of all the jeeps still serviceable, get the wounded on board, and make a dash for it to our own lines." The advancing Germans were barely thirty yards away when the ragged convoy screeched away in headlong retreat. "I never thought the old jeeps were so slow," wrote Poat. "50 mph seemed like snail's pace."

Mackenzie, the tough little Scottish gunner who had predicted his own death, was shot in the armpit and would undoubtedly have bled to death had Seekings not stuffed a field dressing into the wound and driven the jeep back to a dressing station. Mackenzie lost his arm, but lived, rather to the surprise of Seekings, whose sense of foreboding grew sharper even as victory seemed more assured.

By April 11, Frankforce had pushed east as far as Esperke, near Celle, and Poat sent back an accounting to the adjutant at SAS headquarters, for all the world as if he was reporting on his holi-day shopping. "To date we have killed approximately 189 enemy, captured 233, and taken much equipment. . . . Well, cheerio for now, let's have your news. I would like you to forward this letter to Paddy who, I believe, is off in battle, though I have no definite news of him."

Paddy Mayne was not merely in battle, but plunging into his last conflict with a fervor that was either supremely brave or sui-cidal, and possibly both.

Two days earlier, two squadrons of 1SAS assembled at the Ger-man town of Meppen, near the Dutch border, to begin what would be the final SAS operation in Europe. The mood was strange. The men knew that the end of the European war was near, but there

were rumors of imminent redeployment to the Far East. Suppressed elation was mixed with a chill of trepidation.

Mayne laid out the mission, code-named Operation Howard.
The two SAS squadrons would press into Germany as the "spearhead" for the 4th Canadian Armoured Division, clearing the way
for the tanks, rooting out remnants of resistance, and conducting
forward reconnaissance while "causing alarm and disorganization
behind enemy lines." They would drive northeast toward Oldenburg, and then continue north to the U-boat base at Wilhelm-
shaven, a potential final target. Intelligence suggested they would
encounter minimal opposition, and it was optimistically predicted
that, with the tank division "on their heels," the SAS should be
able to cover as much fifty miles a day. The Canadians cheerfully patronized the SAS in their jeeps, referring to them as "our
friends in the little mechanized mess tins." But they had a point:
tanks were far better equipped for what lay ahead.

The terrain south of Oldenburg was far from ideal for jeep
warfare. "Crossed and re-crossed by dykes and canals" that made
navigation difficult, it was too wooded and boggy to permit the
vehicles to operate effectively off-road. Some thought the mission misguided, the men inadequately trained and underarmed for
their allotted role. Still, when the plan had been put to Mayne by
the Canadian commander of the 4th Armoured Division, he had
"accepted with alacrity and enthusiasm." Mayne had not been in
the thick of the action since Termoli. He was itching for a fight
and, like Farran, he had brought along his own musical accompaniment. The windup gramophone player had survived the French
campaign and was now installed in the back of his jeep with a
loudspeaker attached: Paddy Mayne would invade Germany to the
strains of his favorite Irish music, the ballads of Percy French.

The troop set off at dawn on April 10, and made good progress,
crossing the river Hase at around midday. Traveling on parallel
roads, the two squadrons, B and C, pressed on toward the town of
Börger. This was grim, low country, suffused with tragic recent

history. In 1933, at nearby Börgermoor, the Nazis had established one of the first concentration camps, holding socialists, communists, and other "undesirables" regarded as enemies of the Third Reich. The prisoners had composed their own song, which became popular as a rallying anthem for German volunteers in the International Brigades during the Spanish Civil War.

> *Up and down the guards are marching,*
> *No one, no one can get through.*
> *Flight would mean a sure death facing,*
> *Guns and barbed wire block our view.*
> *We are the peat bog soldiers,*
> *Marching with our spades to the moor.*

On the very day that the SAS set off on Operation Howard, the prisoners of Börgermoor were assembled and began a grueling death march to another camp farther east, at Aschendorfermoor, which only a few would complete. The SAS was entering a world of horror.

Squadron B, under the command of Major Dick Bond, was approaching Börger when suddenly the middle of the jeep column came under fire from Panzerfaust rockets, machine guns, and snipers. Some of the shooting emanated from the second of two farm buildings, ranged in an L-shape on the right-hand side of the road, as well as from a dense copse of trees behind and a little way beyond the farmhouse. Bond and the three men in his jeep baled out and scrambled into a deep drainage ditch on the other side of the road, where they were joined by the men from three other jeeps. The vehicles ahead of the attack accelerated out of range and came to a halt. Those behind reversed quickly.

Bond was a recruit from the Auxiliary Units, formed to resist the Nazi invasion of Britain that never happened. Separated from the rest of the men, he attempted to scramble over a large drainage pipe running at right angles into the waterlogged ditch, but as he did so, his head appeared above ground level: a single sniper's bullet killed him instantly. Bond's driver, a Czech Jew named Mikheil Levinsohn, attempted to reach him, also by climbing over the pipe, but the sniper now had a perfect bead on the spot. Levinsohn was also shot dead. Two men south of the drainage pipe managed to scramble down the ditch to where the rest of the column was waiting and reported what had happened. A radio message was immediately sent to Paddy Mayne, who arrived within ten minutes of the ambush. "Poor Dick," he repeated quietly. "Poor Dick."

Mayne's driver, a fellow Ulsterman from the Shankill Road named Billy Hull, had come to know his commander well and understood his moods. "Mayne was in one of those silent rages," said Hull. The commander of 1SAS picked up a Bren gun and magazine. "Poor Dick," he muttered again. Hull followed him with a tommy gun. Eight men, two of them seriously wounded, were still lying in the ditch, pinned down by sporadic fire from one of the farm buildings and the woods. On Mayne's instruction, Hull entered the adjacent farmhouse, climbed the stairs, and fired a single burst from his tommy gun at the windows of the second building. This drew a hail of fire in response, as Hull flattened himself on the floor. "Bullets were ricocheting off the walls and ceiling, and in seconds the ceiling was set on fire by tracers." But the ambushers had now revealed their positions. On the ground, Mayne raised the Bren gun to his shoulder (no easy task with a weapon almost a yard long and weighing more than twenty-five pounds) and began firing "burst after burst" into the house, which gave Hull time to escape and rejoin the main party. Having apparently silenced the attackers, either by killing them or forcing them to retreat through the back door, Mayne beckoned for a jeep with a twin Vickers to come forward to take up his position and continue pounding the German positions. Then he walked back to the squadron.

Firing continued from the German forces concealed in the copse. "Who wants to have a go?" Mayne asked.

John Scott, a young lieutenant recruited from the SBS who had been commissioned the previous November, immediately stepped forward. He was never quite sure why. During an earlier firefight, Scott had come across a German, badly wounded in the stomach; instead of getting the man medical attention, he had shot him. "I regretted it, but I suppose my nerves were frayed at the time." Scott had also ordered Levinsohn to try to reach Bond in the ditch, and had inadvertently sent him to his death. Two different strains of guilt seem to have impelled him to volunteer.

Mayne took the wheel of a jeep, and Scott clambered into the back and manned the twin Vickers. Mayne said nothing. "There was a coldness about Paddy, and it was that coldness that allowed him to sum things up quickly," Scott later observed. Mayne had calculated that it would be impossible to outflank the Germans in the woods, so the only way to relieve the trapped men would be to blast them out. At little more than walking pace, Mayne drove up the road while Scott poured fire into the trees and buildings on the right. As they passed the pinned-down men in the ditch, Mayne shouted above the din: "I'll pick you up on the way back."

These Germans were not the uniformed civilians of the home guard, but remnants of the 1st Parachute Division, the hardened force last encountered by the SAS in Italy—soldiers who, as the report of the engagement later acknowledged, "fought well and even fanatically." They responded to Mayne's assault in kind, pouring down fire on the lone jeep; miraculously, neither man was hit, as Mayne continued to give "cool, precise orders" to his gunner. "There can be only one explanation why Colonel Mayne was not killed," wrote one of his officers. "The sheer audacity and daring which he showed in driving his jeep across their field of fire momentarily bewildered the enemy." One hundred yards beyond the abandoned jeeps, Mayne performed a U-turn. Scott swapped the Vickers for the .50-caliber Browning, a heavy machine gun capable of firing up to six hundred rounds a minute, and moved into the passenger seat. Then they performed the same procedure as before, but in reverse, while Scott continued to blast away at the woods. The German firing slowed; then their guns fell silent. "By this time half their number must have been wiped out," wrote one eyewitness. "By now the enemy had had enough." Mayne drew parallel with the stranded men and stopped. Scott wrote: "He jumped out of the jeep giving me orders to continue firing, lifted the wounded out of the ditch, placed them in the jeep and drove back to the main party." The rescue operation had taken less than four minutes. This action was later described, in official reports, as "virtually suicidal," but Mayne would later insist that he had weighed up the odds: "People think I'm a big, mad Irishman, but I'm not. I calculate the risks for and against and then I have a go."

"Throughout the entire action Colonel Mayne showed a personal courage that it has never before been my privilege to witness," wrote Scott, whose own astonishing bravery has never been fully recognized, largely because he hid it. "I don't think that my part in the action was worth mentioning," he said later.

Bond and Levinsohn were buried a few miles from where they had died, and the SAS pressed on, through the village of Esterwegen and into the flooded woodland beyond, terrain so waterlogged that it was, in Mayne's words, "absolutely bloody to work in." By the afternoon of April 11, they were just thirty-five miles west of Bremen. A sudden mortar attack offered a reminder of how deeply they had penetrated into Germany. Two jeeps were destroyed. An eight-man patrol that attempted to move forward on foot was surrounded and captured by men of the German 7th Parachute Division, which had been deployed to halt the Allied advance. The remaining German forces were said to be massing around Oldenburg for a counterattack. In a dense patch of conifers, a sniper shot one trooper through the head and badly injured two more. The roads were heavily mined, requiring the SAS to pick their way forward. The Canadian tanks had yet to turn up, and the unit was running low on food and ammunition. "Enemy opposition was far stronger than had been anticipated [and] no deep penetration was possible."

Mayne sent back a message to HQ: "The battle is turning into a slogging match and ourselves into mine detectors." He called a halt and waited for the tanks to catch up. In all, the Canadians reported, the SAS had taken "over 400 prisoners of assorted shapes and sizes, disarmed the lot and held about 100 of the toughest type, mostly paratroopers."

Mayne was recommended for a Victoria Cross, the highest British award for valor. The citations competed to laud his feats during the fight outside Börger. "By a single act of supreme bravery [he] drove the enemy from a strongly held village, thereby breaking the crust of the enemy defences in the whole of this sector," wrote the new SAS brigade commander, Mike Calvert. "His cool and determined action and his complete command of the situation together with his unsurpassed gallantry, inspired all ranks. Not only did he save the lives of the wounded but also completely defeated and destroyed the enemy." Major General Christopher Vokes, the commander of the Canadian 4th Armored Division, praised his "leadership and dash" and added, "this officer is worthy of the highest award for gallantry." Field Marshal Montgomery himself signed the medal recommendation.

And yet Mayne was not awarded the Victoria Cross; instead, "VC" was crossed out, without explanation, and "bar to DSO" was added. Mayne had accumulated a DSO and three bars, each bar indicating that he had met the medal criteria in different theaters of war. He was now one of the most highly decorated soldiers in the British Army.

Why Paddy Mayne was denied the VC was, and remains, a source of deep controversy. Jim Almonds, now a commissioned officer, was baffled: "He earned it more than once. Probably his character was against him. His face didn't fit, but his actions did." David Stirling later described the omission as a "monstrous injustice," and with his characteristic eye for an official conspiracy blamed "faceless men who didn't want Mayne and the SAS to be given the distinction." Perhaps Mayne's history of drinking and brawling counted against him. He had few supporters among his superiors. Perhaps the rumors of his homosexuality had reached higher up. But the explanation may be more mundane: there was an understanding that, to merit a VC, the recipient should have materially assisted the outcome of a battle, with actions verified by independent witnesses. In SAS operations—covert, fast moving, and self-regulating—such criteria were often hard, if not impossible, to fulfill. Mayne may have been denied this venerable honor because he was fighting a new sort of war.

The action for which many believed Paddy Mayne should have won the VC took place at the precise moment another special forces soldier was winning that medal in the final weeks of the Italian campaign. Major Anders Lassen was a twenty-four-year-old Dane who had signed up with the commandos in 1940 and joined the Special Boat Service when it was still attached to the SAS. In April 1944, he had led a highly successful raid on the Axis-held Greek island of Santorini, eliminating most of the garrison and blowing up the radio station. A year later, at Lake Comacchio in Italy, Lassen was ordered to lead a raid with just eighteen men that would give the impression that a major landing was under way. The raiding party immediately ran into entrenched German positions. Like Mayne, Lassen favored the direct approach. The subsequent citation read:

> Major Lassen himself then attacked with grenades, and annihilated the first position containing four Germans and two machine guns. Ignoring the hail of bullets sweeping the road from three enemy positions, he raced forward to engage the second position under covering fire from the remainder of the force. Throwing in more grenades he silenced this position which was then overrun by his patrol . . . Lassen rallied and reorganized his force and brought his fire to bear on the third position. Moving forward himself he flung in more grenades which produced a cry of "Kamerad." He then went forward to within three or four yards of the position to order the enemy outside, and to take

their surrender. Whilst shouting to them to come out
he was hit by a burst of Spandau fire from the left of the
position . . . By his magnificent leadership and complete disregard for his personal safety, Major Lassen
had, in the face of overwhelming superiority, achieved
his objects. Three positions were wiped out, accounting for six machine guns, killing eight and wounding
others of the enemy, and two prisoners were taken.

Lassen was the only non-Commonwealth soldier in the Second
World War to be awarded the VC. But, unlike Mayne, he did not
survive: Anders Lassen refused to be evacuated, insisting that this
would endanger his men, and died of his wounds.

On April 21, a week after the end of Operation Howard, a message was relayed to SAS units in the field: "David Stirling in great
heart sends many messages and congratulations to all, and hopes
to come out and visit you soon."

Stirling was free, and back on the warpath.

Chapter 23

LIBERATION

T HE SMELL HIT THEM FIRST. ON APRIL 15, 1945, THE SAS jeeps were driving through the dense woods of pine and silver birch outside Celle, heading for Lüneburg Heath, when they caught the first whiff, a cloying stench of rot and excrement that seemed to hang in the air like a plague miasma. The reek of pure evil, it grew steadily stronger as they advanced. "We'd been coming up through the forest," said Reg Seekings, "and for a day or so we'd had this horrible stink."

Lieutenant John Randall and his driver were on a reconnaissance foray ahead of the main force when they came to a pair of impressive iron gates, standing open at the entrance to a sandy track. Randall was intrigued, wondering if this might be the gateway to some grand country house, and ordered the driver to turn in. After half a mile, they reached a barbed-wire fence ten feet high, and another gate. If this was a POW camp there might be Allied servicemen inside awaiting liberation. The smell grew ever more powerful. A handful of SS guards stood idly by, and stared listlessly as the SAS jeep drove through. Machine-gunners in the watchtowers spaced along the fence looked down but made no move. Randall drew his revolver as a precaution. He was struck by the neatly tended flowerbeds on either side of the gate, and the gleaming whitewashed curbstones.

One hundred yards beyond, they entered a surreal tableau. In a wide clearing, beside rows of low, shuttered huts, wandered an aimless army of ghosts, shuffling, withered semiskeletons with sunken eyes and parchment skin, some clad in black-and-white striped prison garb, but many almost naked. The prisoners converged on the jeep, plucking at the men's uniforms in supplication, speaking a multitude of languages, including English, pleading for food, help, protection. "There were hundreds of them and an overpowering stench," recalled Randall. The guards looked on, without apparent interest. A little farther on was what Randall initially took to be a potato patch, which some of the starving, half-naked figures seemed to be picking over, as if in search of sustenance. On drawing closer, Randall saw it was a pile of dead bodies; the living were pulling off the ragged garments of the dead to clothe themselves. Some fifty yards beyond that was a spectacle that made Randall gasp and retch: a vast pit, fifty feet square, containing a contorted mass of bodies, a charnel pit filled to overflowing with the dead, and the main source of the appalling smell.

Randall and his driver were the first Allied soldiers to enter Bergen-Belsen concentration camp, a place that would become synonymous with Nazi barbarity. Some 60,000 prisoners were still packed into a camp designed to accommodate 10,000; the bodies of another 13,000 people lay all around the site, victims of disease, starvation, and brutality. Some 70,000 people perished at Belsen. Just over a month before the arrival of the SAS, the fifteen-year-old Anne Frank had died here, most probably of typhus, leaving behind a diary that would go on to become the most widely read testament to the crimes of the Holocaust.

A few minutes later Randall was joined by others from the troop: Reg Seekings and Johnny Cooper, along with the chaplain, Fraser McLuskey, and Major John Tonkin, the commander of Operation Bulbasket. "We stood aghast," wrote Cooper. "We simply could not comprehend how it was possible for human beings to treat their fellow men in such a brutal and heinous way." The remaining prison guards, either oblivious to the arrival of Allied soldiers or unconcerned by it, were carrying on the business of murder as usual. Taking advantage of the distraction caused by the arrival of the British soldiers, "a woman prisoner thrust her hand under the wire to try to grab a rotten turnip." A guard stepped forward and casually shot her dead. The padre had been standing just a few dozen feet away. Cooper saw the look on his face, as the woman slumped. McLuskey had wondered long and hard about whether he could ever take up arms. "McLuskey would have shot the first German he could have got his hands on that day," thought Cooper.

At that moment there appeared a smiling figure in SS uniform who introduced himself as Hauptsturmführer Josef Kramer, the commandant of Bergen-Belsen. Alongside him stood a blond woman in the neat dark-blue uniform of a female camp guard: he introduced her as Irma Grese, the warden in charge of women prisoners. Kramer politely inquired if the visitors would like a tour of the camp. "He seemed most willing to oblige," wrote Cooper, "and declared that he was not responsible for the condition of the inmates."

Kramer ushered his visitors into the nearest hut. It was gloomy inside, and eerily silent, save for the occasional groan. "We were overpowered by the stench," recalled Randall. "Emaciated figures peered out at us, in fear and surprise, from the rows of bunks. Lying among them, on the same bunks, were dead bodies."

The SAS men reeled back out into the sunshine, to be met by another shocking sight. In the yard, a camp guard was methodically beating a prisoner with a rifle butt. Cooper glanced across to his old friend. "The effect on Reg Seekings was one of utter rage. I could see that he was on the verge of pulling out his pistol and shooting." Instead, Seekings turned to Tonkin and asked for permission to "teach the guard a lesson." Tonkin nodded his assent. Seekings walked up to the SS guard and punched him in the face with all the power and precision of a regimental boxing champion, combined with the fury of a man whose core morality has been outraged. When the man had staggered back to his feet, Seekings punched him again. This time he did not get up. Tonkin gave orders to arrest Kramer and Grese, and lock them in the guardroom: "We are now in charge, not you, and any guard who attempts to treat a prisoner with brutality will be punished." It would have been only too easy to unleash the SAS on the remaining SS inside the camp; instead, calmly and quietly, Tonkin chose to demonstrate what civilization means. Eight months later Kramer and Grese, nicknamed the "Beast of Belsen" and the "Beauty of Belsen," were tried, convicted of crimes against humanity, and then hanged in Hamelin prison.

The rest of the patrol set about distributing whatever rations they had to the prisoners, while an intelligence officer tried to explain in English, French, and German that they were now free. He was struck by the apparent lack of response to this moment of liberation: "Their faces were dull, exhausted, emotionless, not capable of expressing joy and excitement as had everyone else in Europe." Cooper fell into conversation with a Jewish Belgian journalist, a prisoner in Belsen for only a few months, who explained: "We might be able to restore some of the inmates to bodily health but their minds would be distorted for years to come—perhaps forever."

The SAS men found it hard to put into words the horror they had witnessed, but a few hours later there arrived at Belsen a man who could. Richard Dimbleby's report for the BBC would stun the world with its vivid, heartsick, furious depiction of Nazi brutality.

> Here over an acre of ground lay dead and dying people. You could not see which was which . . . The living lay with their heads against the corpses and around them moved the awful, ghostly procession of emaciated, aimless people, with nothing to do and with no hope of life, unable to move out of your way, unable to look at the terrible sights around them . . . Babies had been born here, tiny wizened things that could not live . . . A mother, driven mad, screamed at a British sentry to give her milk for her child, and thrust the tiny mite

into his arms, then ran off, crying terribly. He opened the bundle and found the baby had been dead for days.

I saw it all—furnaces where thousands have been burnt alive . . . The pit—15 feet deep—as big as a tennis court, piled to the top at one end with naked bodies . . . The British bulldozers, digging a new pit for the hundreds of bodies lying all over the camp days after death . . . The dark huts piled with human filth in which the dead and dying are lying together so that you must step over them to avoid the sticks of arms that are thrust imploringly towards you.

This day at Belsen was the most horrible of my life.

The SAS soldiers who had stumbled on the camp shared that sentiment. "I had been in action for three years and was no stranger to violent death, but what I saw in that camp will stay with me forever," wrote Cooper. It took days before Randall could get the smell of death out of his hair and remove the lingering stench from his clothing. He could never expunge it from his memory. "The smells and the sights of these dead bodies haunted me."

ON THE DAY that Belsen was accidentally liberated by the SAS, David Stirling perched on the ramparts of Colditz Castle, watching the US First Army steadily advancing into the town in the valley below. This was not an entirely sensible lookout point since the Americans, unaware that the forbidding castle on the cliff top was a prison camp, had begun shelling it. The prisoners had quickly painted a Union Jack and raised it from the tower, and spread bedsheets with "POW" written on them in the courtyard in the hope these would be spotted by American reconnaissance planes. That seemed to have stopped the bombardment, for now. Stirling was pleased with his "bird's eye view" of the advance and, as usual, entirely immune to any sense of peril.

Two days earlier, on the direct orders of SS chief Heinrich Himmler, the most prominent prisoners in Colditz, including members of the British royal family and a nephew of Winston Churchill's, had been collected together and shipped to Laufen in southern Germany. The following day the camp commandant, Oberstleutnant Gerhard Prawitt, received an order to send all remaining British prisoners to the east. Assuming, rightly, that they were to be used as hostages, if not murdered, the senior British officer, Lieutenant Colonel William Tod, simply refused to comply. "There was nothing the Commandant could do short of slaughtering us all," Stirling recalled cheerfully. "Willie then demanded that the Commandant surrender the castle to him." Prawitt did so, though he asked that the surrender remain a secret for the time being, in case the die-hard SS in the town found out and decided to take over the camp themselves. That evening, as US forces neared the castle, the guards began to slip away.

On the morning of April 16, a four-man American reconnaissance team entered the castle, led by Private Alan H. Murphey of the US 9th Armored Division—whereupon Hauptmann Eggers, the most senior guard remaining in what had once been Germany's most escape-proof prison, immediately and gratefully surrendered. "Somehow it seemed an anti-climax," said Stirling, as acutely tuned as ever to the irony of every situation.

Stirling was flown back to Britain, placed in a camp outside London, and then, to his intense annoyance, interviewed to establish what psychological damage he had suffered in captivity. "We had to be examined and talked to by a psychoanalyst. They patronized us rotten . . . I was impatient to see my family and get back to the SAS."

There were 186 Allied escape attempts from Colditz. Some 316 POWs had tried to get away, and 32 had made it home, the highest total of any camp. David Stirling had tried to escape from every camp he had ever been placed in, with a complete lack of success.

But he had one more escape attempt in him. On the evening of

April 18, the day after arriving in Britain, he broke out of the psychiatric evaluation camp and, under the cover of darkness, made his way to London, where, revealing an interest hitherto hardly mentioned, he had sex.

"By twelve o'clock that evening I was in a nightclub. By 2 a.m. I was having my first roger for years."

THE WAR FINISHED for the SAS, as most wars do, not in a blaze of glory, but in a flurry of paperwork, loose ends, and inadequate farewells.

By the end of April, the fighting had all but petered out. Even the SS were giving up in large numbers. On May 3, 1SAS reached Lübeck and was ordered to accompany the British 11th Armoured Division on to Kiel. Seekings and Cooper decided to drive on ahead of the main force. Suddenly, they found themselves surrounded by Germans, only this time the surrendering sort. Cooper nearly drove into "two German generals with their hands up," who pointed to a nearby field packed with soldiers, mostly officers. "We parked our jeep and started to accept the capitulation of about five hundred German officers. Each came forward in order of rank from general down to lieutenant to place their revolvers on the jeep." It was a bizarre closing scene for Seekings and Cooper. For four years they had been trying to kill these men, and doing so in large numbers. Now they were being saluted by them. Cooper knew he ought to feel jubilant, or triumphant; instead, he found the situation merely "embarrassing." He was still only twenty-two years old.

Fraser McLuskey made his way back west to Wuppertal, his wife's hometown, to inquire about her family. There the padre learned that her parents had been killed, along with other members of the Calaminus family, in the last Allied air raid of the war.

The Second World War in Europe came to an end on May 8. Frankforce had begun pulling out to the west the day before, through Bremen and on to the rendezvous point at Poperinghe in Belgium. There were celebrations, songs, toasts, amid encouraging rumors that the SAS would find another lease of life in the Far East, where the Pacific war raged on. In May, the newly released David Stirling and brigade commander Mike Calvert met Winston Churchill in Downing Street and obtained permission to begin planning a new SAS mission in China, aimed at severing Japanese supply lines to Malaya. But on August 6 the United States dropped the atomic bomb on Hiroshima. Japan's surrender nine days later brought to an end the Second World War, and with it Stirling's plan for a final offensive operation. "They dropped the bomb," said Jim Almonds, "and that finished it." Instead, 1 and 2SAS were deployed to Norway, to help with the disarming and processing of 300,000 German occupation troops. The weather was warm, the beer plentiful, and the Norwegian women, at least in the recollections of later life, most welcoming. But it was not war. The three months spent in Norway were, in the estimation of Reg Seekings, merely an exercise in "flag-flying."

Mike Calvert commended his troops for their "offensive spirit, drive, and willingness to fight in difficult conditions." He told them: "You have reason to be proud of yourselves. I am proud of you." The message had an unmistakably valedictory ring to it. The more observant members of the regiment knew exactly what was coming. With peace, Britain was dismantling its vast war machine with bleak bureaucratic efficiency. Cooper knew that "the writing was on the wall as soon as the war was over." For some, the prospect of peace was considerably more alarming than that of war. "The more I think of being a solicitor again," admitted Paddy Mayne, "the less I like it."

The end of the wartime SAS came in a crisp, unemotional memo from the War Office: "It has been decided to disband the Special Air Service regiment." Some, as usual, detected a conspiracy, an animus against a regiment that had always bucked the rules and had never been fully accepted by the more conventional senior officers. "A lot of high-powered people had no time for it," grumbled Seekings. In reality, with the dropping of the bomb, military planners saw a new kind of war in prospect, one that could be won by nuclear fission and would have no need for highly specialized troops trained to operate behind the lines. That assumption was, of course, entirely wrong.

In September, the Belgian SAS was absorbed into the reconstituted Belgian army. Soon afterward, the French 3 and 4SAS ceased to be British forces and were handed over to the French army.

On October 1, 1945, the SAS paraded for the last time at Hylands House, the large estate near Chelmsford that had served as the regiment's headquarters since March 1944. The men wore the red beret of airborne troops.

Paddy Mayne, alone, wore the original SAS beret, the color of desert sand.

Chapter 24

WHO DARES SURVIVES

T HE SAS OFFICIALLY CEASED TO EXIST IN OCTOBER 1945.
The men returned to their regiments, or entered civilian life.
David Stirling's grand experiment was over.

Except it wasn't. One small fragment of the regiment endured, secretly, unofficially, and quite possibly illegally. After five years of war, the regiment survived the coming of peace.

Brian Franks, commander of 2SAS, had long pondered the fate of the men left behind on Operation Loyton, that brutal, running fight with the retreating German army in the Vosges Mountains. Some thirty-one men were thought to have been captured, but only one had returned, Sergeant Kenneth Seymour, bringing with him a doubtful story of personal fortitude. In November 1944, just a month after the end of the operation, Franks began searching for evidence that the men might have been murdered in captivity. Six months later, he received a report of a mass grave near the Gaggenau concentration camp, in the French occupation zone of Germany east of the Vosges; thirty-seven bodies had been found, some of which had been identified as British servicemen. Franks sent Major Eric "Bill" Barkworth to investigate.

Barkworth had a personal interest in the fate of the missing men. As 2SAS's chief intelligence officer, he had briefed the officers before Operation Loyton, and warned them of Hitler's Commando Order, demanding the execution of all soldiers captured behind the lines. Barkworth, tall, spruce, and intense, spoke

French and German fluently. He also had the important knack of listening intently to his superior officers, and then doing exactly what he wanted to do regardless of their orders; he tended to avoid official channels if unofficial ones seemed more likely to work.

An estimated 250 Allied servicemen, including downed airmen, perished under Hitler's Commando Order. The vast majority of these, and certainly the SAS soldiers, were wearing uniform and identification tags and ought, therefore, to have enjoyed protection under the Geneva Convention. The Germans themselves had deployed parachute troops, and yet they had chosen to define all Allied parachutists as spies and terrorists. For Barkworth, Hitler's execution order was not just illegal, hypocritical, and abominable, but an immoral barbarity that demanded a full legal accounting.

There was something almost messianic about the way Barkworth set about his job: hunting down evidence about the Nazis who had killed SAS personnel, one by one.

In May 1945, Barkworth, Sergeant Major Fred "Dusty" Rhodes, and four SAS troopers climbed into a truck and a single jeep, and headed for the Continent: this was the War Crimes Investigation Team (WCIT), but in effect it was the last wartime mission of the SAS, unauthorized, unconventional, and therefore, in a way, entirely apt.

For the next three years, Barkworth and his rogue unit gathered evidence of murder: interviewing witnesses, compiling dossiers, combing prison camps, taking statements, locating suspects. They traveled through the British, French, and Soviet occupation zones of Germany, as well as the areas in France and Italy where SAS men had been killed. The investigation swiftly expanded beyond Operation Loyton to include Bulbasket, Houndsworth, and the many smaller operations in which men had been captured and never seen alive again. Some of the work was grim in the extreme. Outside the town of Moussey they searched for an unmarked mass grave. Dusty Rhodes, a gardener in civilian life, spotted a patch of undergrowth that appeared slightly different, less dense and tangled than the surrounding vegetation. Beneath the patch they dug up eight bodies of slain soldiers and resistance fighters. Another twenty-eight bodies, the victims of the Bulbasket massacre, executed after Tonkin's forest camp had been overrun, were exhumed at Saint-Sauvant, before being reburied at Rom. The body of Lincoln Bundy, the cowboy from Arizona, was immediately identifiable from his French civilian clothing.

Barkworth and his men continued to wear uniform with SAS insignia, even though the regiment had ceased to exist. It operated as if on official war crimes business, without any official authority whatever.

That Barkworth was able to do this was due to a Russian prince of royal blood. Captain Prince Yuri Galitzine could trace his lineage back to the Grand Dukes of Lithuania, the royal family of Poland, and the Tsars. With the Bolshevik revolution, the Galitzine dynasty had seen harder times: after schooling in England, Galitzine himself had become a glove maker and then an apprentice at an aircraft factory. During the war he served as a liaison to the Free French, and then in the Allied military propaganda unit, where he had witnessed Nazi barbarity at first hand as one of the first British soldiers to enter the Natzweiler-Struthof concentration camp. The end of the war saw him working in the War Office, in the Adjutant General's Branch 3—Violation of the Laws and Usages of War. Galitzine and Franks shared a conviction that, with so many other horrors emerging from the ruins of Nazi Germany, the fate of British soldiers murdered in defiance of international law was being overlooked.

After a lunch with Franks, Galitzine agreed to keep the unit going by means of some subterfuge. "Because there was obviously quite a lot of administrative confusion, one managed to keep the momentum going of pay and rations and everything else." With Galitzine arranging administrative and logistical support, the SAS war crimes unit was maintained and paid directly by the War Office, long after the SAS itself had been disbanded. Through Franks, a direct radio link was maintained between London and the hunters in the field. Galitzine was impressed by the zeal of the unit—"The SAS team are all personal friends of the missing men and are inspired by the esprit de corps of their regiment"—but he was particularly struck by Barkworth's sense of mission, describing him as "a mystic, a thinker," with an otherworldly air that appealed to the Russian's sense of magic.

At one point, Barkworth's spiritualism got out of hand, when he resorted to an Ouija board in an effort to track down suspects. The Ouija, or talking board, is marked out with the letters of the alphabet through which departed spirits communicate with the living by guiding a heart-shaped piece of wood toward individual letters. Galitzine, initially skeptical, soon became an enthusiastic supporter of this unlikely form of Nazi-hunting. Barkworth insisted, "If people were killed, presumably they want to tell us what happened to them." The team later claimed that two bodies were located in this way, along with a prisoner accused of war crimes—though not one they were looking for, which suggests that the spirits may not have been very good at spelling. The higher-ups were not impressed by Barkworth's resort to spiritual assistance, and Galitzine was accused of "conduct unbecoming in an officer and a gentleman."

In a memo sent to Franks, Barkworth laid out the mounting evidence so painstakingly assembled, and expressed the high moral purpose of his endeavor. The legal proceedings against the accused, he wrote, "will be conducted in such a manner that when the popular clamour of this century has been replaced by that of another, the proceedings will be regarded as an example of strict impartial justice and not of revenge."

But justice can be a messy business, particularly in the aftermath of war. "Nazi-hunting" may sound glamorous and dangerous. In fact, much of the work was boring and frustrating. Many suspects and witnesses had vanished. Those that could be identified were often wholly unreliable, lying as if their lives depended on it, which they did.

Oberleutnant Vogt, the former clergyman who had organized the executions of the Bulbasket prisoners, was dead. The intelligence officer Erich Schönig, his immediate boss, was found to be working as a dentist in Ebingen and arrested in October 1946. General Gallenkamp, their corps commander and the senior officer in charge, was already in custody, picked up by British troops in May 1945. His chief of staff, Colonel Herbert Köstlin, who had witnessed the executions, was also arrested. The case split into two: the executions of the captives in the Saint-Sauvant forest, and the killing by lethal injection of the three SAS prisoners too badly injured to leave the hospital. Shortly before their trial was due to start, General Gallenkamp attempted suicide and failed. In his suicide note he insisted, "My voluntary departure from this life takes place under the impression of the terrible things which have happened in the Corps HQ which I commanded." He admitted authorizing the killings by lethal injection of the three hospital inmates, but insisted that this was an act of mercy as he had been told the wounded men were "beyond saving." He denied ordering the other executions. The trial, in March 1947, was a clutter of claim and counterclaim, with the accused blaming one another and using the familiar defense that they had been obeying orders that could not be refused. "An order of the Führer was binding on those to whom it was given," said Gallenkamp's lawyer, "even when the order was contrary to international law or other traditional values." Köstlin insisted that the crime in question was "incompatible with his Christian belief" and had been carried out only because Gallenkamp had issued "a very clear and unmistakable order." Erich Schönig did not deny involvement, but declared, "I was frankly revolted."

Gallenkamp was sentenced to death, along with the doctor accused of administering the lethal injections. Köstlin got life in prison, while Schönig was sentenced to five years. But on review the Commando Order was accepted as a mitigating factor: Gallenkamp's death sentence was commuted to life in prison, and the hospital doctor was freed. A petition requesting clemency for Gallenkamp was signed by thirty-one former German generals. The sentence was reduced to ten years, and in 1952 Gallenkamp was released on grounds of ill health. He died in 1958.

The Loyton case was not much more definitive, though the hangman claimed some victims. Wilhelm Schneider, the Gestapo officer who had interrogated Kenneth Seymour, was executed in January 1947 in Hamelin prison. Barkworth and Rhodes witnessed the execution of Heinrich Neuschwanger, the officer convicted of the killings at Gaggenau, but it appears to have afforded them little satisfaction, as the murderer seemed blithely unrepentant: "Right up to the moment he was hung I don't think it worried him one little bit." Karl Haug, the executioner of Pat Garstin and the other captives taken in Operation Gain, met the same fate.

Many of those involved in the SAS killings were given light sentences, or escaped justice completely. But, just as John Tonkin had prevented reprisals against the camp guards at Belsen, so Barkworth had insisted that his investigation be carried out with judicial impartiality and without revenge; and in that he had succeeded. The War Crimes Investigation Team stood down in 1948.

By that time, the SAS itself had come back to life. With British military commitments changing in a postwar world, the authorities had belatedly realized that a long-term, deep-penetration fighting unit would be not only useful but essential. The 21SAS Regiment (so called because it amalgamated 2 and 1SAS) came into being in January 1947, as part of the Territorial Army. A squadron became the Malayan Scouts (SAS), renamed 22SAS Regiment in 1952. The SAS regiments would go on to see action around the world, becoming increasingly active in counterterrorism operations and hostage-taking situations during the 1970s.

The SAS idea swiftly spread. The Canadian Special Air Service Company was formed in 1947, the New Zealand Special Air Service Company in 1955; Australia's 1st SAS Company was created in 1957, becoming the Australian Special Air Service Regiment seven years later. The Special Forces Group of the Belgian army, with the same cap badge as the British SAS, traces its origins to the Belgian wartime volunteers of 5SAS. The French 1st Marine Infantry Parachute Regiment has the motto *Qui ose gagne* (Who dares wins), and is directly descended from the French wartime 3 and 4SAS. Israel's special forces unit Sayeret Matkal is modeled on the SAS, as is Ireland's Army Ranger Wing.

In 1962, a young US Army officer, Captain Charles Beckwith, served with 22SAS as an exchange officer. On his return to the US, Beckwith began a long campaign to persuade the US military of the need for a similar unit. "What the [SAS] regiment ended with, I thought, were men who enjoyed being alone, who could think and operate by themselves, men who were strong-minded and resolute," he wrote. "These were the characteristics I thought should be transferred to the U.S. Army's Special Forces." Beckwith envisaged small, autonomous teams of men highly trained in combat, reconnaissance, hostage-rescue, and counterterrorist missions. The 1st Special Forces Operational Detachment–Delta (1st SFOD-D), better known as Delta Force, was finally formed by Beckwith in November 1977.

In tactics and intentions, American and British special forces still follow the principles pioneered by the SAS in the desert more than seventy years ago: attacking the most valuable strategic targets without warning and then melting away again, forcing the enemy to remain on constant, debilitating alert.

The SAS changed the face of warfare, by pioneering techniques of long-term, deep penetration that are more important today than ever. The experience of the SAS proved that, as the Second World War wore on, growing grimmer, bloodier, and more ruthless, the need for a specialized and sometimes brutal form of fighting became ever more urgent. The SAS began the war fighting a gentlemanly foe, and ended it locked in a struggle with the pure evil of the SS. If there were ever doubts that SAS tactics were justified, they evaporated in the mephitic horror of Bergen-Belsen concentration camp.

The postwar history of the SAS lies outside the remit of this book, but the style and secrecy of the wartime SAS endured. In

1989, Stirling wrote an address to be delivered to the SAS sergeants' mess that seemed to capture the essence of the regimental ethos:

> Let me remind you that you must never think of yourselves as an elite. To do so would be bad for you and bad for your relations with the army and it would undermine those splendid qualities, to which you are wedded, of humility in success, and of a constant sense of humour. No, you are not an elite force. You are something more distinguished. Something of which you can be far more proud. The SAS establishment constitutes the smallest Corps in the British Defence Forces but with a special strategic role which is probably unique among all the armies of the world, and one which could save an incalculable number of lives. Hence the need for you to keep a "low profile," for reticence, and for the practice of security at all times.

On January 16, 1944, the *Sunday Graphic* ran the headline "Secret Airmen: They Will Amaze the World." The report, long on drama but notably short on detail, promised that "the exploits of men in Britain's Special Air Service whose work is a close secret will make amazing reading after the war . . . the day-by-day history of the Service will be published after the war."

It has taken more than seventy years for the SAS to end its reticence, and for that promise to be made good.

Acknowledgments

THIS BOOK WAS made possible by the full cooperation and assistance of the SAS Regimental Association. I am particularly grateful to Chris Dodkin, Howard Ham, Tracy Hawkins, Terri Hesmer, and the SAS Association archivist. Gavin Mortimer kindly read the manuscript at various stages of writing, and Alan Hoe and Gordon Stephens cast expert eyes over it at the end, identifying a number of important errors and omissions. The remaining mistakes are entirely my own. I would also like to thank the following for contributing, variously, their expertise, hospitality, memories, and other assistance in the making of this book: Kildare and Sarah Bourke-Borrowes, Robert Hands, Keith Kilby, John Lewes, John McCready, Martin Morgan, Mike Sadler, Alison Smartt, Archie Stirling, and Edward Toms, as well as the numerous individuals who helped but have asked not to be named. Caroline Wood performed great feats of picture research. My publishers at Viking and Crown have been remarkable in their efficiency, imagination, and patience: Joel Rickett, Venetia Butterfield, Poppy North, Peter James, Molly Stern, and Kevin Doughten. It has been a pleasure to tackle this project in concert with a most talented BBC team: Matthew Whiteman, Eamon Hardy, Katie Rider, and Martin Davidson. Ed Victor, my agent, has been, as ever, a fund of enthusiasm and good judgement. I am indebted to my friends and colleagues at *The Times* for their encouragement, and above all to my beloved family, for their unfailing tolerance, support, and humor.

Afterlives

David Stirling was appointed OBE in 1946 and initially settled in Rhodesia, where he became president of the newly founded Capricorn Society, an idealistic scheme to unite Africans without regard to racial, political, and religious divisions. When that failed (he blamed the Colonial Office), Stirling returned to the UK and set up a series of television stations around the world, mostly in developing countries, another project that was as imaginative as it was unprofitable. "I had the biggest collection of the most bankrupt television stations in the world," he said. Later he ran Watchguard (International) Ltd., a secretive company through which he helped train security units for Arab and African countries. He was also associated with several instances of covert military action in the Middle East. In the aftermath of the 1974 miners' strike, he set up GB75, "an organization of apprehensive patriots" who would help keep essential services, such as power stations, running in the event of a general strike. He then turned to fighting left-wing extremism in trade unions, by backing the Movement for True Industrial Democracy (Truemid). In 1984, he gave his name to the Hereford headquarters of the SAS, the Stirling Lines. He was knighted in 1990, and died later that year.

Paddy Mayne never adjusted to peacetime and civilian life. After the war he joined a geographical expedition to the South Atlantic to survey the Falklands region, a project calling for "able-bodied men with the ability to survive in difficult conditions." But after a month he was invalided home on account of the back injury that had been sustained while parachuting in the desert, worsened by subsequent jumps and seldom mentioned to anybody. Mayne became secretary of the Incorporated Law Society of Northern Ireland, and spent much of his time looking after his infirm mother. He drank far too much, and not happily. In an entry for the *Dictionary of National Biography*, George Jellicoe wrote, "Mayne was an unusual and complicated person . . . The life of this normally gentle giant of a man was also punctuated from time to time by acts of sudden, often inexplicable, violence—usually associated with an over-generous intake of alcohol." His back pain became so acute that he could no longer play rugby, or even watch the sport as a seated spectator. He rarely spoke about his war service, and increasingly gave way to "brooding, and strange sensitivity." On December 14, 1955, in his hometown of Newtownards, after a Masonic dinner followed by an evening of drinking and playing poker, he climbed into his red Riley sports car and headed home. He crashed into a stationary lorry at 4:00 a.m. and was found dead at the wheel with a fractured skull. The line of mourners at his military funeral, conducted by the Reverend Fraser McLuskey, was over a mile long.

After a period as an instructor at Sandhurst, **Roy Farran** joined the counterinsurgency police squads in Palestine. In May 1947, his team intercepted an unarmed Jewish schoolboy, Alexander Rubowitz, distributing anti-British propaganda for a proscribed underground organization. During the ensuing interrogation, in a deserted area outside Jerusalem, Farran allegedly killed the boy by smashing his skull with a rock. Farran fled custody twice, but was finally acquitted for lack of admissible evidence. The following year, a parcel bomb addressed to "R. Farran" was opened by his brother Rex, who was killed in the resulting explosion. Roy Farran then worked as a quarryman in Scotland, and ran unsuccessfully as a Conservative parliamentary candidate. In 1950, he emigrated to Canada, where he became a dairy farmer, founded newspapers, wrote two best-selling books about his wartime exploits, entered municipal politics, and eventually became Alberta's solicitor general.

Brian Franks, the commander of 2SAS, lobbied to preserve the skills of the wartime SAS after the regiment's disbandment in 1945. He founded the SAS Regimental Association, and it was partly through his efforts that the Artists' Rifles, a Territorial Army battalion, was redesignated as 21SAS, a combination of 1 and 2SAS. Franks commanded the unit until 1950, before going on to become colonel commandant of the regiment. He was managing director of the Hyde Park Hotel from 1959 to 1972.

Henry Druce was awarded the Croix de Guerre with Palm for his wartime actions with the French resistance. After the war, he rejoined MI6, the British intelligence service, first in Holland and then in Indonesia. Having left government service, he worked in Anglo-Dutch plantations in Java until 1951 and then moved with his family to Canada. There he built up a shipping business in Newfoundland, and later in Quebec and the Cayman Islands, before retiring in 1981 and settling in British Columbia to collect stamps, play golf, and speculate on the stock market, where his "predilection for risk" proved rather less profitable than it had in Nazi-occupied France.

Bob Lilley rejoined the SAS, becoming regimental sergeant major of 21SAS, and later ran a pub in Folkestone, where he would occasionally regale drinkers with the story of the time he strangled a lone Italian soldier in the middle of the desert. In special forces jargon the term a "Boblilley" is now used to describe a commando hit-and-run operation. **Alex Muirhead,** the mortar expert, became a GP and then served for eighteen years as the BBC's chief medical officer. **Harry Poat** returned to the family tomato-farming business in Guernsey, and died in 1982 at the age of sixty-seven. **Mike Sadler** accompanied Mayne on the expedition to the Antarctic, and then joined the Foreign Office. He still lives in Cheltenham.

Pat Riley, the American-born desert veteran, joined the Cambridge police in 1945 but found police work too sedate and volunteered as a captain with the Malayan Regiment. He worked closely with the newly formed Malayan Scouts, which became 22SAS, in operations against communist insurgents. He left the army in 1955 and became landlord of the Dolphin Hotel pub in Colchester, Essex, before joining Securicor, the security firm, where he held various senior positions until his retirement in 1980. After a period on secondment with the British Military Mission to Ethiopia, **Jim Almonds** served with the Eritrean Police Field Force and then returned to the SAS. He left the army in 1961 as a major and retired to the house in Stixwould, Lincolnshire, where he was born. **Tony Greville-Bell** became a Hollywood scriptwriter, and wrote the 1973 horror-film classic *Theatre of Blood*, starring Vincent Price and Diana Rigg. He later became a professional sculptor. His bronze of a wounded soldier being helped to safety by a comrade stands in the SAS Garden of Remembrance.

On demobilization, **Reg Seekings** returned to Cambridgeshire and took over the Rifleman's Arms pub in Ely with his new wife, Monica, which they ran for the next nine years. They then emigrated to Rhodesia to farm tobacco. During the period of the Rhodesian Bush War in the late 1960s and 1970s, he became an inspector in the police antiterrorist unit, formed by the white minority government to fight African communist guerrillas. Seekings returned to East Anglia soon after Zimbabwean independence.

Johnny Cooper rejoined the family wool business and, predictably enough, found it hard to settle down. In 1951, he took an extended short-service commission with 22SAS, for which he was appointed MBE. He served in the Sultan of Oman's armed forces before being recruited by David Stirling to help resist the Egyptian-backed coup in North Yemen. In 1966, he retired with the rank of lieutenant colonel, and moved to Portugal.

After the war, **Fraser McLuskey** traveled throughout Britain visiting the families of SAS soldiers killed in action and telling relatives about the circumstances of their deaths. He helped to set up the Royal Army Chaplains' Training Centre, before returning to Scotland as minister in Broughty Ferry and then Bearsden in Glasgow, to tend to one of the largest congregations in Scotland. He met the young American evangelist Billy Graham and began a lifelong friendship. In 1960, McLuskey moved to St. Columba's in Knightsbridge, remaining there until his retirement in 1986. He was moderator of the General Assembly of the Church of Scotland in 1983–84.

John Tonkin took part in the Antarctic expedition with Mayne and Sadler and fell down a glacier, requiring a long and perilous rescue, which, as usual, he found quite funny. He traveled widely, and eventually moved to Australia, where he became a mining engineer and successful businessman.

In 1943, **Fitzroy Maclean** led Churchill's liaison mission to Yugoslavia's partisan leader General Tito; he described his role as "simply to find out who was killing the most Germans and suggest means by which we could help them to kill more." Randolph Churchill was also a member of the mission, and brought in the novelist Evelyn Waugh. After the war, Maclean was promoted to the local rank of major general, and returned to the UK to take up his parliamentary seat. He served as an MP until 1959, while administering the family estate in Argyll and running a hotel on the shores of Loch Fyne. In 1949, he published his acclaimed memoir, *Eastern Approaches*, which included a description of his time in the SAS. His decorations included the Order of Kutuzov (Soviet Union), the Croix de Guerre (France), and the Order of the Partisan Star (Yugoslavia). He was also appointed a Commander of the Order of the British Empire (CBE) in 1944, honored with the baronetcy of Maclean of Strachur and Glensluain, and made a knight of the Most Ancient and Most Noble Order of the Thistle. He was also, according to some, a model for Ian Fleming's James Bond.

Bill Fraser won no such recognition. One of the bravest soldiers in the SAS, wounded three times, he ended the war with the rank of major, and won the Military Cross with bar and the Croix de Guerre with palm. He rejoined the Gordon Highlanders, but the demons that had stalked him in the last days of the war finally seized him. He was court-martialed for drunkenness and reduced to the ranks, and appears to have left the army soon afterward. There were rumors that he had been seen sleeping rough in parks. In 1954, Paddy Mayne wrote: "Poor old Bill Fraser has collected a three-year prison sentence for breaking into 30 odd houses." On his release, Fraser found work in a bakery and later as a costing clerk. He died in 1975.

After leading the Special Boat Service in a series of operations along the coasts of Italy and Yugoslavia, **George Jellicoe** was among the first Allied soldiers to enter German-occupied Athens. One of the longest-serving parliamentarians in the world, he was a member of the House of Lords for sixty-eight years. In 1973, he resigned as leader of the House of Lords after admitting "some casual affairs" with call girls, but went on to become chairman of the council of King's College London, chairman of the Medical Research Council, and a trustee of the National Aids Trust. He was also president, among other institutions, of the Royal Geographical Society, the Institute of British Geographers, the Anglo-Hellenic League, the Kennet and Avon Canal Trust, the UK Crete Veterans' Association, the British Heart Foundation, and, not least, the SAS Regimental Association.

Alan Samuel Lyle-Smythe, the eccentric, tweed-wearing intelligence agent encountered by Malcolm Pleydell in the Jebel Mountains, became a big-game hunter in Ethiopia, founded a Shakespeare Company in Tanganyika, wrote under the pen name Alan Caillou, and finally evolved into a successful Hollywood actor. He penned fifty-two mildly saucy novels with titles such as *The Love-Hungry Girl at the "Billion Dollar" Oasis*, and appeared in numerous television series in the 1960s and 1970s, including the *Man from U.N.C.L.E.*, *Daktari*, and *The Six Million Dollar Man*. His most alarming role was in *Quark*, a short-lived 1978 science-fiction series in which he played the master of the galactic government and appeared only as a gigantic disembodied head.

Theodore Schurch, alias John Richards, the fascist spy, was arrested in Rome in March 1945. Six months later he was tried by court-martial in London, found guilty on nine counts of treachery and one count of desertion with intent to join the enemy, and sentenced to death. David Stirling gave evidence at his trial. Schurch was hanged, by executioner Albert Pierrepoint, on January 4, 1946, at HM Prison Pentonville. He was twenty-seven. Schurch was the only British soldier executed for treachery committed during the Second World War.

Markus Lutterotti, the German doctor who had escaped from the SAS in the desert, survived the war and returned to his country estate at Fontanasanta in the South Tyrol. With the coming of peace, his interests shifted from tropical medicine to the ethics of euthanasia, a legacy of the soldier whose suffering he had brought to an end in a desert ditch in 1942. An opponent of medically assisted suicide, he founded the ecumenical hospice movement in Germany and dedicated the rest of his life to providing palliative care for the dying. He never forgot his brief sojourn with the SAS in the desert, and the English doctor, the enemy who had befriended him. "It was a gentleman's war in Africa," he said.

Malcolm Pleydell worked in a hospital on Malta until the end of 1943, when he was himself hospitalized with a gastric ulcer. While recuperating, he wrote *Born of the Desert*, the finest firsthand account of the SAS in North Africa. He returned to the UK, recovered in body but suffering from what would be diagnosed today as post-traumatic stress disorder. Ever the acute self-chronicler, Pleydell knew that the experience of desert war, so exciting at the time, had also left invisible wounds: "I felt an alien, totally out of place in this new environment . . . I still found myself avoiding social gatherings years after that because of the accumulation of my traumatic experiences." He devoted the rest of his life to the National Health Service. In 1991, he wrote: "My life has come full circle. I am retired, and out of doors as much as possible [where] I can sense again the wide sweeps of desert, in which I used to commune with the universe and tell the time by the sun by day, and the stars by night."

Wartime SAS Operations

Op Name	Regiment	Date	Location	Remarks
Squatter	L Det	16–17 November 1941	N. Africa	First-ever SAS operation
Agheila raid	L Det	15 December 1941	N. Africa	
Sirte–Tamet raid	L Det	15 December 1941	N. Africa	
Agedabia raid	L Det	22 December 1941	N. Africa	
2nd Sirte raid	L Det	27 December 1941	N. Africa	
2nd Tamet raid	L Det	27 December 1941	N. Africa	
Nofilia raid	L Det	29 December 1941	N. Africa	
Marble Arch raid	L Det	29 December 1941	N. Africa	
Benina raid	L Det	15 March 1942	N. Africa	
Berka raid	L Det	15 March 1942	N. Africa	
Barce raid	L Det	15 March 1942	N. Africa	NZ LRDG
Slonta raid	L Det	15 March 1942	N. Africa	
2nd Benina raid	L Det	15 March 1942	N. Africa	
Benghazi raid	L Det	13 June 1942	N. Africa	
Heraklion raid	L Det	13 June 1942	Heraklion, Crete	
Fuka/Bagush/Sidi Haneish	L Det	July 1942	N. Africa	
Sidi Barrani	L Det	12/13 July 1942	N. Africa	
Bigamy	L Det	14 September 1942	N. Africa	
A and B Sqdn. raids	L Det	November 1942–January 1943	N. Africa	Multiple locations. David Stirling captured on raid in January 1943. In addition to those raids recorded above in N. Africa there were many other small raids, the location/dates of which are not known with any degree of accuracy.
A, B, and C Sqdn. raids	L Det	1942 and 1943	N. Africa	

Op Name	Regiment	Date	Location	Remarks
Snapdragon	2SAS	28 May 1943	Pantelleria	
Marigold	2SAS	30 May 1943	Sardinia	
Hawthorn	2SAS	30 June–7 July 1943	Sardinia	
Narcissus	2SAS	10 July 1943	Sicily	
Husky	SRS	10–12 July 1943	Sicily	
Chestnut	2SAS	13 July–14 August 1943	Sicily	
Speedwell	2SAS	7 September 1943	Italy	
Taranto landings	2SAS	9 September 1943	Italy	
Baytown	SRS	12 September 1943	Italy	
Begonia	2SAS	2 October 1943	Italy	
Jonquil	2SAS	2 October–25 December 1943	Italy	
Devon	SRS	3–6 October 1943	Italy	
Devon	2SAS	3–6 October 1943	Italy	
Candytuft	2SAS	27 October–2 November 1943	Italy	
Saxifrage	2SAS	14 December 1943–end date unknown	Italy	
Sleepylad	2SAS	18 December 1943–end date unknown	Italy	
Maple/Driftwood	2SAS	7 January 1944	Italy	
Maple/Thistledown	2SAS	7 January 1944	Italy	
Pomegranate	2SAS	12 January 1944	Italy	
Baobab	2SAS	29 January 1944	Italy	
Titanic	1SAS	6 June–10 July 1944	France	
Bulbasket	1SAS	6 June–6 August 1944	France	
Dingson/Grog	4SAS	6 June–18 August 1944	France	French
Samwest/Wash	4SAS	6 June–18 August 1944	France	French
Houndsworth	1SAS	6 June–6 September 1944	France	
Cooney	4SAS	8–15 June 1944	France	French
Gain	1SAS	14 June–19 August	France	

Op Name	Regiment	Date	Location	Remarks
Lost	4SAS	23 June–18 July 1944	France	French
Haft	1SAS	8 July–11 August 1944	France	French
Dickens	3SAS	16 July–7 October 1944	France	French
Defoe	2SAS	19 July–23 August 1944	France	Defoe also had breakaway ops of Dodo and Swan
Rupert	2SAS	23 July–10 September 1944	France	
Gaff	2SAS	25 July–13 August 1944	France	
Hardy/Robey	2SAS	26 July–14 September 1944	France	
Chaucer	5SAS	27 July–15 August 1944	France	Belgian
Shakespeare	5SAS	31 July–15 August 1944	France	Belgian
Bunyan	5SAS	3–8 August 1944	France	Belgian
Dunhill	2SAS	3–24 August 1944	France	
Moses	3SAS	3 August–5 October 1944	France	French
Derry	3SAS	5–18 August 1944	France	French
Marshall	3SAS	9–24 August 1944	France	French
Samson	3SAS	9 August–27 September 1944	France	French
Haggard	1SAS	10 August–23 September 1944	France	
Loyton	2SAS	13 August–16 October 1944	France	
Snelgrove	3SAS	13–24 August 1944	France	French
Barker	3SAS	13 August–9 September 1944	France	French
Harrod	3SAS	13 August–24 September 1944	France	French
Kipling	1SAS	14 August–25 September 1944	France	
Jockworth	3SAS	15 August–9 September 1944	France	French
Abel	3SAS	15 August–22 September 1944	France	French
Trueform	2SAS	16–26 August 1944	France	
Trueform 2	5SAS	16–26 August 1944	France	Belgian
Noah	5SAS	16 August–13 September 1944	France	Belgian

Op Name	Regiment	Date	Location	Remarks
Newton	3SAS	19 August–11 September 1944	France	French
Wallace	2SAS	19 August–17 September 1944	France	
Benson	5SAS	28 August–1 September 1944	France	Belgian
Wolsey	Phantom Regt	28 August–1 September 1944	France	Phantom/British
Spencer	4SAS	29 August–14 September 1944	France	French
Berbang	5SAS	2–12 September 1944	France	Belgian
Brutus	5SAS	2–18 September 1944	France	Belgian
Caliban	5SAS	6–11 September 1944	France	Belgian
Pistol	2SAS	15 September–14 October 1944	N. Italy	
Regent	5SAS	27 December 1944–15 January 1945	Belgium	Belgian
Galia	2SAS	27 December 1944–15 February 1945	Italy	
Cold Comfort	2SAS	17 February–30 March 1945	Italy	
Tombola	2SAS	6 March–24 April 1945	Italy	
Fabian	5SAS	19 September 1944–14 March 1945	France	Belgian. The operation was also known as Regan
Gobbo	5SAS	19 September 1944–14 March 1945	France	Belgian. The operation was also known as Portia
Keystone	5SAS	19 September 1944–14 March 1945	Holland	Belgian
Archway	1SAS	25 March–3 May 1945	NW Europe	
Archway	2SAS	25 March–3 May 1945	NW Europe	
Larkswood	5SAS	4–18 April 1945	Holland	Belgian
Howard	1SAS	10–14 April 1945	NW Europe	
Keystone	2SAS	11–18 April 1945	Holland	
Amherst	3SAS	7–15 April 1945	Germany	French
Amherst	4SAS	7–15 April 1945	Germany	French

Regimental Roll of Honor

(1SAS and 2SAS)

NAME	SAS UNIT
ADAMSON, Edward Young, Pte	1st SAS
ALLAN, William Watt, MM, Cpl	1st SAS
ALLEN, Patrick Joseph, Gnr	1st SAS
ANDREWS, Vincent, Pte	1st SAS
APPLEYARD, John Geoffrey, DSO, MC & Bar, Maj	2nd SAS
ARBUCKLE, James Fleming Spiers, Pte	1st SAS
ASHE, Christopher, Pte	2nd SAS
ASHLEY, Alan George, Pte	1st SAS
ASPIN, James, Pte	1st SAS
ASTELL, Norman Francis, Maj	RSR
AUSTIN, Frederick Leonard, Pte	2nd SAS
BAILEY, Christopher Sidney, Capt	1st SAS
BAKER, James Henry Malcolm, LCpl	1st SAS
BALERDI, Justo, Pte	2nd SAS
BALL, John Henry, LBdr	1st SAS
BANNERMAN, Peter, Sigmn	2nd SAS
BARKER, Thomas James, Pte	1st SAS
BARRETT, Donald, Tpr	RSR
BATEMAN, Charles John Reidel, Rfn	2nd SAS
BATEMAN, Kenneth, Cpl	1st SAS
BENNETT, James William Robert, Pte	2nd SAS
BENNETT, Leslie Charles, Pte	2nd SAS
BENSON, Robert Thomas, Sgt	2nd SAS
BENTLEY, John William, Cpl	1st SAS
BETTS, Arthur, Gnr	2nd SAS
BINTLEY, Thomas Norman, Pte	2nd SAS
BIRNIE, Ronald Jack, Lt	2nd SAS
BISHOP, Langslow Thomas, Gdsm	SBS
BLACK, James Desmond, Lt	2nd SAS

BLAKENEY, James, Pte	1st SAS
BOLDEN, Stanley, MM, Cpl	2nd SAS
BOLLAND, Stanley, Gdsm	L Det, SAS Bde
BOND, Charles Frederick Gordon, Maj	1st SAS
BOWEN, John Seymour, Pte	1st SAS
BOXALL, Robert Charles Thomas, Pte	2nd SAS
BRADFORD, Laurence Roy, Capt	1st SAS
BROOK, Harold, LCpl	1st SAS
BROPHY, Michael Joseph, Pte	1st SAS
BROWN, Eric Ernest, Cpl	RSR
BROWN, Leslie Jock, Cpl	1st SAS
BROWN, Selwyn Percival, Pte	2nd SAS
BRUNT, Bernard Oliver, Gnr	2nd SAS
BRYSON, William, Cpl	1st SAS
BUCK, Herbert Cecil, MC, Capt	1st SAS
BUDDEN, Gordon Hubert Frank, Pte	1st SAS
BURY, Robin Cyril Lindsay, Lt	SBS
CAIRNS, Leslie George, Lt	1st SAS
CARMICHAEL, James Alexander, Fus	SBS
CARTER, Stanley Arthur Sidney, Gnr	RSR
CASE, Robert Anthony, Capt	SBS
CASS, George Edward, LSgt	SBS
CASSIDY, George, Pte	1st SAS
CASTELLAIN, Geoffrey Charles, Lt	2nd SAS
CATON, Geoffrey, Bdr	1st SAS
CHAMBERS, Terence Frederick Thomas, Capt	1st SAS
CHEYNE, John, Sgt	L Det, SAS Bde
CHICK, Reginald, Cpl	1st SAS
CHISIM, John Dorman, LCpl	HQ Raiding Forces
CHURCH, Reginald Stanley, Pte	2nd SAS
CLARIDGE, John Henry, Pte	2nd SAS
CLYNES, Charles Maurice, MC, Capt	SBS
COGGER, George Oliver, Pte	1st SAS
COLLIGAN, William Harold, Sgt	RSR
COLLIS, Reginald William, LCpl	RSR
CONWAY, John Joseph, Pte	2nd SAS
COOPER, Samuel, Pte	1st SAS
CORNTHWAITE, Leslie, Cfn	SBS
CREANEY, William John, Pte	1st SAS
CRISP, Clarence, LBdr	1st SAS
CRISP, Richard, Lt	1st SAS
CROSIER, Jack Stanley, Pte	2nd SAS
CROUCH, Alfred John, Tpr	SBS
CROWLEY, Joseph Patrick, Cpl	2nd SAS
CURRIE, Donald Cameron, Pte	2nd SAS
CURTIS, Leonard William, Pte	2nd SAS
DAVIDSON, Alexander, LSgt	1st SAS
DAVIES, Roy David, Pte	1st SAS
DAVIS, Gerald Donovan, Sgt	2nd SAS

DAVISON, Sydney, Pte   1st SAS
DENCH, Arthur Thomas, Gdsm   2nd SAS
DEVINE, William Henry, Cfn   1st SAS
DILL, David Gordon, Lt   2nd SAS
DODDS, William, Spr   2nd SAS
DOWLING, James Frederick, Pte   2nd SAS
DOWNEY, James, Pte   2nd SAS
DREW, Edward, Pte   2nd SAS
DRONGIN, Anthony, Cpl   1st SAS
DUDGEON, Patrick Laurence, MC, Capt   2nd SAS
DUFFY, Joseph Aloysius, Pte   L Det, SAS Bde
DUNCAN, Allan, Pte   1st SAS
DUNKLEY, Frank Wilfred, Sgt   1st SAS
EADES, Leslie Ronald, Pte   1st SAS
ECCLES, Douglas, Sgt   1st SAS
EDGE, Robert, WOII   RSR
EDWARDS, Alfred Ronald, Spr   2nd SAS
ELLIOTT, John Herbert, LCpl   2nd SAS
ERLIS, Harold, Dvr   2nd SAS
EVANS, Augustus George, Pte   SBS
EVANS, John, Pte   2nd SAS
FAIRWEATHER, David Calder, Pte   SBS
FASSAM, Joseph William, LBdr   1st SAS
FENWICK, Ian, Maj   1st SAS
FERGUSON, Douglas, MM, Pte   1st SAS
FIELD, Timothy Joseph, Pte   1st SAS
FINLAY, John Summers, Sgt   1st SAS
FISHWICK, William Owen, Pte   SBS
FITZPATRICK, Michael Benedict, MM, Sgt   2nd SAS
FOSTER, William Johnstone, Sgt   2nd SAS
GALE, Donald Maurice, Pte   1st SAS
GARNHAM, Leonard, Gnr   2nd SAS
GARSTIN, Patrick Bannister, MC, Capt   1st SAS
GLEN, William Osborne, Sgt   2nd SAS
GLYDE, John, Pte   1st SAS
GODDARD, Peter Holland, Lt   1st SAS
GOSLING, John William, Pte   1st SAS
GOTTLIEB, Eliahu, Pte   L Det
GOVAN, James Chisholm Wilson, MM, Cpl   1st SAS
GRANT, Charles Martin, Cpl   1st SAS
GRANT, Ian Maxwell, Lt   2nd SAS
GRANT-WATSON, Robert de Merve Low, Capt   L Det, SAS Bde
GRAY, David, Pte   1st SAS
GREAVES, Sydney, MM, Cpl   SBS
GRIFFIN, Maurice Arthur, Pte   2nd SAS
GRIMSDALE, Stanley David James, Lt   RSR
GRIMSTER, Edgar, Pte   1st SAS
GUARD, Ronald, Pte   1st SAS
GUNN, Philip McLean, MC, MB, ChB, Maj   HQ SAS Bde

GUNSTON, John St. George, Capt	2nd SAS
GURNEY, Hugh Christopher, Lt	2nd SAS
GUSCOTT, Sidney Elliott, Sgt	2nd SAS
HAAS, Petr, Cpl	L Det
HALL, James, LCpl	1st SAS
HALL, Wallace Albert, Pte	2nd SAS
HAMMOND, Joseph, Sgt	2nd SAS
HARRIS, Henry, Pte	SBS
HAWKES, Ernest Henry Albert, Sgt	SBS
HAWKINS, Edward James, Gnr	RSR
HAY, Ralph, Sgt	2nd SAS
HAYDEN, Hugh, Gnr	RSR
HAYES, George Malgwyn, Pte	1st SAS
HEAD, Terence Alexander, Gnr	RSR
HEARN, William Herbert, Pte	1st SAS
HEAVENS, Robert Eric, Sgt	1st SAS
HENDERSON, John Brown, LSgt	1st SAS
HENDERSON, Stanley, Pte	2nd SAS
HENSHAW, James Cyril, Lt	SBS
HERSTELL, Ernest Maxwell, Gnr	1st SAS
HILDRETH, Sydney James, LCpl	L Det, SAS Bde
HILL, Harry, Pte	1st SAS
HODGKINSON, John Owen, LBdr	1st SAS
HOLLAND, William Charles, Pte	2nd SAS
HOLMES, John, Bdr	2nd SAS
HOLT, Desmond Campbell, Capt	SBS
HORE-RUTHVEN, the Hon Alexander Hardinge Patrick, Capt	1st SAS
HOWELL, William Kitchener, Pte	1st SAS
HOWELLS, Ellis, LCpl	SBS
HUGGINS, Stanley A., Dvr	HQ SAS Bde
HUGHES, Stanley Raymond, MM, Fus	SBS
ION, John, Pte	1st SAS
IRELAND, Richard Frederick, Pte	2nd SAS
IVISON, Thomas, Cpl	2nd SAS
JACKSON, Peter Harold, MC, Lt	2nd SAS
JAMES, Trevor John, Gnr	2nd SAS
JESSIMAN, John Russell, LSgt	1st SAS
JOHNSTON, George Gourlay, Sigmn	2nd SAS
JONES, Raymond Walter, MM, Gnr	SBS
JOUGHIN, John, Bdr	SBS
KALKSTEIN, Joachim, Pte	2nd SAS
KASPEROVITCH, Boris, Cpl	2nd SAS
KEANE, Peter John, Lt	RSR
KEEBLE, John, Spr	2nd SAS
KEITH, Douglas, Pte	L Det, SAS Bde
KENDALL, Stanley Vincent, Tpr	1st SAS
KENNEDY, Douglas Stewart, Lt	1st SAS
KENNEDY, Thomas Joseph, DCM, Capt	SBS
KENT, Thomas Henry, Pte	1st SAS

KERLEY, Gerald Charles, Tpr .... 1st SAS
KINGSTON, Frank Charles Norton, Sgt .... SBS
KINNIVANE, John, Cpl .... 1st SAS
KITCHINGMAN, Thomas, Mne .... SBS
KNAGGS, Albert Ernest, Gnr .... RSR
LAMBIE, David, WOII .... 1st SAS
LAMONBY, Kenneth Butler, Lt .... SBS
LASSEN, Anders Frederik Emil Victor Schau, VC, MC & 2 Bars, Maj ... SBS
LAW, George Dalton, Pte .... 1st SAS
LEACH, Wilfred, Sigmn .... 2nd SAS
LEADBETTER, William, Cpl .... 1st SAS
LEES, James, Capt .... SBS
LEIGH, David Blair, 2/Lt .... 2nd SAS
LEWES, John Steel, Lt .... L Det, SAS Bde
LEWIS, Donald, Pte .... 2nd SAS
LEWIS, Michael, Pte .... 1st SAS
LITTLEJOHN, Ross Robertson, MC, Maj .... 2nd SAS
LIVINGSTONE, Donald Macphail, Pte .... 1st SAS
LLOYD, Leonard Edwin Charles, Pte .... 2nd SAS
LOCKERIDGE, Alan, Spr .... 2nd SAS
LODGE, Robert, DCM, Sgt .... 2nd SAS
LONG, Leslie Charles, Cpl .... 1st SAS
LOOSEMORE, Herbert, Pte .... 2nd SAS
LUTTON, Howard, LCpl .... 1st SAS
MacFARLANE, Charles, Pte .... 1st SAS
MALLORY, Harry, MM, Gdsm .... 2nd SAS
MANNION, John Joseph, Sgt .... L Det, SAS Bde
MARLOW, William, Dvr .... 1st SAS
McALPIN, William Muir, Pte .... 1st SAS
McBRIDE, Dominic, Pte .... 1st SAS
McDONALD, John, LCpl .... 1st SAS
McEACHAN, Ronald George, Sigmn .... 2nd SAS
McGONIGAL, Eoin Christopher, Lt .... L Det, SAS Bde
McGOVERN, Peter, Pte .... 2nd SAS
McGUIRE, John, LCpl .... 2nd SAS
McKAY, Douglas Hays, Sgt .... 2nd SAS
McKENDRICK, Robert Alexander, LCpl .... SBS
McKERRACHER, Duncan, Sgt .... SBS
McLAUGHLAN, Benjamin Thomas, Pte .... 1st SAS
McLEOD, Alexander, Pte .... 1st SAS
McMAHON, Ernest, Gnr .... RSR
McNINCH, William Matthew, MM, LSgt .... 1st SAS
MELOT, Robert Marie Emanuel, MC, Maj .... 1st SAS
MILLER, George William John, MM, LSgt .... SBS
MILLER, Ronald, Sgt .... 1st SAS
MOORE, Frederick George, Spr .... SBS
MORRIS, Alfred Dayrell, Capt .... 2nd SAS
MORRIS, Thomas, Pte .... SBS
MORRISON, William, Pte .... SBS

MULLEN, Henry, Pte	1st SAS
MUNRO, George, Sgt	SBS
MURPHY, Denis Luke Maurice, Capt	1st SAS
NEVILL, Walter Henry Edgar, Sgt	2nd SAS
NIXON, Malvern, Pte	1st SAS
O'DOWD, Christopher, MM, LSgt	1st SAS
OGG, Joseph, Pte	1st SAS
O'REILLY, James, Pte	1st SAS
PACKMAN, Leslie Herbert William, Pte	1st SAS
PARRIS, Thomas Alfred, Pte	1st SAS
PASCOE, Henry James, Pte	1st SAS
PASKELL, Percy Edward, Gnr	RSR
PATTERSON, Ian Norman, MC, Maj	SBS
PHILLIPS, Donald, Pte	1st SAS
PHILLIPS, Reginald Roy, Mne	SBS
PINCI, Michele Arthur Kennedy, Lt	2nd SAS
PINCKNEY, Philip Hugh, Capt	2nd SAS
POCOCK, Emrys, Pte	1st SAS
PRICE, Charles William, Tpr	2nd SAS
PUGH, Albert Henry, Bdr	2nd SAS
PUTTICK, Frederick Arthur, Pte	2nd SAS
RAWLINSON, Frank William, Gnr	1st SAS
REILLY, James William Beattie, Pte	2nd SAS
REYNOLDS, Denis Bingham, Maj	2nd SAS
REYNOLDS, Maurice Joseph, Gdsm	2nd SAS
RICCOMINI, James Arthur, MBE MC, Lt	2nd SAS
RICE, Leo Gerard, Pte	SBS
RICHARDS, Charles Teverson, LCpl	1st SAS
RICHARDSON, Nelson David, Gnr	RSR
RICHARDSON, William Ernest Liddell, Pte	1st SAS
ROBERTS, Edward, Cpl	SBS
ROBERTSON, Kitchener Steven, Sgt	1st SAS
ROBINSON, George, LCpl	2nd SAS
ROBSON, John William Robert, LBdr	L Det, SAS Bde
ROGERS, John Kenneth, Pte	1st SAS
ROGERSON, Arthur, LCpl	1st SAS
ROSENSTEIN, Nathan, Pte	L Det
ROUSSEAU, Joseph Maurice, Lt	2nd SAS
RUDD, Leonard Charles, Pte	2nd SAS
RYLAND, Sidney Jack, Pte	1st SAS
SALTER, James, Pte	2nd SAS
SCHERZINGER, Robert Joseph, LBdr	1st SAS
SENIOR, Fred, LSgt	1st SAS
SHARMAN, Allan, Cpl	1st SAS
SHAW, George, Pte	1st SAS
SHORTALL, James Patrick, Cpl	2nd SAS
SHORTEN, Raymond Herbert, Lt	1st SAS
SILIFANTS, Simon Aron, Gnr	1st SAS
SILLETT, Thomas John, Pte	1st SAS

SILLY, James Lovitt, Lt	2nd SAS
SIMMONS, Eric George, Pte	1st SAS
SIMPSON, James, Pte	2nd SAS
SINCLAIR, Archibald Roy McGregor, Sgt	SBS
SKINNER, Alexander Grant, MM, Spr	1st SAS
SLATER, George Frederick, Capt	HQ SAS Bde
SMITH, Jack William, Pte	2nd SAS
SPARROW, Aylmer Knox, Sigmn	1st SAS
SPOONER, Anthony John, Pte	1st SAS
SQUE, Eustace Arthur Nicol, WOII	1st SAS
STEPHENS, Tomos Mansel, Lt	1st SAS
STEWART-JOHNSON, William, Gnr	1st SAS
STONE, Sidney James, Sgt	L Det, SAS Bde
SWANSON, David, Gnr	RSR
SWORD, John Moore, Sgt	RSR
SYMES, Felix John Stewart, Capt	2nd SAS
TAYLOR, Lachlan, Sigmn	2nd SAS
TERRY-HALL, Frank Ernest, Sgt	2nd SAS
THOMAS, Leonard, Gdsm	SBS
THOMAS, William Henry, Gdsm	SBS
THORNTON, Thomas Frederick George, Capt	RSR
THORPE, Percy Roy, MM, Sgt	2nd SAS
TOBIN, Charles Francis, Gdsm	1st SAS
TYSON, Martine Edward, Pte	2nd SAS
VAREY, Thomas, Sgt	1st SAS
WALKER, Joseph, Pte	1st SAS
WALSHAW, George William, Cpl	SBS
WARBURTON, Kenneth, Pte	L Det, SAS Bde
WARD, George Richard, Lt. (QM)	1st SAS
WEAVER, Edwin Thomas, Pte	2nd SAS
WEBSTER, James Walter, Sgt	1st SAS
WERTHEIM, Gerhard, Pte	2nd SAS
WHATELY-SMITH, Anthony Robert, Maj	2nd SAS
WHITE, Roger, MM, LBdr	2nd SAS
WHITE, Victor Owen, Pte	1st SAS
WIDDRINGTON, Edward Antony Fitzherbert, MC, Maj	2nd SAS
WILKINSON, James Kenneth, Pte	2nd SAS
WILKINSON, John James Hamilton, Cpl	1st SAS
WILLIAMS, John Reginald Bernard, Cpl	1st SAS
WILSON, Alexander Melville, Lt	1st SAS
WINDER, Harry, Cpl	2nd SAS
WORTLEY, Reginald Josiah, Sgt	1st SAS
YOUNG, William Pearson, Pte	1st SAS

Selected Bibliography

Almonds Windmill, Lorna, *Gentleman Jim: The Wartime Story of a Founder of the SAS and Special Forces*, London, 2001

———, *A British Achilles: The Story of George, 2nd Earl Jellicoe*, Barnsley, 2005

Asher, Michael, *The Regiment: The Real Story of the SAS*, London, 2007

Bagnold, Ralph, *Sand, Wind and War: Memoirs of a Desert Explorer*, Tucson, Ariz., 1991

Beevor, Antony, *Crete: The Battle and the Resistance*, London, 1992

Buckmaster, Maurice, *They Fought Alone: The True Story of SOE's Agents in Wartime France*, London, 1958

Caillou, Alan [Alan Samuel Lyle-Smythe], *The World Is Six Feet Square*, London, 1954

Close, Roy, *In Action with the SAS: A Soldier's Odyssey from Dunkirk to Berlin*, Barnsley, 2005

Cooper, Artemis, *Cairo in the War, 1939–1945*, London, 1995

Cooper, Johnny, *One of the Originals: The Story of a Founder Member of the SAS*, London, 1991

Cowles, Virginia, *The Phantom Major: The Story of David Stirling and the SAS Regiment*, London, 1958

Dillon, Martin, and Roy Bradford, *Rogue Warrior of the SAS: The Blair Mayne Legend*, Edinburgh, 2012

Extraordinary Editions and SAS Regimental Association, *The SAS War Diary, 1941–1945*, London, 2011

Farran, Roy, *Operation Tombola*, London, 1960

———, *Winged Dagger*, London, 1998

Ford, Roger, *Fire from the Forest: The SAS Brigade in France, 1944*, London, 2003

Hafen, Lyman, *Far from Cactus Flat: The 20th Century Story of a Harsh Land, a Proud Family, and a Lost Son*, St. George, Utah, 2006

Hastings, Max, *Das Reich: The March of the 2nd SS Panzer Division Through France, June 1944*, London, 1983

Helm, Sarah, *A Life in Secrets: Vera Atkins and the Lost Agents of SOE*, London, 2005

Hoe, Alan, *David Stirling: Founder of the SAS*, London, 1992

James, Malcolm [Malcolm Pleydell], *Born of the Desert: With the SAS in North Africa*, London, 1945

Jefferson, David, *Tobruk: A Raid Too Far*, London, 2013

Jones, Tim, *SAS: The First Secret Wars*, London, 2005

Kemp, Anthony, *The Secret Hunters*, London, 1988

———, *The SAS at War, 1941–1945*, London, 1991

Lewes, John, *Jock Lewes, Co-founder of the SAS*, London, 2000

Lewis, Damien, *The Nazi Hunters: The Ultra-Secret SAS Unit and the Quest for Hitler's War Criminals*, London, 2015

Liddell-Hart, Basil, *The Rommel Papers*, Cambridge, Mass., 1991

Lloyd Owen, David, *Providence Their Guide: The Long Range Desert Group*, London, 1980

Maclean, Fitzroy, *Eastern Approaches*, London, 1949

Mather, Carol, *When the Grass Stops Growing*, London, 1997

McClean, Stewart, *SAS: The History of the Special Raiding Squadron, "Paddy's Men,"* Stroud, 2006

McCue, Paul, *SAS Operation Bulbasket: Behind the Lines in Occupied France, 1944*, London, 1996

McLuskey, Fraser, *Parachute Padre: Behind German Lines with the SAS in France, 1944*, London, 1951

Molinari, Andrea, *Desert Raiders: Axis and Allied Special Forces, 1940–43*, Oxford, 2007

Montgomery, Field Marshal the Viscount, *Memoirs*, London, 1958

Moorehead, Alan, *The Desert War*, London, 1965

Morgan, Mike, *Sting of the Scorpion: The Inside Story of the Long Range Desert Group*, Stroud, 2010

Mortimer, Gavin, *Stirling's Men: The Inside History of the SAS in World War II*, London, 2004

———, *The SAS in World War II: An Illustrated History*, London, 2011

———, *The Men Who Made the SAS: The History of the Long Range Desert Group*, London, 2015

O'Dowd, Gearóid, *He Who Dared and Died: The Life and Death of an SAS Original, Sergeant Chris O'Dowd, MM*, Barnsley, 2011

Peniakoff, Vladimir, *Popski's Private Army*, London, 1950

Pleydell, Malcolm, *see* James, Malcolm

Ross, Hamish, *Paddy Mayne: Lt. Col. Blair "Paddy" Mayne, 1 SAS Regiment*, Stroud, 2004

Scholey, Pete, *SAS Heroes: Remarkable Soldiers, Extraordinary Men*, Oxford, 2008

Seymour, William, *British Special Forces*, London, 1985

Stevens, Gordon, *The Originals: The Secret History of the Birth of the SAS*, London, 2005

Strawson, John, *A History of the SAS Regiment*, London, 1984

Warner, Philip, *The SAS*, London, 1971

Waugh, Evelyn, *The Letters of Evelyn Waugh*, ed. Mark Amory, London, 1982

Photography Credits

Every effort has been made to contact all copyright holders. The publishers will be happy to make good in future editions any errors of omission or commission brought to their attention.

All photographs are from the SAS Regimental Association Archive unless otherwise noted.

FIRST PHOTO INSERT
Page 3: *(center)* © IWM
Page 4: *(top left, top right)* © National Museums Scotland; *(center left)* Getty Images/Popperfoto; *(center right)* private collection; *(bottom right)* Alison Smartt [née Pleydell]
Page 5: *(top left)* © National Museums Scotland; *(top right)* private collection; *(center right)* Getty Images/Keystone-France
Page 6: John Lewes Archive
Page 9: *(top)* © IWM; *(bottom)* Getty Images/Keystone
Page 12: *(top)* Nicola von Lutterotti;
Page 14: Alison Smartt [née Pleydell]
Page 15: *(top right)* private collection; *(bottom)* Getty Images/Keystone

SECOND PHOTO INSERT
Page 2: *(top, bottom right)* private collection
Page 8: *(top)* De Agostini Picture Library/A. Dagli Orti/Bridgeman Images
Page 11: *(top)* private collection
Page 12: *(top)* © IWM; *(bottom)* Getty Images/Universal History Archive
Page 14: *(top)* Getty Images/George Rodger; *(bottom)* © IWM
Page 15: *(top)* SAS Regimental Association Archive/Mirrorpix; *(bottom left, bottom right)* The National Archives UK WO 204/13021
Page 16: *(top right)* private collection; *(bottom left, center right)* © IWM

Index

THE SAS WAR DIARY
1941-1945

A unique opportunity to acquire one of the few remaining full-scale reproductions of this extraordinary record of SAS history, published in a never-to-be-repeated limited edition to mark the seventieth anniversary of the SAS and to raise funds for its Regimental Association.

In early 1946, only months after the end of the Second World War, a former SAS soldier undertook a final mission. His task: to find and preserve whatever documentation he could before the SAS was forgotten and its story lost forever.

The soldier tracked down and copied the top secret order authorizing the very first SAS operation. He sought out photographs of the original members of 1SAS and somehow acquired the after-action reports from the few who survived. Then, with more photographs, operational orders, reports, and maps, he traced the story of the SAS through North Africa, Sicily, Italy, and France, all the way to Berlin, and to the final march-past when the SAS was briefly disbanded in October 1945.

By mission end, that soldier had produced something extraordinary—the first ever history of the SAS, in their own words.

He collected his work in a single massive war diary, measuring 17" × 12" × 4" and weighing over twenty-five pounds. He bound it in a leather casing "liberated" from Nazi Germany and then gave it to the SAS Regimental Association. Its existence remained a secret for sixty-five years.

In 2011, Extraordinary Editions published the diary, with the Regimental Association, who agreed to publication so that the stories of their wartime members would be properly acknowledged. The diary started that process, and now Ben Macintyre's magnificent authorized history has concluded it.

Every page of the original diary has been scanned and then printed on specially made, heavyweight, archival-quality acid-free paper, in order to reproduce it as closely as possible, in full size and with stunning clarity.

Each copy is hand-bound in a full-leather binding replicating the original and then blocked with a new design featuring the regimental badge and wings.

There are six different editions of the diary, all individually numbered, and they range in price from £975 for the Anniversary Edition to £2,500 for the magnificent signed and boxed Originals Edition. Most are in the hands of special forces families, institutions, and collectors worldwide, and only a few remain for sale.

The lion's share of the proceeds goes to the welfare fund of the SAS Regimental Association.

You can find out more about the diary at:
www.extraordinaryeditions.com
or e-mail **mm@extraordinaryeditions.com**
for more information.

EXTRAORDINARY
EDITIONS